Compliments to our brave architect!

The Nederlands' First
Women Architects

Erica Smeets-Klokgieters

nai010 publishers

Compliments to our brave architect!

Contents

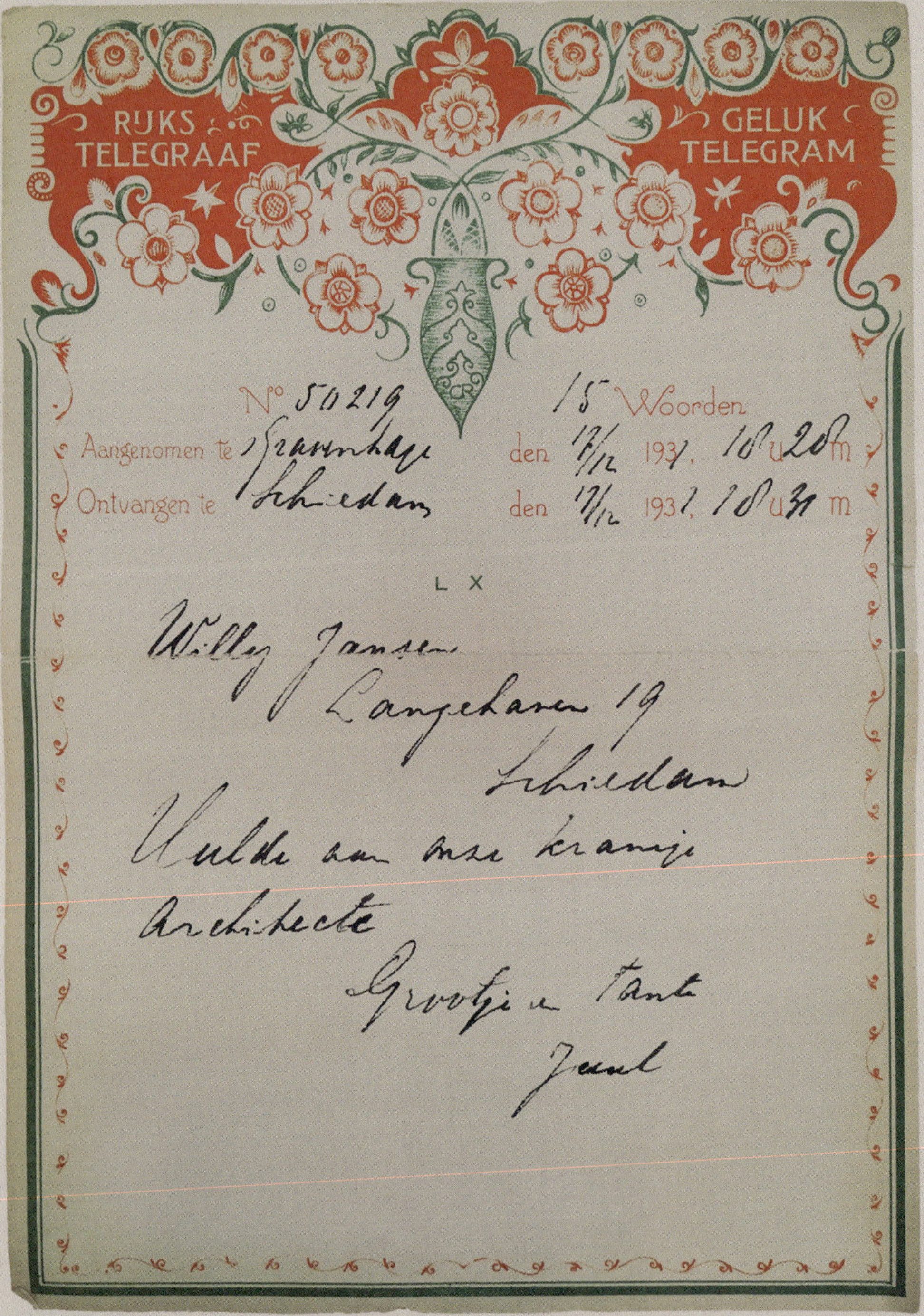

RIJKS TELEGRAAF

GELUK TELEGRAM

No 50219 15 Woorden

Aangenomen te 'sGravenhage den 17/12 1931, 18 u 20 m

Ontvangen te Schiedam den 17/12 1931, 18 u 31 m

L X

Willy Jansen
Langehaven 19
Schiedam

Hulde aan onze kranige
Architecte

Grootje en tante
Jeanl

1

Foreword

When I graduated in 2016 from Utrecht University with a Master's thesis entitled *Women in Construction: The emergence of the first women architects in the Netherlands*, I could not have conceived of how relevant this theme would become in the years that followed. These days, we are flooded with initiatives, publications, exhibitions, podcasts, documentaries and projects, all intended to reveal or showcase women from history.

When I chose this topic for my Master's degree in architectural history and historic buildings and monuments, I was initially inspired by my interest in women throughout history who commissioned building projects. For my Bachelor's degree, I had already researched the role of women in residential architecture by H.P. Berlage and Victor Horta. However, when I set out to find a similar subject for my Master's thesis, it became apparent that it could be extremely interesting to focus not on the women who *commissioned* projects, but on the possibility of women who *carried out* such projects: women architects. One thing was clear: there was no comprehensive overview in the Netherlands of early women architects. A few women architects had gained some degree of fame, but might there be more – possibly even many more? And if so, who were they? Had they had formal training, and if so, which degree programme? Had they been officially enrolled in the programme? More and more interesting questions were emerging. It was clear that I had discovered a *niche*. Desk research soon confirmed that: an overview of the first women who pioneered in the field of architecture was not published until the start of this century, and only focused on the United States of America. A similar publication for the countries around us, or for the Netherlands, was nowhere to be found.

1 Congratulatory telegram from 'Granny and Aunt Juul' to Wil Jansen, dd. 17 December 1931, the day she graduated.

In my view, these blank spaces were sufficient reason to embark on this research. Along the way, I discovered so many more research questions that I decided to conduct more in-depth research after graduation. I obtained my PhD in this field and published a dissertation in 2022. I have established contact with family members who were willing to answer my questions and were able to tell me far more; I gained access to previously undisclosed archives, including one in a bunker in the Geniemuseum of the Dutch Army Corps of Engineers in Vught. During the COVID-19 pandemic, I discovered vast amounts of digital information, often thanks to assistance from eager volunteers from regional museums, local history experts, and municipal and regional archives.

And that's how my quest started, searching for women that I didn't even know existed yet, knew nothing about – but now, after four years of research, I am keenly aware of how important they are to the canon of Dutch architectural history. Some were successful, while others were hardly able to practise their profession, or never managed to work as architects. They all chose a profession that was anything but an obvious choice for women at the time. And that was made painfully clear to them before and during the programme, but was also rubbed in over and over later. Even so, this resistance did not keep these women from choosing to pursue the profession of architect. Bold, strong women, in other words. It inspired me to apply the text from a congratulatory telegram, sent to one of these women on the occasion of her graduation from university, extending its sentiments to all the women in this study: 'Compliments to our brave architect!'.

1 Introduction

Recent years have seen a growing interest in topics relating to women in artistic professions, as evidenced by the many initiatives showcasing little-known contemporary women in the arts, as well as women from the past who have gone unnoticed by history until now. 2019 can be seen as a turning point in this regard. Since then, there has been a steadily rising tide of expositions and projects raising the visibility of the woman in art. Take, for example, the recent exhibition 'Women, Art and Power' at the Musée d'Orsay in Paris, devoted to works by women working as painters, sculptors, graphic artists, and in the applied arts between 1848 and 1914.[1] In parallel, the museum also presented an exhibition on the work of Berthe Morisot (1841–1895) who, unlike her famous Impressionist contemporaries like Claude Monet (1840–1926) and Pierre-Auguste Renoir (1841–1919), never became a household name or indeed enjoyed very much recognition at all. Also in Paris in 2019, the Fondation Louis Vuitton presented a major exhibition of the works of French designer Charlotte Perriand (1903–1999). Dutch national newspaper *NRC Handelsblad* found that this woman was such 'a leading figure' in the field of design and architecture that it devoted a two-page spread to her and this exhibition.[2] In that same year, the newspaper also printed a story entitled 'Tracking down the forgotten women painters', in which the author highlighted the Advancing Women Artists (AWA) foundation in Florence, which is dedicated to restoring 'forgotten works' by 'forgotten women painters'.[3] In 2021, the Rijksmuseum Twenthe in the Dutch city of Enschede followed Rome, New York, Milan and London in presenting a retrospective of paintings by Italian master Artemisia Gentileschi (1593–1653).[4] Due to its great success, that exhibition was extended several months, into the following year. Less than a year later, the museum became the first in the Netherlands to present a solo exhibition of Italian Renaissance painter Sofonisba Anguissola 1531/1532?–1625).[5] Meanwhile, the Kunsthal Rotterdam presented a 'celebration' of over four hundred women entitled 'Here We Are! Women in design 1900 – Today'.[6]

Also notable are the cooperative projects that have been launched to raise the visibility of women in Dutch art history, such as 'The other half: women's participation in the Dutch art world', put on by the Netherlands Institute for Art History (RKD) in cooperation with the Rijksmuseum, the Stedelijk Museum and the University of Amsterdam.[7] In 2021, the Rijksmuseum began a three-year research programme into its own collection, the *Women of the Rijksmuseum* project.[8] The Cultural Heritage

Agency, too, has been researching its own collection, prompted in part by the increasing number of requests from museums for the loan of works by women.[9] The results of the latter revealed that the Cultural Heritage Agency was in the possession of the works of just under 1,600 women – compared to its collection of works by 9,000 men.

Likewise, in architecture there have been initiatives for discovering (and rediscovering) women in the field from the past. Het Nieuwe Instituut (the Museum for Architecture, Design and Digital Culture, often abbreviated as HNI) in Rotterdam is taking a critical look at its own collection policy in its architecture collection, in the project *Collecting Otherwise*.[10] Under the title *Seen/Unseen*, that institution is looking at the issue from a number of perspectives, including the representation of women in the collection.[11] In 2019 art magazine *See All This* published a special edition, in anticipation of the centenary of women's suffrage in the Netherlands, heralding the '99 geniuses' among contemporary women in the arts.[12] These 99 women included only one architect: Francine Houben. Born in 1955, over her career she has attained the status of '*starchitect*', winning high-profile projects around the world and being granted an honorary doctorate from Utrecht University in the Netherlands. Houben is among the small group of women who are registered architects in the Netherlands – of the over ten thousand in the registry, women make up just 29%.[13] And very little is known of these women, with a few notable exceptions, such as Houben or Nathalie de Vries. In early 2021, online magazine *A.Zine* published a special edition entitled *Mevr. de Architect* ('Ms Architect'), featuring nineteen interviews with contemporary women architects.[14] The launch of this print edition was in parallel with an online debate on the importance of visibility, as well as a call for rewriting architectural history to create a place for the unsung women architects of the past. This call is emblematic of the current status of the Dutch canon on the subject of women architects.

Abroad, women have only begun to take their place in the historiography of architecture in recent decades. In the United States, for example, it was not until the rise of feminism in the 1970s that the first research into the number of women in architecture appeared.[15] In that study (*Women's Places: Architecture and Design 1860–1960*), the authors began from the perspective of what had been 'hidden from history': they went looking for women of significance who had remained outside the canon.[16] 1973 saw the publication of *From Tipi to Skyscraper: A History of Women in Architecture*. In it, author and architect Doris Cole explained that she intended this publication to be 'only a first step' in the research into the status of women in architecture.[17] This was followed in 1977 by the volume *Women in American architecture: A Historic and*

Contemporary Perspective, edited by Susana Torre.[18] The fact that this book was sponsored by the Architectural League of New York should underscore how much interest there was in the field for more knowledge about the place of women in architectural history. Torre's research led to the establishment of the Women in Architecture Archive.[19] In her contribution, 'On the fringe of the profession: women in American architecture', Gwendolyn Wright highlighted a number of women architects who had spent their careers working primarily behind the scenes.[20] But it was not until 2008 that the seminal work on the subject was published: *The First American Women Architects* by Sarah Allaback, a compilation of profiles of some 75 important women architects of the 1920s and their work.[21] Of the over 200 women architects practising in the United States at that time, Allaback selected these 75 as the most important pioneers.

In 2017, the Paul Mellon Centre for Studies in British Art and the Architectural Association in London organized the conference *AA Women and Architecture in Context 1917–2017* on the occasion of the centenary of the first admission of women to London's Architectural Association School of Architecture.[22] This conference led to the publication of an internationally oriented printed volume in which, in over 1,300 pages, the Netherlands was not represented at all.[23] At that conference, the publication of *The Bloomsbury Global Encyclopedia of Women in Architecture* was announced, originally intended for publication in 2021.[24] That encyclopaedia, however, was limited to the period of 1960–2015.

In *Breaking Ground: Architecture by Women*, Jane Hall presented a woman's perspective on 150 iconic works by women architects. In it she calls attention to women architects who created buildings in partnerships with men, but who themselves remained out of the spotlight. In Hall's book, some of those male partners, as co-architects of the selected buildings, even go unnamed: for example, Rem Koolhaas, co-founder of the Office for Metropolitan Architecture (OMA), is not named in the discussion of the building he and his fellow OMA architect Ellen van Loon designed together.[25]

Published in 2021, the book *Women in Architecture: Past, Present and Future* discusses 36 contemporary women architects and their projects, including one Dutch work by Nathalie de Vries. The book begins with examples of women from the history of architecture in the United States and in various European countries, including Italy, Germany, France, England and Austria. In this account, the Netherlands is represented as barely a footnote, in the person of Truus Schröder-Schräder (1889–1985), as commissioning client for her own home, better known as the Rietveld Schröder house.[26]

In the history of architecture in the Netherlands, Margaret Staal-Kropholler (1891–1966) is considered to be the first woman architect.[27] She owes this distinction to a review of her first work, a number of villas built in the town of Bergen in 1917. In that review, architect and critic Hendrik Wijdeveld (1885–1987) refers to her as such.[28] A monograph published about her in 1991 names fourteen other women architects whom Staal-Kropholler approached around 1950 for a survey about their work.[29] Unlike Staal-Kropholler herself, who did not have a degree, twelve of these fourteen women had completed university studies in architecture between 1920 and 1945.[30] Before this publication, virtually all of these women had been essentially unknown.

The lengthy *Vrouwen in de vormgeving 1880–1940* ('Women in design 1880–1940') by Marjan Groot, reprinted in 2023, presents an overview of women in the applied arts and industrial design in the Netherlands. This overview does not, however, include women architects, excepting those who were also active as interior designers or designers of furniture, like Staal-Kropholler.[31] The explanation of the absence of architects can be found in Groot's assertion that Staal-Kropholler remained the 'only prewar woman architect'[32]; while in 1908 (according to Groot), women in Germany were being admitted into university programmes in architecture, the Netherlands was 'not nearly there yet' at that time.[33] But the research that led to the book you are now reading has revealed that in this area, the Netherlands was actually ahead of not only the United Kingdom, but Germany as well.

It is striking to note how scant and how fragmentary the writing on the professional history of women architects in the Netherlands remains in the literature of the field. Until now, no general overview on this history was available. Who were the women who had graduated from university, having earned the title of architectural engineer, that Staal-Kropholler approached? Were there perhaps others in that same period, or even earlier, who had studied architecture and worked as architects after completing their degrees? What did such programmes look like? What were the options for these women in a field that at the time was practised only by men? Could they even work in that field, and if so, how? These were the questions underlying the research that went into this book.

Woman and profession: the gender perspective

The rise of the woman architect must also be seen against the background of the history of gender. 'Gender' should be understood to represent the totality of social and cultural characteristics of a sex, as opposed to only the physical. The women's movement that emerged in societies around the world between ca. 1860 and 1920 is now recognized as the first wave of feminism.[34] Women's participation in education, paid work, science or politics was anything but a given. The first woman who studied at university in the Netherlands was Anna Maria van Schurman (1607–1678), who was admitted to what was then known as the Rijksuniversiteit Utrecht in 1636.[35] She took courses in theology, the humanities and medicine. But it would be another two hundred years before the first woman in the Netherlands completed a university degree[36]: that was Aletta Jacobs (1854–1929), who graduated from the University of Groningen in 1878 and defended her dissertation one year later.

Around the late nineteenth and early twentieth century, it was still a commonly held opinion that the woman was 'a weak creation, and ill-suited for the rigours of study'.[37] On the occasion of the inauguration of the new rector magnificus at the University of Amsterdam in 1904, a professor of chemistry stated in no uncertain terms: 'Among the current newly registered students, I have even found 14% women among the students; and among the 58 auditors, there are no fewer than 25. It would appear to me that these high numbers, and their sharp increase, point to very serious disruptions in the natural state of our society.'[38]

Likewise, women faced resistance when attempting to enter the labour process, particularly in those fields and professions considered typically reserved for men. Women were expected to marry, raise a family, and take care of their husbands, children and the house. That a woman's place was in the home (certainly within the affluent sectors of society), where she could devote herself to furnishing and decorating, was reinforced in all manner of novels, handbooks and journals, such as *De Vrouw en haar Huis* ('The Woman and her House'). Single women who had to support themselves worked in what had traditionally been women's jobs: teachers, nurses, and the like. Women lower on the social ladder worked in factories in various industries, making textiles or cigars. In 1898, in The Hague, there was a 'National Exhibition of Women's Labour', calling attention to industry, art, science and social work being done by women, and which had the explicit goal of enabling women to 'hold meetings to discuss all that could be beneficial to the expansion of the working spheres of the woman in the Netherlands' – in short, an early and textbook example of a networking platform.[39] This exhibition was to be presented in a new exhibition space to be built for the purpose, but there was no woman architect to be found to design it. After the turn of the century, however, that situation had improved slightly, because for an Amsterdam exhibition entitled 'The Woman 1813–1913', Margaret Staal-Kropholler did have the opportunity to design the '1913 House' for that component of the exhibition, including the interior design.[40]

In the early decades of the twentieth century, women began to enter professions for which a university education was required. In those days, women who completed a university degree in the Netherlands were seen as extremely exceptional, and were listed in an annual publication entitled *Vrouwenjaarboekje voor Nederland* ('Women's Yearbook for the Netherlands').[41] With Aletta Jacobs in the vanguard, there were just over 90 professionally active women doctors in 1915, along with some 90 pharmacists, 50 dentists and 20 attorneys. But there were, of course, more graduates in these disciplines than those numbers suggest: some were registered as not practising, which could mean that they had since married, or that they were unable to find work. Still more of the women who graduated ended up in jobs that were far from the fields they had studied – often in non-academic positions such as administrative assistants or secretaries.

A milestone was reached in 1919 when women won the right to vote. In the years that followed, the feminist movement dwindled somewhat, in part because of the financial crashes of the 1920s and the Second World War following shortly thereafter; it would only regain steam when the second wave of feminism arose in the 1960s. Meanwhile, in 1924 it was ordered by royal decree that married women in government jobs were to be dismissed en masse, as part of an effort to reduce the number of civil servants at the national level. Moreover, during the years of the crash, unmarried women working as civil servants also had to relinquish their jobs to make way for men in the workforce. The Ministry of Social Affairs at the time was even working on a bill that would have prohibited all married women from holding jobs of any kind; that bill, however, never made it past the High Council for Labour. In 1955, a member of Parliament named Corry Tendeloo (1897–1956) gave an impassioned plea on the floor of the house to restore the employability of engaged and married civil servants.[42] In it she noted that government orders for the dismissal of women always coincided with economic downturns, and moreover that they were always defended with 'arguments of principle', namely that 'a woman belongs in her family and in her home, and not on the labour market'.[43] A few months before Tendeloo died in 1956, the ban on engaged and married women in government jobs was abolished, as was women's legal incapacity.[44]

The *Handboek genderstudies in media, kunst en cultuur* ('Handbook of gender studies in media, art and culture'), published in 2015, places the third feminist wave at the beginning of the 1990s.[45] This handbook discusses theories and key concepts on gender, applied from various perspectives in specific disciplines in cultural studies. Conspicuously, within the realm of the arts, this handbook restricts its discussion of themes in gender to the visual arts, and does not devote one word of that discussion to architecture.

The research

How did the professionally educated woman make her entry into the field of architecture in the Netherlands? This was the primary research question that led to this publication. To answer it, I structured my research around several themes.

In the Netherlands, there were also a number of other architecture-adjacent fields that were historically practised by women, such as furniture designer, interior designer and garden architect.[46] In Chapter 2 I outline developments in these fields in order to put the rise of the woman architect in perspective.

Who were the first women to seat themselves at the architect's table? That question I answer in Chapter 3.[47] An architect is a structural designer of a building or complex of buildings and monitors the process of the construction.[48] The title of architect has been legally protected in the Netherlands since 1988. However, the origins of the modern practice of the architect's profession and the relevant course of education date back to the nineteenth century. Because I could not rely on the official registries of architects to give an account of the first women architects, I estimated based on the programmes in architecture studies that existed at the time. The first women who successfully completed these programmes made up the research group.

I looked into the women alumni of what was then the Technische Hogeschool in Delft, the first university-level programme in architecture, as well as the women who graduated from the Voortgezet en Hooger Bouwkunst Onderricht (VHBO) in Amsterdam (what would now be considered a 'university of applied sciences'), the first higher education programme offering a qualification as architect. These were the only two academic programmes in architecture of their kind in the Netherlands in the first half of the twentieth century.[49] The various schools that offered training in drawing and applied arts and crafts did not qualify as full-fledged architecture programmes, due to their relatively low level and limited curriculum, so I left them outside the scope of my research. That means that any women who may have pursued a programme in these schools and then later became active in architectural engineering and design are not included in this research.

I did not, however, limit myself in this research to women architects of Dutch nationality who pursued their education in the Netherlands (and who may then have pursued their careers in other countries). My research also includes women who were born in other countries but were educated in the Netherlands. The period of my research begins with the founding of the Technische Hoogeschool in 1905 (the VHBO came shortly after, in 1908), and ends with the year 1945. After the Second World War, the education system changed, and specializations such as city planning began to emerge. Moreover, my focus in this research is on the *emergence* of women in the field of architecture.

For the research into the women alumni of the Technische Hogeschool in Delft, I relied on student administration records in the National Archive in The Hague and, to a lesser extent, in the City Archive of Delft. By 1946, nineteen women had graduated as architectural engineers. Unfortunately, information such as exam questions and results were lost in a 2008 fire in the architecture faculty. For the inventory of the women who graduated from the VHBO, I was able to use the complete publication Dave Wendt produced for the centenary of the VHBO (later the Academie van Bouwkunst) and the archive of the academy at Het Nieuwe Instituut in Rotterdam.[50] At the end of the Second World War, only two women had earned diplomas from the VHBO. Consequently, the total research group consisted of 21 women who had received a diploma or a university degree in architecture studies.

In Chapter 3 I present a description of these two programmes that produced the first women architects, and in this description I consider what it was like to participate in these programmes as a woman, addressing issues such as accessibility and interpersonal conduct. For this I consulted various resources, including annual reports and yearbooks, study guides, student almanacs and student newspapers of the Technische Hoogeschool. As women's organizations and institutions emerged, they began producing guides and yearbooks intended to help girls and women in their choice of programmes and professions. These publications, supplemented with statistical information on professions practised by women, offered a treasure trove of information. They also contain assessments of the future expectations of certain fields for women. The practice of the profession of architect was not seen as a choice that offered much potential.

Chapter 4 presents an overview of the professional practice of the women architects in the research group. How did their careers progress over time? Were they able to find work as architects? And if so, were they independent or employed? Were these women's skills and potential truly appreciated? The list of names issued by the Vereeniging van Delftsche Ingenieurs ('Association of Delft Engineers'), which I was able to consult at the Royal Institution of Engineers in The Hague, and which list the jobs held by alumni by year of graduation, was an important resource. A thesis from 1982 on the work experience of women architectural engineers offered starting points for further research in the form of interviews with four early graduates who were still alive at that time.[51]

Thanks to the women's rights movement, a number of general women's rights organizations emerged, and along the way women also gained access to professional associations and advisory committees. The extent to which these memberships played a role in the first women architects' transition into the profession is also addressed in Chapter 4. For this I once again relied on a number of resources, including archives and membership registers of these associations, some of which are held by Atria, the knowledge institute for emancipation and women's history in Amsterdam. Finally, Chapter 4 concludes with a look at the extent to which women architects received attention in the media.

Chapters 5 and 6 are monographs of two such women who had remained unsung until now. Grada Wolffensperger (1887–1965) was the first woman in the Netherlands to graduate with a degree in architectural engineering. It seemed to me that investigating her story was a priority. That proved quite challenging, but in retrospect this was quite understandable. The information that the search produced, in the archives of the Province of Noord-Holland in Haarlem, proved to be the only evidence of what turned out to be an unfortunate and short career.[52]

I was prompted to investigate Riné Boerée (1898–1995) by a note written by Staal-Kropholler on her list of colleagues to write to, asking questions about their work. The word 'concrete' that she scribbled in the margin alongside Boerée's name piqued my interest.[53] That led to an interesting search for a woman who, by specializing in an area of the field that was completely virgin territory for a woman, revealed a striking career in which she distinguished herself not only from other women in the field, but the men in her profession as well.[54] The research also took me to an archive at Het Nieuwe Instituut that was inventoried, but as far as I could determine only rarely consulted. This archive, which featured drawings and lecture notes made by Boerée during her studies, also gave me a better picture of the architecture programme at the Technische Hoogeschool in Delft. Boerée's further career at the Genie (Army Corps of Engineers) came to light thanks to further research in the National Archives in The Hague, the Netherlands Institute for Military History in The Hague, and last but not least the Geniemuseum in Vught, where I found, in a bunker where some of the archive was stored, the indisputable proof that Boerée's specialization made her an indispensable asset to her employer: she had been assigned to the construction of barracks complexes and, later, military runways.

Another woman who distinguished herself from her colleagues was Wil Jansen (1904–1989). She is the subject of Chapter 7. Jansen was the only woman from the research group who succeeded in independently maintaining an architecture practice, and with a well-filled, wide-ranging portfolio of orders at that. Her crowning achievement, a flat complex for single working women in Rotterdam, was the subject of a publication.[55] But her other work remained completely unknown, discovered in the Municipal Archives of Schiedam, which had been handed over by her nephew in 2011. Jansen had also left her mark in the field of non-residential construction, an area in which it was, if anything, even more unusual for a woman to work. Jansen was also active in the first Women's Advisory Commission, which was created in Rotterdam after the Second World War, a body that advised the municipality on residential construction.[56]

In order to write these three monographs, I had the privilege of consulting very interesting primary sources held by descendants of these three women architects, as well as friends and acquaintances from their inner circles. These persons were not only willing to speak to me about their memories, but also opened their collections of priceless materials that had *not* been handed over to the archives, such as personal documents, photos and design materials. For Chapters 5 through 7, I selected three cases of three hitherto virtually unknown women, all very different. Together, these chapters also present a contextual picture of the time in which their education and careers played out.

Chapter 8 discusses a select group of five women from the research group who all married architects, who they then worked closely with in their own joint architecture practices. The chosen composition of this group also offered the potential to investigate the models of partnerships between men and women working as architects who were both spouses and colleagues. I was curious: was there any mutual recognition and inspiration? This group included both Koos Pot-Keegstra (1908–1997) and Lotte Stam-Beese (1903–1988), the two VHBO graduates. Stam-Beese is one of the few women from the research group who enjoyed some standing in the architecture world; she was the subject of two monographs.[57] Although she became a city planner (a domain that falls outside the framework of this research), she did work with her spouse in their architecture firm until they divorced. By including her in this chapter, I was able to look at her in a different light than would have been possible with a pure analysis of her city planning oeuvre. The archives in the possession of Het Nieuwe Instituut were a valuable resource on Stam-Beese and Pot-Keegstra. Of two other architect couples, Van Rood-van Rijswijk and Kammer-Kret, the HNI retains only the archives of the man's work. In fact, in the case of Jan Kammer-Kret (1906–1984) the drawings that she made during her studies, as well as the complete works of both her and her spouse, are filed in his archive – and thus under his name. One of their daughters, a retired architectural engineer and now very old, was willing to share memories, photographs and documentation about her parents with me. The Lammers-Koeleman couple remained childless, and their architecture firm was eventually taken over by another firm; none of their archives remain. In the cases where no archives were available, the personal reporting that Staal-Kropholler made at the time about their works was retained at Het Nieuwe Instituut, and this provided very interesting information.

In Chapter 8, we will also discover that the women who were married to architects produced an oeuvre quite surprising for the time, both typologically and stylistically. Of course, from this oeuvre I had to make a selection.

For a complete list of the 21 women in my research group, please see the entries at the back of this volume, in which I have catalogued all the information I uncovered during my research, including personal data, education, overall career and relevant ancillary activities, along with references to sources. Regarding the three women who are the subject of the monographs in Chapters 5, 6 and 7 (Wolffensperger, Boerée and Jansen), the entries at the back of this volume contain limited information. I made a deliberate choice to indicate in these entries whether the women in the research group did or did not have children, with the idea that any descendants might potentially be able to play a role in future research.

Perhaps the elephant in the room is the question of whether the work that these women architects produced was fundamentally different than that of their male counterparts; that question remains difficult to answer. Like the men in their field, these women followed the rationalistic philosophy of 'het Nieuwe Bouwen' (hereinafter referred to as the Modern Movement), which began to emerge in the 1920s. But that architectural style generally evokes much more masculine connotations.[58] According to author Hanneke Oosterhof, Staal-Kropholler was much better suited to this environment, because it allowed her to apply the decorative Amsterdam School style, which (according to her) was much more readily associated with the feminine. But were these styles first pursued and developed by men working as architects only for the simple reason that there were virtually no women architects in this period? It can be said that anything developed or produced by these women could, at the time, have been seen as a departure from anything that had been built up to that point. For women, this 'New Building' movement presented opportunities for creating efficient, functional floor plans in buildings to make life easier for the ones devoting themselves to the housekeeping: women. This attention to efficiency and functionality was not merely limited to residential construction, but we can also see it expressed in the non-residential works that a few of these women architects produced.

It is also evidenced in the physical appearance of the buildings. The dictates of efficiency can also be seen in the use of new, industrially produced construction materials. There were women who were committed to building sound and sustainable homes.[59] This will become clear in Chapters 7 and 8, in which we will also see that designs by women won architectural prizes in contests where the jury was labouring under the misconception that the submission was a man's. One of the few direct citations I came across from a woman architect about the architectural differences between designs by men and women came from Wil Jansen. 'The interior is where most of the differences come to light. There are so many of the small things that a man finds unimportant, but a woman does not.'[60] But it seems that not all of the women working in her field agreed. Pot-Keegstra described her spouse and partner as the one who was most concerned with the 'fine details', while she herself was mainly occupied with the big picture.[61]

References to persons and professions

For the most part, I refer to the women in the research group by their surnames. In the portions of the text concerning their youth or education, I opted to use their given names, to maintain the atmosphere; likewise in situations in which their fathers, brothers or spouses appear, I did so to avoid confusion. Persons such as family members, teachers, professors and male architects are referred to by their full names the first time they are mentioned in any chapter. Where the name that a person went by is unknown, I opted to use all given names or, in some cases, the initials.

To highlight the distinction from men who were architects, wherever possible I tried to use the term 'woman architect' rather than simply using the word 'architect', which from a gender equality perspective would have been an equally valid choice. The same can be said for the references to other related professions, such as architectural engineer.

2 The rise of women in furniture design, interior architecture and garden architecture

In the early decades of the twentieth century, women made their way into disciplines that were closely related to architecture, but for which there were no university programmes. Within the realm of design, women initially focused on crafts such as needlepoint, lacemaking, batik and weaving.[1] These crafts were almost by nature associated with femininity, and so this was compatible with the prevailing image of women in society. As time went on, however, women began to be associated with certain characteristics that drew them into new areas within the field of design. In various newspapers, men in design professions expressed positive opinions about the role that women could play in interior decoration, furniture design and even interior architecture, with their sense of intimacy, atmosphere and colour. Because specializations and higher education programmes in those specializations emerged gradually, these different disciplines were not sharply delineated before the Second World War. As a result, furniture makers could easily develop into interior designers, and in Margaret Staal-Kropholler's case, she was trained as a decorative artist, then moved into furniture design and interior architecture, and finally into architecture. Women's participation was also on the rise in garden architecture. The art of gardening was seen as a 'beautiful pursuit' for women, one in which attributes like taste, colour selection and an 'almost motherly care' for raising flowers and shrubs were valuable assets.[2]

This chapter describes the rise of the woman in these architecture-adjacent disciplines and, in so doing, serves to put the rise of the woman architect in perspective. The research reveals that academically trained women architects were also active in these disciplines, whether forced into them by economic circumstances or not.

Women in interior architecture and furniture design

In the early decades of the twentieth century, there was no specific definition of the job of interior architect, and there was certainly no legal protection on the title.[3] In fact, legal protection of that title (as well as that of architect) only entered into effect by law in 1988.[4] Interior architecture became a profession and a career only very slowly. The association VANK (Vereeniging voor Ambachts- en Nijverheidskunst, or Association for Craft and Industrial Arts) was founded in 1904, but only began to be concerned with the lack of standing rules, codes of conduct and fee tables for the practice of the craft around 1918. The calls for an educational programme coordinated to the field were loudest outside VANK itself, and when such a programme did emerge, it was something of an amalgam of existing industrial arts education. As a result of the financial crises of the 1920s coupled with various budget-cutting measures, in 1924 a number of industrial arts schools in Amsterdam (the Kunstnijverheidsschool Quellinus, the Rijksnijverheidsschool, the Dagteeken- en Kunstambachtschool voor Meisjes and the Teekenschool voor Kunstambachten) were merged into the Instituut voor Kunstnijverheidsonderwijs ('Institute for Industrial Arts Education'). After this merger, the Institute offered a class in 'Interior Architecture'.[5] The Haagse Academie van Beeldende Kunsten followed in 1931 with a programme in Furniture Construction and Interior Art. This department was formed under the management of interior architect and industrial designer Cor Alons (1892–1967).

In 1940, VANK adopted a regulation defining the qualification of 'VANK Interior Architect': 'To qualify as a VANK interior architect, a person must be engaged in the design of furniture and other elements of the interior and, moreover, have mastered the creation of an interior in the broadest sense of the word. He must possess sufficient architectural knowledge with all the requirements of professional expertise associated therewith, insofar as this is necessary for the interior.'[6] A draft fee system produced by VANK and dating from 1941 makes a distinction between the 'free interior architect', who implements his design work 'under his own leadership, by third parties'; the 'businessman-interior architect', who has his designs implemented 'in his own or another's workshops' and who delivers them directly to the client; and the 'civil servant-interior architect', who cooperated with or was associated with an 'industrial company'.[7]

VANK's attempts to regulate and define the profession reflected the situation in those years. That situation was succinctly described by furniture designer and interior architect Cornelis van der Sluys (1881–1944) in his notes for a report on this subject, also drafted in 1941.[8] In them Van der Sluys makes a distinction between a furniture designer and an interior architect. According to him, the furniture designer was the person who '...knows the furniture maker's trade through and through, both the old craft (handmade work) and the machine labour', and who had completed trade school 'after Mulo or HBS', two years of apprenticeship, 'and then a drawing school'.[9] For the programme in interior architecture, he compiled a list of points for attention and requirements: 'In the main, first as a furniture draughtsman, supplemented with building and architecture studies, knowledge of construction materials, and of lighting and heating techniques. Study of paintwork and colour harmony. (...) The interior architect must have knowledge of metal and metalworking, must be able to design objects such as lamps and wrought ironworks (...). Most importantly, he must also have knowledge of fabrics, linoleums, carpets. (...) He must be able to evaluate locks, hinges and other fittings, and much more.'[10] According to Van der Sluys, drawing schools or academies could only 'do something primary', but a 'temporary working situation with an architect or builder would be most useful'.[11] In his opinion, it was not a mistake to initially classify interior architecture within the field of architecture, possibly 'because in the past the architect knew more, or had less to do', but in the present, he believed, the architect lacked the elementary knowledge and the time to 'care for the details'.[12] 'An object of furniture designed by an architect is even infamous and a total failure,' Van der Sluys wrote.[13] Despite all the attempts to define and regulate the field, in the course of the Second World War VANK was disbanded, and Van der Sluys' notes were never published.[14] In 1945 a new association for furniture designers, interior designers/retailers and interior architects was founded: the Vereniging van Beoefenaars der Gebonden Kunsten (GKf). That association lasted until 1975, when it was incorporated into the Professional Association of Netherlands Interior Designers (Bond van Nederlandse Interieurarchitecten) – which still exists today.

Neither the regulations drafted by VANK nor Van der Sluys' notes give any indication of an expectation that women might be practitioners in the field; in any case, these texts are written using exclusively masculine pronouns. Nonetheless, in her overview work *Vrouwen in de vormgeving in Nederland 1880–1940* ('Women in design in the Netherlands 1880–1940'), Marjan Groot names seven women who were visibly active as furniture designers and interior designers in the Netherlands from the 1910s on.[15] It could be that in Van der Sluys' view, these women fell under the following description from his notes: 'The woman who has taste or believes herself to have taste "advises" and arranges homes, without having any professional knowledge.'[16]

Because of the less than clearly defined disciplines and a lack of registration, it is impossible to give a precise picture of the total numbers of professional practitioners in the first half of the twentieth century, and the same goes for any attempt to determine the precise share of women in that number. Looking at the current situation: as of 31 December 2021 there were 1643 interior architects registered in the Dutch national registry of architects, of which 56% are women.[17] It is entirely possible that more women were active in this profession at the time, but evidently not so many that they captured Groot's attention. What Groot does not say in her book, but which is relevant for this research, is that at the time there was also no specific professionally oriented programme in interior architecture at the higher education level. Consequently, as compared to the group of graduate women architects, this group of professional practitioners went through an entirely different path of education.

Of the seven women named in Groot's overview work who were active as furniture designers and interior designers, three received their education abroad[18]: Gertrud Arper (1894–1968), Truus Schröder-Schräder (1889–1985) and Lotte Stam-Beese. Stam-Beese later went on to study architecture in Amsterdam, and so falls under the group of women who graduated with a degree in architecture. She will be discussed in more detail in Chapter 8. Because the research focuses on the rise of women architects who pursued and completed their education in the Netherlands, the other four of the women identified by Groot are the most relevant for the discussion in this chapter and for framing a perspective for this research. This is because these four women studied industrial arts (at least partly) in the Netherlands. Three of them were active in both furniture and interior design.

One of the first women to move in both circles was Margaret Kropholler. She earned her diploma in 1907 from a girls' art school in Amsterdam, the Dagteeken- en Kunstambachtsschool voor Meisjes, where she took courses in hand drawing and decorative drawing, and principles of style and ornamentation.[19] Before devoting herself to architecture, she designed furniture and interiors in the firm run by her brother (Alexander Jacobus ['Co'] Kropholler, 1881–1973) and his business partner (and her later husband) Jan Frederik ('Frits') Staal (1879–1940). In 1910 she took a course in architecture at the School voor Kunstnijverheid in Haarlem, in which the emphasis was on aesthetic design and which linked constructional designs to decorative paintings, sculpture and furniture and interior design.[20] For the exhibition 'The Woman 1813–1913' in Amsterdam, she provided not only the interior layout but the complete furnishing of the exhibition section 'The House'.[21] Although this was an outstanding opportunity to showcase and profile her work, she presented her design under the pseudonym 'Greta Derlinge'. It may be that she did not want to risk being confused with her brother, with whom she had had a difficult relationship ever since she began her relationship with Staal, who was married at the time. She had a daughter with Staal, but continued her work, and later successfully profiled herself as a working architect.

Jo van Regteren Altena (1876–1954) studied at the School voor Kunstnijverheid in Haarlem in 1903.[22] Initially she worked as an embroiderer, seamstress and batik artist. Later she designed and produced lampshades. From the late 1920s on, she was increasingly active in advising on and designing interiors **[fig. 1]**. In an interview in the magazine *Binnenhuis en Buitenwereld*, she revealed her modest

1

1 Interior (ca. 1939) from a design by Jo van Regteren Altena.

approach by stating that she would not claim the title of interior architect.[23] Van Regteren Altena organized exhibitions for women at her home. She had even done so while living with her parents at their home, where she had set up a room for the purpose. Later she exhibited her work in her own Haarlem industrial arts gallery, where other women also exhibited, as well as in retail outlets of colleagues in the industrial arts trade that she had met through her membership in VANK and various VANK committees. She participated in exhibitions organized by VANK, and worked closely with architects.

Ida Liefrinck (1901–2006), who began studying interior architecture, furniture design and ceramics at the Kunstnijverheidsschool Quellinus in Amsterdam in 1918, worked in the Rotterdam architecture firm operated by J.J.P. Oud (1890–1963), and also participated in research into the kitchen designs of German workers' houses.[24] After studying furniture-making in Germany, she returned to the Netherlands. In 1933 she married an electrical engineer, Otto Falkenberg, but she continued her own work after marriage. An interior she designed in 1938 for the single working woman, commissioned by Amsterdam firm Metz & Co. (the well-known luxury department store for home furnishings), led to a long-term collaboration with that firm's in-house interior architect, Elmar Berkovich

zit-slaapkamer
ontwerp
Ida Falkenberg-
Liefrinck

2

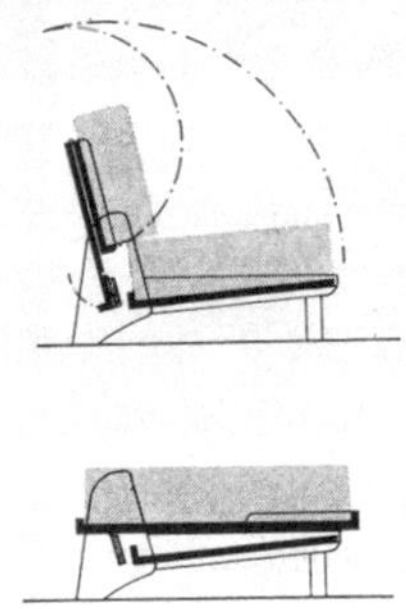

verstelbare zit-slaap-bank

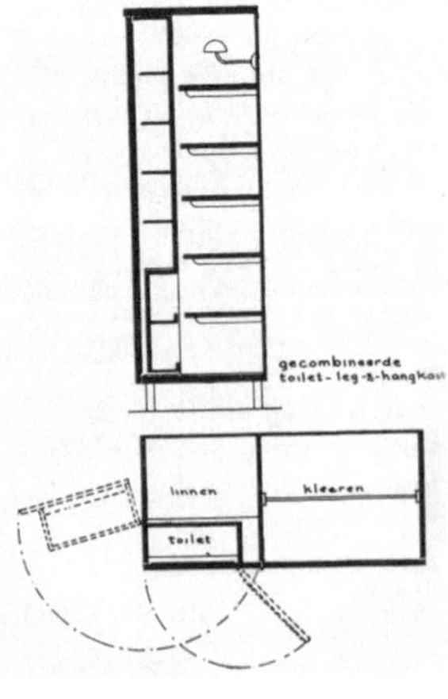

(1897–1986) **[fig. 2]**. Going by the draft system of VANK discussed above, Liefrinck would have fallen under the category 'civil servant-interior architect', and would have had to have been paid accordingly.[25]
Out of extreme dissatisfaction with the rattan furniture in the shop below her home, Liefrinck decided to design her own rattan chairs. Her modern, minimalist models, produced not only in rattan but also in reed and wood, were highly sought after and exhibited by men working in her field. Liefrinck did not operate in VANK-related circles, but found other publicity channels. As a board member of Opbouw, a Rotterdam association of practitioners of 'building and related arts', she was partly responsible for a change in course in 1929 that attempted to engage with the Modern Movement, also known as 'New Objectivity'.[26] Cooperation with the Amsterdam group De 8 led to the creation of the avant-garde magazine *de 8 en Opbouw*, in which she was published frequently and for which she served as editorial secretary from 1934 to 1939.[27] In one of her articles, she called for a new culture of living with practical and affordable furniture instead of elite and pricey 'furniture art'.[28]

Phemia Molkenboer (1883–1940), whose father was director of the Rijksnormaalschool voor Teekenonderwijzers in Amsterdam, earned a diploma in hand drawing from that school in 1905 and went on to study at the Rijksakademie voor Beeldende Kunsten.[29] Alongside giving lessons and drawing, she also produced illustrations and designed children's furniture. She used her illustrations and exhibitions to generate publicity for her children's furniture. From 1915 to 1925 Molkenboer developed wooden toys and children's furniture for Amsterdam toy factory Olanda, and with them was exhibited successfully at the 'Exhibition of aesthetically produced consumer products' in Haarlem in 1919. She was active as a board member of an art circle, and in 1919 also joined VANK.

2 Design (1938) by Ida Falkenberg-Liefrinck of a sitting room/bedroom for a working woman, as appeared in *de 8 en Opbouw*.

From this small group of professional women, it is difficult to draw broad conclusions. And yet, there is a consistent picture to be found in the careers of these women. All four managed to be successful in disciplines like furniture design and manufacture, interior design and interior architecture, professions that until then had only been practised by men. To all appearances, it seems that Van Regteren Altena and Molkenboer, both single, were able to earn their own living. Alongside giving drawing lessons, which must have provided Molkenboer with a regular income, she was also a successful children's furniture maker and managed to find the right channels for their sale.

Within the field, it seems that these women did not encounter any particular resistance; in fact, quite the contrary, we see that their work was appreciated and valued by the men working in their field. One would expect that their arrival on the labour market would have been perceived as unusual, at the very least, or even a threat, by the men working in their field. In particular, whereas the single women evidently succeeded in practising their profession independently, when we compare this to the group of women architects, we see that almost none of them managed this. Some of them made certain attempts, but they failed to achieve what the women furniture designers and interior architects did: find ways to promote their own work and leverage professional networks and sales channels. Most likely, it was harder to accept that women could prove themselves in the skillsets of domains like building and architecture than that women could excel in areas that they were already closely involved in, such as interior design. The fact that most women architects in this research study also had university degrees was hard to reconcile with the societal image. That was not an issue for the phenomenon of women becoming educated in the industrial arts.

Women in garden architecture

Those with the title of garden and landscape architect (legally protected since 1988) designed gardens, parks and urban green spaces, including the planning, layout and design of the landscape.[30] Until 1945 there was no specific higher education programme for garden architecture.[31] Consequently, they cannot effectively be compared to women who earned a diploma in architecture in tertiary education before 1945. I present the following description to offer a picture of the education available to women who wanted to enter the field of garden architecture. Around 1900, there were secondary education programmes in garden architecture in a few cities, like Aalsmeer and Tiel. Of the students who completed these programmes, few if any were women. Occasionally, a young lady would take a number of courses out of personal interest or as a way of spending time. Higher education in garden design first became possible in 1904, when it was offered at the Rijks Hoogere Land-, Tuin- en Boschbouwschool in Wageningen.[32] From the very beginning, only a few women attended this school, and that was still the case in the 1940s. The students were separated: women sat apart from men, assigned to the front row.[33] Some women opted to only take the courses in garden architecture.[34] In 1918, this institution was legally granted the academic status of 'university', and changed its name to the Rijks Landbouw Hooge School. It is relevant to note for the purposes of this research that the level of education was equivalent to that of the Technische Hogeschool (TH) in Delft. The major in 'Garden and Landscape Architecture' was first offered in 1945; this means that until then there were no garden architects (men or women) with a university degree.[35] The first woman garden architect to receive this degree was Deni Hartelust (1928–1982).[36] She graduated in 1955.

3

3 Teacher at the Middelbare Tuinbouwschool Voor Meisjes Huis te Lande in Rijswijk, 1930.

→
4 Students of the Middelbare Tuinbouwschool Voor Meisjes Huis te Lande in Rijswijk, 1928.

Beginning in 1907, girls from affluent families could pursue secondary education in garden design at the Middelbare Tuinbouwschool Voor Meisjes Huis te Lande ('Huis te Lande Horticultural School for Girls') in Rijswijk.[37] One of the founders of this school was Jacoba Hingst (1871–1950), who set up the school in her villa. Initially, the programme was not intended to educate 'girls from polite society' to enter the field of garden architecture as a profession, but rather to teach them the skills of growing flowers, vegetables and fruits for later use in their own gardens.[38] The girls attended courses in garden design, plant knowledge, art history and flower arrangement, and went on study trips to France and England to visit famous growers **[Figs. 3 and 4]**. In 1941 the objective of this programme was, to some degree, adjusted to the following: 'to give girls such knowledge of and skills in the work of gardening so that later in life they will be able to have practical use of it, whether they wish to seek a position in gardening in another's or their own company, or whether they wish to apply their knowledge usefully within their own circles'.[39] One year later, typing was also added. This three-year programme initially accepted a maximum of six students per year; after the First World War, that number varied from 8 to 23. It is not clear how many women earned this diploma before 1945. One source gives an indication, stating that in this period,

twelve women had gone from this programme to working at Huis te Lande as garden architects.[40] This does not say for certain that all twelve of these women actually completed the programme.

In their ambition to become independent garden architects, women faced a barrier in the form of the recommendation from the government to nonetheless work first as an assistant so they could experience whether they found it objectionable to 'work with labourers, due to their physiology'.[41] The profession of garden architect was mentioned for the first time in a professions guide for girls dating from 1914, and it was only recommended for 'strong and not impecunious girls, who can afford to wait and see whether the number of jobs will be sufficient to make a living'.[42] The Society for Gardening and Botany (Maatschappij voor Tuinbouw en Plantkunde) discouraged women from seeking to earn a living in the gardening world.[43] They were also warned that the income would be low, and very irregular.[44] Nonetheless, many women were not scared off by these warnings. In the period up to 1945, we know that 20 women were active in garden architecture.

The women who had made the profession their own (whether or not they had studied garden architecture or earned a degree and it) and were active in the field demonstrated their knowledge and expertise at exhibitions. For the exhibition 'The Woman 1813–1913', a 'Ms J.G. van Zijdveld' (1875–1958) produced the design for the exhibition site.[45] At the exhibition, earlier designs of other women were on display and visitors could read in the exhibition catalogue about what 'some' women had achieved in garden architecture up to that point.[46] Unfortunately, they were not identified by name. For the site design for the exhibition, the organization could choose from nine women who had presented themselves as garden architects. Their names, however, are similarly unknown.

Jeanette van Zijdveld, the tenth child of the family of a civil-law notary, established her own growing business in Laren in 1907, in partnership with her friend Cornelia Spoor (1885–1950); that business grew into a profitable firm with 12 employees.[47] It is not known whether either of these women had studied garden architecture. They were able to take advantage of the artists in the local region, who were their clients. In 1915, Van Zuidveld talked about her experience that potential clients had doubts about whether she had the same qualities as the men working in her field.[48] She also noted that dealing with men as employees was a completely new experience for her. Nonetheless, she believed that 'both of these objections were easy to deal with'.[49] Van Zijdveld and Spoor published about their work in *De vrouw en haar huis* and also worked with other garden architects.

Tine Cool (1887–1944), a single woman who had not studied the profession, gained experience by working in a market gardening company, then began garden design as an independent professional, and advertised herself as a garden architect in newspapers in Bussum.[50] More than actual work in garden design, she wrote a large number of articles in magazines like *Buiten, Het Landhuis, Floralia, Onze Tuinen en Bouwkundig Weekblad Architectura*.[51] This may have also been related to the fact that her health was poor. But Cool was in close contact with her fellow garden architects.

Renske Boon (1900–1985), daughter of a wealthy landowner in Groningen, began the programme at Huis te Lande in the early 1920s.[52] She later returned to her parents' home in Hoogezand and began her own company there, while her sister took care of the housekeeping. The new garden that Boon created there was the calling card for her business. She won commissions for villa gardens, farmyards, pleasure gardens, cemetery landscaping and city parks. Boon ultimately left behind an oeuvre of some two hundred projects. Another woman with her own garden design company was Iep Faber (1899–1983), who earned a diploma from Huis te Lande.[53]

Mien Ruys (1904–1999), daughter of a market gardener in Dedemsvaart, was given the opportunity to study at the first technical college for garden design in Berlin, Germany.[54] In the early 1930s, she audited classes at the Technische Hoogeschool in Delft and discovered, in her own words, 'the broader connection (...) between urban design, architecture, and garden and landscape architecture'.[55] Ruys established herself as an independent professional in Amsterdam and had a lively portfolio of orders, thanks in part to her father's market gardening operation. She sought to move in Amsterdam architecture circles, and enjoyed some recognition there. After the war, Ruys seems to have worked with architect Ko Mulder, who worked in the department of urban development. Ruys' projects included the development of green spaces in neighbourhoods such as Slotervaart.

Despite the negative career advice, the women described here were apparently able to provide for themselves reasonably well as independent professionals, thanks in part to their creativity in finding promotional opportunities, networks and clients. Because prior to the Second World War the field was still emerging, there were still no specific positions available with the government. Architects in the employ of the municipal authorities, like Ko Mulder (1900–1988), were assigned projects in gardening and landscape architecture under their management because there were still no specialists in the field of landscape architecture.

In 1922 Bond van Nederlandsche Tuinarchitecten (BNT), or 'Association of Dutch Garden Architects', was established. It is interesting to note that alongside garden architect Leonard Springer (1855–1940), there were a number of women involved in the foundation of this organization, including Jo Bouwens (1895–1962), Jacoba Hingst, Tine Cool and Jeanette van Zijdveld.[56] The object of this association was 'the development and appreciation of the art of gardening as an independent art', as well as promoting the interests of the members and education.[57] Over ten years after its founding, the then-chairman of the BNT, in his efforts to obtain protection for the title of garden architect, made an apt comparison with architecture when he argued that 'the difference between garden art and garden architecture (...) is just as big as the difference between architect and builder'.[58] There was also more than a hint of envy in the quest to position the field on an equal footing with architects. Immediately following Springer's arguments in the journal *Bouwkundig Weekblad Architectura*, architect and garden architect Johan Pieter Fokker (1889–1963) called for his fellow members of the association to 'agitate for garden architects to be given all the work that they are, in fact, entitled to (...)'.[59] Fokker argued that the garden-technical knowledge was lacking among architects, 'who only had education in construction', and that many architects 'nonetheless make forays (...) into the field of garden architecture where they do not belong and that the garden architects are bitter about this'. In Chapter 7, we will see that architects like Wil Jansen who were active in garden architecture were primarily prompted to do so by the economic conditions. The importance of partnerships with architects was also underscored by Iep Faber in an article in the weekly *Onze Tuinen* in 1928.[60] The fact that both disciplines could be complementary is evidenced by the partnerships between Mulder and Ruys in Amsterdam, as already mentioned above. Ruys became a board member of the BNT in 1941.

Of any supposed resistance that women might have experienced when they entered the world of garden architecture professionally, there are virtually no examples to be found. As already cited, only Van Zijdveld expressed any doubts experienced on the part of clients concerning whether they should hire a woman, and about learning to deal with men as employees. And even these objections seemed to not be insurmountable for Van Zijdveld. While young women were still discouraged from pursuing education in horticulture by voices in the field, whenever they entered the labour market in spite of this discouragement there seems to have been little to no overt objection or opposition from men working in their field. Fokker, for example, expressed the opinion that 'engaging in the minutiae of the small crop' was well-suited to the 'female temperament'.[61]
He also cited examples of what he saw as well-lain borders by women, for example those of Tine Cool.[62]

Earlier acceptance

Women on the rise in interior and garden architecture found themselves more readily accepted by clients and colleagues then their contemporaries working as women architects, as the following chapters will show.

This can be partly explained by the fact that professions such as interior designer, furniture designer and garden architect tended to be associated with characteristics considered 'feminine', such as a keen sense of colour, detail and atmosphere. By contrast, women who wished to become architects and who became proficient in technical skills at the academic level had a difficult path ahead of them. For centuries, architecture has been a profession traditionally assigned to and performed by men. By comparison, professions such as interior architect and garden architect were still emerging, so there was no long-established order to upset.

3 The pioneering women architects

The word architecture comes to us from the Greek *architektón*, which is a compound of two Greek words, *archi* (principal, master) and *tektón* (carpenter).[1] In the early decades of the nineteenth century, it was the master builders – primarily craftsmen who had developed practical skills from working as plasterers or carpenters – who drafted building plans and oversaw their execution.[2] By the second half of the nineteenth century, a rapidly growing population and expansion of the cities were driving a dramatic increase in demand in the building sector, particularly for the various types of public building.[3] The design process for such buildings and the use of new materials such as iron, glass, zinc and concrete demanded specialist knowledge that the craftsmen and master builders did not possess.

An institution founded in 1842, the Maatschappij tot Bevordering der Bouwkunst, recognized the importance of separating the design process and the actual construction, and advocated for a special educational programme leading to the title of professional architectural designer.[4] That institution published professional journals and organized lectures and discussion meetings. Five years later, the Royal Dutch Institute of Engineers (KIVI) was established to pursue similar activities.[5] Engineers focused primarily on infrastructure projects like harbours and bridges, as well as roads and waterways, but also on building construction.

This chapter outlines a general picture of the first university-level programme in architecture, given at the Technische Hogeschool in Delft, as well as the first programmes in higher vocational education for the qualification of architect (Voortgezet en Hoger Bouwkunst Onderricht, VHBO), given in Amsterdam. These two programmes produced the first women architects. In addition, this chapter also looks at the degree to which these programmes were accessible to women, and the experiences of some of them in regard to the programme itself and how they were treated as women as they pursued it.

Education in Delft

By virtue of the Secondary Education Act of 2 May 1863, the university chair in 'bouwkunde' (architecture) was granted to the Polytechnic School in Delft, which was founded in 1864. This was the start of the first official architecture programme in the Netherlands. With the arrival of the Polytechnic, the Royal Academy in Delft was closed; the latter had been

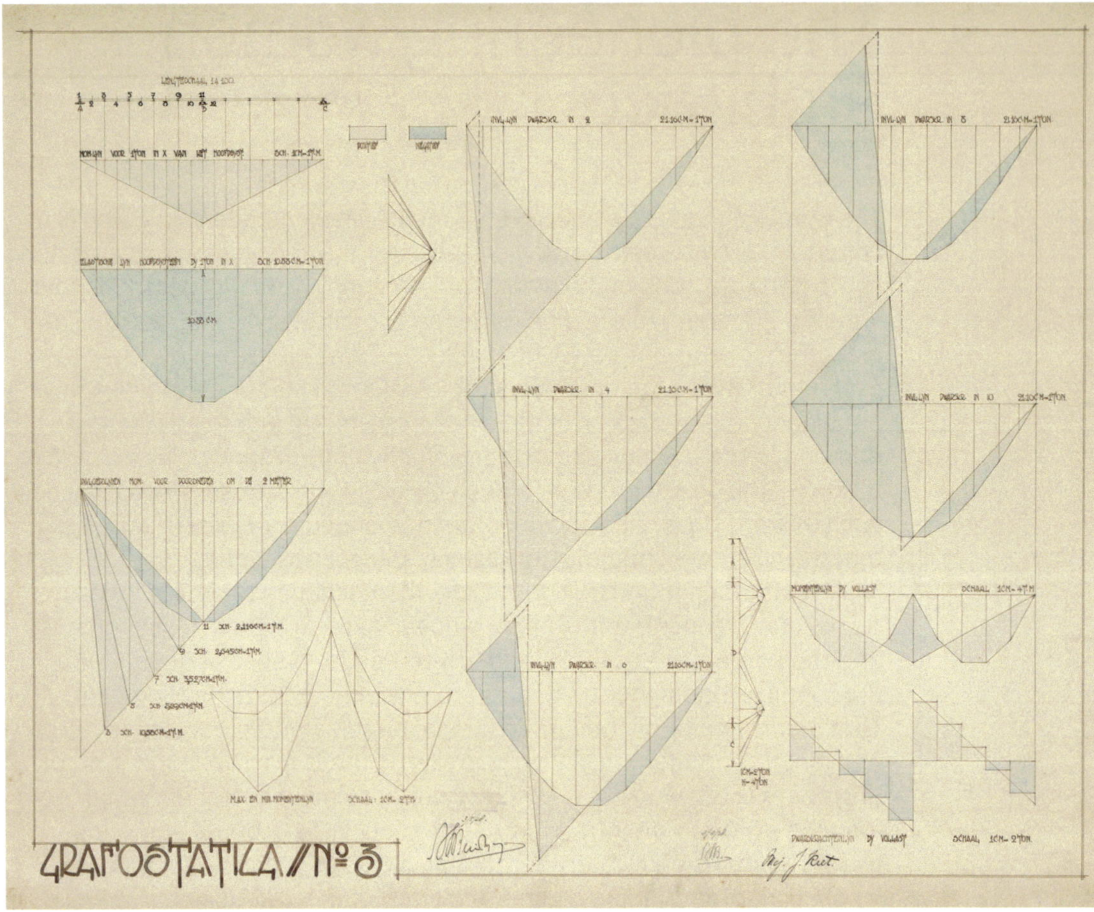

1a

1a Drawing was considered to be of paramount importance. J. Kret, *Grafostatica no. 3*, Delft 1928.

1b

1b J. Kret, *Gemeenlandshuis Maassluis*, Wil Jansen, Delft, second year of study 1925–1926.

established by Royal Decree in 1842 by King Willem II, with the official name of 'Royal Academy for the education of civil engineers, both for service to the country and for the industries and apprentices in the trades'.[6] At the Royal Academy, the architecture course was at that time still a component of the curriculum in the Roadworks and Hydroengineering department.[7] For the students at the Polytechnic, the four-year programme in architecture initially largely coincided with the civil engineering programme. A change in the law in 1901 created an independent programme with the qualification of 'architect or architectural engineer'.[8] This architecture programme took on its permanent form in 1905 when the Polytechnic School became the Technische Hogeschool (TH), raising the level of the qualification to a university degree. After the passage of the Higher Education Act in 1985, the school became the Technical University.

A prerequisite for sitting the final examinations in the architecture programme at the Technische Hoogeschool was a final diploma from the appropriate secondary school: a five-year course at the hogereburgerschool (HBS) or gymnasium-B.[9] The five-year architecture programme consisted of technical components on the one hand and art history and design courses on the other. The addition of this last element had its origins in the objections of the executive board of the Technische Hoogeschool

2a

2b

2a Beginning in the second year of study, modelling was a component of the curriculum. W.C.M. Jansen, model of a design for a museum, Delft, undated.

2b W.C.M. Jansen, model of a design for a city hall, Delft, undated.

→
3a 'Girls in the drawing hall', department of Architecture, Oude Delft, 1909. It is not known whether this depicts the four female students of the 1909–1910 academic year, which would have included Grada Wolffensperger (not identifiable in the photo).

to an initial impetus to place the architecture programme in the Rijks-akademie van Beeldende Kunsten in Amsterdam.[10] The examination for the introductory level (propaedeutic exam) was taken in three components: theoretical and applied mathematics, theoretical and applied physics, and architecture, technical drawing and hand drawing. The drawing component was considered to be the most important **[fig. 1a and 1b]**. By the mid-1920s, outdoor drawing was added to the programme.[11] Chemistry was also among the first-year courses, but there was no examination in this subject.

3b

Officially, the programme allowed three years for passing the candidate exam, which was also a three-component exam. The curriculum was expanded with courses such as mechanics, 'land surveying and levelling', administrative law and constitutional law, hydroengineering, road and bridge construction, knowledge and research of construction materials, technical hygiene, modelling and sculpture, decorative art and art history **[Figs. 2a and 2b]**.[12] For the technical fields, the students had to 'work primarily in the drawing auditoriums under the continuous supervision of professors and assistants', in which there was also opportunity to 'enrich knowledge of the literature, which is necessary for broad edification' **[Figs. 3a and 3b]**.[13] For the candidate exam in the third year, students had to design residential homes and small public buildings **[fig. 4]**.[14] Professors of architecture at the Technische Hoogeschool included Henri Evers (1855–1929), Adrianus van der Steur (1865–1945) and Richard Schoemaker (1886–1942).[15] Karel Sluyterman (1863–1931) taught decorative art and ornamentation, and Arend Odé (1865–1955) taught modelling and sculpting.

3b Woman and architecture student, Delft, year and name unknown.

→
4 For the candidate exam, students had to design a small public building. C.H.M. Boerée, *Hotel Café Restaurant*, front elevation and floor plan, Delft 1924.

The programme in the final year further included a striking number of new subjects that did not require final examinations, such as mechanical engineering, mechanical technology, economics, commercial law and accounting. In order to graduate, the students first had to pass theoretical exams in thirteen subjects.[16] The graduating assignment consisted of creating a design for a public building **[fig. 5]**. The design sketch had to be made in one day and was then sealed. On the basis of that design sketch, a total design would then be developed over several weeks, as well as a component for the decorative art course.

The inclusion in the curriculum of subjects such as administrative and commercial law, business and accounting is an indication of a programme that was more oriented towards preparing students for the practice of a profession as an independent architect than as an architect in the employ of a firm. Others reached the same conclusion, including Ko Mulder, who later went to work for the municipality of Amsterdam and eventually became a city planner. She noted that the programme was not particularly good preparation for professional practice.[17] Initially, there was no option to specialize within the programme.[18] All architecture students sat the

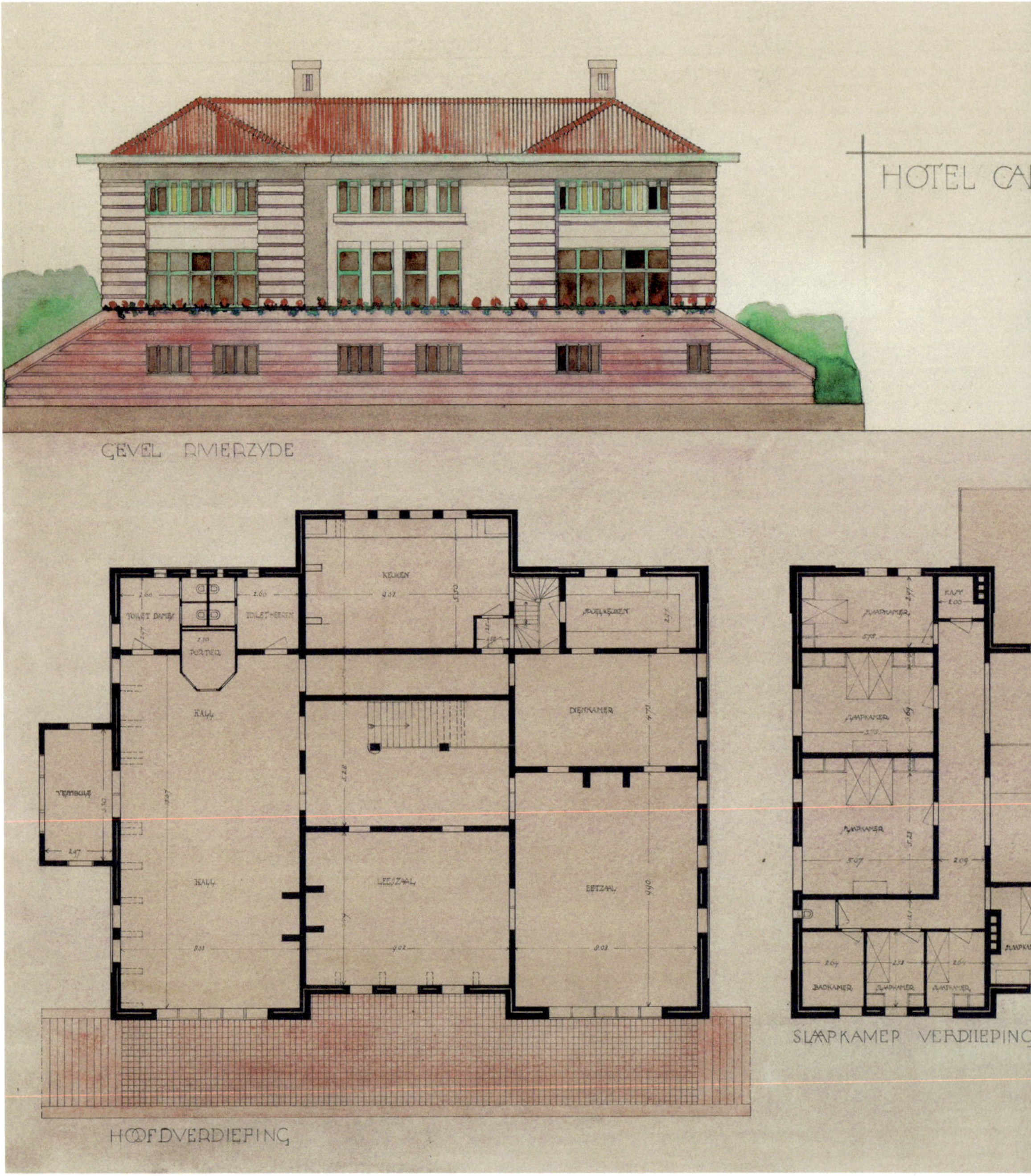
GEVEL RIVIERZYDE
HOOFDVERDIEPING
SLAAPKAMER VERDIEPING
KEUKEN
TOILET DAMES
TOILET HEEREN
PORTIER
SPOELKEUKEN
HALL
VESTIBULE
DIENKAMER
LEESZAAL
EETZAAL
SLAAPKAMER
BADKAMER
KAST

4

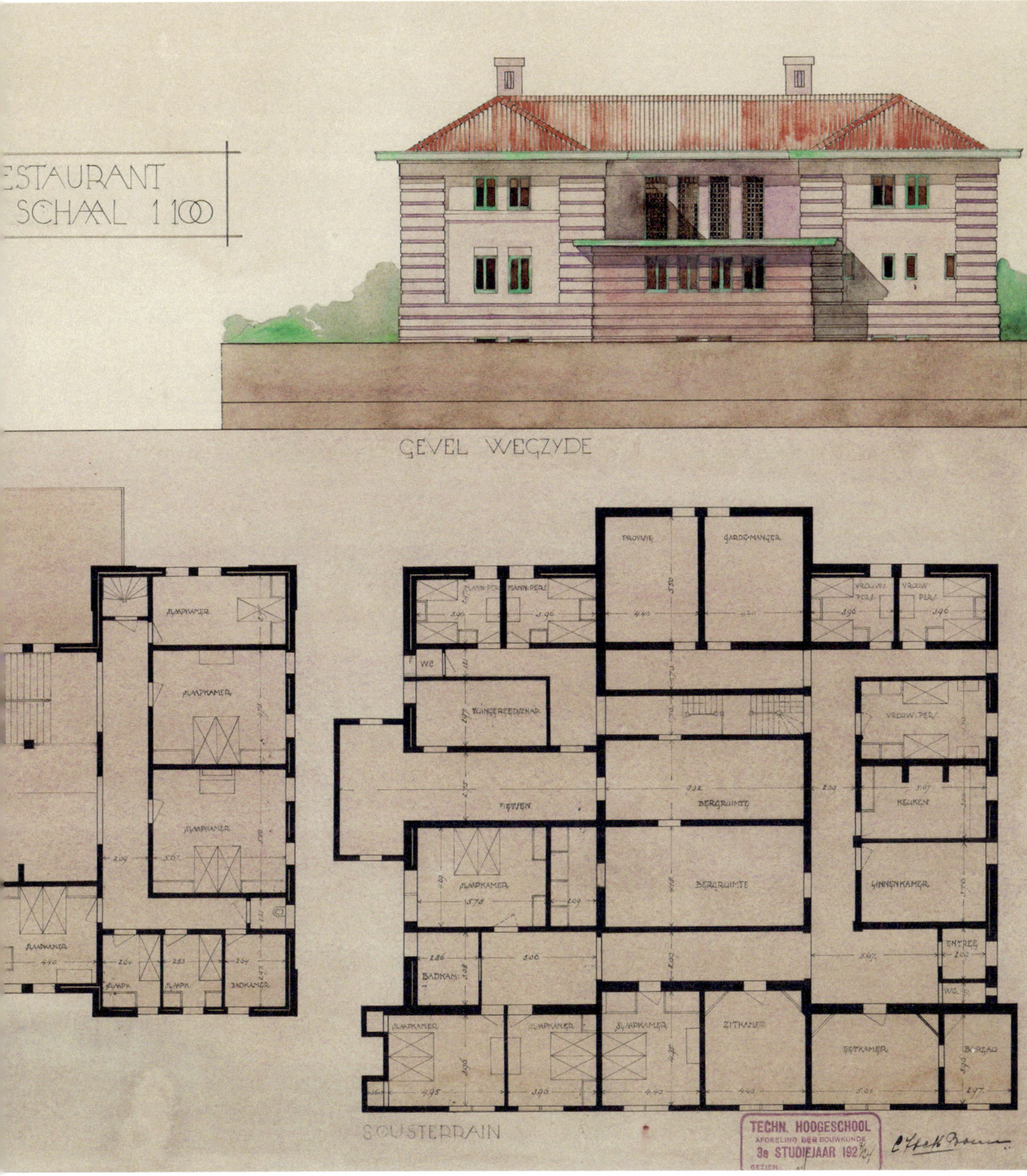
ESTAURANT
SCHAAL 1 100
GEVEL WEGZYDE
PROVISIE
GARDE-MANGER
SLAAPKAMER
TUINGEREEDSCHAP
FIETSEN
BERGRUIMTE
KEUKEN
LINNENKAMER
ENTREE
BADKAMER
ZITKAMER
EETKAMER
BUREAU
WC
SOUSTERRAIN
TECHN. HOOGESCHOOL
AFDEELING DER BOUWKUNDE
3e STUDIEJAAR 192

5

same final examinations. In the 1920s, students in the final year could choose to specialize in non-residential construction, monumental architecture or urban development **[fig. 6]**.[19] This last course was taught as a component of the architecture programme by architect and city planner Marinus Jan Granpré Molière (1883–1972). Granpré Molière, who remained at the Technische Hoogeschool in Delft as a full professor until 1953, represented the Delft School, which was generally perceived as very traditional.[20] The first full professor of urban design was appointed in 1947, but it was only in the 1960s that urban design became an independent discipline.

Along with the participation in study trips under the supervision of the professors, both in the Netherlands and abroad, working in practice was strongly recommended as 'a virtually indispensable element of an architect's education' **[fig. 7a-7c]**.[21] That practical experience – usually unpaid – was to be done during the summer holidays. In some cases a lecturer or professor would recommend such a temporary work-study position to help the student better master specific skills.[22]

In Chapters 6, 7 and 8 we will take a closer look at the substantive side of the Technische Hoogeschool's programme in architecture from the perspective of professional practice.

5 Design for a public building, graduating assignment. J. Kret, *Bank building*, Delft 1930–1931.

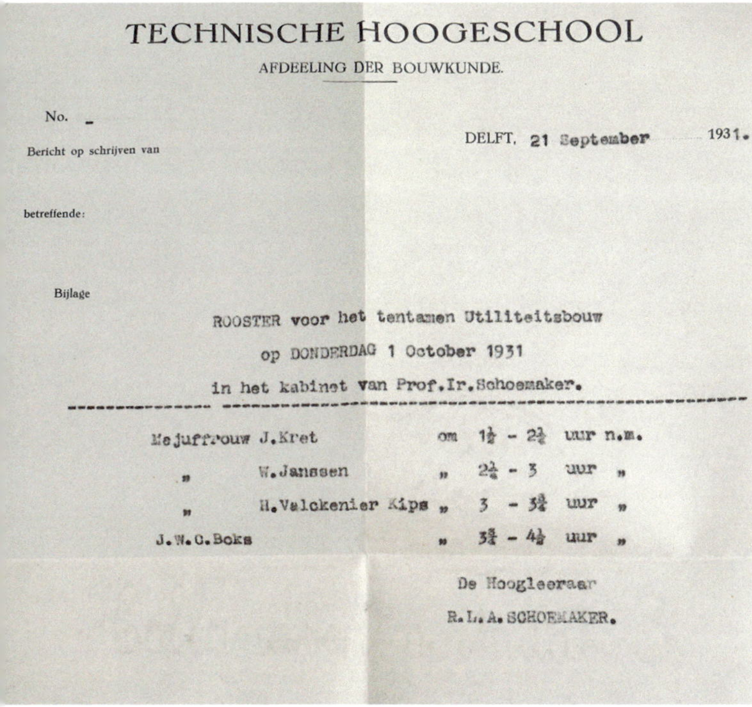

TECHNISCHE HOOGESCHOOL

AFDEELING DER BOUWKUNDE.

No. –

Bericht op schrijven van

betreffende:

Bijlage

DELFT, 21 September 1931.

ROOSTER voor het tentamen Utiliteitsbouw

op DONDERDAG 1 October 1931

in het kabinet van Prof.Ir.Schoemaker.

Mejuffrouw J.Kret	om	1½ - 2¼	uur n.m.
" W.Janssen	"	2¼ - 3	uur "
" H.Valckenier Kips	"	3 - 3¾	uur "
J.W.C.Boks	"	3¾ - 4½	uur "

De Hoogleeraar

R.L.A.SCHOEMAKER.

6

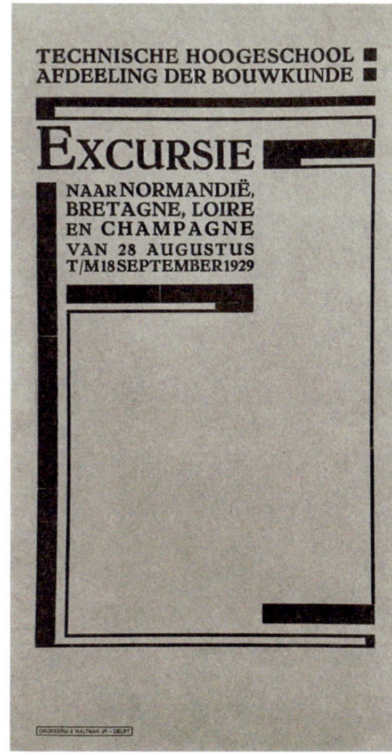

TECHNISCHE HOOGESCHOOL

AFDEELING DER BOUWKUNDE

EXCURSIE

NAAR NORMANDIË, BRETAGNE, LOIRE EN CHAMPAGNE

VAN 28 AUGUSTUS T/M 18 SEPTEMBER 1929

7a

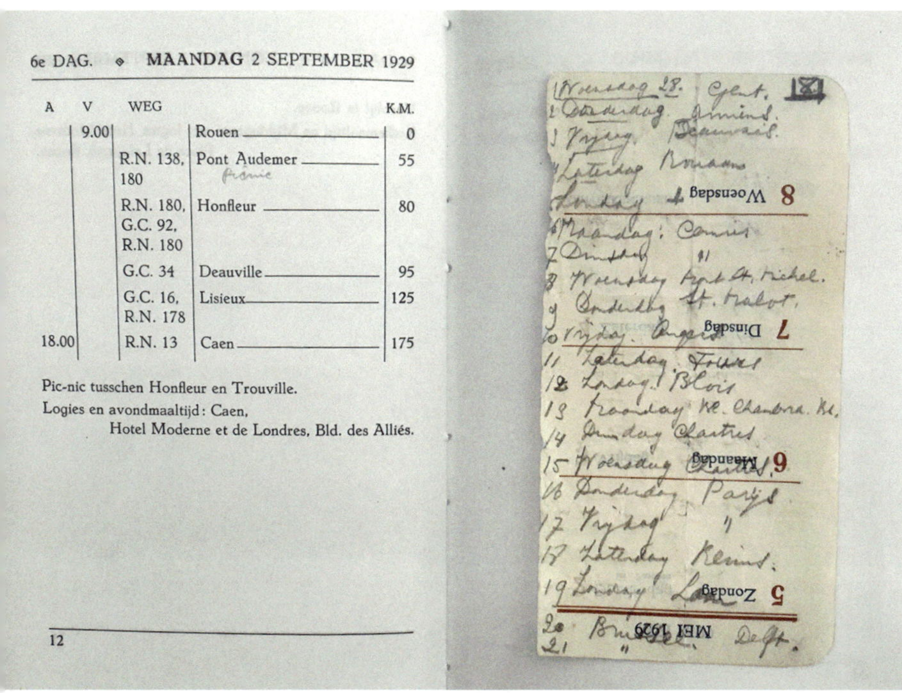

6e DAG. ◆ MAANDAG 2 SEPTEMBER 1929

A	V	WEG		K.M.
	9.00		Rouen	0
		R.N. 138, 180	Pont Audemer	55
		R.N. 180, G.C. 92, R.N. 180	Honfleur	80
		G.C. 34	Deauville	95
		G.C. 16, R.N. 178	Lisieux	125
18.00		R.N. 13	Caen	175

Pic-nic tusschen Honfleur en Trouville.
Logies en avondmaaltijd: Caen,
Hotel Moderne et de Londres, Bld. des Alliés.

12

7b

6 Roster for the exam in non-residential construction, 1931.

7a Title page of the programme of the architecture department's excursion to France, 1929.

7b Programme component, with notes by Wil Jansen.

→
7c An excursion to Middelburg, 1927.

The first women architectural engineers at the Technische Hogeschool in Delft

At the end of the nineteenth century, women, in any cases daughters of professors in Delft, were attending classes (then at the Polytechnic School) as part of their general education, as a way of passing the time, and presumably also in the hopes of finding a suitable candidate for marriage.[23] The first woman to be admitted to study in Delft was a Russian student from Zurich, who came to the Polytechnic School in 1873 to continue her education.[24] However, her name is not included in the list of graduates.[25] The first women who graduated in Delft earned the title of 'technologist' (chemical engineer). Marie Bes (1882–1936) was the first woman to complete this programme at the Polytechnic School, in 1904.[26] That programme proved to be far and away the most popular of the technical studies pursued by women in Delft. By 1946, some 160 women had graduated from the programme with the title of technologist. The women technologists found work in a government job (as long as they remained unmarried), in large private companies such as factories, or in teaching. As far as other disciplines aside from architecture, 19 women graduated in electrical engineering, six in civil engineering, five in physical engineering and one in mechanical engineering.[27]

For the less affluent, undertaking studies at a university was not an option: tuition fees amounted to some three hundred guilders a year.[28] The 19 women in the research group who completed their studies in architecture came from wealthy families, with fathers who were in good jobs – accountants, military officers, teachers or university professors. There are no known examples of women studying architecture whose fathers were architects. The men in the student cohort, however, did include several architects' sons.[29]

For women, there was very little encouragement to become an architect. In a contribution to the encyclopaedic handbook *De vrouw, de vrouwenbeweging en het vrouwenvraagstuk* ('The woman, the women's movement and the woman issue'), a good portion of which was devoted to 'The woman and future offspring (upbringing, teaching, study)', one woman technologist presented an overview of 'The study of women at the Technische Hoogeschool'.[30] For the woman architectural engineer or architect, she saw only limited career prospects, namely to work out 'detailed blueprints of designs made by others'.[31] She believed that with enough artistic acumen, the women 'artist-architects' would be able to find a 'broad working sphere', but only in the decoration of buildings and ships, 'particularly with respect to the interiors, insofar as this is not done by the builder himself'. The *Leidraad voor Nederlandsche meisjes bij de keuze van een beroep* ('Guidebook for Dutch girls in the choice of a profession'), written by the director of the National Bureau for Women's Labour and published in 1928, described the future prospects of a woman architectural engineer succinctly as 'not favourable'.[32]

The Technische Hoogeschool itself was likewise anything but inviting when it came to admitting women to the study of architecture. The report for the 1908–1909 academic year stated that the performance of the job of architect was too physically demanding for women and that any woman who nonetheless did wish to become an architect could better focus on 'the internal decoration of buildings, an orientation to which the woman is by nature well-suited. The question arises, however, of whether five of them shall find enough to make a reasonable living in that line of work.'[33] Even a full professor of architecture, Granpré Molière, was known to hold the opinion that women really should not go to university.[34] In the depths of the economic crisis following the crash of 1929, there did not appear to be a particularly rosy future for any of the students coming through the Technische Hoogeschool. For example, in a review of a pamphlet published by the Central Committee for Academic Interests, *De spiegel*, a body of the Delft Student Corps, called the pamphlet's tone 'dismal'. And that went for most programmes, including architecture. The reviewer considered it 'more than necessary, now that the prospects for the engineer are so poor (...) to warn the parents or guardians of the incoming student. We hope that these warnings will be heeded, but will not stop those who actually possess the characteristics (...) from studying in Delft,' was the dour conclusion.[35] Those characteristics that were necessary to succeed as an engineer were, in the opinion of the committee, a combination of (in part) 'courtesy, general interest and education, perseverance, strength of character, in a word: civility'.

Clearly, the women who enrolled as full-time students in the architecture programme at the Technische Hoogeschool must have been highly motivated, and have had a clear vision of working as a professional architect. Several graduates later indicated that they received particular support from their parents in their choice of study.[36] According to Beb Zeeman (1895–1990), whose father was a professor in Leiden, her parents were extremely progressive for the time and supported her choice. The parents of Toki Koeleman (1911–2000) expected her to make a choice of career that would enable her to be financially independent, which did mean that she had to abandon her first choice of study: sculpting. She began her studies in 1931, in the heart of the financial crisis. Jan Kret's father, who was a clerk in a commercial enterprise, actually encouraged her to study architecture, and Wil Jansen's otherwise generally conservative father expressed pride in his daughter as the only one of the eight children in the family who went to university.[37]

The fact that these women met the entrance criterion of having a diploma from an HBS or gymnasium (the most academically rigorous secondary school) indicates that there had already been a choice in these women's lives to pursue a higher level of education, something still unconventional for the time. In 1870, Aletta Jacobs had been the first girl to be admitted to the Hogereburgerschool (HBS).[38] That form of education had been introduced in 1863 by the Secondary Education Act. Until 1906, admission of a girl to the HBS still required individual ministerial consent. In 1893, there were 64 girls in gymnasium and 342 girls in HBS in the Netherlands, amounting to 2.5% and 5% of students respectively **[fig. 8]**.

In 1904, the Polytechnic School allowed enrolment of the first two women to study architecture. They began their studies in 1905, the year in which the Technische Hoogeschool was launched, together with an additional woman newly registered as a student.[39] These three women, Johanna Victoire Blankenberg (1886–1918), Johanna Gesina Gratama (1886–1965) and Louise Betsy van der Spil (1884–ca. 1967), none of whom completed their studies, were among a total of 32 students who were registered for the architecture programme that year. In that same year, twenty women also audited a few courses. According to the annual report of the Technische Hoogeschool, these women primarily attended art-related courses like art history, decorative art and modelling, which was seen as a testament to 'the love and inclination of Dutch women towards these subjects'.[40] But it was not only women who came to simply 'attend a few courses': in 1915, for example, there were 38 men and 24 women who registered to audit the architecture programme.[41] It is not known which courses the men audited.

← **8** Jan Kret (front row, third from right), with four fellow female students in the fifth-year class of the HBS, 1923.

In 1917, Grada Wolffensperger became the first woman to graduate in architecture, with the title of architectural engineer.[42] In that year, 13 women were enrolled in the architecture programme as full-time students, out of a total of 70.[43] 1921 saw a high watershed of women registered in the programme: 18 out of a total of 117 architecture students.[44] Beginning in 1931, when four women graduated in architecture at the same time, the number of female students gradually declined, hitting a low point in 1940 with two women out of a total of 129 students.[45] The crisis years, and perhaps also the dwindling women's movement, took their toll. In the 1930s, the question was being openly asked within the Technische Hoogeschool whether, in view of the terrible economic conditions, women should have the ambition to study engineering at all, because they would be taking places that could be better occupied by men.[46]

At that time, Frida de Jong wrote in an article that women studying full-time at the Technische Hoogeschool and who were therefore making a deliberate choice to pursue an academic education in preparation for a profession, were being seen by male students as potential competition on the labour market.[47] However, she did not substantiate this with examples. But interviews dating from the 1980s with four women architectural engineers who graduated between 1920 and 1940 reveal that these women did not experience any sensitivities among the men studying alongside them in regard to their participation in the programme.[48] One of the interviewees even stated that in her experience, it was 'not an issue' for them that there were 'girl students' **[fig. 9]**.[49]

These interviews are more noteworthy for the picture they present of the way in which professors treated the women in their classes. A few examples stand in sharp contrast to the foregoing, and give indications of an outspoken hostility. One interviewee, for example, indicated that although 'most of the professors' were 'very nice', it was 'only Professor Evers (...) who [treated] the girls extremely disparagingly, because he didn't take female students seriously'.[50] 'For example, when the girls were at the practice tables in the afternoon – all five of us together – then Professor Evers called all the girls by the same name, the name of whichever of us was in the front.'[51] Another noted that 'the girls' were, from a practical perspective, tested more harshly than 'the boys'.[52] As an example she mentioned Schoemaker, professor of architecture and non-residential buildings, who often put various types of door and window hardware on their drawing tables for them to identify. In Jan Kret's third year of study, Granpré Molière advised her to drop out. Although in his opinion she had mastered residential architecture to a certain degree, she could, he said 'better leave the major projects to others'.[53] Kret did complete her studies, however, and became a practising architect.

→
9 Drafting studio, Delft first year, 1915–1916. The names of the two female students are unknown.

In contrast, we have the positive experiences of one of the very earliest women who studied architecture. When asked, Beb Zeeman, who began her studies in 1913, stated that she had never felt treated differently as a woman at any time during her studies. Likewise, even Ko Mulder later admitted that despite the conduct of Evers as she described it, she didn't feel discriminated against. Evers was, according to Mulder, 'just an old man'.[54] It is difficult to establish whether these examples might be the result of differences in personal perception, but the unpleasant experiences with certain professors, as cited here, speak for themselves.

Not all women, by any means, elected to take the option to gain practical experience during their studies. Grada Wolffensperger, for example, was convinced that it would be equally useful for her to learn to draw at home during the holidays.[55] For a woman as an architectural engineer in the making, finding a place to get work experience was no simple matter. Toki Koeleman, who was advised by an instructor to gain practical experience with making designs, was told by one architect that he didn't want any female students in his firm, but she was nonetheless able to convince him.[56] Beb Zeeman worked for one summer in the construction firm of Professor Evers, whose

design had just recently been selected as the winning design for Rotterdam's new City Hall.[57] As the only woman in the office, she was stationed not in the large drawing hall, but in a side room. Over the next three summers, Zeeman obtained practical experience in the office of the architect for municipal works in Utrecht, S.F. Loeb, under whose supervision she had worked in Rotterdam. For Zeeman, these work weeks bore little resemblance to the study assignments at the Technische Hoogeschool, which in her eyes had little connection with actual practice. As an example, she referred to the design of a doctor's office on a city square, for which the dimensions were already set. Zeeman graduated in 1920 and became the second woman architect to earn the title of architectural engineer, after Grada Wolffensperger.

In the period up to 1946, a total of 19 women graduated as architectural engineers, this out of the 81 who had registered to study architecture full-time since 1904.[58] The length of time that this group of graduates needed to complete their studies varied, from 6 to 13 years. Most of the information, such as exam questions and results, were lost in a 2008 fire in the architecture faculty. Not one woman architectural engineer completed a doctorate in the first half of the twentieth century. Partly in view of the attitude of certain professors, it remains a question whether there were any women who wanted to do so, and if so whether they were discouraged from doing so within the programme. Particularly between 1929 and 1938, women would have sought to deepen their knowledge, in view of the difficult labour market brought on by the financial crisis.[59] Evidently, for the eight women architectural engineers who graduated from the architecture programme in this period, this argument did not apply. There were women who earned doctorates in chemical engineering, Jeane van Amstel (1888–1929) being the first to do so in 1912. After her, ten other women followed in the period up to 1946.[60]

The Delftsche Vrouwelijke Studenten Vereeniging

To get a good picture of where the women studying architecture were positioned amongst the men who were their fellow students, we will here make a slight digression into the role that the Delftsche Vrouwelijke Studenten Vereeniging (DVSV), a student association for women in Delft, played in their lives. The DVSV was established in 1904, because women were prohibited from becoming members of the Delft Student Corps.[61] The first woman who graduated from the programme, Marie Bes, was also the first member of the DVSV. Out of the women studying architecture, all the women in the research group joined the DVSV **[fig. 10]**. Along with facilitating contact with women studying other fields (of the members, the technologists and chemical engineers represented a significant majority), the association

10

10 Front page of the DVSV member list, 1919.

also served the architecture students in other ways, such as providing an opportunity to practice drawing together at the student society.[62] Many were active in committees and on the board of the association **[fig. 11a-11e]**.

The association must have offered these students something to hold onto. It not only helped them navigate this new phase of their lives, as could be expected from any student association at any university, then and now, but in this case also finding a place for women as a minority among the vast majority of male students. In her address in 1913, the DVSV chairwoman offered the new members the following perspective: '(...) you, who up to now have done virtually everything under male supervision, will now learn your own initiative and to supervise yourself here. (...) This does not mean that I intend to make man-haters out of you (...) far from it! But the Delft academic and student life must become for you the way to achieve, for yourself, that: either you can hold an independent place in society or, if you marry, can become not only your husband's wife, but also his support, a support that he will be able to count on at all times.'[63] This last proclamation may not sound particularly emancipated, but should be seen in light of the society of the time.

The fact that there was initially virtually no contact between the newly established DVSV and the Delft Student Corps is evidenced

11b

11c

11d

←
11a Beb Zeeman (middle) as chairwoman of the DVSV board 1917–1918.

11b Ko Mulder (middle) and Paula Rooseboom (second from left), respectively chairwoman and first secretary of the DVSV board in 1924–1925.

11c Wil van den Broek d'Obrenan (far right) as DVSV board member 1925–1926.

11d Chairwoman Toki Koeleman (middle) and Greet van der Poest Clement (left) on the DVSV board 1936–1937.

→
11e To Strumphler (left) as DVSV board member 1934–1935.

from a report of Delft student society life written by a technology student, in which she states that the DVSV was initially considered a quantité négligeable. 'Currently, the relationship is polite but cold.'[64] Still, there was encouragement from the student world for the female students to let themselves be heard more, and one female student joined the editorial board of the student weekly magazine. At the same time, in that same report the author states, with some resignation: 'Some complain that those in the student world take so little notice of us – but what do they want? There is still such a small group in Delft, what possible influence could 30 or 40 girls have on + 1,100 young men?'[65]

The first women to graduate from the VHBO in Amsterdam

In 1908 the Genootschap Architectura et Amicitia in Amsterdam established the Cursus Voortgezet en Hooger Bouwkunst Onderricht (VHBO), or 'course in secondary and higher architecture education', later the Academie van Bouwkunst.[66] Like the Maatschappij tot Bevordering der Bouwkunst, from its very beginnings the Genootschap served as a discussion platform for currently practising architects and architects in training at a time when there was no fully accredited architecture programme in the country. It provided a friendly atmosphere in which its members could share knowledge in various ways, including excursions, literature exchanges and contests.[67] Both associations advocated good architectural education and positioned themselves against the architecture programme at the Delft Polytechnic School, which according to them was extremely interwoven with the other engineering programmes in the school and, moreover, was not sufficiently focused on the aesthetic aspects of architecture. These objections disappeared with the establishment of the architecture programme at the new Technische Hogeschool, but the general opinion was that a school for higher education in architecture was essential in a city of Amsterdam's stature.

Candidates for the programme had to have a final diploma from a suitable secondary education institution with the appropriate prerequisite knowledge and at least two years of practical experience.[68] This latter admission requirement was intended to prevent 'dilettantes, ladies, etc. [sic] from registering'.[69] It was a three-year course given evenings in several locations in Amsterdam (the Rijksakademie van Beeldende Kunsten, the Kunstnijverheidsschool Quellinus and one of the rooms of the Genootschap Architectura et Amicitia in Hotel Parkzicht).[70] The tuition was fifty guilders for the entire course, significantly lower than the three hundred guilders for the programme at the Technische Hoogeschool – and intended to attract as many students as possible

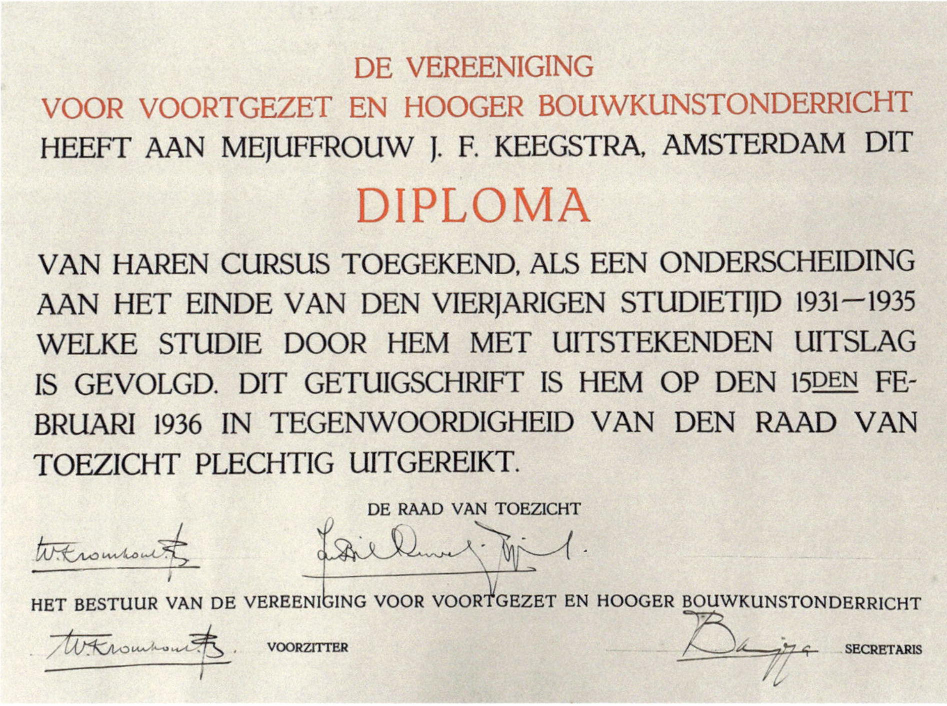

DE VEREENIGING
VOOR VOORTGEZET EN HOOGER BOUWKUNSTONDERRICHT
HEEFT AAN MEJUFFROUW J. F. KEEGSTRA, AMSTERDAM DIT

DIPLOMA

VAN HAREN CURSUS TOEGEKEND, ALS EEN ONDERSCHEIDING AAN HET EINDE VAN DEN VIERJARIGEN STUDIETIJD 1931—1935 WELKE STUDIE DOOR HEM MET UITSTEKENDEN UITSLAG IS GEVOLGD. DIT GETUIGSCHRIFT IS HEM OP DEN 15DEN FEBRUARI 1936 IN TEGENWOORDIGHEID VAN DEN RAAD VAN TOEZICHT PLECHTIG UITGEREIKT.

DE RAAD VAN TOEZICHT

HET BESTUUR VAN DE VEREENIGING VOOR VOORTGEZET EN HOOGER BOUWKUNSTONDERRICHT

VOORZITTER SECRETARIS

12

12 In 1936, Koos Keegstra became the first woman to receive her VHBO diploma.

(and specifically men). Private contributions and grants were expected to cover the costs. Hendrik Petrus Berlage (1856–1934), as chairman of the association, was closely involved in the design of the VHBO and also attached to the programme as an instructor.

Initially, the course launched with 50 students. Its goal was to 'introduce architecturally inclined students, who already possess the craft and the breadth of architectural knowledge, to the domain of art'.[71] The material consisted of 36 courses subdivided into seven 'groups', or main topics. These seven 'groups' were: 'Artistic Architectural Components; Architectural Compositions; Nature of Construction Works – Use; Art History; Technical Sciences, Craftsmanship and Ornamentation; Composition'.[72] Throughout the entire course, the majority of the time was devoted to the primary subject of artistic architectural components: 60 evening sessions of two hours each. In the final year of the programme, each student had to produce a major design of a 'complete monumental project, with all details, calculations, decorations, ornamentation, etc.', which would be assessed primarily on its artistic merit.[73] In 1912, the evening course became a four-year programme.

The annual guide published specially for women by the National Bureau for Women's Labour, which contained all the programmes that could be followed and professions that could be practised, did include the architect's

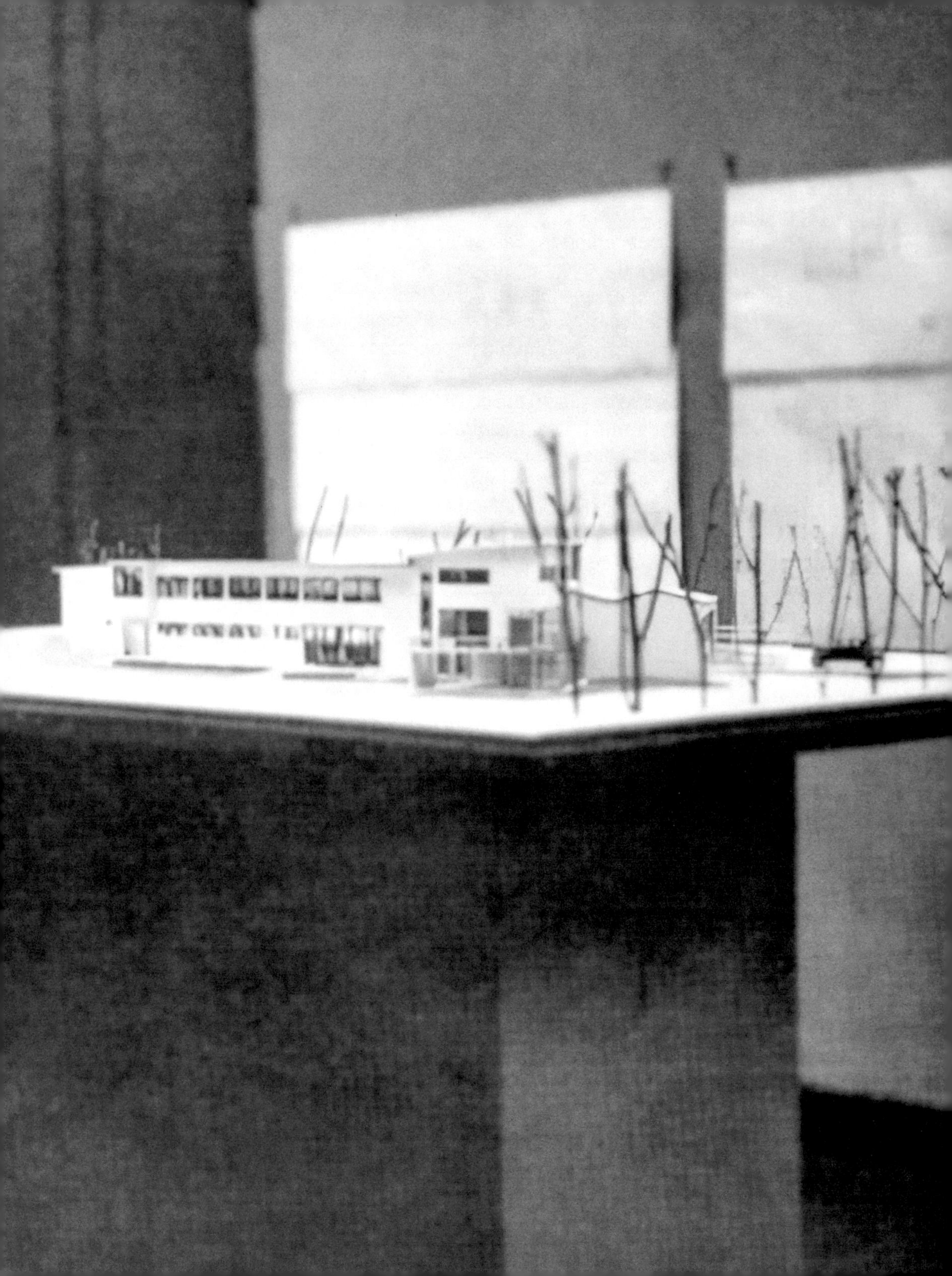

profession, although the VHBO was not mentioned.[74] In the 1914–1915 academic year, the VHBO registered the first woman enrolled, among a total of 19 new registrants: that student was Margaret Staal-Kropholler.[75] She attended the programme for two years, and so never received a diploma. After Staal-Kropholler, Alida (Lidy) van Waveren-Scheltema (1899–1977) was the second woman to register for the VHBO, in 1926.[76] She, too, dropped out after two years.

In the 1920s the VHBO was forced to present the disclaimer that the VHBO course was not a fully fledged higher education programme in architecture. This was a capitulation to pressure from the Bond van Nederlandse Architecten, or BNA ('Association of Dutch Architects'), which was seeking legal protection of the title of architect and did not consider the VHBO diploma to be title-worthy.[77] It was not until 1936 that new management of the VHBO began making adjustments to the curriculum in order to become accredited at that level. In the meantime, the diplomas the VHBO issued were 'not an architect diploma', but rather 'a positive proof of sufficient architectural aptitude to be able to develop into an architect in practice' and 'along with Delft, the only diploma in our country that marks the holder as a person with developed architectural aptitude'; so said the chairman at the time, Adrianus van der Steur, in the commencement ceremony on 19 February 1938.[78] It is not clear whether the VHBO diploma was ever considered title-worthy, and if so, from when.

Two years earlier, Koos Keegstra had become the first woman to complete the VHBO programme, which for 27 years had only produced male graduates **[fig. 12]**.[79] Her progressive parents had found it a matter of course that their daughter should learn a profession, but when after earning the HBS diploma she declared that she wished to become an urban designer, and to that end intended to follow Cor van Eesteren's (1897–1988) advice and go to Paris to study, they would not allow her to be quite as progressive as that.[80] After first being rejected in Utrecht, Keegstra went to the Middelbare Technische School (MTS) in Haarlem, the only girl among a student body of 300 boys. Keegstra had been rejected in Utrecht because their female students did not sit for the final exams. The headmaster in Haarlem placed a condition on her admission, which was that she would not marry immediately after graduation, as a previous girl had done. The school's infrastructure was not set up to accommodate girls, for example in the matter of bathroom facilities. The inconvenience with respect to girls at the school is also evidenced from the director's very strong recommendation to Keegstra that during breaks she immediately repair to the concierge's lodge and wait there until class resumed. During the first carpentry class, she was tested before the eyes of all the boys by having to demonstrate that she could saw through a plank. After the MTS, Keegstra worked in an architecture firm and for the municipality of Amsterdam. This ultimately satisfied the admission requirements for the VHBO. She completed the programme, although it took her an extra year because though she clearly saw the big picture, she 'neglected the details'.[81]

Keegstra earned her diploma under the supervision of Frits Eschauzier (1889–1957), an architect who was known for being a traditionalist. Her graduating assignment was a 'Home for an art collector' **[fig. 13]**. 'This assignment presented significant difficulties, because it became clear that the term "home" had become much more unstable than had been, in the whirlwind speed at which our culture is "advancing",' noted Eschauzier in *Bouwkundig Weekblad Architectura*.[82] 'That a different kind of building should emerge from a confused concept of family life is understandable, and we see the dismal result in our modern residential architecture. But where a house for a family, in the full sense of the word, was now being requested as an academic exercise, we could nonetheless still assume that it should stand firmly on its own merits and in balance with itself. In fact, this could never be a building without tradition, because no one is without tradition.' The weekly magazine published four of the designs, including Keegstra's. Eschauzier did not otherwise go into the details of the individual cases, but Keegstra's outspokenly modern design set itself apart from the others, which were much more traditional. In Chapter 8 we will see that Keegstra continued to build a modernist oeuvre throughout her career.

← **13** Koos Keegstra and her final exam work, *Home for an art collector*, Amsterdam 1935.

The contrasts between the graduating assignments published in *Bouwkundig Weekblad Architectura* could well be considered emblematic of the situation in which the VHBO found itself at that time. The criticism that the Modern Movement was insufficiently represented was something that the executive board tried to counter with a team of lecturers that was as balanced as possible, with place for both adherents of the more traditional and also followers of the more avant-garde movements.[83] This balance was also taken into account in the assignment of supervisors of the graduating assignments.

Whereas in the early 1920s, the VHBO was still attracting something on the order of 70 students per year, this proved to be the prewar maximum; the absolute low point came in 1936 when the programme registered only 31 students.[84] During the Second World War, the numbers began to climb again. Due to lack of work, the attendees had time to devote to education, especially programmes such as this that inspired confidence that they would be able to play their part in post-war reconstruction. A record number of women were enrolled in 1943, four in total: three first-year students and one fourth-year, Lotte Stam-Beese. She was the second woman (after Koos Keegstra) to complete the entire programme, receiving her diploma in 1945.

Stam-Beese attended the VHBO during the war years, a period in which the group of instructors consisted of representatives of the Modern Movement. This meant she had classes in natural lighting and circulation in buildings from Albert Boeken (1891–1951), leader of the Groep '32. Willem van Tijen (1894–1974), Stam-Beese's supervisor in her final year, taught classes on residential community planning, and Jan Bijhouwer (1898–1974) taught classes like urban green spaces and garden landscaping.[85] Van Tijen and Bijhouwer both moved in the circles of De 8 and Opbouw. Neither urban design, the subject that would occupy Stam-Beese after the VHBO, nor landscape architecture existed as specific disciplines at the time, but in 1944 subjects such as the history of garden architecture and principles of garden architecture were added to the curriculum.[86] Another component of the programme was characteristics of styles. This series of classes, on the history of architecture, was given throughout the entire programme by historian Willem van der Pluym (1879–1960).[87] After 1944 there was a stronger focus on aspects of craftsmanship and industry. For example, such subjects as sculpture and painting were no longer approached from a purely art historical perspective, but also taught as a separate craft subject.[88] In 1957 a new department was established: Higher Education in Urban Design (Stedebouwkundig Hoger Onderricht, SHO), where Stam-Beese taught design classes until around 1965.[89]

The fact that few women enrolled in the VHBO course (exact numbers cannot be given, because the archives are incomplete) can be primarily attributed to the admission requirement of at least two years of practical experience, a requirement that had the object of keeping women out of the programme. For a woman, and particularly a woman without a diploma, it was virtually impossible to gain any practical experience. There is nothing known about the treatment of the female students by instructors or fellow students in the course of this programme. In the various interviews that Pot-Keegstra later gave, she speaks exclusively about her experiences at MTS as the only female student.

4 The professional practice of the first women architects in the Netherlands

Architects in the second half of the nineteenth century practised their professions independently, in their own architecture firms.[1] Typically, this would be a small firm that employed a handful of draughtsmen and surveyors. Depending on the order portfolio, these firms might grow into successful enterprises, gaining more employees as they grew.

In the first half of the twentieth century, architects were faced with daunting tasks.[2] Alongside commissions from affluent private individuals, with the introduction of the Housing Act (1901) municipalities also became a major client. The Housing Act was intended to put an end to the harrowing living conditions across the country, particularly of the working class in the cities, and to promote the construction of good housing. The first professional association for architects, the Bond van Nederlandse Architecten (BNA), was established in 1908.[3] The BNA distinguished itself from the Maatschappij tot Bevordering der Bouwkunst (Society to Promote the Architectural Arts), which at that time also admitted builders along with architects, as well as the more artistically minded. These two bodies merged in 1919.[4] The BNA consistently lobbied for legal protection of the profession of architect, and in 1946 established a registry of architects. To be registered, an architect had to fulfil a number of requirements in terms of professional skills and also adopt a code of conduct, which among other things prohibited the architect from having financial interests in the performance of the construction and requiring the architects to act as an independent expert for the client. The profession of architect was finally protected by law in 1988, and now only architectural engineers or graduates from an accredited university of applied sciences (HBO) can be given the title of architect.

In the early twentieth century, a need for specialists in urban design emerged, particularly in the biggest cities.[5] Because the specialism of 'urban designer' did not yet exist, the response to this need fell to the architect. A similar development was seen in landscape architecture, which came into demand as cities expanded and needed to create green features like city parks. Gradually, local authorities and institutions began opting to take such specialists into their own employ.

As already discussed in Chapter 3, women were not encouraged to go into architecture. In a brochure published by the Central Committee for Academic Interests at the Technische Hoogeschool of Delft, Professor

Adrianus van der Steur enumerated a long list of practical problems for the woman architect.[6] There was, for example, interacting with contractors and workmen which, in his view, demanded a forceful attitude; then there was the climbing on scaffolding and roofs, which women were not suited for. Sometimes, however, the reality proved stubbornly different: 'The primary difficulty of this job for a woman is that you might not always be able to exert enough authority over contractors and workmen, not that I ever had trouble with that: if you demonstrate that you actually know what you're doing, you'll get what you want to be done,' according to architect Koos Keegstra, who was for a time employed as a draughtswoman and technical surveyor at the Service of Public Works in Amsterdam.[7] Much later, looking back at her career in an interview in *Het Parool*, she would reiterate that, man or woman, you simply have to know your job. 'A male architect (...) could also get thrown off the scaffolding, back in the day, if he was a bungler.' **[fig. 1]**.[8] Around the same time, Grada Wolffensperger's male colleague at the Department of Public Works in Haarlem, Jan Buijs, for whom she had to clear out to benefit his career, similarly discouraged his niece from going into architecture, because builders wouldn't listen to a woman 'and climbing up scaffolding in all manner of inclement weather is likewise nothing for a woman'.[9] That niece was Kitty van der Mijll Dekker (1908–2004) who, on the recommendation of the same uncle, went to the Bauhaus. She became a hand loom artist and textile designer, and her work was displayed in national and international exhibitions.

←
1 Pot-Keegstra at a construction project, undated.

While the two women from the research group with VHBO diplomas (one of them Keegstra) had already been professionally active before their study (which was a prerequisite for admission) and continued their professional activities during their study, the nineteen architectural engineers were left to find their own way in the field after graduation. These women then faced the difficult challenge of how to practice their profession and gain a place for themselves among their male colleagues. Margaret Staal-Kropholler was still dealing with this as late as 1951, when she wrote: 'The unusual breeds mistrust, and the only way to win trust is to demonstrate achievements. But one needs commissions to do that, and those are only given to architects that people trust. That's why it's much more difficult for a woman architect to find work, as opposed to a woman painter or sculptor, who can also start without commissions.'[10] Alongside these social obstacles, in the 1930s some of the women architects also struggled with the difficult economic conditions, which did not make it any easier for anyone to find work and win commissions.

When the first women graduated as architectural engineers in 1917, there were three options for working in the field of architecture: finding a government job, joining an architecture firm or working as an independent architect. In this chapter we will look at whether and to what extent these options were open to women. A number of women architects looked beyond the bounds of their own field: the second section of this chapter presents a picture of the architecture-adjacent side activities that these women conducted within professional associations, interest organizations or advisory committees. The last section of this chapter will look at whether and to what extent the women architects captured the attention of the media in the practice of their profession, or whether they had to generate that attention themselves by writing articles.

A government job

As from 1924, only unmarried women were permitted to hold government jobs. As soon as they married, dismissal followed. Single women in government jobs became even more vulnerable in the years of the financial crisis, when they were the first to be fired in order to keep men in the workplace.[11] This is what happened to Koos Keegstra at the Public Works Department in Amsterdam.

The first two women to graduate as architectural engineers, Grada Wolffensperger and Beb Zeeman, worked briefly in the early 1920s as adjunct architects: Wolffensperger in the Department of Public Works in Haarlem and Zeeman in the same department in Amsterdam. In the wake of the First World War, the construction sector had ground to a near halt due to supply chain difficulties and high costs of construction materials, but as the situation improved, the demand for personnel in the industry exploded as builders tried to work through the accumulated backlog of the war years. Both Wolffensperger and Zeeman had this to thank for their jobs. In both of their cases, they were the only women in their departments. Alongside 14 fellow draughtsmen who were men, Zeeman produced design drawings and occasionally visited construction sites. But both of these women's careers ended prematurely. Wolffensperger had to step aside so that the aforesaid Jan Buijs could keep his job (see Chapter 5); Zeeman married and moved to the Dutch East Indies with her husband.

Seven women from the research group were able to pursue their careers in government jobs. Some, like Riné Boerée, first found temporary work in government institutions; in her case, she first worked at the Government Building Agency (Rijksgebouwendienst) and later worked at the Army Corps of Engineers (Genie) as an expert in concrete (see Chapter 6). Ko Mulder and the divorced Lotte Stam-Beese both had distinguished careers as city planners, the former in Amsterdam and the latter in Rotterdam. In 1928 the urban design division of the Public Works Department in Amsterdam offered Mulder a golden opportunity to specialize in city

planning and landscape architecture, despite her having not specifically studied these specializations **[fig. 2]**. As already discussed, these two disciplines only began to take root in academic education after the Second World War. Stam-Beese primarily benefited from the post-war reconstruction. The same can be said for the other four women from the research group: Wil van den Broek d'Obrenan (1905–1966), Sophie Heyting (1894–1988), Greet van der Poest Clement (1912–1976) and To Strumphler (1911–1981). All of them became municipal architects or took jobs as engineers in municipal or provincial planning departments.

2 Working in an architecture firm

It is likely that a woman architect, after completing her studies, would have aspired to a full-time, high-level job commensurate with her level of education. For a position in an architecture firm, this would mean that she would form a partnership with one or more colleagues who were already employed. For male architects, entering into such partnerships had more or less become the norm over time. This was how a twenty-year-old Co Kropholler, brother of Margaret, and his colleague Frits Staal, three years his senior, came to establish an architecture firm in Amsterdam in 1902. Johannes Albertus Kuiper (1907–2003), who in 1937 married Ada Struyk (1908–1985), a woman architect who had graduated in that same year, began an architecture firm in 1940 with Pieter Verhagen (1882–1950).[12]

2 Ko Mulder at the drawing board, undated.

For women architects, entering into this kind of association with one or more male colleagues proved not to be a realistic option. For one thing, there was the generally prevailing conception that the woman's role was subservient, that she belonged at home and that her duties were to spouse and family. This was difficult to reconcile with the idea of allowing a woman to become a partner in an architecture firm.

Then there was the already noted unease and even active resistance to the presence of women on a construction site. Ko Mulder was rejected by an architect who gave the reason that he simply could never send a woman up a scaffold.[13] And, as also already mentioned, a woman supervising a construction site, and having to deal with all the contractors and workers accordingly, presented another obstacle. On the other hand, Wil Jansen saw the formation of a partnership as the answer to these objections: '(...) not all women have the same capacities in the business area – negotiating with contractors. Association with male colleagues has the advantage that the men can to some extent take that aspect on themselves.'[14] It should be noted that Jansen herself, as will be described later, worked as an independent architect.

The third likely reason for resistance to admitting a woman as a partner in a firm was the possibility that she might have attained a higher level of education than the male partners. Remember that at the time, by no means all working architects had actually studied at university.

Absolutely none of the group of these first women architects became a partner in a firm. Where cooperation on an equal footing proved to be impossible, some of them joined firms as employees, but in subordinate roles. In these cases, they were temporary positions in which, as far as is known, they only performed tasks that were below their level of education. Ko Mulder initially worked as a draughtswoman at an architecture firm in The Hague, run by Gerretsen & Wegerif – both men were friends of hers – where she primarily worked out detailed designs from drawings. After graduating in 1920, Beb Zeeman was briefly the only woman working in **3**
an architect's office, officially in the position of engineer, but here too her work was limited to working out the details of his sketches.[15] Immediately after graduating in 1921, Marie Snethlage (1893–1998) found work as an engineer in the brand-new firm of architect A.A. Kok in Amsterdam. Abel Kok (1881–1951) gained a reputation primarily as a restoration architect, and in the year that Snethlage came to work for him he had an impressive list of commissions, including the restoration of the Agnietenkapel on Oudezijds Voorburgwal in Amsterdam.[16] But within three years, Snethlage was out of a job.

These temporary and undervalued positions in architecture firms stand in stark contrast to the positions that the women architects held in governmental agencies. There, these women were able to develop and specialize in domains like urbanism, city planning and landscape architecture.

3 Pot-Keegstra working, undated.

An independent practice

As I have pointed out, not one woman architect became a partner in an independent architecture firm. By contrast, marrying an architect opened the possibility for some of them to operate a firm jointly with their spouse. Five women in the research group worked closely with their husbands. These five cases are discussed in more detail in Chapter 8. These women were able to develop as fully fledged partners in their architecture practices. And from that position most of them produced an interesting oeuvre **[fig. 3]**.

A few single women from the research group made attempts to establish themselves as independent architects (see the individual entries on them) – at least, they were registered as such, but virtually none of their oeuvre seems to be traceable. The only woman who succeeded as an independent, working architect and had a successful career was Wil Jansen, who was unmarried.

As what we would now call a freelancer or independent contractor, Jansen built up a substantial and impressive portfolio of orders, filled

in part by commissions from the family business run by her brothers. In the stormy financial weather of the 1930s, her brother-in-law helped her, particularly in the area of landscape architecture. Over the course of her career Jansen worked on both residential and non-residential buildings, as well as interior design and furniture design. Perhaps the high point of her career was the completion of a residential building for single women in Rotterdam (see also Chapter 7).

Architect, but...

Of the nineteen women architectural engineers and two qualified architects, thirteen were able to practice their profession. For eight of them, all architectural engineers, there was little to no work for them to be found in their field. We will see in Chapter 5 that Grada Wolffensperger remained unemployed for the rest of her life. Beb Zeeman, who graduated after her, and who worked briefly in a government job until she married, became a maths teacher after her husband's death. At that time, there was no possibility of obtaining a teaching position for her at the Technische Hoogeschool itself, for example as lecturer. In 1935, a private tutor in psychotechnology briefly worked at the Technische Hoogeschool. Within the Technische Hoogeschool, there were functions occupied by women who graduated in disciplines other than architecture; these included assistant, head assistant or conservator. The first woman lecturer was not appointed until 1947, in the field of theoretical and applied physics.[17]

After leaving the Kok architecture firm, Marie Snethlage never again found work in her field. She ended up working in administration, and went through a series of jobs, from correspondent at a banking house to librarian at the Academie van Beeldende Kunsten in The Hague to, finally, administrator within the archive of the Chief Government Architect. She certainly did not lack ambition to find work in her field. Eight years after graduation, she went back and completed another entire academic year in architecture at the Technische Hoogeschool in Delft, possibly to keep her knowledge current.

Four women – Ina Groenevelt (1898–1977), Co van der Kloet (1896–1959), Loes Pomes (1905–1964) and Ada Struyk – married fairly quickly after graduation and insofar as is known never worked in their field at all. Struyk became a politician and at one point had public housing in her portfolio.

Competitions: a first step to visibility?

Competitions, usually put on by the trade associations, offered principally young graduate architects the opportunity to gain experience and potentially acquire some name recognition as an award-winner. Generally, there

4

4 Wil Jansen did not disclose that she was competing as a woman in the contest of the Genootschap Architectura et Amicitia, 1932. Tube containing competition materials.

was also a modest financial sum attached to these 'study competitions'. The women architects also took part in these, submitting designs for consideration in the competition.

After graduating in 1926, Ko Mulder sent a submission to a study prize contest offered by the Rotterdam association 'Architecture and Friendship'. Her winning design, for a fire station, was praised for its 'rugged, manly spirit'.[18] At the award ceremony, the all-male jury was stunned to find that 'architectural engineer Mulder' was actually a woman. Over ten years later, Mulder herself was on a jury for another study competition offered by the Genootschap Architectura et Amicitia. In that competition Koos Keegstra, who had just recently earned her VHBO diploma, won second prize in collaboration with her future husband Joop Pot (1909–1972).[19] Wil Jansen's submission for the 1932 edition of that same association's competition was ruled as one of the 10 best, and eligible for publication in professional weekly *Bouwkundig Weekblad* (see Chapter 7). Jansen, the only woman in contention, did not announce herself as such, possibly for fear of not being evaluated on her merits **[fig. 4]**.

It would go too far to conclude that participation by these women architects in such study competitions led to more name recognition for them. However, it must certainly have contributed to their efforts to profile themselves as architects, even if only to demonstrate that they were capable of competing with their male colleagues.

Interest groups, professional associations and committees

Under the influence of the women's movement, from around the turn of the century a whole spectrum of broadly oriented associations seeking to promote the interests of the professional woman began to emerge. Around this time, other existing professional associations also began to admit women to their membership. Additionally, women began to set up advisory committees to let their voices be heard on topics like housing construction. Here I will address the question of whether the women architects in the research group were members of such professional organizations and committees, particularly at the start of their careers, whether they played active roles in them, and the extent to which such side activities played a role in the professionalization of these women. We will first look at the most significant general interest associations, then the professional associations and a few select committees.

An association to promote the interests of women with higher education was founded in 1918: the Vereeniging van Gestudeerde Vrouwen, or 'Association of Learned Women'. In the early 1920s, this association changed its name to the Vereniging van Vrouwen met een Academische Opleiding (VVAO), or 'Association of Women with an Academic Education'. That association still exists today, under the name Vereniging van vrouwen met hogere opleiding ('Association of women with higher education'), and numbers approximately 3,500 members.[20] One of the very first members was Aletta Jacobs. One of the association's most significant activities was giving academic and professional advice to women. Ko Mulder, Wil Jansen and Ada Kuiper-Struyk were all active in the administration of the broadly oriented association, so the field of architecture was well-represented. Jansen travelled all over the country giving public lectures, usually about interior architecture. The network that she built in and around the VVAO was what eventually brought her the commission for her celebrated residential building for single women in Rotterdam (see Chapter 7).

During the National Exhibition of Women's Labour in 1898, there was an initiative that led to the founding of the Nationale VrouwenRaad (NVR), or 'National Women's Council', with the goal of pooling women's knowledge and expertise in various areas. The NVR still exists as the Nederlandse VrouwenRaad (having changed its name in 1974).[21] A large number of general and professional associations dedicated to the improvement of women's position in society joined this Women's Council: not only women's associations like those for women who were factory workers, teachers and midwives, but also organizations like the Dutch Vegetarians' Federation and the Anti-Sugar Tax Federation, have had representation in it. But architecture associations – notoriously old boys' networks – most likely never saw any interest in joining.[22] It was not until after the Second World War that the field of architecture became an area of attention for the Council. It was then that architecture was grouped together with other fields, including painting, sculpture, music, theatre and dance, into a Committee for Art, whose members included Margaret Staal-Kropholler.[23] Over a number of years, she approached women architectural engineers with questions about the work they produced, and reported on the responses annually in the Council.[24]

Most women who graduated as architectural engineers were members of the Vereeniging van Delftsche Ingenieurs (VDI).[25] This association was founded in 1853 to promote the interests of the alumni of the Royal Academy, the predecessor of the Polytechnic School. Since 1886 the association had published the weekly journal *De Ingenieur*, which in 1900 also became the periodical of the Koninklijk Instituut van Ingenieurs (KIVI); that institute would later absorb the association (in 1961). The VDI, whose members were mostly men, did not actually exclude women; in 1919, Grada Wolffensperger became the first woman architectural engineer to become a member, but she had been preceded by a few women technologists and one electrical engineer. The length of the VDI membership of some women architectural engineers was in parallel with periods in which they had no work or made efforts to establish themselves as independent architects. They may have been hoping to get work or obtain commissions by building up a network. Nonetheless, it is likely that however accepted they may have felt by their fellow students who were men during their studies, as soon as it came to finding work, the relations became considerably more sensitive. But the establishment of informal contacts in the hopes of finding work was not the only reason for these women to join the VDI. We see the evidence of this in a notice from the VDI published in *Bouwkundig Weekblad Architectura*, in which the Department of Architectural Engineers publicized its placement agency which mediated in finding jobs for architectural engineers.[26] The agency had the goal of notifying all architectural engineers who graduated in Delft of any job openings, and requested associations such as the BNA to give notice of them whenever possible.

Becoming a member of the VDI was more opportune than the BNA. The latter association accepted both architects with private practices and in government employ.[27] In 1931 Ko Mulder, by that time working in the Department of City Development in Amsterdam, became the 'first woman in the BNA', a fact that the chairman was extremely pleased about.[28] After that, no other women architects are found in the membership records until 1950.[29]

Only a few women architects ever registered as members of the Genootschap Architectura et Amicitia, which was primarily interested in getting young architects and draughtsmen interested in educational meetings – meetings that were also intended to promote connections and friendship among colleagues. Marie Snethlage was a member for ten years after she graduated, a period in which she tried in vain to find work as an architect.[30] It may be that membership provided her with an environment in which she could feel connected with the field. Ko Mulder had been a member since 1915, even before she started her studies, and she would remain so until 1942.[31]

None of the women architects from this research group are to be found in administrative functions within the professional associations. The 'old boys' networks', which the associations were for so long, were most likely not open to the idea. It is, however, conceivable that there were women with administrative ambitions. Eleven of the women from the research group were active during their student years in the administration of the DVSV, five of them as chairwoman. They were, in order: Beb Zeeman, Sophie Heyting, Ko Mulder, Wil Jansen and Toki Koeleman.[32]

When it came time for reconstruction after the Second World War, numerous women sought to have their say in the construction of new housing. Some formed councils, study groups and committees to make recommendations on issues such as more efficient home layouts and practical floor plans, domains in which women were of course understood to be more at home in. The most practical possible layout of a home increased its utility and reduced the burden of housekeeping. One organization, the Nederlandse Huishoudraad, set up a housing committee, the membership of which included both housewives and a few women architects from the research group. These were Ada Kuiper-Struyk, Sophie Heyting, Toki Lammers-Koeleman and Jeanne van Rood-van Rijswijk.[33]

In 1946, the first women's advisory committee or Vrouwen Advies Commissie (VAC) was founded in Rotterdam; this was a municipal advisory body for issues relating to housing construction, housing layout and the living environment. After Rotterdam, women began forming VACs in other municipalities. These local committees can still be found today, in their previous forms or as housing advisory committees known as a Woonadviescommissie (WAC).[34] Since 2000, men have also been allowed join these advisory bodies. Wil Jansen and Ada Kuiper-Struyk were very active within the Rotterdam VAC, and for Jansen in particular this led to an interesting network of contacts, including avant-garde architect Willem van Tijen. This was her introduction to modern architecture. As we will see in Chapter 7, together with the practical insights that she gained during her years of work for the VAC, this is reflected in the work that she produced in her own practice.

For these women who alongside practising their profession were active in ancillary activities such as this, the two factors together reinforced each other: the women who were professionally active were better positioned for professional associations and committees; meanwhile, the ancillary activities that these women pursued were of benefit to their own professional development, as we see in Wil Jansen's case.

Women architects in the media

Did the early women architects who succeeded in practising their profession also succeed in gaining media attention? For example, was the fact that a woman was working as an architect newsworthy in itself? Did the media report on the work that these women were doing or about their careers in general? Or did the woman architect create her own media presence by doing things like writing articles?

When Grada Wolffensperger became the first woman to graduate as an architectural engineer in 1917, this was reason enough for the weekly magazine *De Amsterdammer* to publish an interview with her.[35] Two other women's journals also covered her, but only with a photograph and a short notice (see Chapter 5). This somewhat tepid interest on the part of the press was typical of the time. While the fact that Wolffensperger was the first woman to graduate in this field was perhaps interesting enough, the general assumption was presumably that she had no professional future.

Three years later, the second woman to graduate as an architectural engineer, Beb Zeeman, spoke to the editors of *Bouwkundig Weekblad* (then still the BNA's own monthly) at their request about her views on the task of women in architecture.[36] This article can be seen as an early contribution to what would now be called the gender issue. It does not, however, present a particularly emancipated vision of it. Zeeman saw a role for the woman architect in contributing solutions to construction problems in, primarily, homes and schools 'more than the pure monumental building or in non-residential works. Those require more of the male strength and power, they need less of the feminine softness and more intimate aspects.'[37] Zeeman did, however, go so far as to say that it was not that the woman would 'walk solely down the path trodden by men, but that she (...) would also leave her own mark (...) on the course of architecture itself'.[38] What exactly those marks would be, she did not say.

In 1936, when Koos Keegstra became the first woman to earn the VHBO diploma, this was reason enough for national newspaper *De Telegraaf* to interview her. Keegstra outlined the course and process of her studies (in the MTS, too, she was the only girl among 300 boys) and also presented her vision of architecture. She was an adherent of New Objectivity, which she believed could strongly improve the layout of the home and thereby the efficiency of the housekeeping for the woman, who in her view 'was still a slave to her house'.[39]

Until the reconstruction, when they began to let themselves be heard from within committees or as practising architects themselves, woman architects were hardly ever the subject of any publicity at all. During the long, difficult years of the 1930s, many of them were not active in the field of architecture due to the lack of jobs or commissions. For most women, their careers only really developed after 1945. While Koos Keegstra and her husband Joop Pot were running their architecture firm together, the couple maintained good relations with the press. Keegstra also gave interviews on her own, in which she shed light not only on her views on architecture but her career as a woman architect (see Chapter 8). As the icing on the cake, and something of a final bow at the end of her career, she was featured in a full-page article in *Het Parool* upon the completion of the Bijlmerbajes, a very large project that she completed alone after the death of her husband Joop.[40] To Strumphler, who went to work for the Provincial Planological Department in Arnhem after the war, is known to have given two newspaper interviews in which she discussed the field of planning.

Another way that they achieved media coverage was by writing articles of their own, sharing knowledge of the field with others. How many men wrote such articles in the total population of architects is unknown. In the pre-war period, a few of the women in the research group did publish under their own names. Here it should be noted that this was still considered the exclusive province of men, who made up the editorial boards of professional journals like *Bouwkundig Weekblad Architectura*, which as from 1924 was the joint architecture journal of the BNA and the Genootschap Architectura et Amicitia, and *Wendingen*, the 'monthly for building and décor'.[41] The aforementioned request from the editorial board of *Bouwkundig Weekblad* to Beb Zeeman to write an article about the task of women in architecture could perhaps be seen as an initial, cautious attempt to give a woman architect a platform.

In the period from 1935 to 1940, before starting her VHBO programme, Lotte Stam-Beese published various articles in *De 8 & Opbouw*.[42] Lotte and her husband Mart Stam (1899–1986) ran their shared architecture firm Stam and Beese Architects in Amsterdam. There the couple found a warm welcome in a community of avant-garde architects united in De 8 & Opbouw, who published an eponymous magazine. Stam-Beese must have been inspired by this environment. In her article, she presented her perspective on subjects like school construction and the need for children's charity homes. In that period Stam-Beese was one of the very few women among the members. In 1936 a woman joined the editorial board of *De 8 & Opbouw*: interior architect Ida Falkenberg-Liefrinck. Before that Liefrinck had written articles for *De 8 & Opbouw*, including one on the education of interior architects. That article ended with an expression of support for her and her work by architect and fellow member Han van Loghem (1881–1940). Around 1929, Liefrinck was on the board of Opbouw, together with Van Loghem and others, including Cor van Eesteren.[43]

It is known that in 1936 Sophie Heyting and Paula Rooseboom (1899–1975), as members of the Building Committee of the Dutch Association of Housewives, were working on a publication entitled *What should you pay attention to when choosing a house?*.[44] This was most likely a small publication that would have been distributed to the members. Unfortunately, no copies were found.

After 1945 there was more interest for the women architects in the press, and from this time on we gradually see their publications appearing in the form of articles in professional journals or other printed media. Alongside promoting architecture at the field in a study guide for women's professions, Ko Mulder published pieces about urban design in general and the Amsterdamse Bos, her own project, in particular.[45] In the run-up to her political career, Ada Kuiper-Struyk did not go unnoticed as an architect, and she wrote an article about 'human dignity and housing of the Dutch people'.[46] The architect couples Lammers-Koeleman and Pot-Keegstra both published about their projects in professional journals.[47] In both cases, my research was unable to establish which of the spouses was the actual author. In 1959, Koos Pot-Keegstra published a one-time article about urban design in *Bouwkundig Weekblad*, specifically about the negative impact of holiday habits on nature and landscape.[48] Notably, she was also the editor-in-chief of the weekly magazine at the time,[49] and both the only woman on the editorial board and the only woman to have an article published in the journal that year.

5 Grada Wolffensperger, the first woman architectural engineer in the Netherlands

'Because she had to pave the road for those who would follow after her from Delft.'

On 29 June 1917, Grada Wolffensperger (1887–1965) wrote history. She was the first woman in the Netherlands to graduate from the architecture programme of what was then called the Technische Hoogeschool (TH) in Delft, as an 'architectural engineer'.[1] In the 1908–1909 academic year, when she enrolled, she was only the seventh woman to study architecture at that level since it was accredited as a university programme in 1905, and the only one who completed the programme at that time.[2] This remarkable fact went largely unnoticed, even in a time when it was far from self-evident that a woman would go to university at all, let alone choose a profession that had traditionally been considered a man's job. That may well be the reason why the public statements by the Technische Hoogeschool did not include any particular mention of her graduation. The only interview with Wolffensperger appeared in the local newspaper *De Amsterdammer*, in the women's section. In that interview, the author expressed the hope that this architectural engineer would get a major commission within the near future, 'because she had to pave the road for those who would follow after her from Delft'.[3] Monthly magazine *De Kroniek* praised Wolffensperger for her presumed talent which would enable her to 'faire de l'architecture un art vivant', and another source expressed high expectations of her future work, 'in view of her expert skills'.[4] Despite all that, her career did not go as expected. The first woman architectural engineer in the Netherlands found it far from easy to practice her profession. Wolffensperger and 18 other women comprised a group of architectural engineers who completed their studies at the Technische Hoogeschool from 1905 until the end of the Second World War, and remained largely unknown.

This chapter will focus specifically on Grada Wolffensperger. We know little about any architecture she may have designed, but we do know how her studies progressed and that she was the first woman architectural engineer to find a job in the Public Works department in Haarlem. It is very likely that this was the only job that this remarkable woman held in her entire life. Sources from the Noord-Hollands Archive give us an impression of how Haarlem's municipal building department functioned shortly after the First World War and what role Wolffensperger played in that context. Based on what we know of the rest of her life, we can extrapolate the limited career prospects that were available at that time for the first university-trained women architects.

Vagaries of fashion

Gerarda Wilhelmina Elisabeth Wolffensperger was born in The Hague on 3 April 1887, the youngest of three daughters, from the second marriage of her mother, Barbera Johanna Woudenberg (1857–1949). Barbera Woudenberg was abruptly widowed six months into her first marriage in 1880; when her first husband died, she was pregnant with a boy, who only survived for a few weeks after his birth. Shortly after these dramatic events, she remarried to Julius Frederik Theodor Wolffensperger (1849–1915). When the family bought a new home on Heemskerckstraat in The Hague in 1902, Grada started attending the Hoogereburgerschool (HBS) as an external student in Delft, at the age of 15. Six years later, she and three other women sat for the final examinations for the 'HBS five-year programme'.[5] The diploma granted access to the architecture programme at the Technische Hoogeschool in Delft, an option that she undoubtedly coveted fiercely; she enrolled that very year. In doing so, this daughter of a 'Certified Clerk' at a mortgage office deviated from the strongly prevailing public opinion that a woman's role was in the home.[6] The book *Van Vrouwenleven 1813–1913* ('On Women's Lives 1813–1913') addressed the 'very difficult question of this time', in which daughters 'succumbed to the vagaries of fashion' and traded their duties at home for work 'for which they had no extraordinary inclination'.[7] The daughters were 'sorely missed' in many households that lacked charm and good cheer, but – it was postulated – the woman also had the right to lead her own life, and it was her parents' duty to ensure that their children would gain economic independence. In any case, Grada's parents did not obstruct her choice, and may even have encouraged her.

That encouragement did not come from the programme itself: the architect's profession was supposedly too physically demanding for women.[8] Moreover, women were not expected to climb the scaffolding and move amongst the builders and craftsmen. When Grada embarked on her university career in the 1908–1909 academic year, she was one of three women in a total of 11 first-year students in the architecture programme.[9] All in all, five women studied architecture at the Technische Hoogeschool that academic year, out of a total of 51 architecture students. Grada completed the requirements of her initial propaedeutic year in May 1910,

1

1 Shortly after successfully completing her final examination on 2 July 1915, Grada Wolffensperger made this drawing of a bell tower in Edam.

2

3

along with four men who were studying architecture.[10] She passed the candidate examinations in summer 1915 **[fig. 1]**.[11], as one of the 17 students in their fifth year (or longer) of architecture, out of a total of 52 students.[12] During her student years, Grada continued living in her parents' home on Heemskerckstraat in The Hague. Several months before she received her diploma, her father died at the age of 65 years. It must have been a very sad time for her. 'It is not possible to await visitors', the newspaper obituary reads.[13]

Although she lived at home, Grada did not lead an isolated life separate from the lively student culture in Delft. In her first year at university, she joined the women's student society that had been established in 1904, the Delftsche Vrouwelijke Studenten Vereeniging (DVSV), located at Oude Delft 123 **[fig. 2]**.[14] At the DVSV she not only met the few other women studying architecture alongside her, but also women studying technology (chemistry) – which was the most popular course of study among women at the Technische Hoogeschool – and eventually also electrical engineering and civil engineering. In the year that Grada joined, this young student society was sceptical about its future prospects. The board noted in its records that 'the number of DVSV members will never significantly exceed its current level, since a course of study at the TH and its application in

2 1917 membership list of the Delftsche Vrouwelijke Studenten Vereeniging, of which Grada Wolffensperger was a member throughout her time as a student.

3 After graduating in 1917, Grada Wolffensperger had her portrait taken by Henri Berssenbrugge. The photo appeared in the monthly *De Kroniek*.

4

4 The graduate Grada Wolffensperger in her living room in 1917, photographed for *De Vrouw en haar Huis*.

practice will always present great difficulties for a woman.'[15] The student society had forty members and offered all sorts of activities, such as theatre and gymnastics. Grada was not listed as an active member of committees or the board. Women studying architecture would not join the DVSV board until later. It is unknown whether there were already options for female students to join the Delft student society for applied studies in civil engineering and architecture, the Delftsch Civiel en Bouwkundig Gezelschap Practische Studie, and whether Grada made use of those options. Established in 1894, that student society emerged from two sub-divisions of the Delftsch Studenten Corps.[16]

The first woman architectural engineer in the Netherlands

On 29 June 1917, Grada Wolffensperger graduated from the architecture programme, becoming the first woman architectural engineer in the Netherlands.[17] Great things were expected of her: Wolffensperger sat for a portrait by none other than Henri Berssenbrugge (1873–1959). This portrait photographer's clientele included many prominent citizens of The Hague, as well as performers and artists whom he received in his studio on Zeestraat, next to Panorama Mesdag.[18] Berssenbrugge felt drawn to the

De Stijl art movement and commissioned architect Jan Wils (1891–1972) and decorative artist Vilmos Huszár (1884–1960) to do the interior of his art studio. Wolffensperger's portrait in profile featured prominently in *De Kroniek* **[fig. 3]**.[19] The magazine *De Vrouw en haar Huis* ('The Woman and her House') put a photo of Wolffensperger on the front page, depicting her reading and surrounded by books at home 'in her living room' **[fig. 4]**.[20] In the caption, the editor (also a woman) expressed the hope that 'practising the profession would eventually elevate her to a height that would compel her male colleagues to express appreciation for women's labour in this line.'

The interview with Wolffensperger in weekly newspaper *De Amsterdammer* not only offers a fairly accurate impression of the general sentiment at the time, but is also the only source that offers some glimpse of how this woman architectural engineer viewed the profession right after graduating.[21] Wolffensperger was interviewed by someone with the byline 'v.T.', who may possibly have been Catharina van Tussenbroek (1852–1925), one of the first women to study medicine, who graduated cum laude in 1887 and went on to become a gynaecologist and publish scientific articles.[22] She was a well-known proponent of women's rights and may have contributed to the women's section of *De Amsterdammer* in that capacity. In the interview, Wolffensperger confessed that she had no idea what her future might hold. The author of the article was convinced that Wolffensperger, despite her lack of experience, would not make the same mistakes as many men just starting out as architects.

'Would a woman ever have allowed a hotel to be built without a kitchen, as – it was immediately noted – the lead architect of the Oranje Hotel in Scheveningen had done? Would a house built by a woman ever have cupboards that were impractical in placement and internal structure? Would the coal cellar, the attic or the basement ever be pushed into such disregard as they are in houses designed by men?'[23]

These questions led readers to suspect that a rosy future lay in store for this newly qualified architect and that, as a woman, she was also considered capable of designing different types of structures than the more obvious private residences. However, over the course of the article, the author lapsed into the prevailing perspectives on the role of women at that time, expecting that Wolffensperger's contribution to the field of architecture would be primarily limited to interior decoration. She could be expected to build 'an ideal little home', easy to live in and charmingly decorated. In addition to practical common sense, the article alleged, the ineffable sense of good taste that any woman would use to add a feminine touch to the home with 'carpets, trinkets and wall decorations' would achieve great things for Wolffensperger. The idea that she could be entrusted with decorating the interior, according to the author, was based in part on the artful style in which the room where the interview took place had been decorated: in a plain manner and with coloured wallpaper with 'a light frieze'. The author also mused that Wolffensperger herself may have designed the armchair in which she had been photographed. The interview was presumably conducted in Grada's own room in her parental home on Heemskerckstraat, which was also the setting depicted in *De Vrouw en haar Huis* **[fig. 4]**.[24]

One possible problem that the author anticipated on Wolffensperger's behalf was interacting with contractors and workers at the site. That context would demand a strong character, although her determination would suggest that she possessed that in spades. Wolffensperger herself held the opinion that no architect had ever completely avoided problems with contractors and, she added contemplatively, 'possibly also with the workers'. She saw no reason that it would be any different for a woman. Wolffensperger had not acquired any practical experience at all during the course of her studies. She stated adamantly in the interview that she had seen no reason to do so. In her view, instead of spending time 'in the workshop', she was convinced that it would be equally useful for her to learn to draw at home. She had seen students waste enough time 'hanging about on the scaffolding and under the platforms'. Although she would have liked to witness a major building project from start to finish, she had not apparently managed to make that happen.

Freshly graduated, and bolstered by the way in which several media outlets focused a spotlight on her, Wolffensperger must have felt hopeful about her future prospects.

Possible directions

The question then was where and how the first woman architectural engineer was going to gain practical experience. The Centrale Commissie ter Behartiging van Studiebelangen ('Central Committee for Representing Study-Related Interests') at the Technische Hoogeschool strongly advised students to pursue practical application during the course of their studies, especially since 'engaging with actual practice cultivates a love of the profession'.[25] There were arrangements in place for each student to do a work placement at least once. Every year, the national government offered several 'Extraordinary Foreman' positions where students could gain practical experience during their summer holidays. It is striking that such an ambitious student as Grada Wolffensperger chose not to pursue this part of her programme.

The committee assessed the future prospects for an architectural engineer as considerably less favourable than for a civil engineer. The latter profession could expect a varied and exciting future working for such employers as the national public works department, the post and telegraph service, the railway and tram companies, the national survey board, the many municipal public works departments, in education, or abroad in the Dutch East Indies. The starting salary for a civil engineer ranged from 1,200 guilders (Assistant at the Technische Hoogeschool) to 2,000 guilders (national public works department) a year, even rising as high as 400 guilders a month for a position on the Triangulation Brigade in the Dutch East Indies. The diploma for an architectural engineer, in contrast, was not specifically required by any job at all, and did not even entitle its holder to teach at a secondary school. All the other final diplomas issued by the Technische Hoogeschool did include a teaching credential.[26] When Wolffensperger graduated, 38 women had obtained an engineering diploma by that point: two civil engineers, three electrical engineers and 33 chemical engineers.[27] Architecture was considered a completely separate course of study, hardly related to any other field of engineering and therefore impossible to combine. There were no options to specialize. The Committee believed that the personal capacities of the architecture student were vitally important. Mediocre students were advised not to enrol in the programme, since they were not expected to achieve much success in the field. It has been impossible to determine whether Wolffensperger was an above-average student. Study results were lost in the big fire in 2008 in the architecture faculty. The programme may have been hard for her, since she took nine years to complete it. It was possible to obtain a diploma as an architectural engineer after five years; on average, students spent seven years studying at the faculty of architecture.[28]

According to the *Encyclopaedisch Handboek* ('Encyclopaedic Handbook'), which devoted a chapter to women attending technical programmes at the Technische Hoogeschool, a woman architect had to be not only practical but also artistic, enabling her to create works that had enduring artistic value and thus distinguishing herself from the civil engineer.[29] But this author, a chemical engineer herself, also followed the stereotypical assumption that a woman 'artist-architect' would be more likely to find employment in decorating the interiors of residential homes and – if she proved capable – of other buildings and ships, 'to the extent that the builder does not do it himself'.[30] The expectation was that a woman architect would not easily be given the opportunity to gain practical experience, and that her work would mainly be limited to working out the details based on designs made by others. Professional interaction with the workers was considered a highlight: they were generally considered to be more well-mannered than their colleagues in civil engineering works.

Looking for work

Although the Netherlands remained neutral during the First World War, the country was dragged along into the all-consuming crisis of those years. The jobs left vacant by the mobilization were taken by women wherever possible.[31] When the supply of raw materials ground to a halt in 1917, however, unemployment spiked. It must have been a difficult time for Wolffensperger for find work. Two years after graduating, she joined the Vereeniging van Delftsche Ingenieurs (VDI), the trade association of engineering graduates established in 1853 to represent the interests of alumni from the Royal Academy, which offered the engineering programme at that time.[32] Since 1886, the VDI had published the weekly journal *De Ingenieur*, which in 1900 also became the periodical of the Koninklijk Instituut van Ingenieurs (KIVI); that institute would later absorb the association (in 1961). The trade association accepted women who had graduated from the programmes.

Wolffensperger may have hoped that the VDI network would help her to find a job. Strikingly, she seemed in no hurry to provide her details to the VDI: after repeated requests to specify her address and place of employment, she was eventually listed in the membership registry for 1919 under 'private practice' in The Hague.[33] This raises the question of whether it was her intention at that time to find work as an independent architect, and whether she expected to find commissions without any prior experience. She may have requested that listing simply because she had not yet found an employer.

Public Works in Haarlem

On 7 February 1919, the Municipal Executive (consisting of the mayor and the aldermen) wrote a letter to the city council of Haarlem describing the extraordinary circumstances in which the Public Works Bureau had been forced to work, especially in the final years of the First World War.[34] The high prices of building materials were a contributing factor in the delay of various works. Now that the war was over, work at the Bureau was expected to pick up rapidly. And the municipality was not alone in these efforts; private contractors were also expected to start working on the accumulated backlog, which would also necessitate digging sewer lines and paving roads. Haarlem also resumed the practice of selling off municipal land, accompanied by quite a bit of administrative paperwork.

The Bureau was in urgent need of more civil servants, and this expanded workforce would be required for an indefinite period. The civil department of the Public Works Bureau consisted of three 'first-class foremen' and four 'second-class foremen'; the latter category needed three more people.[35]

The architectural department consisted of an assistant architect, a structural engineer, three first-class foremen, one second-class foreman, a clerk and several temporary draughtsmen. An additional two draughtsmen and another clerk initially seemed sufficient for this department. The city council agreed and provided a budget of 8,000 guilders. On 1 December of the same year, the Municipal Executive asked the city council to approve an additional expansion for Haarlem's Public Works Bureau – no longer making any distinction between civil and architectural departments – with the addition of an assistant director, a foreman, four draughtsmen, an assistant draughtsman and an assistant clerk.[36] Once again, the council approved the request: an amount of 17,300 guilders was made available, which included promotions for several civil servants. It would appear that the city council only had a say in permanent hires, because the Public Works Director, L.C. Dumont (1865–1935), repeatedly requested permission from the Municipal Executive to hire personnel 'in unattached employ' with the aim of 'achieving a more structured course of affairs'.[37] The Municipal Executive approved each request without involving the city council.

Although Dumont's 1905 expansion plan for the city of Haarlem was unsuccessful, the city council then approved his revised General Plan for Expansion in 1919. This plan, which included the construction of several residential neighbourhoods, was undoubtedly at least partly why Dumont needed additional staff.[38] New temporary employees were hired again in early 1920. On 15 March of that year, the correspondence log of the Municipal Executive mentions five 'unattached civil servants': an 'aspiring draughtsman', two site foremen and two assistant architects.[39] One of the two assistant architects hired at that time was Grada Wolffensperger.

Royally rewarded

Sadly, Wolffensperger's personnel file was not found in the records of the Public Works Bureau, but letters exchanged between Director Dumont and the Municipal Executive paint a picture of her working environment. The Dutch efforts to catch up after the difficult years of the First World War resulted in labour shortages. In a letter that Dumont sent to the Municipal Executive around the same time that Wolffensperger was hired, he once again requested permission to temporarily expand the Public Works Bureau with another six employees, 'since so much work is and will be on our slate simultaneously'.[40] Dumont doubted whether he could still find suitable technically trained employees and noted in advance that he might need to make alternative proposals, not least in view of 'the preferability of also significantly expanding the permanent staff in the near future'. In other words, the situation offered Wolffensperger every opportunity to prove herself.

D. *Openbare werken.*

1°.	Adjunct-directeur	*f* 2,700.—	tot	*f* 3,500.—
2°.	Adjunct-architect	〃 2,000.—	〃	〃 3,000.—
3°.	Ingenieur	〃 2,000.—	〃	〃 3,000.—
4°.	Administratief technisch ambtenaar ...	〃 1,600.—	〃	〃 2,200.—
5°.	Opzichter 1ste klasse...............	〃 1,600.—	〃	〃 2,200.—
6°.	〃 2de 〃	〃 1,300.—	〃	〃 1,800.—
7°.	Adjunct-commies	〃 1,100.—	〃	〃 1,600.—
8°.	Klerk.............................	〃 1,000.—	〃	〃 1,400.—
9°.	Onder-opzichter	〃 1,000.—	〃	〃 1,400.—
10°.	Adjunct-klerk	〃 600.—	〃	〃 1,000.—

5

The last letter from Dumont referenced above offers an extensive overview of the current and expected work activities for Public Works, which Wolffensperger was no doubt aware of when she started her new job on 1 May. The department's work list included embankments, sewerage and shoring for a playground and for purchased land, renovating and expanding the police headquarters, renovating a school and the Municipal Power Company, building the substructure of a bathing and swimming facility, building 89 workers homes on Slachthuisstraat, etc.

Wolffensperger's salary followed the guidelines of the bylaw for remuneration of civil servants **[fig. 5]**.[41] The bylaw, which applied to civil servants in permanent employment, offers a decent impression of the jobs at the Public Works Bureau and the salaries paid to Wolffensperger's colleagues. The assistant architect was positioned quite high in the departmental hierarchy, right below the assistant director, at an annual salary of 2,000 to 3,000 guilders. Wolffensperger's annual salary was 3,000 guilders, as was noted when she was hired.[42] It is notable for that time that she earned exactly the same amount as the man who was appointed to the role of assistant architect, both of them hired on a definite employment contract.[43] This colleague, Jan Buijs (1889–1961), had graduated from the TH in Delft in 1919 and had obtained the position thanks in no small part to the warm recommendation of his architecture professor, Adrianus van der Steur.[44] The 1921 *Haarlem Address Book* provides an overview of Wolffensperger's colleagues at that time from among the permanent staff of Public Works at 'Bureau Prinsenhof' **[fig. 6]**.[45] The list consists exclusively of men, and Dumont was the only architectural engineer.[46] In other words, Wolffensperger held the same credentials as the director – and her arrival must have caused quite an uproar among her fellow architects who had not received university training **[fig. 7]**.

5 Grada's remuneration as deputy architect for Public Works was fully in line with salaries for civil servants. The overview also offers a glimpse of the hierarchy as it applied at that time.

A year after she was hired, Wolffensperger and several other colleagues in temporary employment were eligible for a periodical raise of 100 guilders;

GEMEENTE ZAKEN. 11

Gemeente-Archief.

Geopend op werkdagen van 9.30—4 uur.

E. Knappert, *Archivaris.*

Mr. J. W. Kool, *Adj.-Archivaris.*

Gemeente-Ontvanger.

Kantoor in het Raadhuis. Ingang Pandpoort.

Geopend dagelijks, uitgezonderd Zaterdags, Zondagen, Nieuwjaarsdag en de algemeen erkende Christelijke en daarmede door Burgemeester en Wethouders gelijkgestelde feestdagen van 9—2 ure.

F. de Jonge, *Ontvanger.*
J. P. de Klerk, *Referendaris.*
D. Andrea, *Commies.*
J. H. v. d. Wateren, *Klerk.*

Belastingkantoor Jacobijnestraat 24.

Voor de ontvangst der plaatselijke directe belasting alleen Maandag, Dinsdag, Woensdag en Donderdag.

J. F. Cramer, *Hoofdcommies.*
P. C. Roodenburg, *Commies.*
A. Koomen, *Adj.-Commies.*
N. C. A. Ockhuijzen Sr., C. J. Grootenboer, C. Vink, *Deurwaarders.*

Openbare Werken.

Bureau Prinsenhof. Geopend werkdagen van 9—12 uur.

Ir. L. C. Dumont *b.i. Directeur.*
Ir. G. W. Ph. Daniëls *c.i. Adj.-Direct.*
Ir. D. N. de Lange *c.i. Ingenieur.*
A. A. Hillebrand, *Architect.*
G. Smits, *Adj.-Architect.*
M. W. C. Visser, *Hoofdinspecteur.*
H. J. Zuurendonk, „
G. A. Degenaar, „
H. C. Sprik, *Hoofdcommies.*
C. F. J. Javaux, *Adj.-Commies.*
L. H. Hamaker, „
L. A. W. G. de Kam, „
P. Looijen, *Klerk.*
D. West, *Adj.-Klerk.*
J. V. Munsterman, *Bouwkundige.*
H. de Lugt, „
E. J. Mühren, *Bouwkundige.*
J. Kampinga, *Teekenaar.*
J. N. Lobel, *Inspecteur.*
J. G. Niesten, „
M. G. Riemens, „
J. Elles, *Opzichter.*
M. L. Lindhout, „
H. I. van Es, „
C. W. E. Kars, „
J. H. Scherpenhuijzen, „
E. J. Kievit, *Onder-Opzichter.*
S. C. Timmerman, „
A. van der Meer, *Bediende.*
M. P. de Ridder, „
H. B. Harmans, „

Bouw- en Woningtoezicht.

Bureau Kruisstraat 45. *Geopend voor het publiek van* 9½—12½ *uur.*

D. Kruijff, *Directeur.*
Iz. van Campen, *Hoofdinspecteur.*
B. Bakker, „
J. J. L. Dalhuisen, „
A. F. P. Onderwater, „
G. A. Brongers, *Inspecteur.*
P. van Driel, „
J. L. van Deursen, „
L. M. v. Buren, „
W. H. Cappelhof, *Opzichter.*
N. J. de Wilde, *Onder-opzichter.*
F. F. de Wilde, „
J. de Vries, *Adj.-Teekenaar.*
M. van Waard, „
J. L. Hulsenboom, *Commies.*
C. Vink Jr., *Adj.-Commies.*
N. J. v. d. Wateren, *Klerk.*
Th. P. Dijt, *Adj.-Klerk.*
S. T. v. d. Veen, „
J. A. Boeser, *Portier.*

6

6 Grada's colleagues in permanent employment at the Public Works department in 1921. Director Dumont was the only male architectural engineer.

7

7 Grada Wolffensperger as the only woman among her colleagues at the Public Works department in Haarlem, 1921. Third from the right is her colleague J.W.E. Buijs; fifth from the left is director L.C. Dumont.

8

8 The 'Dice' at the Grote Houtbrug bridge, 1909.

at that time, her annual salary was no less than 3,800 guilders.[47] Clearly, her salary had already been structurally increased over time. It is worth noting that Buijs, who still worked in the same department, was not on that short list of periodic raises. Several months before that, Dumont had hired another two draughtsmen and a site foreman on a temporary basis, offering them more than minimum wage, for which he had been reprimanded by the Municipal Executive.[48] The chronic staff shortages had to be resolved, no matter what the cost. And thus Grada Wolffensperger continued to enjoy job security, and was well rewarded for her work.

Dice

During the course of 1921, however, the steady flow of new hires in Public Works was reversed, and Dumont even started dismissing temporary employees. Various draughtsmen and site foremen were dismissed in November, after which a list was produced in December of the five (!) temporary employees still in the department: two site foremen, an inspector and the two assistant architects, Wolffensperger and Buijs. Dumont had to provide an account of their work activities to the Municipal Executive.[49]

9

9 The Stedelijk Gymnasium school on Prinsenhof for which Jan Buijs designed a new wing. It was built on the left side, where a vestige of the Public Works Bureau can still be seen (ca. 1923).

Wolffensperger was responsible for 'developing a drawing for the Traffic Commission' and for the specifications and drawings of small buildings near Grote Houtbrug. These small buildings mostly likely refer to the former customs houses, known as 'commizienhuisjes'. After the Grote Houtpoort was torn down in 1824, these tollhouses were occupied by customs officers or 'commiezen' who collected tolls, excise duties and import duties on incoming goods.[50] The two small structures situated on either side of the bridge dated back to 1826 and were designed by architect T.F. Suys (1783–1861). Nicknamed the 'Dice' because of their cubical shape, they lost their function when municipal import duties were abolished in 1865 **[fig. 8]**. Local cultural heritage associations Bond Heemschut and Vereniging Haerlem managed to keep the city from tearing them down in 1917, but in 1922 the city council once again decided to demolish the customs houses 'in view of the changing conditions of modern traffic since 1917'.[51] Despite the best efforts of the Municipal Executive to widen the sidewalks and install a subterranean urinal and toilet – while preserving the 'Dice' – the customs houses were eventually demolished in 1928 to make way for a wider Grote Houtbrug. Wolffensperger may well have spent time in 1921 on redeveloping or renovating the buildings. Her colleague Buijs was overseeing the sizable renovation plan for the Stedelijk Gymnasium school building situated next to the Public Works Bureau, and would presumably have been assigned to draft a plan 'for restructuring the trade school into a building for the Inspection Service' **[fig. 9]**.[52] Was Buijs already placed in a privileged position by taking on these projects?

A letter stored in the Noord-Hollands Archive dated 19 April 1922 is addressed to the directors of a series of municipal bodies, including the dune water company, the gas company and the Public Works Bureau.[53] The Municipal Executive announced a continuation of temporary employees for the time being, making it possible to postpone dismissal until 1 June 1922 of those civil servants who 'absolutely could not be missed'. It was clear that cutback policies were in play that affected not only Public Works, but all municipal services. Dumont replied by return letter that he had already dismissed the five remaining temporary civil servants as of 1 May. Despite the leeway offered by the Municipal Executive, Dumont opted to uphold the dismissal of two civil servants: one 'G. Wolffensperger, architectural engineer' and inspector.[54] In the correspondence that was found, this was the first time that Wolffensperger had been referred to by her official title. The records show that she received an honourable discharge from service.[55]

Why did Dumont opt not to make use of the postponement offered by the Municipal Executive to keep Wolffensperger on? One possible reason could be that Dumont wanted to trade favours with the Municipal Executive. The two site foremen were allowed to stay on longer than that ultimate deadline of 1 June, since they were apparently indispensable in the course of the work. For 'civil servant J. Buijs', as Dumont referred to him in his letter about Wolffensperger's dismissal, Dumont had already come up with an alternative proposal in March: Buijs could stay on until late 1922.[56] In the end, he continued working for the public works department until 1924, focusing on the renovation and partial new building for the Stedelijk Gymnasium school.[57] After that, he established a practice as an independent architect in The Hague and went on to work closely with Joan Lürsen, who had briefly worked alongside Buijs on the draughting team at Public Works. Wolffensperger got the short end of the stick here.

Crisis and war

In the membership lists of the Vereeniging van Delftsche Ingenieurs (VDI), Grada was only listed as 'Assistant Architect in temporary employ at the Public Works department in Haarlem' for two years.[58] After 1922, she was no longer a VDI member, but was still included in the list of all engineers with degrees, which the association published annually. Year after year, she was registered as an architectural engineer without position, residing in The Hague.[59] What attempts might she have made to find a new job after her dismissal?

The increasingly stringent cutback policies implemented by the national government to reduce the number of civil servants culminated in 1924 in a Royal Decree stating that women in civil service had to be dismissed once they were married. A new job in government service was therefore not an obvious choice for a candidate like Wolffensperger, who may have been 35 by then, but was still considered marriageable. She may have tried to get a job at an architecture firm. These firms listed job openings in the *Haagsche Courant*, a local newspaper in The Hague, for such positions as architectural draughtsman or technically trained administrative employee, but Wolffensperger would presumably have initially hoped to find a job at her own level.[60] This raises the question of whether she would have wanted to work at an architectural firm as a business partner, or as an employee. It would have been a ground-breaking challenge to gain access to the male-dominated environment that architecture practice simply was at the time. However, no evidence was found to suggest that Grada Wolffensperger worked at architecture firms, at least not for extended periods, since those positions would show up in the VDI yearbooks.

In 1932, she was listed for the first time in the telephone book of The Hague, as was her mother. At that time, Wolffensperger lived on Boreelstraat, number 12, while her mother still lived on Heemskerckstraat. As in the VDI lists, her entry in the phone book stated that she was an independent architect. By that time, she must have abandoned those ambitions, in view of her very limited experience and the financial crisis that was in full swing. She does appear in the architects' registry, which was created in 1934, but that presumably did not bring her any commissions either **[fig. 10]**.[61]

During the Second World War, Boreelstraat was in a German restricted zone; it is very likely that Wolffensperger moved in with her mother, who died in 1949 at the age of 91. Wolffensperger never married and did not have any children, nor did her oldest sister Mien, with whom she lived out the rest of her years in their parental home on Heemskerckstraat. It must have been an egregious affront to Wolffensperger that she was unable to pursue a government career despite being unmarried.

Her youngest sister Barbera, who was also unmarried, died at the age of 35.[62] It is not known whether Grada's sisters attended any further education; in any case, neither obtained a university degree.

A close friend of the family described Grada as a tall, slim, tastefully dressed woman with a delightful sense of humour, open-minded and averse to posh pretension.[63] The family was well off, and Grada was able to lead a good life with her sister even without a job. The two were

10

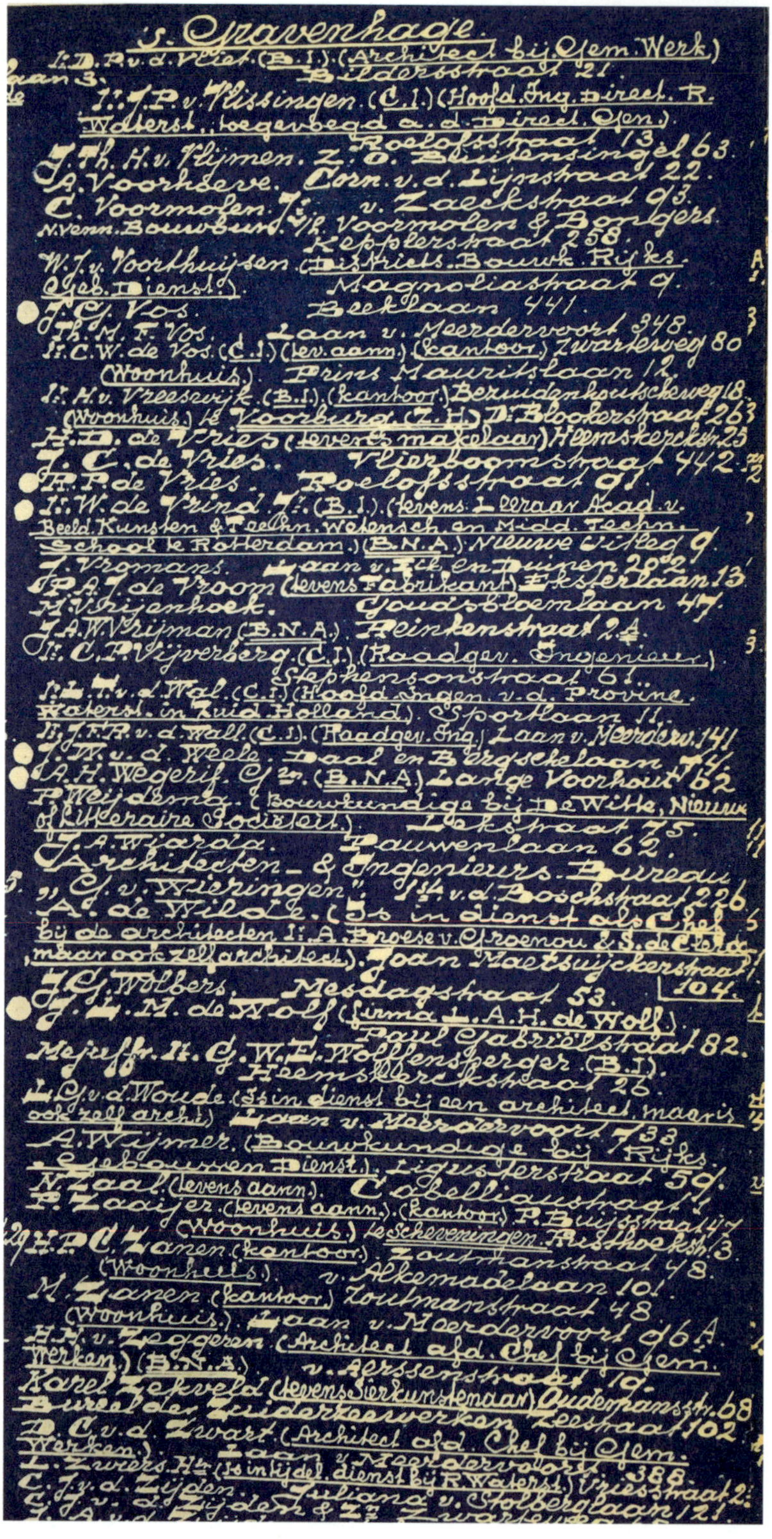

's Gravenhage.
Ir. D. P. v. d. Vliet. (B.I.) (Architect bij Gem. Werk.) Bilderdijkstraat 21
Ir. J. P. v. Vlissingen. (C.I.) (Hoofd. Ing. direct. R. Waterst., toegevoegd a. d. Direct. Gen.) Roelofsstraat 13
J. Th. H. v. Vlijmen. Z. O. Buitensingel 63.
A. Voorhoeve. Corn. v. d. Lijnstraat 22.
C. Voormolen Jr. v. Zaeckstraat 93.
N.Venn. Bouwbur. v/h. Voormolen & Bongers. Kepplerstraat 258.
W. J. v. Voorthuijsen (Districts. Bouwk. Rijks. Geb. Dienst.) Magnoliastraat 9.
J. G. Vos. Beeklaan 441
Th. M. F. Vos. Laan v. Meerdervoort 348.
Ir. C. W. de Vos. (C.I.) (lev. aann.) (Kantoor) Zwarteweg 80 (Woonhuis) Prins Mauritslaan 12.
Ir. H. v. Vreeswijk. (B.I.) (Kantoor) Bezuidenhoutscheweg 18. (Woonhuis) te Voorburg (Z.H.) D. Blookerstraat 263
H. D. de Vries (tevens makelaar) Heemskerckstr. 25
J. C. de Vries. Vlierboomstraat 442.
R. P. de Vries. Roelofsstraat 91.
Ir. W. de Vrind Jr. (B.I.) (tevens Leeraar Acad. v. Beeld. Kunsten & Techn. Wetensch. en Midd. Techn. School te Rotterdam.) (B.N.A.) Nieuwe Uitleg 9.
J. Vromans. Laan v. Eik en Duinen 202
P. A. J. de Vroom (tevens Fabrikant) Eksterlaan 13.
M. Vrijenhoek. Goudsbloemlaan 47.
J. A. W. Vrijman (B.N.A.) Heinkenstraat 24.
Ir. C. P. Vijverberg (C.I.) (Raadgev. Ingenieur.) Stephensonstraat 61.
Ir. L. T. v. d. Wal. (C.I.) (Hoofd Ingen. v. d. Provinc. Waterst. in Zuid Holland). Sportlaan 11.
Ir. J. F. R. v. d. Wall. (C.I.) (Raadgev. Ing.) Laan v. Meerderv. 141
J. W. v. d. Weele Daal en Bergschelaan 74.
A. H. Wegerif. G zn. (B.N.A.) Lange Voorhout 62
P. Weijdema. (Bouwkundige bij De Witte, Nieuwe of Litteraire Societeit.) Lekstraat 75.
J. A. Wiarda. Pauwenlaan 62.
Architecten- & Ingenieurs-Bureau „G. v. Wieringen" Ir. v. d. Boschstraat 226
A. de Wilde. (Is in dienst als Chef bij de architecten Ir. A. Broese v. Groenou & S. de Clercq, maar ook zelf architect). Joan Maetsuijckerstraat 104.
J. G. Wolbers. Mesdagstraat 53.
J. L. M. de Wolf (firma L. A. H. de Wolf.) Paul Gabriëlstraat 82.
Mejuffr. Ir. G. W. E. Wolffensperger (B.I.) Heemskerckstraat 26.
L. G. v. d. Woude (Is in dienst bij een architect, maar is ook zelf archit.) Laan v. Meerdervoort 733
A. Wijmer. (Bouwkundige bij Rijks Gebouwen Dienst.) Ligusterstraat 59.
N. Zaal. (tevens aann.) Cabelliaustraat 1
P. Zaaijer. (tevens aann.) (Kantoor) P. Buijsstraat 47 (Woonhuis) te Scheveningen Risthoekstr. 3
H. P. C. Zanen (Kantoor) Zoutmanstraat 48. (Woonhuis) v. Alkemadelaan 101
M. Zanen (Kantoor) Zoutmanstraat 48 (Woonhuis) Laan v. Meerdervoort 26 A
H. W. v. Zeggeren (Architect afd. Chef bij Gem. Werken.) (B.N.A.) v. Aerssenstraat 19.
Karel Zekveld (tevens Sierkunstenaar) Oudemansstr. 68
Bureau der Zuiderzeewerken Zeestraat 102
D. C. v. d. Zwart (Architect afd. Chef bij Gem. Werken.) Laan v. Meerdervoort 388
L. Zwiers. Hz. (Is in tijdel. dienst bij R. Waterst.)
C. J. J. v. d. Zijden. Juliana v. Stolberglaan 121 / Vriesstraat 2
J. A. v. d. Zijden & Zn. Zwarteweg

←

10 *Registry of all Dutch Architects etc.*, 1934, which lists Grada Wolffensperger.

inseparable; when Mien died in 1964, Grada spent the last year of her life alone in the Heemskerckstraat house, huddled frightened and lonely on her chair by the fireplace day and night. She died on 12 February 1965. She had managed to complete her studies, but a career was not in the cards for her. Even so, the very first steps had been taken towards 'paving the way' for the women who came after her.

As the first woman architectural engineer in the Netherlands, Grada Wolffensperger did not have an illustrious career. After her nine years studying architecture at university, the opportunities available to her proved extremely limited, despite the talents attributed to her and the soaring expectations expressed in various media. The massive surge in construction directly after the First World War offered her the opportunity to gain practical experience as an assistant architect working for the local government in Haarlem, where she received a salary even higher than the level dictated by the bylaws determining the salaries of civil servants. Even so, she had to make way for a male colleague. Whether this policy was based on a fair and honest performance review in the workplace is unclear. Wolffensperger did not find any other post with the government. Although married women were not permitted to work in government service from 1924 on, the fact that Wolffensperger was unmarried did not seem to have helped her career.

There are no records that she was able to carry out commissions as an independent architect. It is very likely that the lack of practical experience played a role there. While joining an architecture firm as a business partner on equal footing may have been a step too far for a woman in those days, she also did not find employment at such a firm at a level appropriate to her qualifications. The later years of financial crisis were a major contributing factor in her inability to fulfil the ambitious expectations.

6 Riné Boerée, concrete specialist with the Army Corps of Engineers (Genie)

Riné Boerée (1898–1995) was one of the first woman architectural engineers who graduated from the Technische Hoogeschool (TH) in Delft in the early twentieth century. In a time when women were supposed to fulfil their designated role as wives and mothers in the home, developing an architecture career was a difficult and sometimes fruitless endeavour for this small group of technically trained women. To the extent that society could even imagine the possibility of a woman architect, the prevailing belief was that they should focus on interior architecture and decoration, designing a kitchen or at most a residence. The concept that a woman would design office buildings or banks, hotels or department stores was unimaginable. The career arc of Riné Boerée unfolded on a completely different level within the world of architecture. As an architectural engineer, she developed her skills in structural engineering in the Dutch armed forces, working for the Army Corps of Engineers – known as De Genie – and specializing in concrete. It must have been challenging for her to prove herself in the men's world of the military.

This chapter covers the extraordinary career of Riné Boerée. Thanks in part to her class notes from university, which were preserved, it is possible to achieve an impression of her architectural studies at the TH. Her career begged for further research: the only known interview with Boerée, a few days before her death, yielded several interesting facts.[1] Based on Boerée's personal archive at Het Nieuwe Instituut (HNI) and retained by her family, among other sources it was possible to map out the early days of her career.[2] It is very likely that her interest in concrete was piqued when she became involved in construction of the Nirwana block of flats in The Hague. It proved impossible to achieve an overview of her later work for the Genie by searching through all the potentially relevant but unstructured files stored in the National Archives (NA). None of the construction drawings that could be consulted in the NA and in the collection of the Netherlands Institute for Military History (NIMH) bore her own signature, although there were a number signed by her male colleagues on the same team.[3] This did not seem surprising as such, in view of the strictly hierarchical and primarily male-dominated command structure in the Ministry of Defence. Research in the Genie Museum in Vught showed that Boerée had worked for the engineering branch of the army in The Hague in the years preceding the Second World War, primarily focusing on calculations and drawings for reinforced concrete structures for the barracks. The trail led back to the NIMH, where a specification drawing by Boerée was found.[4] Finally, her career at the Genie began to take shape.

Thanks to the diary kept by her sister Mia (1900–1987), with whom she shared a home throughout her life, we know that Boerée temporarily worked for a concrete company during the Second World War. From the Second World War until her pension, Boerée was able to deploy her expert knowledge of concrete in the construction and maintenance of military airfields.

This chapter also attempts to offer an impression of the architectural departments in the Army Corps of Engineers where Boerée worked and which projects she must have encountered, as one of the first women architectural engineers.

Shining example

Chathariné Heripsimé Marie Boerée was the oldest daughter of career soldier Henri Rijnier Boerée (1873–1949) and Helena Gerardina Scholten (1876–1918). Her first two names came from her Armenian grandmother on her mother's side. Riné and her sister Mia were born in Naarden. In 1903 the family moved to The Hague, where Henri Boerée was a first lieutenant posted to the Second Field Artillery regiment. He was promoted to captain at the Hogere Krijgsschool (a military academy for higher general staff education) in 1912 **[fig. 1]**.[5] The many transfers he had already made by then were familiar territory; his father Hendrik (1843–1918) had been an engineering foreman at the Directorate-General for Public Works and Water (Rijkswaterstaat) and was regularly stationed at various locations, including Zierikzee and Meppel. In the winters of 1902–1903 and 1903–1904, Hendrik was stationed in Kampen due to ice formation and 'high surface water' in the river IJssel.[6] Henri's youngest brother, Theodoor Alexander (1879–1968), was also a soldier and was stationed in The Hague around the same time as Henri, with the Second Fortress Artillery regiment.[7]

While in The Hague, Riné attended Higher Civic School (HBS) from 1911 to 1916. After earning her final diploma, she started studying architecture at the Technische Hoogeschool (TH), travelling back and forth to Delft from her parental home on Valeriusstraat in The Hague. Her grandfather Hendrik served as a shining example in her choice of study.[8] In the 1916–1917 academic year, five more women and eight men enrolled in the architecture programme.[9] Of those five women, two graduated: Ina Groenevelt in 1923, Co van der Kloet in 1926.[10] Boerée completed her studies in 1929 **[fig. 2]**. It took her thirteen years to complete the five-year programme, whereas the average completion period was seven years. 'More than in any other department, the students in the department of Architecture exceed the study period specified in the regulations,' stated the Centrale Commissie

1

2

1 Henri Rijnier Boerée.

2 Riné Boerée in her final year of study, 1928.

voor de Studiebelangen (Central Committee for Academic Interests at the Technische Hoogeschool), attributing this delay largely to a 'wrong structure of the lesson materials by the students'.[11] Student records show that Riné 'withdrew' from her propaedeutic exams on more than one occasion, so that she did not complete her propaedeutical requirements until in 1921.[12] Her mother's death in 1918, at the age of 42, undoubtedly played a role. Her candidate examinations were also less than ideal, and Riné did not pass all the exam components.

When Henri Boerée remarried in 1921, that must have prompted Riné to spread her wings and move forward. In 1923 she and her sister Mia bought a home together in Oegstgeest at Burgemeester De Kempenaerstraat 74; it was jointly owned and both would continue living there for the rest of their lives. The three blocks of twelve houses were completed in 1921, based on a design by architects A.Th. Kraan and M.E. Groenewegen from Leiden. The back of the properties bordered on a beautifully landscaped park garden, which is now the Hendrik Kraemerpark.[13] Mia, who was studying law in Leiden, already lived on Kempenaerstraat at number 54. Henri Boerée had his daughters' best interests at heart and must have not only paid their tuition, but also covered the costs of their joint residence. He had four more children with his second wife, all sons.

3

Architecture in Delft

The examination for the introductory level (propaedeutic exam) was administered in three components.[14] In the third component, the emphasis was on technical drawing and hand drawing, two subjects that were considered vitally important **[fig. 3-7]**. Boerée took more than three years to complete the third component, which she initially did not pass due to 'insufficient technical skills'.[15]

The curriculum for the candidate examination also consisted of three parts. She was better at drawing technical specifications by that time: in June 1924, she completed the second part of the candidate examination with an 8/10. A few of her courses were not specifically part of the architecture department. For example, Boerée took classes in mechanical engineering from Professor Albert Sybrandus Keverling Buisman (1890–1944) and learned about building materials from Professor Christiaan Kornelis Visser (1877–1957). Both of these university lecturers were civil engineers affiliated with the Roadworks and Hydroengineering department.[16] This programme was an artefact from the time when the four-year architecture programme at the former Polytechnic School still overlapped significantly with the civil engineering

3 C.H.M. Boerée, entrance, 1921.

4 C.H.M. Boerée, ornament, 1921.

5 'RB', *Drommedaris gateway to Enkhuizen*, undated. This drawing may also have been a practice exercise (see also 6 and 7).

6 'RB', *Carillon bell tower in Edam*, undated. Grada Wolffensperger drew a detailed version of the same object (see Chapter 5, 1).

7 Unsigned, *St. Mary's Church Choir* (location not legible), undated.

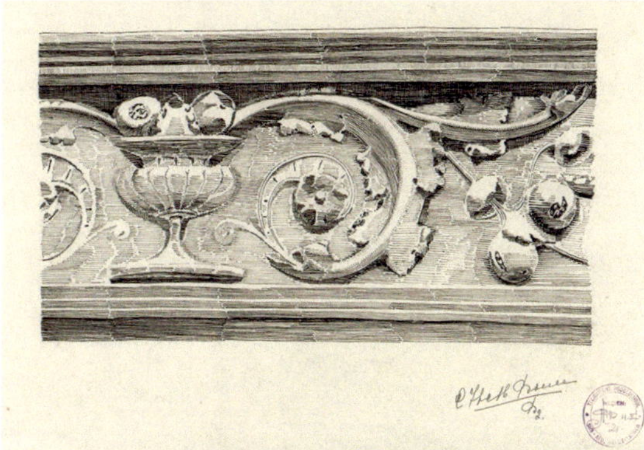

4

5

6

7

8

programme. It is likely that these civil engineering courses were particularly relevant to Boerée's work at the Army Corps of Engineers later on. She passed the building materials course with a 9/10.

The addition of art history and design courses to the architecture programme, which had been an independent study since 1905, had its origins in the objections of the executive board of the Technische Hoogeschool to an initial impetus to place the architecture programme in the Rijksakademie van Beeldende Kunsten in Amsterdam.[17] Architecture encompassed theory of architectural forms, structural building practices and the history of architecture. Boerée took classes from Professors Henri Evers (1855–1929) and Adrianus van der Steur (1865–1945) **[fig. 8]**. One of her fellow students, Ko Mulder, characterized these gentlemen as professors who were prominent in their field and made no secret of that fact.[18] She described Evers as a fascinating storyteller.

The notes that Boerée took in class offer an impression of the topics covered in those days. The first lines she wrote in 1919 during Professor Ever's class on the history of architecture read: 'Architecture starts in the first degree of civilization, when mankind roamed nomadically, and sought shelter from the weather'.[19] These do not appear to be her own observations, but direct quotes from the professor. In a separate notebook, she made

8 Prof.Ir. J.A.G. van der Steur as Rector Magnificus of the Technische Hoogeschool Delft, 1922.

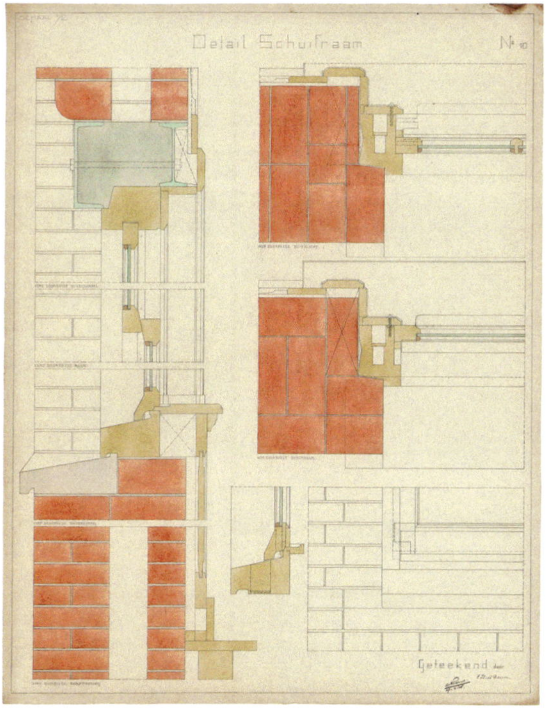

9

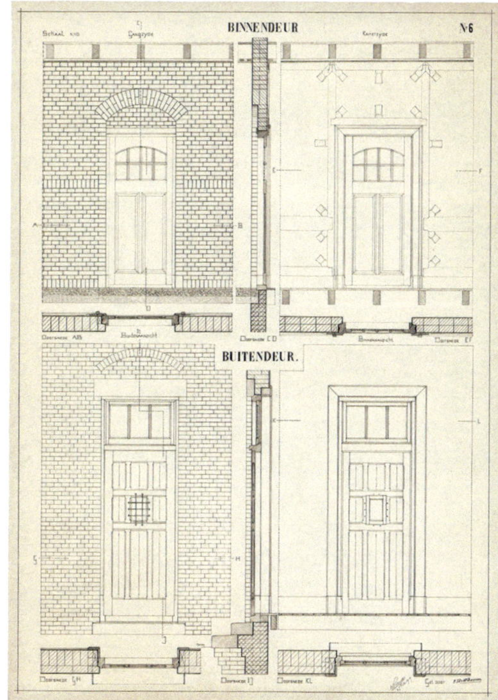

10

9 C.H.M. Boerée, *Detail of sash window*, 1918.

10 C.H.M. Boerée, *Interior door exterior door*, 1919.

notes on such topics as 'Byzantium', 'Islamic Architecture', 'Architecture in Europe – Romanesque France' and 'Gothicism in Italy'.[20] The architecture course also covered the topic of residential buildings. The class notes describe every conceivable type of room and aspects of the house, such as a gentlemen's room – 'much needed' –, boudoir, pantry, polishing room, hall, floor-to-floor height, cupboards and flooring.[21] For her propaedeutic examination, Riné produced 32 meticulously numbered drawings of doors, windows, staircases, foundations and roofs **[fig. 9-10]**.[22]

Boerée's notebooks also place her university studies in an interesting historical context. Van der Steur, who had been trained by Evers, taught classes on Dutch architecture. The notes that Riné took in his class on 12 February 1925 read: 'Our architecture is minimally appreciated abroad. (...) Our people's nature is contemplative, rejecting pomp and circumstance, with few monumental features in our buildings.'[23] The reading list that Van der Steur assigned to the students was very limited, since 'there is essentially no reference book on our architecture'.[24] The short list mentioned only a more catalogue-style 'and not yet very reliable' work by Weissman, a 1914 publication by Kalf, and several publications by Vermeulen that had been released, regarding which Boerée noted: 'started, several volumes published, dangerous theories'.[25] These words

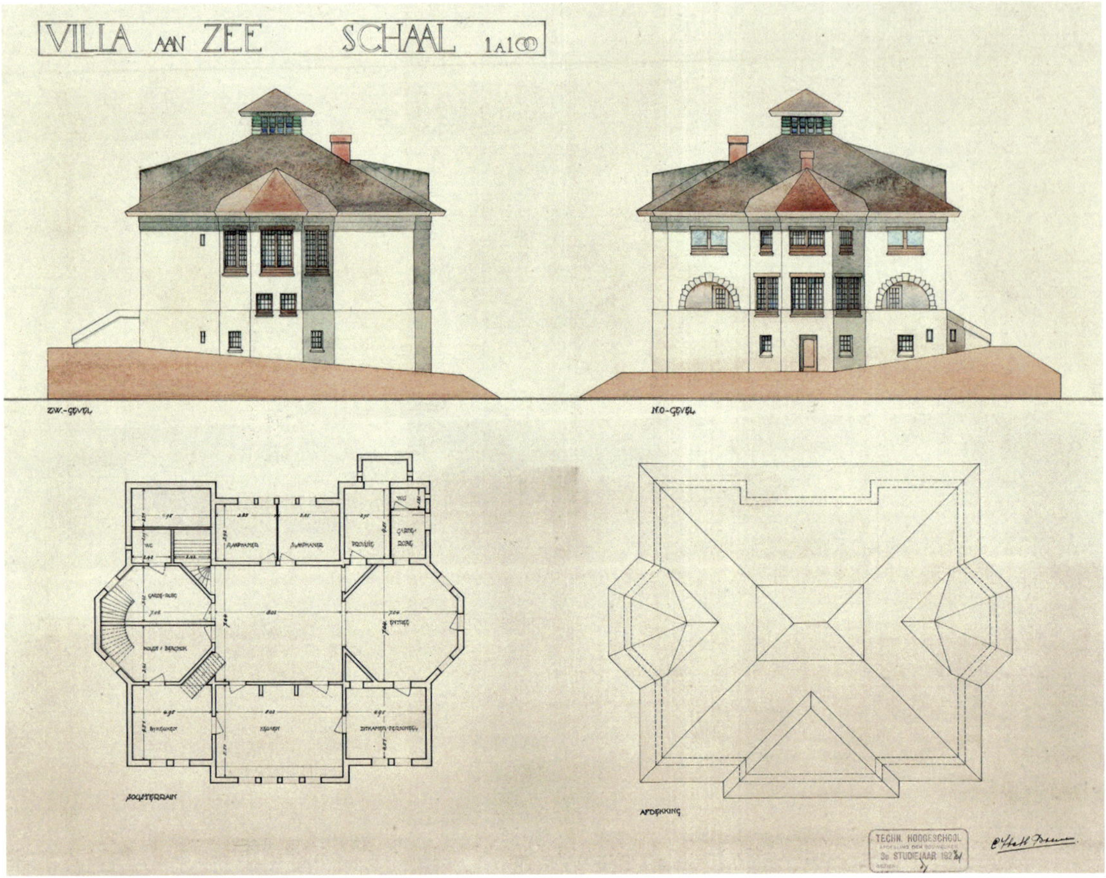

11

11 C.H.M. Boerée, *Seaside villa*, facade and floor plan, 1923–1924.

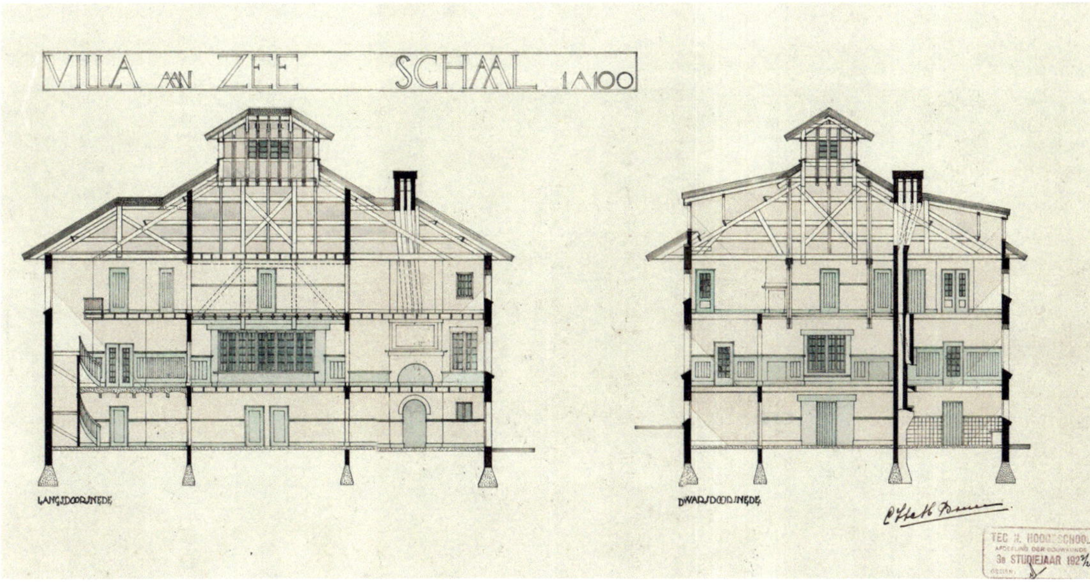

12

12 C.H.M. Boerée, *Seaside villa*, longitudinal and cross-section, 1923–1924.

seem to have been dictated directly by Van der Steur and are particularly noteworthy because the ideology of the architectural historian referenced here, F.A.J. Vermeulen, who later became a notorious collaborator during the German occupation, was already characterized as 'dangerous' then.[26] The 'several volumes' refers to the first sections that were published in 1925, in anticipation of a handbook on the history of architecture that would later be published in six volumes.[27] Dressed in his perpetual garb of tailcoat, breeches and gaiters, Van der Steur caused many students' in-class drawings to vanish entirely below his corrections applied in heavy pencil on tracing paper.[28] There was hardly any discussion.

From 1922 to 1925, Boerée took classes in decorative art and ornamental drawing from Karel Sluyterman (1863–1931). Fireplace mantelpieces, furniture, Egyptian art, modern industrial art and other topics were covered on Tuesdays from 13:00 to 14:00. Sluyterman was considered friendly and charming, for example because he introduced himself to the students – which his colleagues Van der Steur and Evers would never have done, in the opinion of Boerée's classmate.[29]

In preparing for the candidate examination, the students practiced designing residential homes and small public buildings **[fig. 11-12]**.[30] Boerée completed the requirements for her candidate examination

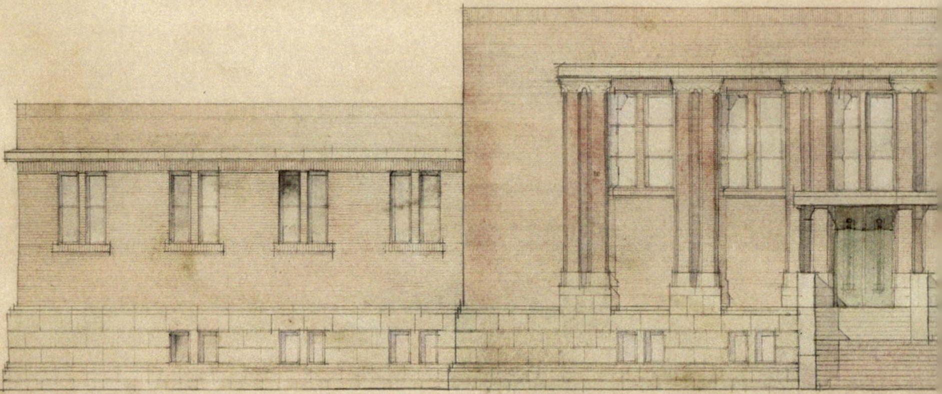

VOORGEVEL

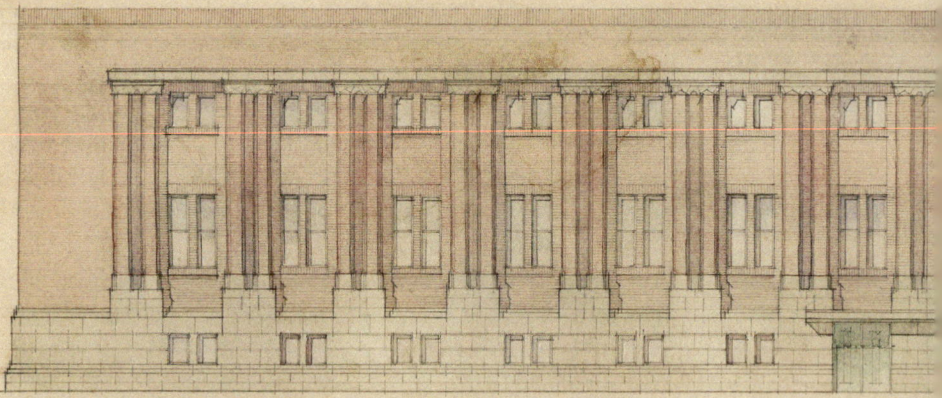

ACHTERGEVEL

GEREC

SCHAAL

TSHOF

1:100

P. Th. H. Broese

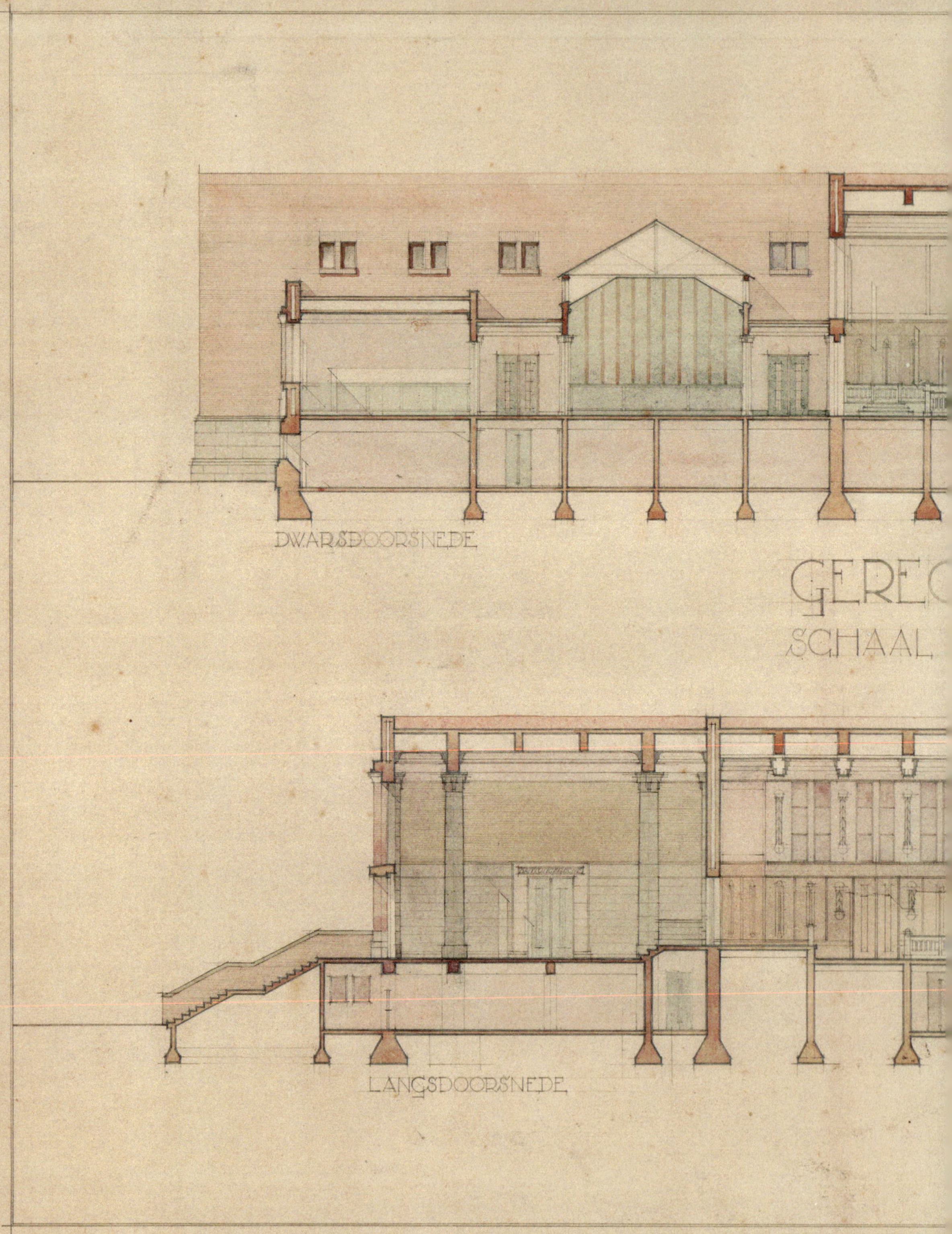
DWARSDOORSNEDE
GEREC
SCHAAL
LANGSDOORSNEDE

TSHOF

1:100

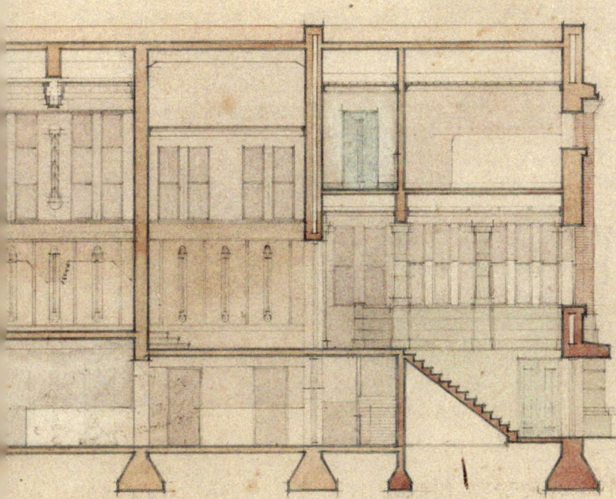

15

in summer 1926. In the final year, they had to create larger designs. The graduation project involved the design of a public building. Unfortunately, many of the student drawings made by Boerée that still remain were undated. Her design for a courthouse may well have been for her graduation project **[fig. 13-14]**. Boerée graduated on 29 June 1929; she was 30 years old at that time.[31]

← ←
13 C.H.M. Boerée, *Courthouse*, front and rear facades, undated.

←
14 C.H.M. Boerée, *Courthouse*, cross-section and longitudinal section, undated.

Tea circles

In her very first year at university, Boerée and two other women in their first year, Ina Groenevelt and Co van der Kloet, joined the Delftsche Vrouwelijke Studenten Vereeniging ('Delft Female Student Society', or DVSV), which had been established in 1904.[32] In those first years, most of the members were technologists (chemical engineers), which was the most popular course of study for women at the Technische Hoogeschool (TH). DVSV gave the women studying at the TH a chance to meet – much needed, since women were not allowed to join the Delfts Studenten Corps.[33] However, courtesy visits did take place back and forth as time passed. For example, the new DVSV board paid an annual visit to the Corps Senate 'to wish them luck on their anniversary'.[34]

When Boerée joined in 1916, DVSV had over 80 members and students from the architecture programme were on the board for the first time, represented by Beb Zeeman and Marie Snethlage.[35] In the 1918–1919 academic year, Boerée was the second secretary **[fig. 15]**.[36]

The DVSV activities consisted primarily of cabaret, theatre, photography, gymnastics and tea circles. The women studying architecture also practiced drawing together.[37] Causeries (literary discussions) took place sporadically, such as the talk by Beb Zeeman on 'Art, the concept in contemporary practice'.[38] The annual reports do not make mention of any lectures by Boerée. From 1925 on, the DVSV published annual overviews of its donors (mostly women), which included a man who clearly held the student society in high esteem: the father of Riné Boerée.[39]

Fort Prins Frederik

In the personal archive left by Riné Boerée at HNI, there is an undated and unsigned map of Fort Prins Frederik in Ooltgensplaat **[fig. 16]**.[40] It not only shows the fort itself, but also the service buildings and in particular the secretary's residence located just outside the fort on Havendijk, where the commander was housed **[fig. 17]**. Once the fort had been abandoned as an active fortification, the municipal secretary moved into the building in 1929, which is where it got its name.[41] The municipal secretary was responsible for overseeing the fort, which was used as summer accommodations for the members of the Vrijwillige Burgerwacht (volunteer civil defence force) of Amsterdam, which had been commanded and chaired by father Henri Boerée since 1923.[42] In 1936, also under Boerée's leadership, the Vereniging voor Nationale Volksopvoeding (association for national public education) set the fort up as a work camp for young and unemployed Roman Catholics and as a summer camp and training centre for the women who led De Graal, a 'young women's movement for Catholic action'.[43] In early 1940, before the Germans invaded, the Ministry of Defence requisitioned the fort again.[44]

15 Riné Boerée (extreme left), second secretary of the board of the Delftsche Vrouwelijke Studenten Vereeniging, 1918–1919.

The floor plans of the ground floor and attic of the secretary's residence are detailed. It is very possible that Henri Boerée nominated his daughter to come up with the design for remodelling the house for the municipal secretary and his family. The Germans tore down the secretary's residence in 1942.

Fuel station

We know very little about the ambitions that Boerée cherished right after graduation. She must have persevered in her pursuit of a degree for good reason. But what options were available to her? Of the eight women archi-

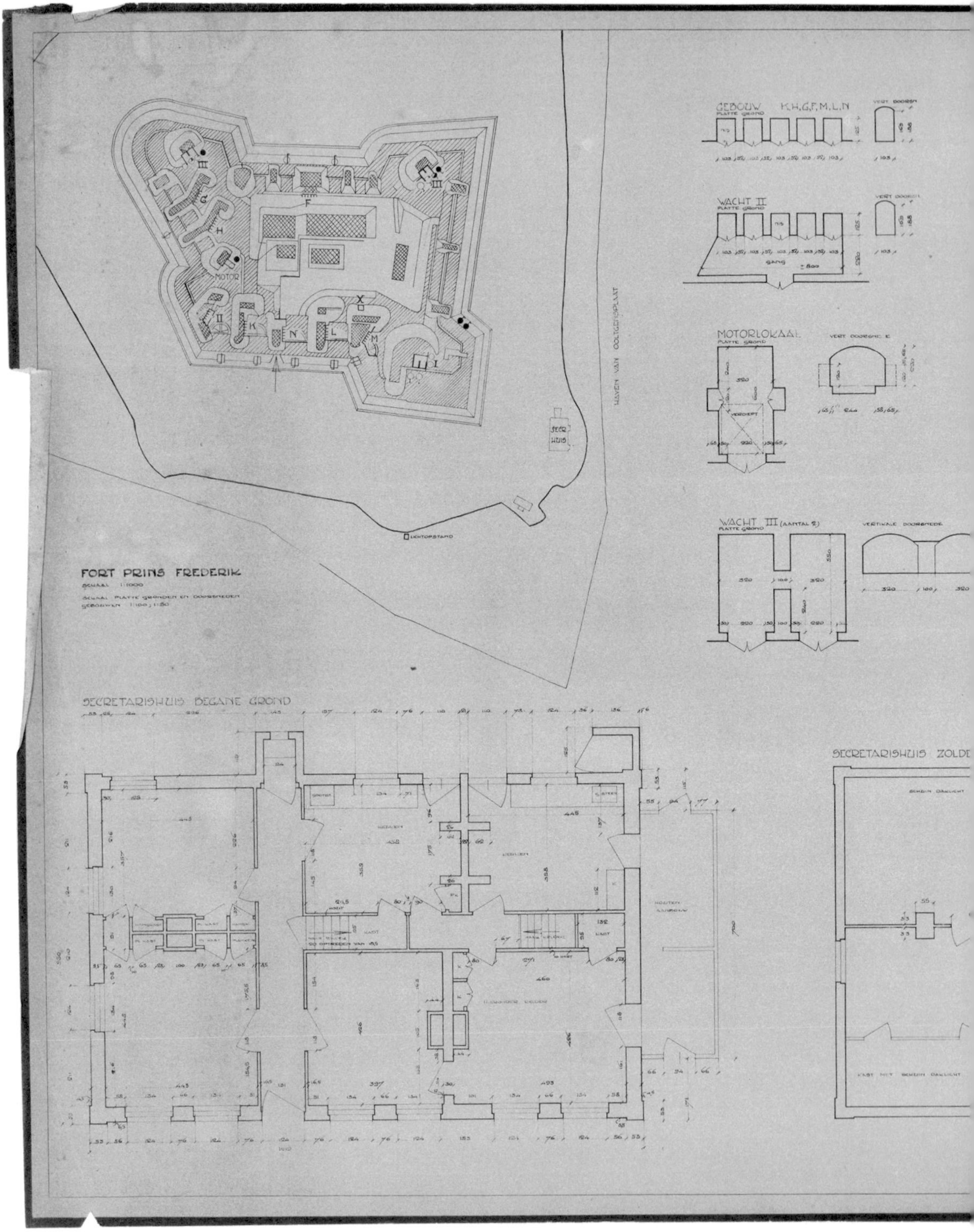
FORT PRINS FREDERIK
SCHAAL 1:1000
GEBOUW K,H,G,F,M,L,N
WACHT II
MOTORLOKAAL
WACHT III (AANTAL 2)
SECRETARISHUIS BEGANE GROND
SECRETARISHUIS ZOLDE
HAVEN VAN OOLTGENSPLAAT

16

16 Unsigned,
Fort Prins Frederik,
Ooltgensplaat,
floor plan, undated.

17

17 Fort
Prins Frederik,
Ooltgensplaat,
1920–1930.

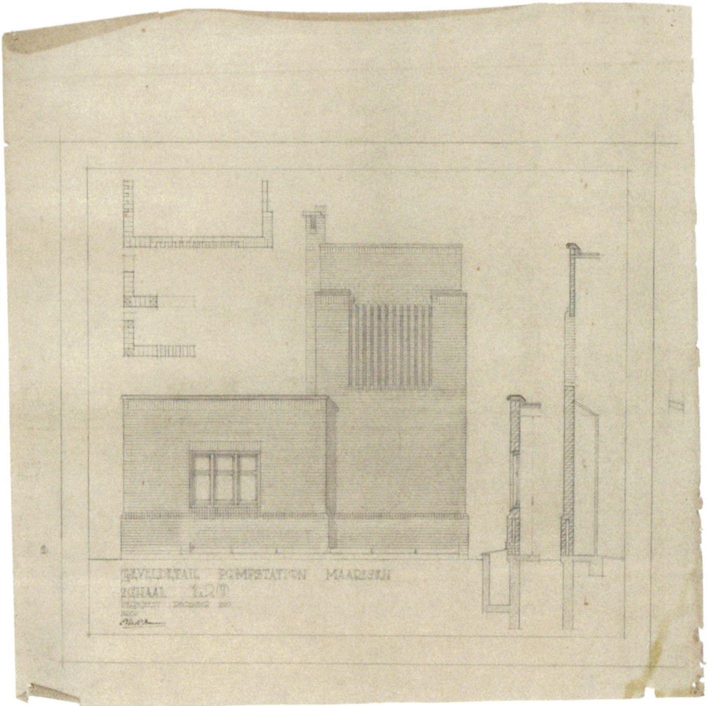

18

tectural engineers who had graduated before her, only one – Ko Mulder – had found a suitable job in government service. The others either got married and thus lost their chance at a government job, or attempted to find work as an independent architect and eventually accepted an administrative position. In a career guide published by the National Bureau for Women's Labour, the prospects for women architects were described as follows: 'in own office, unfavourable; likelihood of placement in architecture firm is minimal'.[45] At any rate, there were very few job openings available for freshly graduated architects, men or women. For example, there were hardly any jobs listed for architectural engineers in trade journal *De Ingenieur* after Boerée graduated in summer 1929.[46] In that year, Boerée spent five months working at an architecture firm in Amsterdam without pay, 'because there was already a young man on the payroll at the firm.'[47] during her time there, she was 'sent out to the work sites'.

A design drawing by Boerée from December 1929 has remained intact, showing a facade detail for an industrial fuel station **[fig. 18]**.[48] This fuel station, which no longer exists, was built on an industrial complex of a metalworks and galvanization company: N.V. Plaatwerkerij en verzinkerij v/h P. Bammens en Zn. This family firm from Geertruidenberg had been relocated by new owners to Stationsweg in Maarssen, suitable location

18 C.H.M. Boerée, *Facade detail of Maarssen fuel station*, 1929.

19

19 The Bammens complex in Maarssen, 1952. The fuel station can still be seen at the top left.

near the Amsterdam-Rhine canal and the railway **[fig. 19]**.[49] It is remarkable that this fairly prestigious company gave the commission to Boerée. She completed the project as an independent architect; the design drawing was signed by Boerée herself in Oegstgeest. Despite the utilitarian nature of the fuel station, Boerée still focused attention on the exterior design and gave both sections of the sleek, modern building a facade featuring neat brickwork. She may have been inspired by the water tower building, where the external appearance received a great deal of attention.

Turning point

Boerée's specialization in concrete constructions very probably originated from a surprising source. In her interview, she was asked which project she considered most characteristic of her preferred work.[50] Other than the Alexanderkazerne (military barracks in The Hague) which will be addressed later in this chapter, she mentioned the Nirwana block of flats (1928–1930) in The Hague, where she was said to have been involved in building the reinforced concrete structure. Designed by Jan Duiker (1890–1935) and Jan Gerko Wiebenga (1886–1974), this eight-storey residential tower was erected on the corner of Van Alkemadelaan and Benoordenhoutseweg

SCHEVENINGEN 4
LOOSDUINEN
HOEK v. HOLLAND 22

[fig. 20].[51] The design was an example of the Modern Movement, in which functional architecture was achieved using modern building techniques. It was the first residential high-rise in the Netherlands to be erected as a reinforced concrete skeleton, such that the outer walls were no longer load-bearing and the facades could be made almost entirely of glass. This significantly increased natural light in the homes. The flat building incorporated all sorts of shared modern conveniences that made it possible to keep household staff to a minimum: hot and cold running water, central heating, a rubbish chute and a laundry chute, and electric lifts for passengers, food and shopping. The kitchens of the spacious flats were also equipped with the latest in technical features.

The plans that Duiker and Wiebenga developed for the Nirwana block of flats were inspired by the high-rise apartment buildings in the USA, where Wiebenga had worked for a year. The two Delft alumni had complementary skills: Duiker was an architectural engineer, while Wiebenga – a civil engineer – was able to contribute his knowledge and expertise to the concrete structure. Their partnership was rocky, however. As a result of individual preferences expressed by the very demanding future occupants, the plans had to be adjusted several times. In the letters that were preserved, Wiebenga complained about the significant amount of extra work that was repeatedly heaped upon him: 'Since mister D. has serious shortcomings in organization and construction (...) I am moreover a victim of his mania for making changes, such that I am forced to redo all the work four or five times. I would therefore prefer to hire cheaper workers to do the drawing from now on (...)'.[52]

← **20** The Nirwana block of flats on Benoordenhoutseweg in The Hague, 1952.

Could this be how Boerée ended up on the project? Her name may have been mentioned in architectural circles in The Hague, leading her to do drawings for Wiebenga.[53] It is striking that each and every one of the many scribbles, calculations and drawings related to the flat block bear Wiebenga's signature, without any exceptions.[54] It seems to have been nearly obsessive on his part. As a result, it is impossible to determine whether hired workers, which may have included Boerée, contributed to these documents. However, in view of the fact that she stated in the interview that she saw this project as one of the most characteristic works in her portfolio, we can say in retrospect that her involvement in the Nirwana block of flats had a huge impact on the rest of her career.

Government Buildings Agency

It is uncertain whether Boerée actually cherished ambitions to establish herself as an independent architect. No other projects were found that were assumed to be designed by Boerée working as an independent architect, other than the aforementioned fuel station in Maarssen.[55]

On 14 November 1930, she started working at the Dienst Rijksgebouwen ('Government Buildings Agency') in The Hague on the draughting team on a temporary basis.[56] In part due to the growing financial crisis caused by the Wall Street crash in the US, she accepted a job for which she was overqualified. In her later interview, she emphasized that it was far from easy to find a job and that she was pleased to be working.[57] The Government Buildings Agency had a rigid downsizing policy during that period, and did not start hiring again until around 1935.

In the *DVSV Almanac*, she did not describe her job as a temporary draughtswomen, but as 'Engineer working for the Government Buildings Agency'.[58] She obtained the position thanks to the government architect, Kees Bremer (1880–1949), who lived next door to her aunt. Bremer had also studied in Delft under Evers, just like Boerée; as the government architect (1924–1946), he also designed buildings independently, such as post offices, tax offices and laboratories.[59] During the period that Boerée came to work at the Government Buildings Agency, Bremer was often in Maastricht. In that city, he would earn acclaim with the Gouvernement (provincial seat of government for Limburg) and residence for the Queen's Commissioner (1930–1935), the construction of the new Wilhemina Bridge (1930–1932) and the restoration of the medieval St. Servatius Bridge (1932–1933). In 1933, he also joined the Rijkscommissie voor de Monumentenzorg, which would later become the Cultural Heritage Agency of the Netherlands. Bremer had a reputation for being good at delegating, often allowing young subordinates to work independently.

Drawings by Boerée were preserved that featured a monumental staircase.[60] These stairs led to a caretaker's residence in the complex of the Head Office of Postal and Telegraph Services (1917–1923) on Kortenaerkade in The Hague.[61] The staircase may have been a supplement to the previous design. The blueprints were signed by Boerée and by 'The Architectural Chief Officer L. Bok'. Louis Bok (1883–1953), Director of Maintenance and Expansion Works, frequently worked closely with Bremer, who was in charge of erecting the buildings for the Head Office on Kortenaerkade, based on an amended design by Marinus Jan Granpré Molière (1883–1972). As a woman surrounded by a large group of fellow architects and construction engineers (all men), Boerée was permitted to sign her own work.[62] Her status as a university graduate and Bremer's delegatory leadership style must have played a role here, rather than the fact that she was Bremer's neighbour's niece.

Unfortunately, this is the only project that Boerée is known to have worked on during that time. Based on this solitary example, it cannot be concluded that she was only assigned to interior renovations in her capacity as a woman at the Agency. On 1 January 1933, Boerée was dismissed from the Government Buildings Agency due to a lack of work and budget.

De Genie

Boerée did not have a long wait before finding new employment. Within two months, she became a temporary site forewoman and draughtswoman at the Army Corps of Engineers (known as De Genie) in The Hague. This was the branch of the Dutch armed forces responsible for design, construction and maintenance of all military works. It is very likely that she obtained this job through her father; although he was living in Bussum by then, he was a retired colonel and commander of the Vrijwillige Burgerwacht (volunteer civil defence force) of Amsterdam and undoubtedly had a large military network.[63] This was the start of Boerée's career at De Genie, where she would work until her pension, interrupted only by the years of the Second World War.

Boerée was also overqualified for her first job with De Genie, but her interest in concrete continued to develop here. At the end of 1933, she took a course in concrete inspection at the Betonvereniging ('Concrete Association') in Rotterdam, possibly facilitated by her employer. The course was taught by Ir. Nicolaas Jakob Rengers (1896–1983).[64] In 1932, the Betonvereniging had given him a golden badge of honour in recognition for his international research on reinforced concrete columns, a topic that (as will become apparent later in this chapter) also captured Boerée's interest. With the course he launched in 1933, Rengers established a solid reputation in the concrete sector. Clearly, his course met a need. In the very first year, independently established and ambitious architect Koen Limperg (1908–1943) also took the course.[65] The organizers do not appear to have anticipated that women would take part: the text on the preprinted certificate states that 'Mr C.H.M. Boerée, engineer' had attended the course **[fig. 21]**.[66] Boerée's interest and specialization in concrete is clearly evidenced by the fact that, in 1935, she became the first woman to join the Betonvereniging.[67]

In the 1937 yearbook of the Vereeniging van Delftsche Ingenieurs ('Association of Delft Engineers'), she had her profession listed as 'Temporary Draughtswoman of barracks building in The Hague'.[68] She was specifically focused on building elements of the barracks, as shown by a working plan for buildings on the site at the intersection of Van Alkemadelaan and Waalsdorperweg in The Hague. The plan consists of a division of tasks for the period from 1934–1935 for two barracks complexes planned for construction: Alexanderkazerne (1935–1938) for the cavalry and Frederikkazerne (1935–1942) for the artillery. The anonymous work plan, with the added comment 'to be discussed with Captain Kok', is apparently written by a subordinate on his orders.[69] Captain J. Kok (1895–1975) was an army engineer and the designer of both barracks complexes.[70] Under his leadership, six site foremen-draughtsmen, two site foremen and an administrator

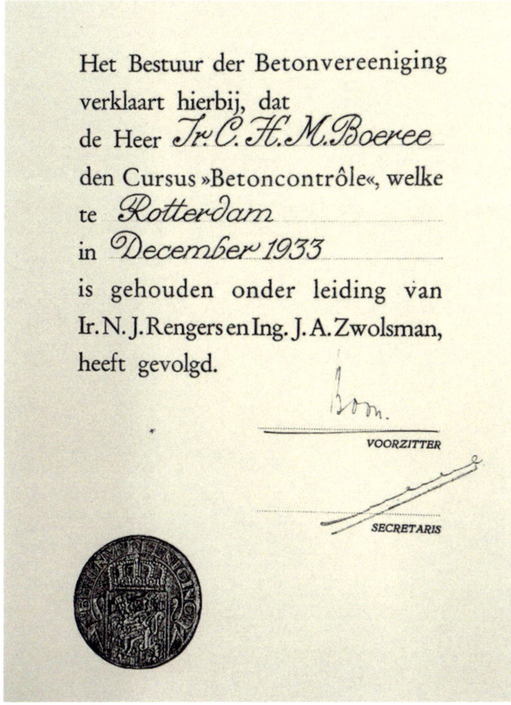

Het Bestuur der Betonvereeniging
verklaart hierbij, dat
de Heer Ir. C. H. M. Boeree
den Cursus »Betoncontrôle«, welke
te Rotterdam
in December 1933
is gehouden onder leiding van
Ir. N. J. Rengers en Ing. J. A. Zwolsman,
heeft gevolgd.

Boon.
VOORZITTER

SECRETARIS

21

21 The diploma for the course in Concrete Control, 1933.

worked on the preparations. On the team of site foremen-draughtsmen, Boerée was responsible for a specific part described as the 'reinforced concrete calculations and drawings for redirecting and expanding Waalsdorperweg (cladding walls)' – the first technical specifications – and the 'reinforced concrete drawings of buildings for second specifications (partially complete, very extensive work)'[71] Comparing this to the tasks assigned to her colleagues, she was the only one specifically focusing on reinforced concrete. The author of the plan emphasized that the design specifications '[proved] very difficult, as in fact the entire preparation (...), related to sand excavation and elevation, etc.' And that it was necessary for 'the leader to have access to sufficient good employees, since the task would otherwise be too burdensome for their leader'. This shows that Boerée was characterized as a competent professional and colleague, and that she was considered a full member of the team, the rest of whom were men.[72]

The second, very extensive technical specifications contained an impressive list of buildings that would be in the barracks complex: 'supply warehouses, workshop building for shoemakers and tailors, double residence with storage shed, privy building, transformer station, weighbridge house, veterinary hospital, quarantine stables, guardhouse,

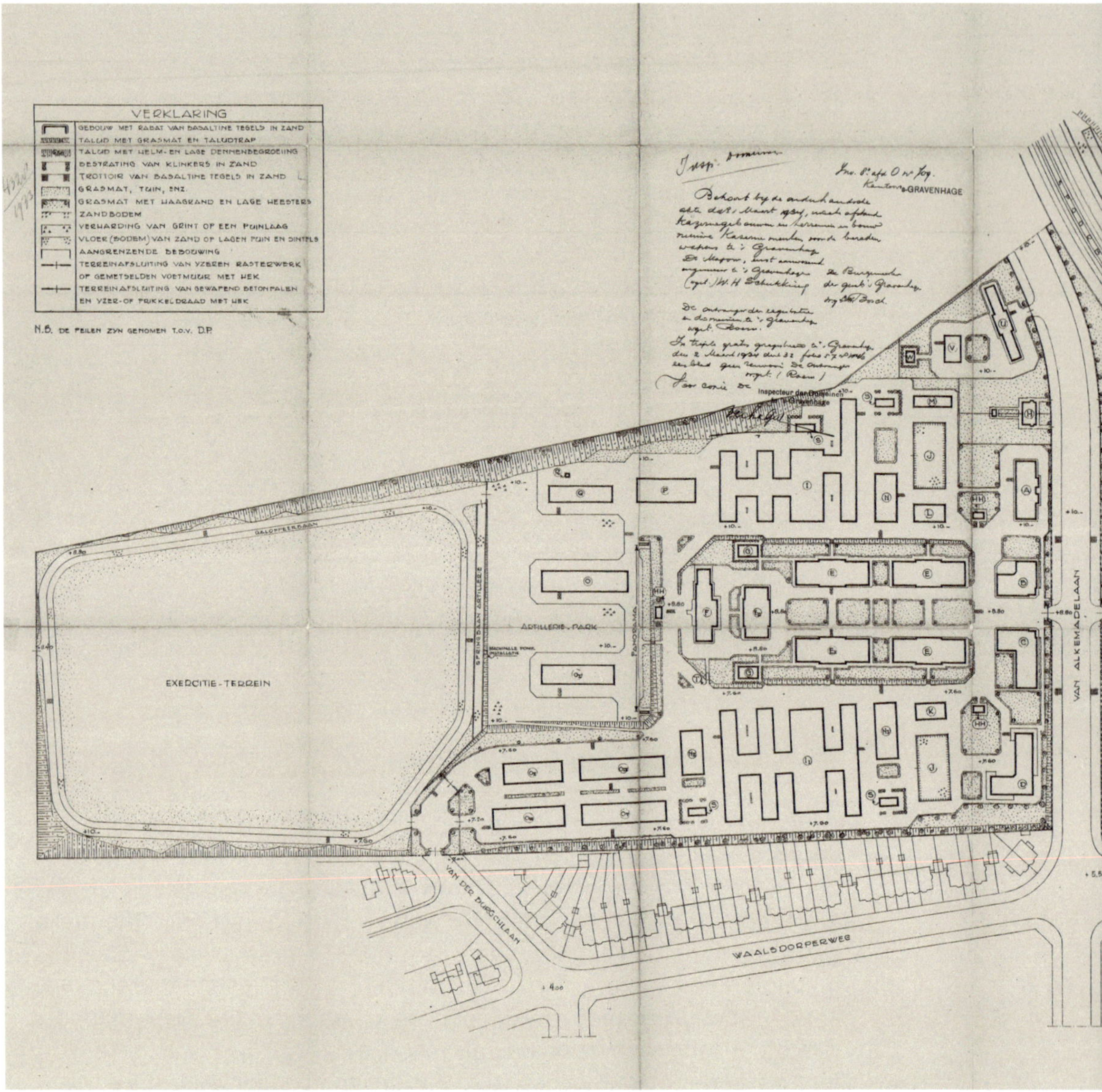
VERKLARING
GEBOUW MET RABAT VAN BASALTINE TEGELS IN ZAND
TALUD MET GRASMAT EN TALUDTRAP
TALUD MET HELM- EN LAGE DENNENBEGROEIING
BESTRATING VAN KLINKERS IN ZAND
TROTTOIR VAN BASALTINE TEGELS IN ZAND
GRASMAT, TUIN, ENZ.
GRASMAT MET HAAGRAND EN LAGE HEESTERS
ZANDBODEM
VERHARDING VAN GRINT OF EEN PUINLAAG
VLOER (BODEM) VAN ZAND OF LAGEN PUIN EN SINTELS
AANGRENZENDE BEBOUWING
TERREINAFSLUITING VAN YZEREN RASTERWERK
OF GEMETSELDEN VOETMUUR MET HEK
TERREINAFSLUITING VAN GEWAPEND BETONPALEN
EN YZER- OF PRIKKELDRAAD MET HEK
N.B. DE PEILEN ZYN GENOMEN T.O.V. D.P.
GRAVENHAGE
EXERCITIE-TERREIN
ARTILLERIE-PARK
GALOPPEERBAAN
VAN ALKEMADELAAN
WAALSDORPERWEG
VAN DER BURCHLAAN

22

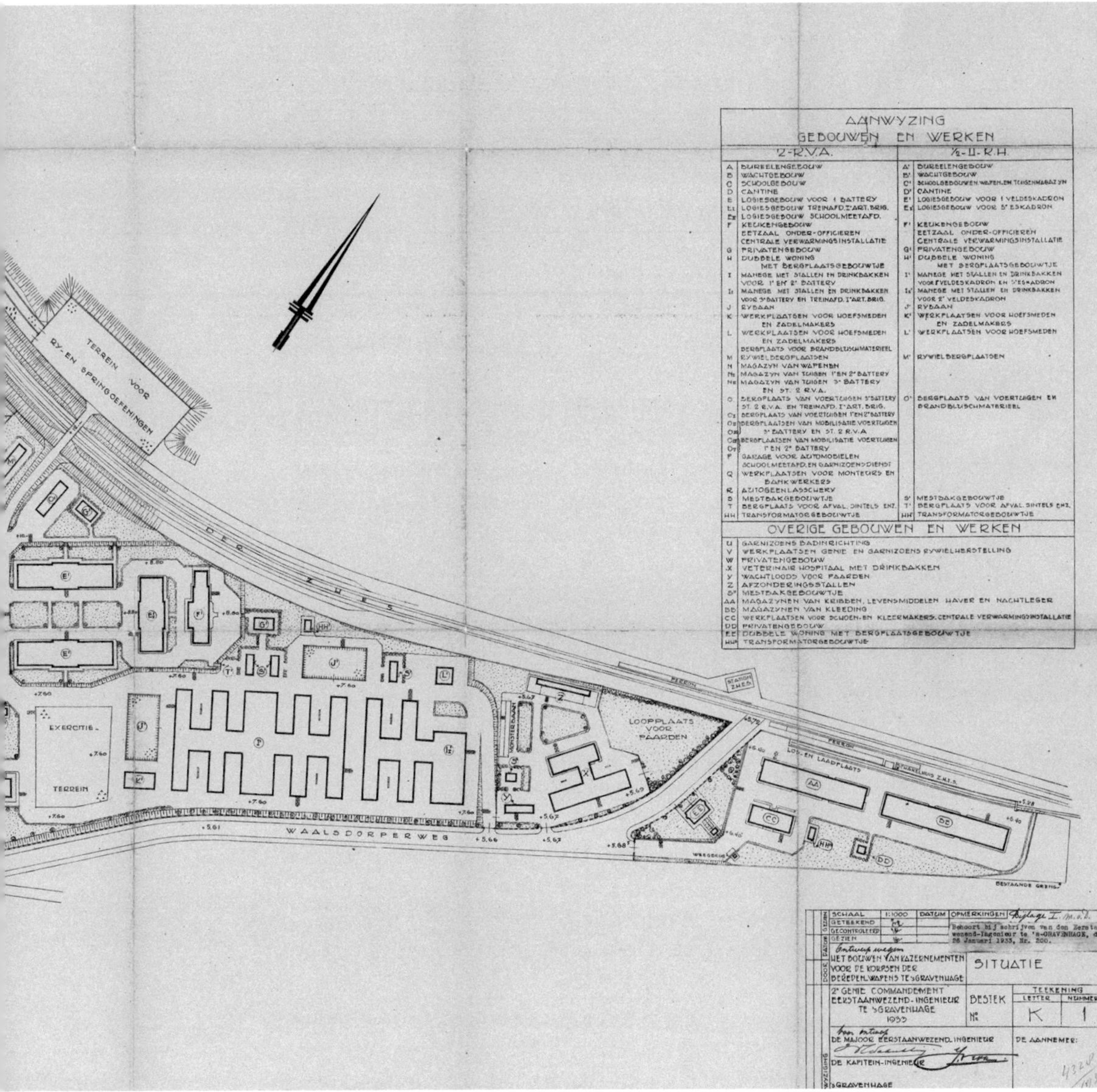

22 *Design for the construction of barracks for the army equestrian unit in The Hague,* or the design scheme for the Alexander barracks and the Frederik barracks, 1933.

manure shed, etc.'.[73] The floor plan from the design of 1933 illustrates the extensive complex that they envisioned and can be considered an urban planning design on a micro level **[fig. 22]**.[74] The plans were apparently not sufficiently comprehensive; an appended document provided a non-exhaustive list summarizing 'more necessary spaces', such as: lodging accommodation with washrooms, drying rooms, night privies; barn and stable complexes with 'regular and officer horse stations', larger stables with emergency facilities for mobilization, hay barns; 'privy buildings for scullery maids'; school buildings with gymnasium halls, signalling rooms and panorama rooms; office buildings for department heads, adjuncts and clerks, and mobilization bureaus for batteries and squadrons; vehicle sheds with cleaning rooms and 'issuing desks'; canteen rooms with verandas, etc. etc.[75]

Some of the items on this wish list can be explained by a growing trend in that period to improve living conditions in the barracks. This was expressed in ministerial decisions that specified separate day rooms and dining halls, but also separate drying and polishing rooms for corporals and soldiers; separate 'sitting rooms provided with coloured walls' for junior officers, and even the installation of doors with padlocks for the 'open cubbyholes'.[76] Kok's plan aimed to achieve military accommodations that allowed the living and sleeping quarters to have optimal access to daylight and fresh air. This was achieved by placing the lodging accommodations along the long sides of the rectangular garden **[fig. 22, see E/F]**. One short side of the square was closed off with a smaller building to provide accommodations for reserve troops, with the service building containing the kitchen and dining room right behind that. This 'pavilion system' originated in the design of hospital buildings, used in the Netherlands from the end of the nineteenth century.[77] Where an entire battalion was once housed in such a building, occupation was now limited to one squadron or battery. 'The overall impression is that light and air pour in abundantly (...)', according to one journalist after the completion of the Alexander barracks.[78]

The lodging accommodations were placed in the centre of the barracks complex, right after the entrance, and the other buildings were situated around that according to their function, based on a clearly structured urban design. In designing his plans, Kok simultaneously had to incorporate the explicit desire expressed by the city of The Hague to ensure that the buildings in the complex would be a good visual match in terms of architectural style and height for the adjacent newly built residential neighbourhood, Benoordenhout. The aerial photo from 1938 shows that much of the design scheme from 1933 was built and that the structure of the lodging accommodations echoes that of the spatial structure of the homes in the Benoordenhout neighbourhood, with wide green strips between the buildings **[fig. 23]**.

23

23 The Van Alkemade complex under construction, 1938.

'The necessary competence'

In May 1935, it was still impossible to issue the tender for construction of the barracks complex due to unforeseen problems in installing the central heating pipes. Among other factors, this meant that the floors at ground level in the buildings that had to be heated would need to be made from concrete, and that the foundations needed to be laid deeper to provide for a crawlspace. That meant making changes in the designs and technical specifications that were already partly finished. To minimize delays in the tender procedure, it was proposed to have 'the site foreman-draughtsman, (...) as soon as one can be missed in the detailed drawing work (...), take on part of the calculation and drawing work, for which this site foreman-draughtsman possesses the necessary competence.'[79] In the margin, this decision was initialled and the chosen candidate was specified: 'Miss Boerée, engineer, will make a general estimate and calculate quantities of reinforced concrete, etc.; other staff will derive their data from these calculations.' This said enough about how much her knowledge was valued.

The fact that Boerée was definitely working on this project is proven by a specification drawing of 30 December 1936 on which she is listed

24

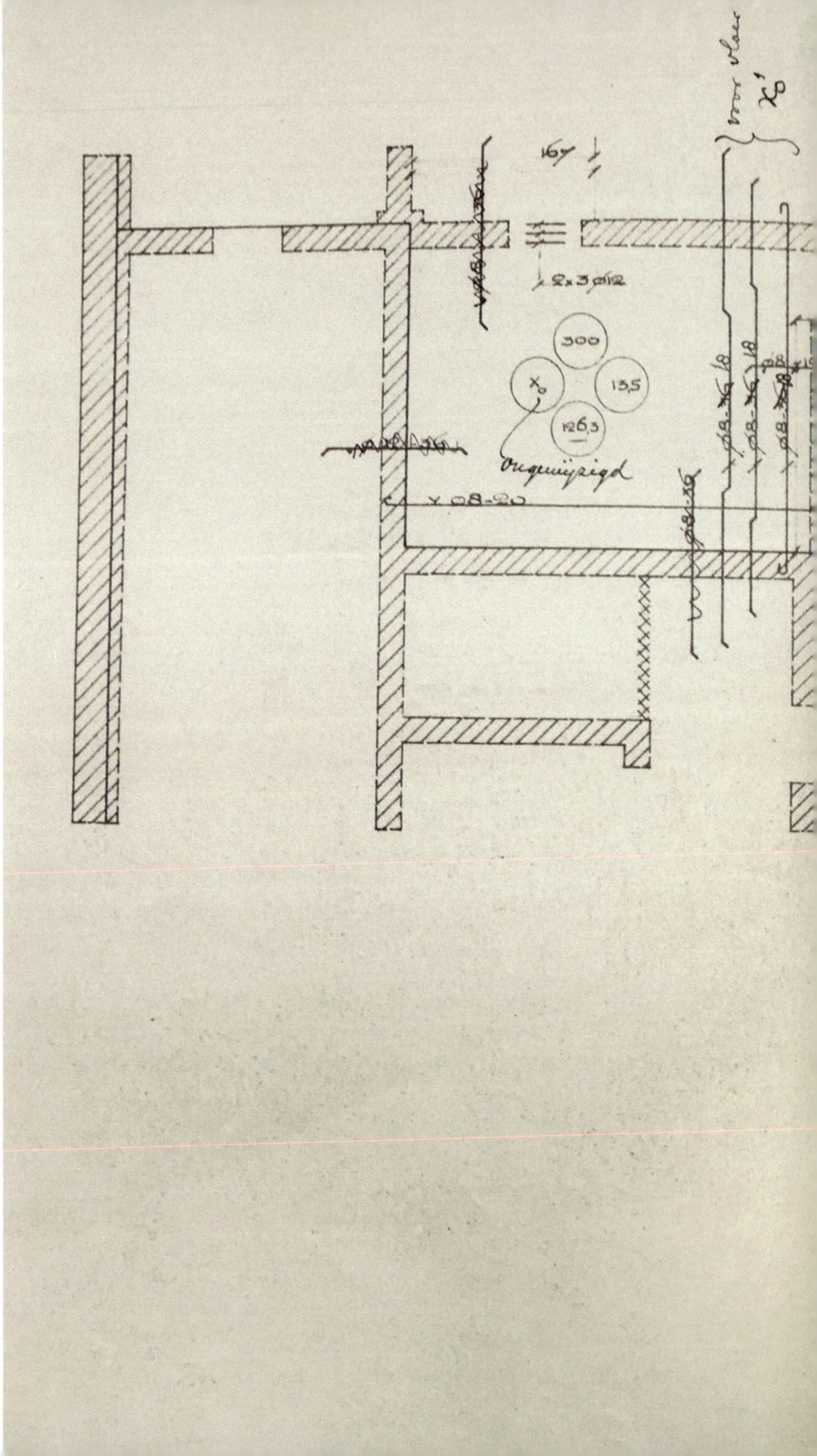

24 Boerée, *The construction of barracks for the army equestrian unit in The Hague, building D1, design scheme*, 1936.

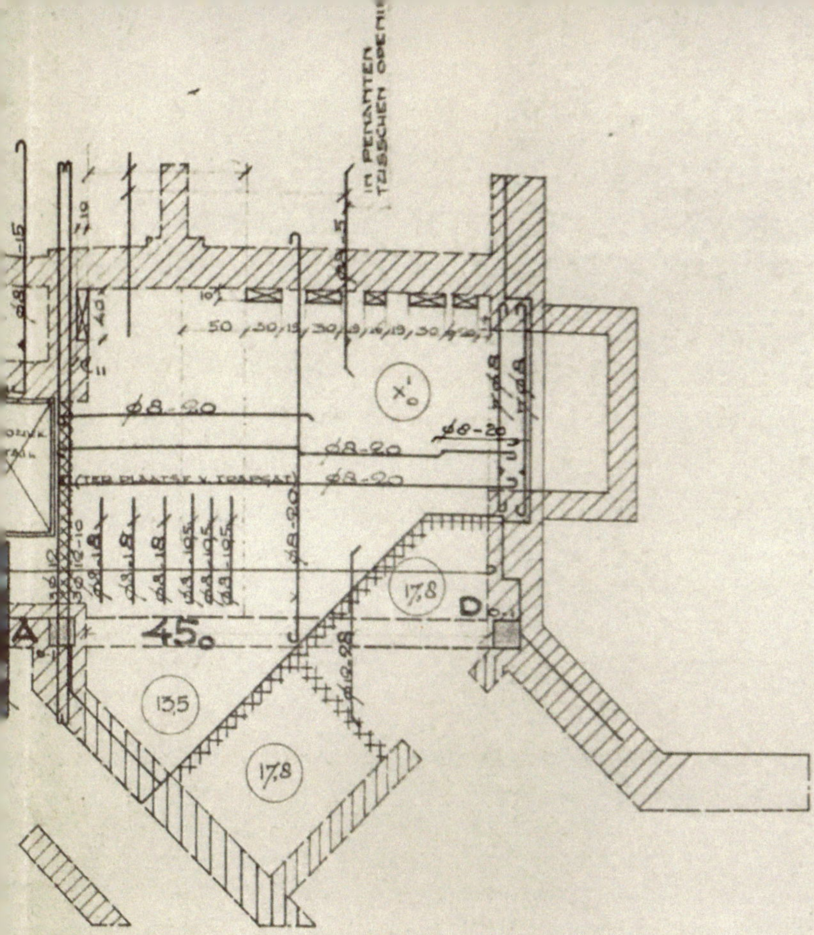

GEZIEN			
SCHAAL	1:50	DATUM	OPMERKINGEN
GETEEKEND	BOEREE	30.12.'36	
GECONTROLEERD		31.12.'36	
GEZIEN		31-12-'36	

LETTER V/. GEBOUW: D'

DATUM: 30.12.'36 — DOOR: B

HET BOUWEN VAN KAZERNEMENTEN VOOR DE KORPSEN DER BEREDEN WAPENS TE 'S GRAVENHAGE.

BEGANE GROND. WIJZIGING VAN VLOER X_0

2E GENIE COMMANDEMENT
EERSTAANWEZEND-INGENIEUR
TE 'S-GRAVENHAGE.
1936

BESTEK № 59/1936

K.B.: 6

...NG VAN K.B. 3

VOOR AFGIFTE.
DE KAPITEIN - INGENIEUR:

VOOR ONTVANGST.
DE AANNEMER:

as draughtswoman **[fig. 24]**.[80] However, the building marked D1 on the drawing does not correspond to the floor plan of the complex from 1933. It can be understood from the drawing that the ground floor of the building had to be changed and that reinforced concrete would be used. The original plan had been to keep Boerée on staff until the estimated tender date of 1 January 1936. Considering when her drawing was dated, the deadline was significantly exceeded. The Alexander barracks was completed in 1938.[81] On the east side of Van Alkemadelaan, which had been extended shortly before that (towards Scheveningen), most of the Frederik barracks was still under construction **[fig. 23]**. That complex rose from the ground in great symmetry with the Alexander barracks **[fig. 22]**.

Boerée stayed much longer than expected in her job – which was still temporary – and was also assigned to work on the rest of the detailed drawings for the complex. Near the site where the barracks complex was being built, Bureau Kazernebouw ('Barracks Building Bureau') was located at Waalsdorperweg 124, where Captain Kok was stationed, and most likely Boerée as well **[fig. 25]**. At the Army Corps of Engineers (De Genie), political developments in Germany and the rest of Europe from 1935 on led to substantial construction activities on new buildings and significant work pressure, which only grew after mobilization was announced on 28 August 1939.[82] On 3 November 1939, Boerée was appointed a 'temporary engineer with De Genie'.[83] Although she still had not received a permanent position, she must have perceived it as proof that her work was appreciated.

By her own account, she was the only one who knew anything about concrete, and was therefore eventually appointed head of the Concrete Department within De Genie.[84] After a young captain became her new boss, a man who had been a concrete technician working on the Dutch railways applied for a job, and the captain considered having him take her place. 'In response to the captain's question, "and where would you go then, madam?", I had no reply at that time,' Boerée said in the 1995 interview.[85] The young captain must have been Captain J. Kok. She was apparently able to retain her position after all.

←
25 Riné Boerée (left of centre with hat) and her colleagues at the Army Corps of Engineers (Dienst der Genie), ca. 1936.

26 Boerée, *Graph for columns with eccentric loads*, undated.

'Good at reinforced concrete'

Until she was very old, Boerée was also captivated by bunkers: after she retired, she finally had time to run the calculations for a prestressed concrete construction for a bunker.[86] Whether she actually had any involvement in such work during her time at De Genie is uncertain, but her interest can be explained at least in part by what was happening at the time. From 1933 on, the Netherlands started building bunkers, following in the footsteps of the French, who built the Maginot Line between 1930 and 1938; in turn, the Germans responded by building the Siegfried Line.

26

EXCENTRISCHE KOLOMMEN MINIMUM WAPENING BETONSPANNING 70 KG/cm² e = αH x = HOOGTE DRUKZÔNE = βH AFMETINGEN KOLOM b×H

$\frac{p}{b \times H}$ =	2	3	4	5	6	7	8	9	10	11	12	13	14	15	16	17	18	19	20	HART WAP TOT BUITENKANT BETON = 0,2 H			σ_b	σ_y
α=1,15 β=0,45														3,584 2,377	4,032 2,546	4,480 2,715	4,927 2,884	5375 3,053	5,823 3,222		DRUK TREK	p= y=	70	837
α=1,20 β=0,44						0,137 1,063	0,604 1,237	1,071 1,412	1,540 1,587	2,008 1,761	2,475 1,936	2,943 2,111	3,411 2,285	3,879 2,460	4,347 2,634	4,814 2,809	5,282 2,984	5,750 3,158	6,217 3,333		DRUK TREK	p= y=	70	859
α=1,25 β=0,44						0,246 1,131	0,729 1,315	1,212 1,500	1,696 1,084	2,179 1,868	2,662 2,052	3,146 2,237	3,629 2,421	4,112 2,605	4,596 2,790	5,079 2,974	5,562 3,159	6,046 3,343		DRUK TREK		p= y=	70	859
α=1,30 β=0,435						0,387 1,166	0,891 1,355	1,394 1,544	1,898 1,735	2,402 1,923	2,906 2,112	3,409 2,301	3,913 2,491	4,417 2,680	4,921 2,869	5,425 3,058	5,929 3,247		DRUK TREK		p= y=		70	881
α=1,35 β=0,435						0,497 1,232	1,017 1,431	1,536 1,630	2,056 1,829	2,575 2,027	3,095 2,226	3,614 2,424	4,134 2,623	4,653 2,822	5,173 3,020	5,692 3,219		DRUK TREK		p= y=			70	891
α=1,40 β=0,43					0,131 1,060	0,642 1,263	1,182 1,466	1,723 1,669	2,263 1,872	2,804 2,075	3,345 2,278	3,886 2,481	4,426 2,684	4,966 2,887	5,507 3,090	6,047 3,293		DRUK TREK		p= y=			70	903
α=1,45 β=0,43					0,197 1,116	0,753 1,328	1,310 1,546	1,866 1,752	2,422 1,964	2,979 2,177	3,535 2,389	4,092 2,601	4,648 2,813	5,205 3,025	5,761 3,238		DRUK TREK		p= y=				70	903
α=1,50 β=0,43					0,292 1,171	0,864 1,393	1,437 1,614	2,009 1,835	2,581 2,057	3,154 2,278	3,726 2,500	4,298 2,721	4,871 2,942	5,443 3,164	6,015 3,385		DRUK TREK		p= y=				70	903
α=1,55 β=0,43					0,387 1,226	0,976 1,437	1,564 1,688	2,152 1,918	2,740 2,149	3,329 2,380	3,917 2,610	4,505 2,841	5,093 3,071	5,682 3,302		DRUK TREK		p= y=					70	903
α=1,60 β=0,425					0,516 1,247	1,127 1,481	1,737 1,714	2,348 1,948	2,958 2,182	3,569 2,416	4,179 2,650	4,790 2,883	5,400 3,117	6,011 3,351		DRUK TREK		p= y=					70	926
α=1,65 β=0,425					0,612 1,300	1,239 1,543	1,866 1,786	2,492 2,029	3,119 2,272	3,745 2,515	4,372 2,758	4,999 3,000	5,625 3,243		DRUK TREK		p= y=						70	926
α=1,70 β=0,425				0,066 1,103	0,709 1,354	1,351 1,606	1,994 1,858	2,637 2,110	3,279 2,362	3,922 2,614	4,565 2,865	5,207 3,117	5,850 3,369		DRUK TREK		p= y=						70	926
α=1,75 β=0,425				0,146 1,148	0,805 1,408	1,464 1,669	2,123 1,930	2,781 2,191	3,440 2,452	4,099 2,713	4,758 2,973	5,416 3,234	6075 3,495		DRUK TREK		p= y=						70	926
α=1,80 β=0,425				0,227 1,193	0,901 1,462	1,576 1,732	2,251 2,002	2,926 2,272	3,601 2,542	4,276 2,812	4,950 3,081	5,625 3,351		DRUK TREK		p= y=							70	926
α=1,85 β=0,425				0,307 1,237	0,998 1,516	1,689 1,795	2,380 2,074	3,071 2,353	3,761 2,632	4,452 2,910	5,143 3,189	5,834 3,466		DRUK TREK		p= y=							70	926
α=1,90 β=0,425				0,387 1,282	1,094 1,570	1,801 1,858	2,508 2,146	3,215 2,434	3,922 2,722	4,629 3,009	5,336 3,297	6,043 3,585		DRUK TREK		p= y=							70	926
α=1,95 β=0,425				0,469 1,327	1,191 1,624	1,914 1,921	2,637 2,218	3,360 2,515	4,083 2,812	4,806 3,108	5,529 3,405		DRUK TREK		p= y=								70	926
α=2,00 β=0,42				0,583 1,336	1,330 1,634	2,077 1,932	2,824 2,231	3,570 2,529	4,317 2,827	5,064 3,125	5,811 3,424		DRUK TREK		p= y=								70	950
α=2,05 β=0,42				0,664 1,380	1,427 1,687	2,190 1,994	2,953 2,301	3,716 2,608	4,479 2,915	5,242 3,222	6,005 3,529		DRUK TREK		p= y=								70	950
α=2,10 β=0,42				0,746 1,424	1,525 1,740	2,304 2,055	3,083 2,371	3,862 2,687	4,642 3,003	5,421 3,318		DRUK TREK		p= y=									70	950
α=2,15 β=0,42			0,031 1,143	0,827 1,468	1,622 1,792	2,418 2,117	3,213 2,441	4,009 2,766	4,804 3,090	5,600 3,415		DRUK TREK		p= y=									70	950
α=2,20 β=0,42			0,096 1,178	0,908 1,511	1,720 1,845	2,531 2,178	3,343 2,511	4,155 2,845	4,966 3,178	5,778 3,511		DRUK TREK		p= y=									70	950
α=2,25 β=0,42			0,161 1,213	0,989 1,555	1,817 1,898	2,645 2,240	3,473 2,582	4,301 2,924	5,129 3,266	5,957 3,608		DRUK TREK		p= y=									70	950
α=2,30 β=0,42			0,226 1,248	1,070 1,599	1,914 1,950	2,759 2,301	3,603 2,652	4,447 3,003	5,291 3,354		DRUK TREK		p= y=										70	950
α=2,35 β=0,415			0,324 1,249	1,194 1,600	2,064 1,951	2,934 2,302	3,804 2,652	4,674 3,003	5,544 3,354		DRUK TREK		p= y=										70	974
α=2,40 β=0,415			0,390 1,284	1,276 1,643	2,163 2,002	3,049 2,362	3,935 2,721	4,822 3,080	5,708 3,440		DRUK TREK		p= y=										70	974
α=2,45 β=0,415			0,456 1,318	1,358 1,686	2,261 2,054	3,164 2,421	4,067 2,789	4,970 3,157	5,872 3,524		DRUK TREK		p= y=										70	974
α=2,50 β=0,415			0,521 1,352	1,440 1,728	2,360 2,105	3,279 2,481	4,198 2,858	5,117 3,234	6,037 3,611		DRUK TREK		p= y=										70	974
α=2,55 β=0,415			0,587 1,386	1,522 1,771	2,458 2,156	3,394 2,541	4,329 2,926	5,265 3,311		DRUK TREK		p= y=											70	974
α=2,60 β=0,415			0,652 1,420	1,605 1,814	2,557 2,208	3,509 2,601	4,461 2,995	5,413 3,388		DRUK TREK		p= y=											70	974
α=2,65 β=0,415			0,718 1,455	1,687 1,857	2,655 2,259	3,624 2,661	4,542 3,064	5,561 3,465		DRUK TREK		p= y=											70	974

BOERKE TABEL 1B

SPANNINGEN TREKWAPENING

GRAFIEK VOOR KOLOMMEN MET EX

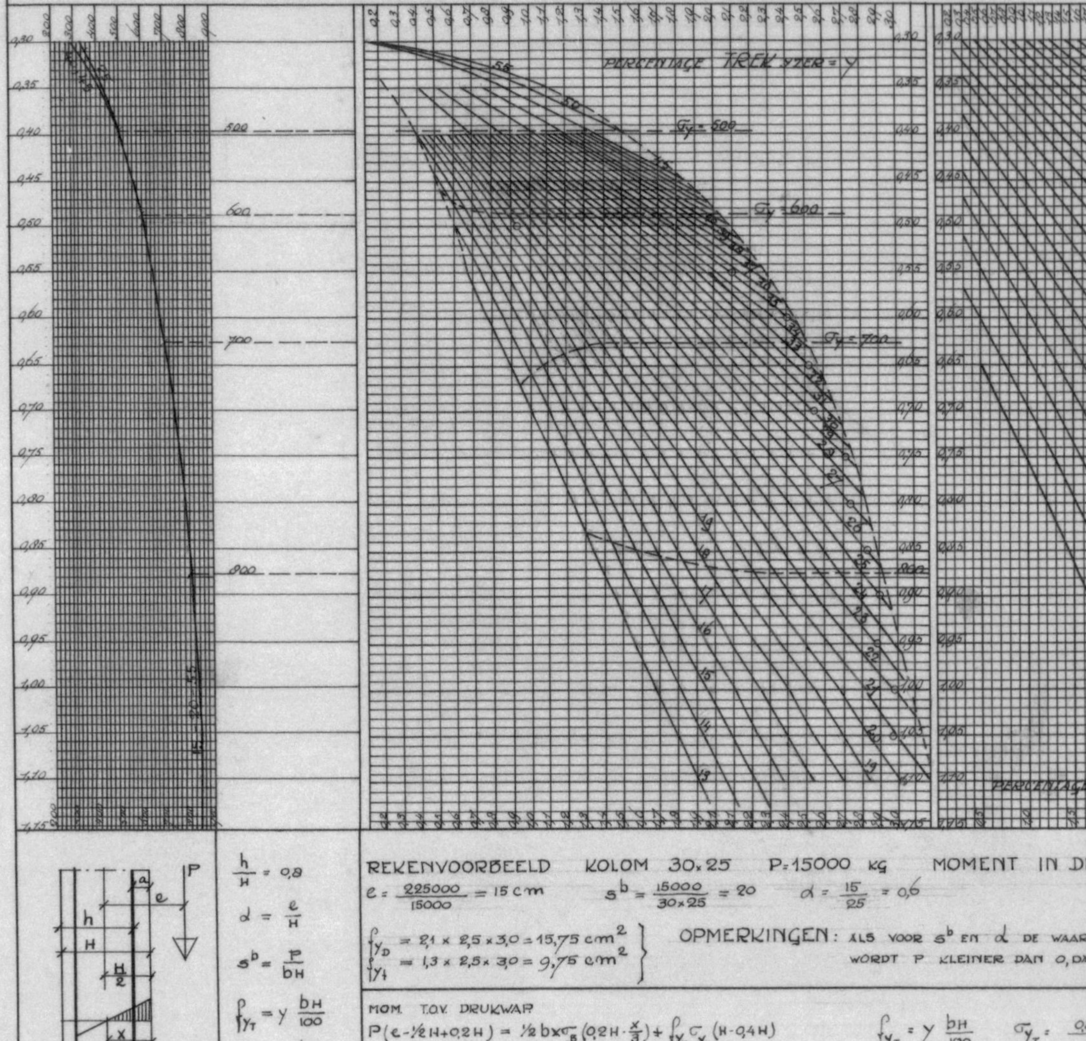

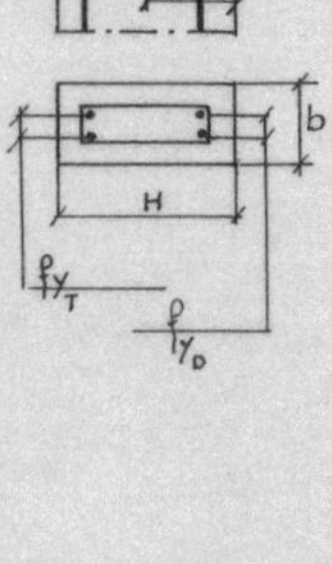

$\frac{h}{H} = 0{,}8$

$\alpha = \frac{e}{H}$

$s^b = \frac{P}{bH}$

$f_{y_T} = y\,\frac{bH}{100}$

$f_{y_D} = p\,\frac{bH}{100}$

$e = \frac{M}{P}$

$a = 0{,}2\,H$

REKENVOORBEELD KOLOM 30 x 25 P = 15000 KG MOMENT IN DE

$e = \frac{225000}{15000} = 15\text{ cm}$ $s^b = \frac{15000}{30 \times 25} = 20$ $\alpha = \frac{15}{25} = 0{,}6$

$f_{y_D} = 2{,}1 \times 2{,}5 \times 3{,}0 = 15{,}75\text{ cm}^2$
$f_{y_T} = 1{,}3 \times 2{,}5 \times 3{,}0 = 9{,}75\text{ cm}^2$

OPMERKINGEN: ALS VOOR s^b EN α DE WAARD
WORDT P KLEINER DAN 0, DAN

MOM. T.O.V. DRUKWAP.

$$P(e - \tfrac{1}{2}H + 0{,}2H) = \tfrac{1}{2}\,b x \sigma_B \left(0{,}2H - \frac{x}{3}\right) + f_{y_T}\sigma_{y_T}(H - 0{,}4H)$$ $f_{y_T} = y\,\frac{bH}{100}$ $\sigma_{y_T} = \frac{0{,}8}{}$

$$y = 100\,\frac{\frac{P}{bH}(\alpha - 0{,}3) - \tfrac{1}{2}\beta\sigma_B\left(0{,}2 - \frac{\beta}{3}\right)}{\frac{0{,}8-\beta}{\beta}\, m\sigma_B \cdot 0{,}6}$$ VOOR $\sigma_B = 70$ IS $y = 100\,\frac{\frac{P}{bH}(\alpha - 0{,}3)}{\frac{0{,}8-\beta}{\beta}\cdot}$

MOM. T.O.V. TREKWAP.

$$P(e + \tfrac{1}{2}H - 0{,}2H) = f_{y_D}\sigma_{y_D}(H - 0{,}4H) + \tfrac{1}{2}\,b x \sigma_B \left(H - 0{,}2H - \frac{x}{3}\right)$$ $f_{y_D} = p\,\frac{bH}{100}$ $\sigma_{y_D} =$

$$p = 100\,\frac{\frac{P}{bH}(\alpha + 0{,}3) - \tfrac{1}{2}\sigma_B\beta\left(0{,}8 - \frac{\beta}{3}\right)}{\frac{\beta-0{,}2}{\beta}(m-1)\sigma_B \cdot 0{,}6}$$ VOOR $\sigma_B = 70$ IS $p = 100\,\frac{\frac{P}{bH}(\alpha + 0{,}3}{\frac{\beta - 0{,}2}{\beta}}$

BETONSPANNING 70 KG PER CM²

27

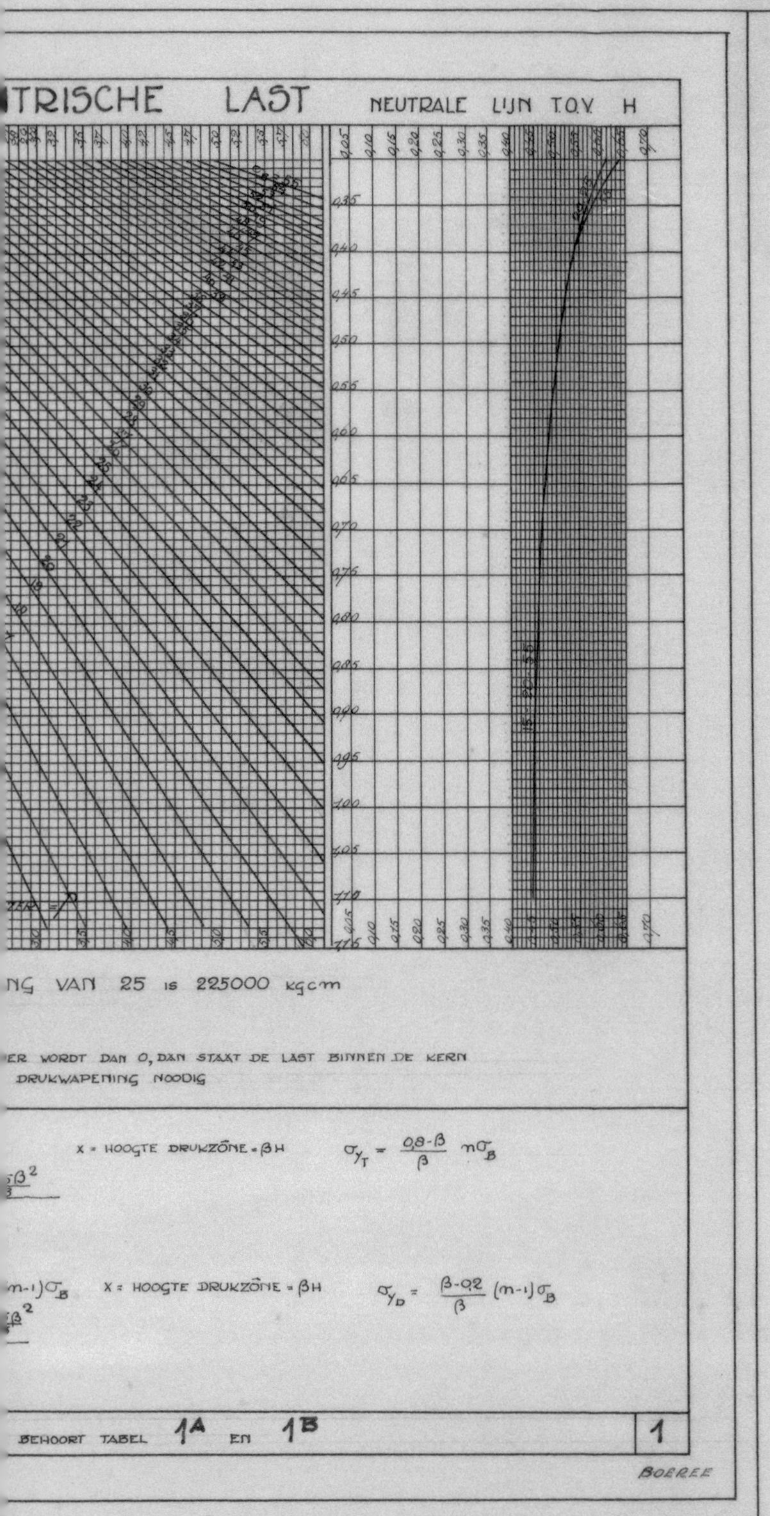

27 Boerée, concrete tension table, undated.

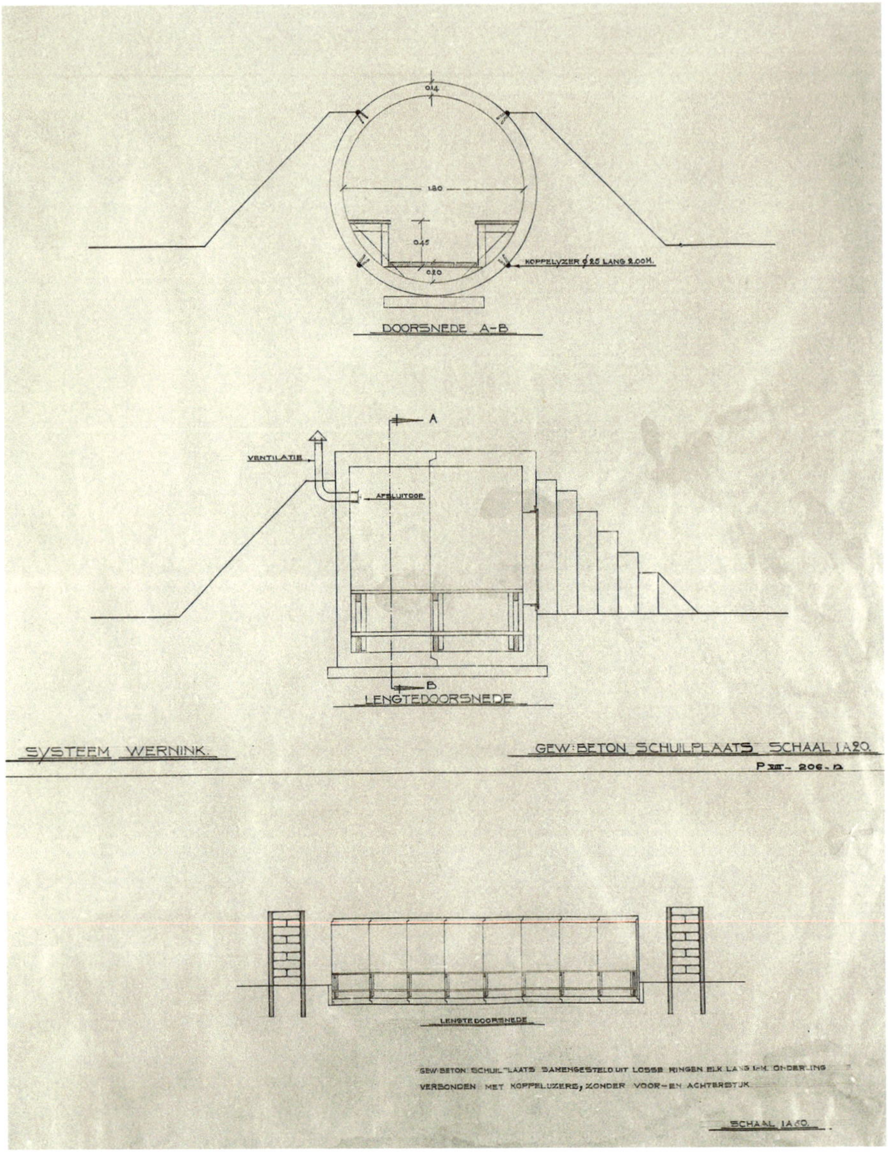

28

28 Reinforced concrete shelter according to the Wernink system.

Boerée's archives included tables worked out on large sheets of paper in the chart of calculations for reinforced concrete columns with eccentric loading **[fig. 26-27]**.[87] Some of the undated calculations are numbered, and all have her last name on them. Since none of them are initialled by teachers, unlike the comments added on her student materials during her time at the Technische Hoogeschool in Delft, the documents appear to have been made during her working career. The meticulously detailed calculations were standard for that time, considering the lack of digital computation resources, but the careful planning and design that went into the overall concept shows her great interest and dedication. In the interview she gave shortly before her death, she indicated that she was 'good at reinforced concrete', echoing the comment written on her engineering examination.[88]

War and more concrete

We do not know exactly when Boerée was dismissed from the Army Corps of Engineers (De Genie) after the start of the Second World War, but in 1941 she listed her profession as an engineer 'without position'.[89] In spring 1943, she started working for a concrete company, N.V. Wernink's Beton Maatschappij, located at Hoge Morsweg 148 in Leiden. The company was established in 1814 at the Woellust outpost in Oudshoorn, where its founder P.A.W. Wernink produced lime mortar in the facility's lime kiln made from raw materials that he sourced from shellfish trappers in Katwijk.[90] After the move to Leiden in 1894, the company was one of the first in the Netherlands to use reinforced concrete according to the Hennebique system **[fig. 28]**. The younger son, P.A. Wernink, believed that concrete was 'the next good thing' and the company soon became succesful.[91] Showing entrepreneurial insight, during the war the company focused on building reinforced concrete shelters and developing a 'Fire Brake' product designed to protect archives and other document repositories from fire resulting from aerial bombardments.[92] The product's success was demonstrated in a fire test on Wernink's company grounds, drawing keen interest from various parties, including the Government Buildings Agency, directors from Municipal Works, the Dutch railways, the building police and the National Bureau for Iron and Steel.[93]

This company must have been a good place for Boerée to work. There are no records on whether she was able to use what she had learned about concrete by then. Thanks to a diary that her sister Mia kept during the final months of the war, in 1945, we know that Riné provided 'prints' at Wernink and was concerned about finding the ammonia she needed: 'nowhere to be found in all of Leiden'.[94] On 11 February 1945, the street was bombed by the British. There was an army engineering site on Morsweg that was used as a transfer point for V1s and V2s, and a bunker that housed a telephone switchboard that was important to the German forces.[95] Despite the windows broken by the bombing, work at Wernink continued as usual, even after a fresh bombardment on 28 February. But Boerée regularly worked less than full-time at Wernink. She spent those hours searching for food and wood to burn; she could often obtain firewood from her employer, who handed out coal to those in need.[96] A few days after Boerée was called to the factory on 23 April 1945 to 'start organizing the card catalogue system', the company was ordered to do excavation work for the Germans. In response, the company decided to close its doors until after the war. Mia's diary entries show that Boerée was not able to avoid administrative duties at her place of employment.

Despite the difficult wartime conditions, both sisters maintained strict personal discipline, determined to keep pursuing personal development. Mia was two years younger than Riné and graduated two years earlier, and went on to become the head of a publishing house in 1935; she studied English and stenography every day, while Riné regularly spent her Sundays 'sketching'.[97] Riné's interests extended beyond concrete structures for barracks or bunkers, also encompassing castles, churches and landscapes which she sketched.[98] Later on, she would also take many snapshots of similar buildings when she went on holiday, going for long walks on her own.

Back at De Genie

The exceptional circumstances caused by the war must have been the reason for Boerée's dismissal from the Army Corps of Engineers (De Genie), rather than any aspect of her performance, because her dismissal was reversed in early 1946 with the note that she 'had effectively remained in service'.[99] Boerée was able to return to De Genie, eventually receiving her permanent appointment on 9 May 1949. Her father died a few months before that. Less than a year later, she was promoted to 'Engineer first class in permanent employment'.[100] This was one of the highest-ranking positions available to a civilian at De Genie.[101] Until her pension in 1964, she worked for the department responsible for construction, management and maintenance of airfields: Bureau Aanleg Beheer en Onderhoud Vliegvelden (BABOV). Established after the war, this unit was part of Dienst Gebouwen Werken en Terreinen ('Buildings, Works and Terrains Department' or DGW&T), the former building agency of the Army Corps of Engineers where Boerée started her career. BABOV fell under the auspices of the Ministry of War and was based in Amsterdam. In 1946, there was still a policy in effect for De Genie as a whole, stating that no more than 59 specialized civilian engineers could be employed on a permanent contract.[102]

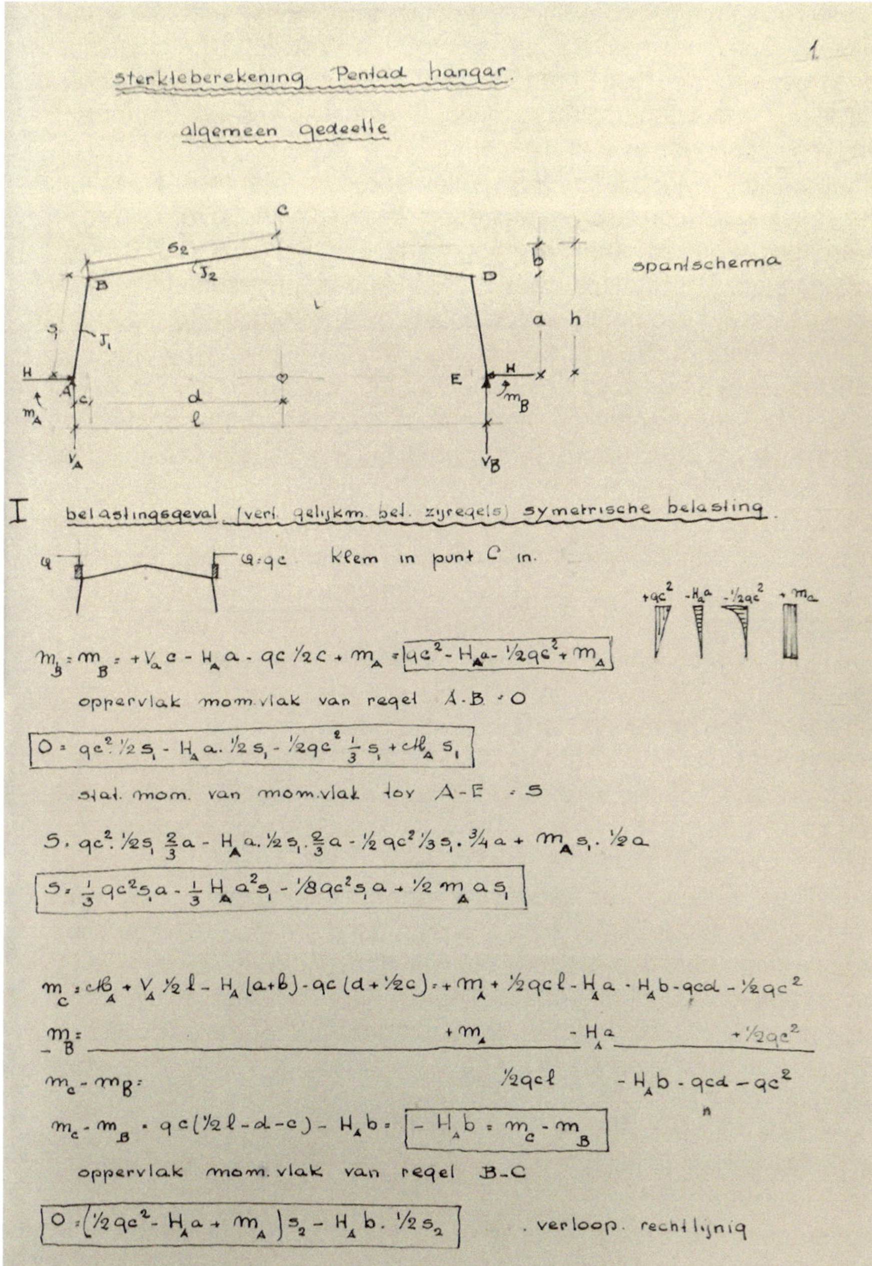

1

sterkteberekening Pentad hangar.

algemeen gedeelte

I belastingsgeval (verl. gelijkm. bel. zijregels) symetrische belasting.

q   Q = qc   Klem in punt C in.

$m_B = m_B = +V_a c - H_A a - qc\,\frac{1}{2}c + m_A = \boxed{qc^2 - H_A a - \frac{1}{2}qc^2 + m_A}$

oppervlak mom.vlak van regel A-B = 0

$\boxed{0 = qc^2 \cdot \frac{1}{2}s_1 - H_A a \cdot \frac{1}{2}s_1 - \frac{1}{2}qc^2 \frac{1}{3}s_1 + m_A s_1}$

stat. mom. van mom.vlak t.o.v. A-E = S

$S = qc^2 \cdot \frac{1}{2}s_1 \frac{2}{3}a - H_A a \cdot \frac{1}{2}s_1 \cdot \frac{2}{3}a - \frac{1}{2}qc^2 \frac{1}{3}s_1 \cdot \frac{3}{4}a + m_A s_1 \cdot \frac{1}{2}a$

$\boxed{S = \frac{1}{3}qc^2 s_1 a - \frac{1}{3}H_A a^2 s_1 - \frac{1}{8}qc^2 s_1 a + \frac{1}{2}m_A a s_1}$

$m_C = m_A + V_A \frac{1}{2}l - H_A(a+b) - qc(d + \frac{1}{2}c) = + m_A + \frac{1}{2}qcl - H_A a - H_A b - qcd - \frac{1}{2}qc^2$

$m_B = \qquad + m_A \qquad - H_A a \qquad + \frac{1}{2}qc^2$

$m_C - m_B = \qquad \frac{1}{2}qcl \qquad - H_A b - qcd - qc^2$

$m_C - m_B = qc(\frac{1}{2}l - d - c) - H_A b = \boxed{-H_A b = m_C - m_B}$

oppervlak mom. vlak van regel B-C

$\boxed{0 = (\frac{1}{2}qc^2 - H_A a + m_A)s_2 - H_A b \cdot \frac{1}{2}s_2}$. verloop rechtlijnig

29 C.H.M. Boerée, *Strength calculation for Pentad hangar*, Deelen airport, 1946–1947.

29

Boerée's archives contained an incomplete booklet that she wrote in 1946–1947, originally 33 pages in total, with strength calculations for a truss structure for a Pentad hangar, designed for the Deelen airbase **[fig. 29]**.[103] Originally a military airfield, Deelen was expanded during German occupation into a huge complex that ate up 2500 hectares of pristine natural forest in the Hoge Veluwe area.[104] After the war, although the airfield had been badly damaged, there were plans to turn it into an alternative airport to handle overflow traffic from Schiphol. Only four of the forty hangars at the complex were still left intact; the rest had presumably been destroyed in demolition campaigns by the Germans at the end of 1944. Boerée's strength calculations, which were in part intended to anticipate any snow build-up on the roof and what member forces might occur under such conditions, were presumably done for verification of an existing hangar structure.[105] Shortly after the war, various British hangars were disassembled, transported to the Netherlands, and assembled here to ensure that Dutch airfields could reopen as soon as possible. Boerée followed her calculations with an advisory addendum that she initialled herself, indicating where structural reinforcements should be applied in such a hangar.

After a reorganisation of BABOV in 1951, Boerée eventually went to work at District West, which included the airbase at Ypenburg, Soesterberg, Hilversum, Den Helder and De Lier. BABOV was located at the Valkenburg military airfield in Leiden, at Morsweg 1, not far from Wernink Concrete, her previous employer, which had suffered major damage from the Allied bombs intended for the airfield. The work at BABOV focused mainly on the take-off and landing runways and taxiways at airbases, but also included the military buildings. BABOV was tasked with implementing new building works, supervising maintenance and promoting site management aspects. Local newspapers occasionally ran calls for tenders so companies could submit bids.[106] The archives kept by Boerée include a newspaper clipping from 1956 that excoriates substandard materials delivered for a hangar to be assembled at the naval airbase at Valkenburg, which had been then been transferred to the Naval Air Force.[107] This also involved a Pentad hangar, of the type that Boerée had been working on for the Deelen airbase. That may have been the reason why she was also involved in this hangar.

For the rest of her life, Boerée also showed a particular interest in landing runways. Given her specific expert knowledge of concrete, this is presumably also what she worked on at BABOV. In the late 1950s, the runway system had to be upgraded and the three existing landing runways at the Valkenburg airfield were replaced by two runways made of concrete.[108] Sadly, no calculations or drawings by Boerée were found for this project.

Boerée retired on 1 January 1964 and lived the rest of her days with her sister Mia in their shared home in Oegstgeest. Riné Boerée died on 24 February 1995, just days after the only known interview she ever gave.

Out of the spotlights

Riné Boerée had a career that was exceptional for that time, thanks in part to her perseverance and thirst for knowledge, but undoubtedly also thanks to her father, who facilitated his daughters' university education and felt it was important for them to be stand on their own two feet. His education at the Royal Military Academy and his subsequent career – in environments that were not known to be supportive of women – did not prevent him from embracing emancipated views regarding the role of women in society. His donations to the DVSV, for example, show how he felt about women at university. In 1938, the Roman Catholic Women's League in Den Bosch decided to establish a group of women volunteers to serve the community in times of need. The initiative was shared by the Nederlandse Vereeniging van Huisvrouwen ('Dutch Association of Housewives') and the Nederlandse Christen Vrouwen Bond ('Dutch Christian Women's League'). During the opening ceremony, Henri Boerée spoke a few words in his capacity as commander of the Vrijwillige Burgerwacht (volunteer civil defence force) of Amsterdam, expounding on the topic of 'the task of the woman in threatening circumstances'.[109] We do not know exactly what he said in his speech, and the title could also be interpreted as stereotyping in relation to the always caring and self-sacrificing role of women in society. However, the fact that he was willing to speak to a women's league and travel to Den Bosch for that purpose could be seen as evidence of his emancipated views. His mindset must surely have encouraged Riné Boerée to go to university and choose a less than easy profession.

Her remarkable career was never showcased, then or later. Besides the brief entry in the publication *Vrouwen in techniek. 90 Jaar Delftse Vrouwelijke Ingenieurs* ('Women in Technology: 90 Years of Women Engineers in Delft'), for which she was interviewed at an elderly age, not one single contemporary medium published an article on her, there were no interviews in the military papers to mark her pension, no *In Memoriam* in trade journals – not even in a magazine like *Beton*, which was published by the Concrete Association.[111] Similarly, she did not publish any technical articles, although this could possibly be attributed to the strict confidentiality probably imposed by the Ministry of Defence. She preferred not to seek the spotlight, which may also be why there are hardly any photos of her. Illustrating her career outside the spotlight, she consistently went unmentioned in the regular updates on 'recent women's work in Architecture' that Margaret Staal-Kropholler (1891–1966) gave in the National Women's Council from 1949 on.[111] Her own correspondence list of the women who graduated as architectural engineers – Staal-Kropholler herself was not among them – did include an address for Riné, annotated in pencil in the margin with the word 'concrete'.[112] However, Boerée never responded to the questionnaires that she sent inquiring about her work.

A remarkable career

Riné Boerée had a remarkable career in many ways. As one of the first women to graduate as an architectural engineer in the Netherlands, she became a specialist in a building technique that was still new at that time: building structures out of reinforced concrete. Most of her career took place within the Dutch armed forces, within the Army Corps of Engineers (De Genie). She deviated from the stereotypically nurturing role that women were expected to adopt within the home, but that was not all. Even within the small group of women architectural engineers who had graduated by then, her track record puts her in an exceptional position.

Her father Henri Boerée played a key role in Riné's development. By paying for her education and buying a house for her and her sister to live in, he encouraged both his daughters to stand on their own two feet. His military career and resulting network probably helped Riné find work, despite the economic crisis and the social and societal limitations and prejudices imposed on working women in those days.

It is striking to note that Riné Boerée's interest and knowledge focused on the structural aspects of architecture, rather than – as was expected of women back then – on the decorative or artistic aspects. Her contribution to the revolutionary Nirwana block of flats in The Hague laid the foundation for her extensive career in the world of concrete. In her work at De Genie, her knowledge was fully recognized. Remarkably, once again, she received the same professional room to manoeuvre as her male colleagues, and was also able to sign building designs with her own name.

Her strong personality was definitely also partly responsible for her successful career. University was not easy for her, and she must have had moments throughout her working life when she had to prove herself to the men she worked with, both colleagues and managers.

And finally, it is remarkable that the extraordinary career of Riné Boerée has remained unmentioned in the annals of architectural history until now. She also did her best to keep it that way. Her work at the Ministry of Defence went largely unnoticed by her peers. When she was actively contacted to say more about her work, she declined the honour.

7 Wil Jansen, an enterprising woman architect from Schiedam

When Wil Jansen (1904–1989) graduated from the Technische Hoogeschool (TH) in Delft in 1931, she joined the ranks of a small group of woman architectural engineers that had graced the Netherlands since 1917.[1] As the youngest scion of a Schiedam manufacturing family that had five sons and three daughters, she was the only one to attend university and complete a degree. As an unmarried, independent architect, Jansen managed to build up a sizable portfolio of orders, a feat that the other women who graduated alongside her never managed in that profession.

Jansen's commissions were not limited to residential interiors, which was the most obvious domain for which a woman could develop concepts in those days. Her brothers involved her not only in renovating their homes, but also in developing the various business premises owned by their entrepreneurial family. Partly compelled by the economic crisis, Jansen mainly focused on landscape architecture in the first few years of her professional practice. However, her portfolio soon filled up with construction and renovation projects commissioned by many different clients; her core clientele consisted of family, in-laws, friends and acquaintances all across the Netherlands. Along the way, Jansen developed into an architect with modernist tastes and opinions.

Those who are still familiar with Wil Jansen's work primarily know her for the Rotterdamsche Verzekering Sociëteiten (RVS) apartment building which she designed (1956–58). Intended for single women working in Rotterdam, this apartment building featured in a publication in 2010 and can be considered her most prominent commission.[2] However, little was known about her career or oeuvre beyond that. In 2011, her nephew H.Th.F. Jansen decided to transfer ownership of his aunt's archive to Schiedam municipal archives. Access was recently provided to Jansen's archive, which contains a wealth of primary sources, including design sketches, building plans, notes and correspondence; these were foundational to this research.[3]

The main question in this chapter is: how did Wil Jansen develop as a woman architect? Did she encounter specific gender-related problems along the way, or was she also able to leverage it to her advantage? This chapter attempts to give an impression of the career and stylistic

1

development of one of the first women architectural engineers in the Netherlands, placed within the context of the architectural era of post-World War II reconstruction. Following a general biographical section, we will look at Jansen's education and the role it played in her later development. The second part of the chapter focuses on her work, illustrating her stylistic development based on a selection of her projects.

Liquor retailer or architect?

Wilhelmina Catharina Maria Jansen was born on 9 January 1904 in Schiedam. She was the eighth child of Jacoba Maria Catharina Beukers (1863–1928), daughter of a 'merchant on Nieuwe Haven', and Hermanus Johannes Jansen (1859–1935).[4] Her father Herman Jansen was a born businessman based in Schiedam.[5] The family distillery he inherited, which dated back to 1777, expanded under his management into an industrial imperium employing his five sons. As a board member of the Chamber of Commerce and co-founder of Vereeniging Schiedam Vooruit ('Association for Progress in Schiedam'), he promoted local economic interests. Herman Jansen was also deeply engaged in society. The ink had barely dried on the 1901 Housing Act to promote the construction of good-quality social housing when he co-founded and sat on the board of the Vereeniging Volkshuisvesting ('Public Housing Association'). The Housing Act meant that housing associations could be eligible for financial support to fund building projects, as long as those projects contributed to improving public housing. Jansen, who owned large tracts of land near Vlaardingerdijk, made plots available where the first homes would be built between 1905 and 1907.[6]

The children in Herman Jansen's devoutly Catholic family, living in a stately residence at Lange Haven 19, were raised by a nanny and sent off to boarding school.[7] As the youngest, Wil was an exception, attending Higher Civic School (HBS) from 1917 to 1923 **[fig. 1]**. As the last child still living at home, she was allowed to join her parents at the table for daily meals, a privilege not granted to the other children until they were 16. Herman Jansen may also have envisioned that his smart youngest daughter would take on an active role in the flourishing family firm, but she decided to head in a completely different direction. In 1924 she enrolled in the architecture programme at the Technische Hoogeschool (TH) in Delft.[8] It was presumably more opportune for Wil to strike out on her own, once her brothers had secured the line of succession within the family firm. Her father respected her decision and was proud that one of his children was going off to university **[fig. 2]**. He had gone to the HBS on Overschiestraat that his uncle had co-founded in 1869, where boys from wealthy bourgeois homes were trained to become future captains of trade and industry.

←
1 Portrait of the Jansen family, ca. 1919. Wil was at a Higher Civic School (HBS) at the time. From left to right, standing: Tup, Pop, Guust, Ida, Dick, Hans; sitting: Nol, mother Jacoba Jansen-Beukers, Wil and father Herman Jansen; lying down: the family dog Tjebbes.

2 Wil Jansen with her father Herman in 1924, the year she began her studies.

2

In choosing to pursue an independent future, Wil went entirely against the grain of prevailing societal opinion. Women were not expected to study at university, let alone practice a profession at that level. Their role was supposed to be at home with the family. Wil's mother was a shining example of this: she ran the household and managed the staff, as evidenced by the hiring ads that appeared regularly in the local newspaper, in which 'Mrs H. Jansen' was looking for a 'proper maid' for Saturday or a 'proper second girl, preferably RC, for day and night'.[9]

When Wil graduated in 1931, the consequences of the stock market crash in 1929 were clearly palpable and building commissions were declining steadily. The government kept building projects going to some extent. However, since 1924, government jobs were no longer open to married women. Unmarried women applying for jobs were equally unlikely to be hired as long as they were still considered potentially eligible for marriage. In view of the entrepreneurial environment in which Wil grew up, it is doubtful whether she had ambitions of a career in government service. Even so, she must have been aware that a woman newly arrived in a pre-eminently male-dominated construction sector would find it far from simple to acquire commissions independently.[10]

After the death of Herman Jansen, the family bought a brand-new duplex in 1939 for Wil and her sister Pop (1899–1974), at Rubenslaan 17 in Schiedam, which she renovated herself on various occasions.[11] Wil would pursue her architecture practice at this address, and continue living there with her sister for the rest of her life. Pop, who gave cooking lessons at a housekeeping school, cooked the daily meals and ran the household. Her culinary talents were probably the reason why family Christmas dinners were always held at the Rubenslaan house.

Ample financial provisions were made for the two unmarried sisters who did not work in the family firm. Wil and Pop were shareholders in the family firm and co-owned various buildings in the Laakkwartier neighbourhood in The Hague in joint ownership with their father.[12] Despite these considerations, Wil wanted to earn her own living. In 1965, she purchased and renovated a summer home called 'Klein Elvenhoef', on Korssendijk by the interlinked rectangular lakes of the Reeuwijkse Plassen, where she spent her summers with Pop and her family.[13]

Studying in Delft

Jansen attended the first academic year of the architecture programme in 1924–1925, with four women and fourteen men in her class. A total of 109 men and twelve women were enrolled in the architecture programme that year.[14] Three of the other women students in Jansen's class – Jan Kret, Willy van den Broek d'Obrenan and Jeanne van Rijswijk

(1904–1960) – also completed their degree. Throughout her studies, Jansen lived in her parental home in Schiedam.[15] That did not keep her from joining the Delftsche Vrouwelijke Studenten Vereeniging ('Delft Female Student Society', or DVSV), whose active members already included several other architecture students.[16] In the 1927–1928 academic year, when Wil was studying for her candidate diploma, she became president of the DVSV, which had forty members at that time **[fig. 3]**.[17] In her speech to the new members, she called on them to make every effort to play an active role in the DVSV, which she saw as excellent preparation for life after university: 'Toss your books aside for a time (...). Because you will not get there by study alone. Here you will also be prepared for life afterwards, in society. And you must ensure that yourself; you will not find any instructions for it on the timetable or schedule.'[18] During her presidency, Jansen's mother died in spring 1928 after a short illness. Jansen passed her candidate examinations over a year later.[19]

In autumn 1929, Jansen took seven fellow students, a woman who was 'an interested party', and a driver on a three-week field trip to northern France, headed by professor of architecture Adrianus van der Steur.[20] The group visited such towns and cities as Amiens, Beauvais, Le Mont-Saint-Michel, Chartres, Paris and Reims, alternating their travel itinerary with relaxing excursions such as a 'pic-nic between Honfleur and Trouville'.[21]

In her final year at university, Jansen sat for her utility building exam with professor Richard Schoemaker. Schoemaker's extensive lectures (which frequently ran long) covered the wooden and steel structures of factories, warehouses, storage facilities and garages, among others, as well as the associated auxiliary rooms: engine rooms, boiler rooms, but also offices, lounges, cloakrooms and toilets.[22] This must have been where Jansen learned the foundational principles of her later designs for the family firm. Two months before graduation in 1931, professor Marinus Jan Granpré Molière notified her 'that despite the insufficient portfolio in Decorative Arts, there is no objection to granting you access to the final examinations in architectural engineering.'[23] Jansen's university diploma was signed by Gerardus Diehl (1882–1938), professor of architecture and head of the architecture department, and department secretary Dirk Frederik Slothouwer (1884–1946), professor in theory of architectural forms and history of architecture.[24]

In 1930, a small group of architecture students demanded their 'right to modernity', protesting what they viewed as overly traditional architectural education.[25] The students advocated exploration of new architectural concepts and organized an international course on new architecture in Delft, featuring such speakers as architect and Bauhaus founding member Walter Gropius (1883–1969), architect and designer Marcel Breuer (1902–1981), urban planner Cornelis van Eesteren, and architects

3

3 Wil Jansen (centre) as president of the Delftsche Vrouwelijke Studenten Vereeniging, 1927–1928.

Gerrit Rietveld (1888–1964), Willem van Tijen and Jan Duiker. These speakers were affiliated with the Congrès Internationaux d'Architecture Moderne (CIAM), launched in 1928. The coursework offered in Delft included a visit to the Van Nelle factory that had recently opened in Rotterdam, an example of the Modern Movement. During their classes, the students had never encountered this new architectural movement based on rational and functionalist principles. 'Should we then, with our engineering diploma in our pocket, make our grand entrance in society completely ignorant of the concepts and theories underlying the many revolutionary directions (...)? Or is it particularly this specific modern movement, that of der Neue Sachlichkeit, which is so unimportant? (...) It surely cannot be disputed that (...) we will eventually encounter it at some point. Can fundamental education at the T.H. then prepare us for this encounter?'[26] University professors attended the course in their own personal time, since the architecture department refused to endorse it. Jansen, who was studying for her final exams at the time, was presumably not part of the protest group, but she must have been aware of the course, and it is very plausible that she would have attended. It would have marked her first cautious forays into modern architecture. Later on, she would have more contact with Willem van Tijen due to her activities in Rotterdam.

Even before graduating, Jansen spent a short time in Paris, where she worked for architects Urbain Cassan (1890–1979) and Louis Victor Plousey (1880–1936), on Avenue Hoche. Cassan was an advisory architect to the Chemins de fer du Nord et de l'État, designing many railway stations during the reconstruction period in France following the First World War. From 1969 to 1972, he took part in efforts to develop the neighbourhood and the Tour Montparnasse in Paris. Plousey primarily constructed residential buildings in the 7th and 15th arrondissements in Paris. Plousey and Cassan sometimes collaborated on projects, such as the Hôpital Beaujon (1933–1934) in Clichy.[27] Considering the pavilion structure still common at the time, this hospital was showcased as the first vertical hospital facility to be constructed in a single innovative block rising thirteen storeys high. At the architecture firm, Jansen shared a room with four colleagues; although she learned to speak French more fluently, she described the work as 'not very interesting': '(...) since everything is reinforced concrete, it's not much more than tracing lines'.[28] The work concerned part of the Gare du Havre-Maritime, a network of railway stations in the port of Le Havre, the terminal station of the railway line from Paris-Saint Lazare. In the house where Jansen stayed during her time in Paris, which she described as enjoying 'some renown', and in the library where she spent many happy hours, she not only met many international colleagues, but also encountered familiar faces from Delft.[29] Jansen graduated on 17 December 1931.

Distinguishing earnest sincerity from frivolous mirth

Jansen's archive contained various sketches and drawings that she made after graduation, both to gain experience and to find clients. For example, in 1932 she submitted a design for a study competition issued by the Genootschap Architectura et Amicitia, the first in a series intended to offer young architects a welcome pastime in 'a period of forced and depressing unemployment'.[30] Moreover, the intention was for the winners of this 'crisis contest' to receive a monetary award as soon as sufficient funds had been found to cover the costs.[31] In addition, the board felt it was important for young architects to have more opportunity to work on modest assignments involving practical solutions, rather than the more customary and more complex competition topics, such as monumental government buildings. This must have appealed to Jansen.

The Review Committee received 81 'serious' submissions; one project was not taken into consideration because the designer 'had not managed to distinguish between earnest sincerity and frivolous mirth'.[32] No winners were announced, but ten of the 21 best designs – including Jansen's submission – were considered eligible for publication in the weekly magazine *Bouwkundig Weekblad Architectura*. Of the ten selected, she was the only architectural engineer and – although she had not notified them of the fact – the only woman.[33] Whether the latter would have influenced the committee's decision in any way cannot be determined, but it did give her a better chance of being assessed on her actual merits. The review committee was headed by Henry Zwiers (1900–1992), who had been working as an independent architect in Haarlem since his graduation from the TH in Delft in 1923. Zwiers would become a professor of architecture at the TH in 1938.[34]

The competition involved designing a residence and workspace for an architect and his family. The envisioned home was situated in a suburb of the city and it had to be feasible to build it with a limited budget. Jansen's design was based on a clearly structured L-shaped floor plan in which she positioned the architect's study in such a way that it was part of the living room and the workspace **[fig. 4a]**.[35] The review committee had almost no critical comments regarding her design. Other than an incorrect position for the garage, they said that 'the entire structure was complete and logical' and the facades were 'sober, but distinguished'.[36]

In their general comments, the committee noted that 30 per cent of the designs received had a flat roof, half of which they considered as belonging to 'the movement of what is known as New Objectivity'.[37] The residence designed by Jansen still had a traditional double-pitched roof; the jury described it as part of the small group of good-quality designs

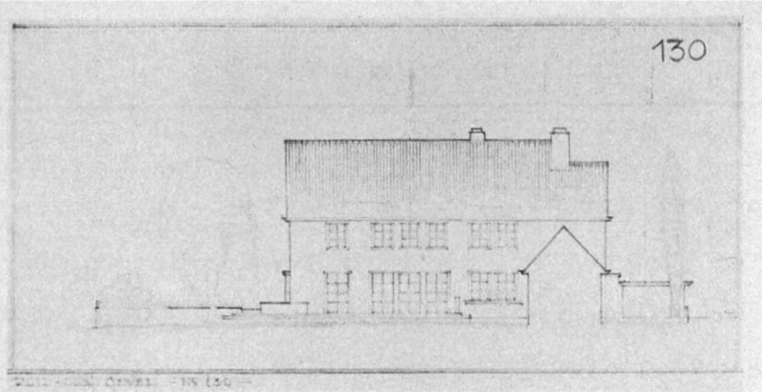

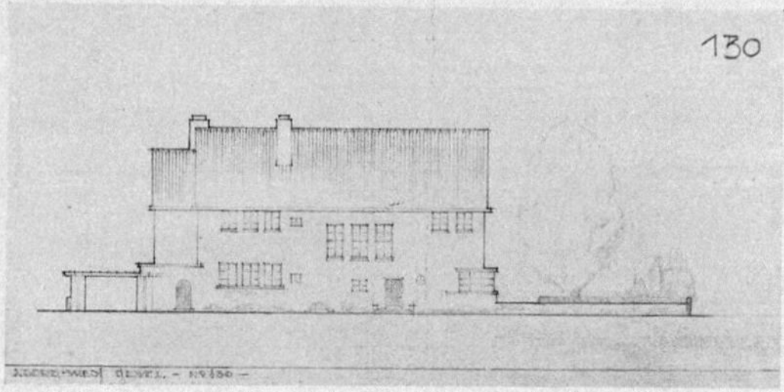

4a

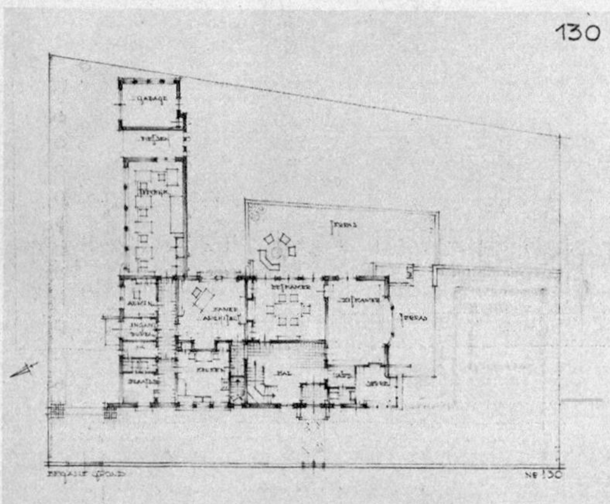

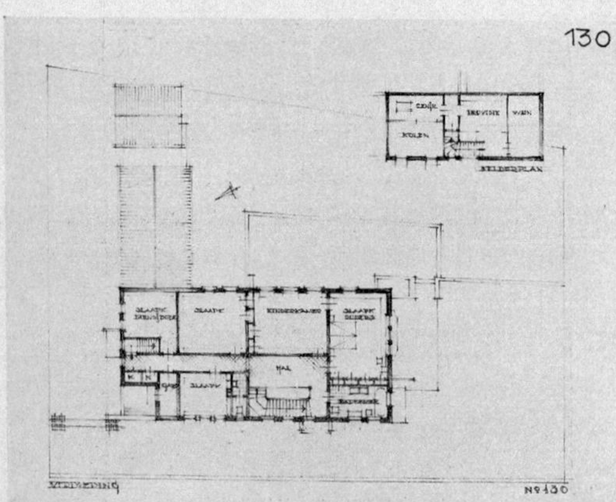

ONTWERP Ir. W. C. M. JANSEN B.I. SCHIEDAM

4b

4a Student competition design of a residence for architects by Wil Jansen, 1932. The entire structure was described by the jury as 'complete and logical'.

4b Sketch of the facade composition of the architect's residence by Wil Jansen, unsigned and undated [1932].

in which the roof construction was well-balanced in proportion to the floor plan **[fig. 4a and 4b]**. Although Zwiers had a reputation for being conservative, modern designs were also included among the ten best, although accompanied by such comments as 'a solid project for its type'.[38]

One notable detail in the general comments from the jury was about the toilet room in the work wing on Jansen's design. According to the assignment, the working area had to include a 'small room for administration' as well as a spacious drawing office.[39] The jury considered it decidedly inappropriate that the toilet room, which would also have to be used by the 'generally female administrative assistants' from the 'small room for administration', had been placed in various designs in the drawing office in which – according to the jury – only men would work.[40] Jansen saw it as an interesting challenge to incorporate the cautious increase in participation by women in what had previously been considered professions reserved solely for men. She adopted a more modern and more practical approach: in her plan, she positioned a ladies' room and a men's room right next to the staff entrance, so uncomfortable situations would never arise. No other designs indicating any further participation in the Genootschap competition series were found in Jansen's archive.

5

Designs for the family firm

As an inexperienced woman architect, and in view of the unfavourable economic climate, it was far from easy for Jansen to launch her architecture practice. From the start, but also throughout her career, her brothers brought her commissions from their various companies, largely based in Schiedam. Circuitously, she was involved in the family firm in a different way. Several of Jansen's earliest work drawings were of the Cartonnagefabriek, a cardboard factory on Nieuwe Haven in Schiedam, on the corner of Oranjestraat. Founded in 1920 by the family, the company produced packing boxes for distilled products and was earmarked for Wil's youngest brother Tup (1902–1993), who was 18 at the time.[41] He started the company in a building beside their parental home on Lange Haven. In 1923, he requested municipal planning permission to expand the company by installing five electric motors.[42] It was probably Wil who took an existing drawing of the facade and added in a site sketch of this factory building, between the family home on one side and the public bathhouse (built in 1911) on the other, with homes on Westvest along the back.[43] Since the rapidly growing business had outgrown the options for expansion at that site, it was relocated in 1930 to a former malthouse (dating back to 1840) at Oranjestraat 8.

Shortly before her graduation ceremony on 17 December 1931, Wil Jansen had her first commission: Tup wanted to quickly expand the factory even more. However, the floor plans she designed, which included snow and wind stress calculations for the roof, were never implemented in that form.[44] The side facade was changed according to her plans, though, to accommodate ground-floor loading for vans and lorries **[fig. 5]**. For the front of the building, she designed facade lettering in modern typography.[45]

In 1935 the city of Schiedam announced plans to replace the Oranjebrug (1885), the bridge over the inner harbour at Nieuwe Haven, beside the cardboard factory. The 'fairly complicated [road] traffic' at that location also demanded a change in the traffic situation in the form of a 'circular traffic intersection' – the prototype of the roundabout – and partial filling of the harbour to widen the road.[46] Wil had requested the plans from the municipality and made her own variation on that **[fig. 6]**.[47] To the west of the envisioned traffic intersection, she added an elongated, tapering parking strip that bisected the road. This showed her focus on green spaces. Some of the buildings along Nieuwe Haven, including the St. Liduina church, were separated from the street by a row of trees in Wil's version. She marked off various strips of greenery, even on the new bridge itself. Wil drew her sketches on exactly the same day that local newspaper *Schiedamsche Courant* announced that the plans for the bridge were completed.[48] What motivated her to make these drawings then, and even make copies of them, is unclear. The municipal documents do not show any evidence of a submission procedure.[49] The plans undoubtedly attracted Jansen's interest because they affected access to the cardboard factory. The parking strip she envisioned may partly have been intended for visitors to the factory. Moreover, the intersection was clearly visible from the factory building, so she wanted to achieve a more pleasant setting by adding urban greenery.

5 The former cardboard packaging factory on Oranjestraat, 1965. The facade changes that Wil Jansen made to accommodate loading facilities for lorries are still clearly visible on the photo.

→
6 Unsigned design by Wil Jansen, *Alternative plan for new Oranjebrug*, 1936.

Although her sketches were not used, they may have also been urban development exercises for this burgeoning architectural engineer, although only on the micro scale, and she hardly focused any attention on it after that. During Jansen's student years, urban design was taught as a component of the architecture programme by architect and city planner Granpré Molière, but it was only in the 1960s that urban design became an independent discipline. The fact that Jansen quickly encountered urban design issues in actual practice, such as the example of the cardboard factory, is indicative of a time when the rapid increase in road traffic demanded urban design solutions. The number of passenger vehicles in the Netherlands had spiked from 35,000 in 1920 to 115,000 in 1930.[50] In towns and cities that also had busy shipping lanes, like Schiedam, increased road traffic also meant making changes to bridges, as also happened between 1925 and 1932 in Rotterdam.[51]

6

When the flourishing cardboard factory outgrew the expansion options at the Oranjestraat site, it later moved to an existing industrial building at Noordvestsingel 75. On 26 October 1951, the municipality issued a permit to change the 'tuitgevels' (traditionally designed funnel-shaped gables).[52] By then, Jansen had been working as an architect for twenty years; the simple plans she designed, which were approved, involved removing the stepped gables to reveal the pitched roof beneath **[fig. 7]**.[53] The factory building was in the 's-Graveland polder on the northern edge of Schiedam, behind a string of buildings situated along the Noordvest waterfront. Exactly how long the cardboard factory was located on Noordvestsingel is unclear, but it is striking that modernizing the exterior – even with such a simple change – was considered important at this remote location. The costs of changing the facade were estimated at two thousand guilders.

The location may have served as a temporary solution for the ever-expanding company; on 11 July 1956, Mayor J.W. Peek sank the first pile for its new premises on an equally new street: Burgemeester Honnerlage Gretelaan.[54] The new site was adjacent to the plot at Noordvestsingel 75, and Tup Jansen had managed to acquire the land by making a deal with the municipality.[55] Building the cardboard factory there meant demolishing 44 condemned houses arranged around courtyards, which had previously been occupied by distillery workers from the malthouses.[56] Tup went all-out for the new factory building. Built on concrete piles and delivered in early 1958, the building was not only modern in its design.[57] To ensure efficiency in business operations, a concrete ramp for lorries was added, providing direct access to the 5,000 m2 factory hall on the first floor. The materials from the ground-floor storeroom were transported up to the factory hall in lifts. Tup proved he was a modern employer who considered the well-being of his employees, who were able to work in natural daylight thanks to the saw-tooth roof, and enjoyed various facilities, including a spacious cafeteria with a bar and stage area, changing rooms and showers, and bicycle sheds. A survey was conducted beforehand so the factory workers could share their preferences.[58]

→
7 Wil Jansen removed the stepped facades of the cardboard packaging factory on Noordvestsingel in 1951.

Tup hired Rotterdam-based architect F.C. de Weger to build this new factory. Frans de Weger (1913–2005) would later be one of the architects who designed the station building at Schiphol Airport (1961–1968), which would become famous for its clear structure. In that period, Wil worked on her commission for the RVS building in Rotterdam; the first pile on that project was also sunk in 1956. It is very possible that her involvement in the RVS flat made her unavailable to provide designs for her brother's new factory. As a result, the media praise showered on the new building was not directed at her. However, her archive contained an interesting set of undated design drawings that may have been her initial ideas for Tup's new cardboard factory, which clearly show her functionalist architectural principles.[59] In these drawings she had also taken women in the workforce into account.[60] The detailed floor plan was intended for a specific plot of land (location not specified) with an oblique angle on one short side. The main entrance was placed on that side. The building consisted of three layers that were cantilevered on the first and second floors. The ground floor had an unspecified large hall – probably the manufacturing room –, storerooms, a shipping room, a garage and a large bicycle shed for employees, which had its own entrance with separate cloakrooms and toilets for men and women **[fig. 8a]**. The first floor only covered the front section of the building; besides offices and archives, it also contained the canteen for the male employees **[fig. 8b]**. The second floor, with even less floor area, had an equally large canteen for female employees and included a balcony **[fig. 8b]**. The women did have to climb stairs to reach that floor, since lifts were not included in the design.

Jansen had given careful consideration to spatial design, organization of the space and routing. The employee facilities may have been the first step towards the premises eventually built on Burgemeester Honnerlagelaan. Modern in appearance due to not only the cantilevers, but also the horizontal and vertical accents, the facade may also have been an inspiration for the later design **[fig. 8c and 8d]**.

In 1952, her brother Hans (1894–1972) asked Wil to take on the renovation of his factory. This first lactic acid plant in the Netherlands had originally been established when Herman Jansen had sold his patent for yeast production, making it necessary to come up with a new company for Hans.[61] Building on the knowledge he had learned from producing yeast, Hans achieved success in producing lactic acid bacteria. The plant was located in a former malting distillery at Noordvest 97. The renovation, which cost about 50,000 guilders, involved 'installation of new wooden beam structures and floors with steel underlayer and pillars', for which Wil did the calculations and drawings.[62] The drawings submitted to the municipality were signed by her, but also list the Schiedam-based architecture firm of Kramers & Willemsen.[63] Coen Kramers (1894–1971) was a good friend of the Jansen family; during busy periods, he loaned them his draughtsman, who came to assist Wil at the Rubenslaan site.[64] Several of her design drawings for the lactic acid plan are signed by one L. Scheffers.

The lactic acid plant was on the Noordvest side next to other companies owned by the family, such as the distillery, the bottle storage warehouse and the branderij ('malting distillery'), headed by Wil's brother Dick (1898–1986).[65] The back of these buildings butted up against the warehouse and the office of the family firm, located at Zijlstraat 6 **[fig. 9]**.[66] The office was in a former residence (ca. 1780) designed by Jan Giudici (1746–1829),

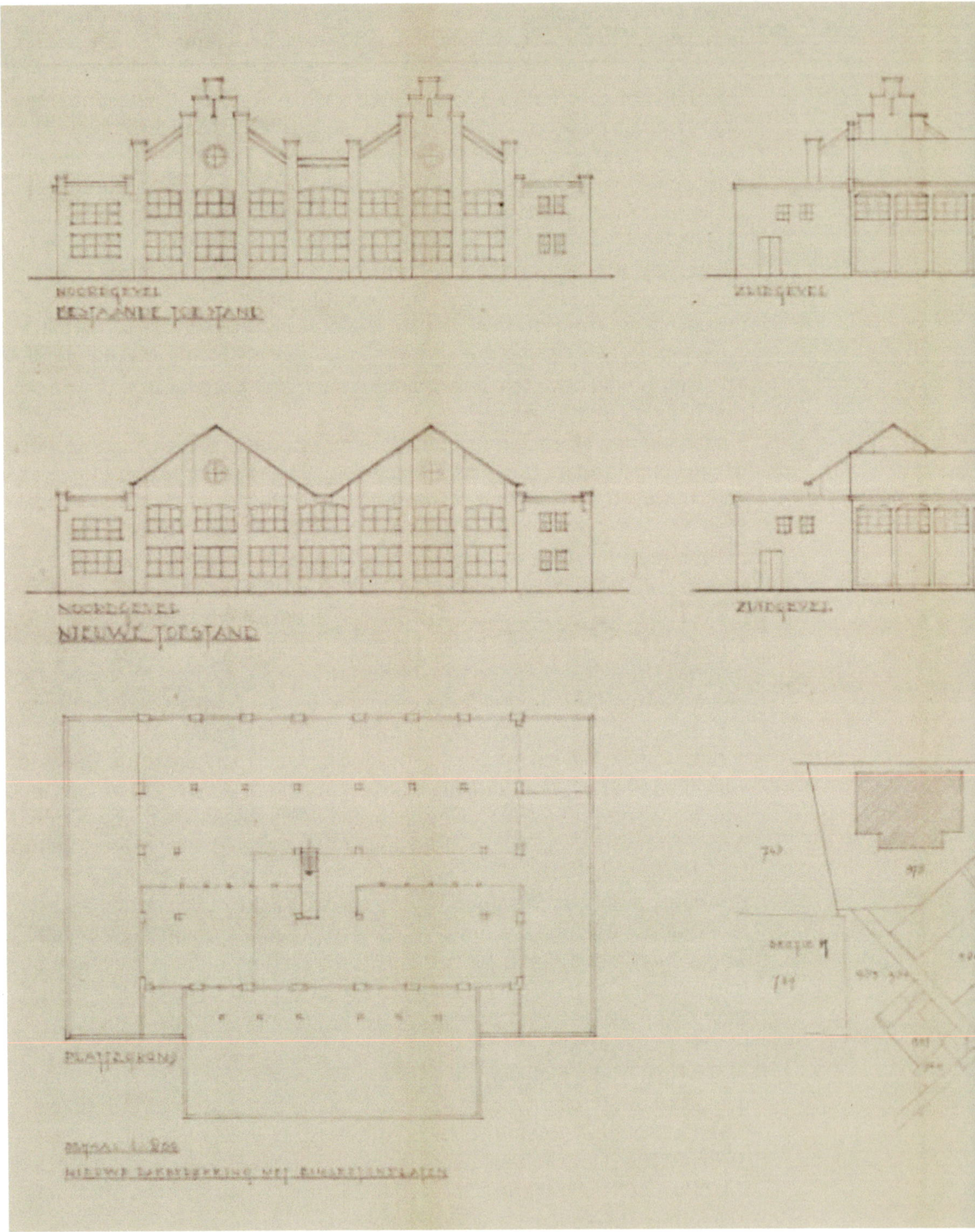
NOORDGEVEL
BESTAANDE TOESTAND
ZUIDGEVEL
NOORDGEVEL
NIEUWE TOESTAND
ZUIDGEVEL
PLATTEGROND

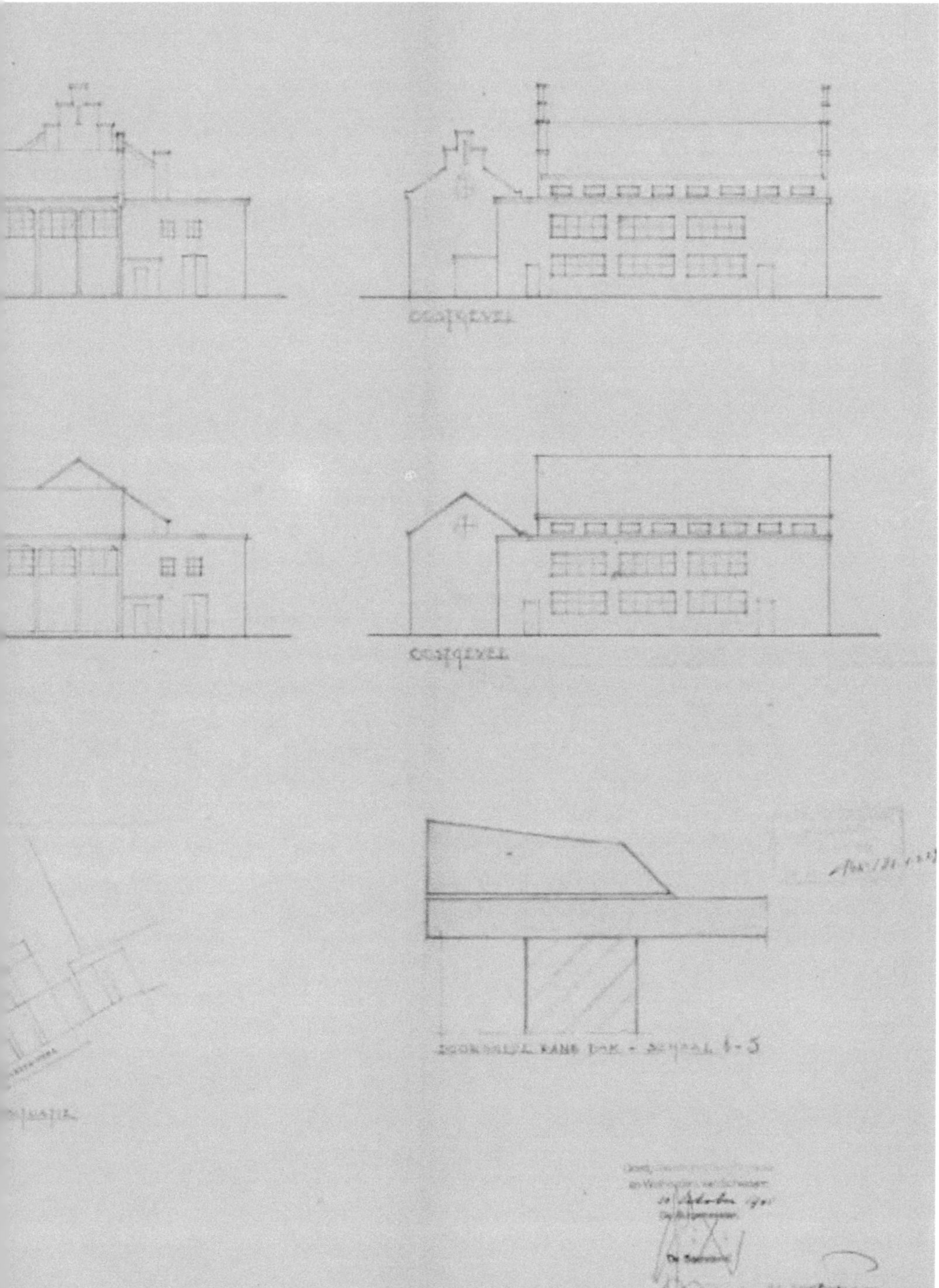

7

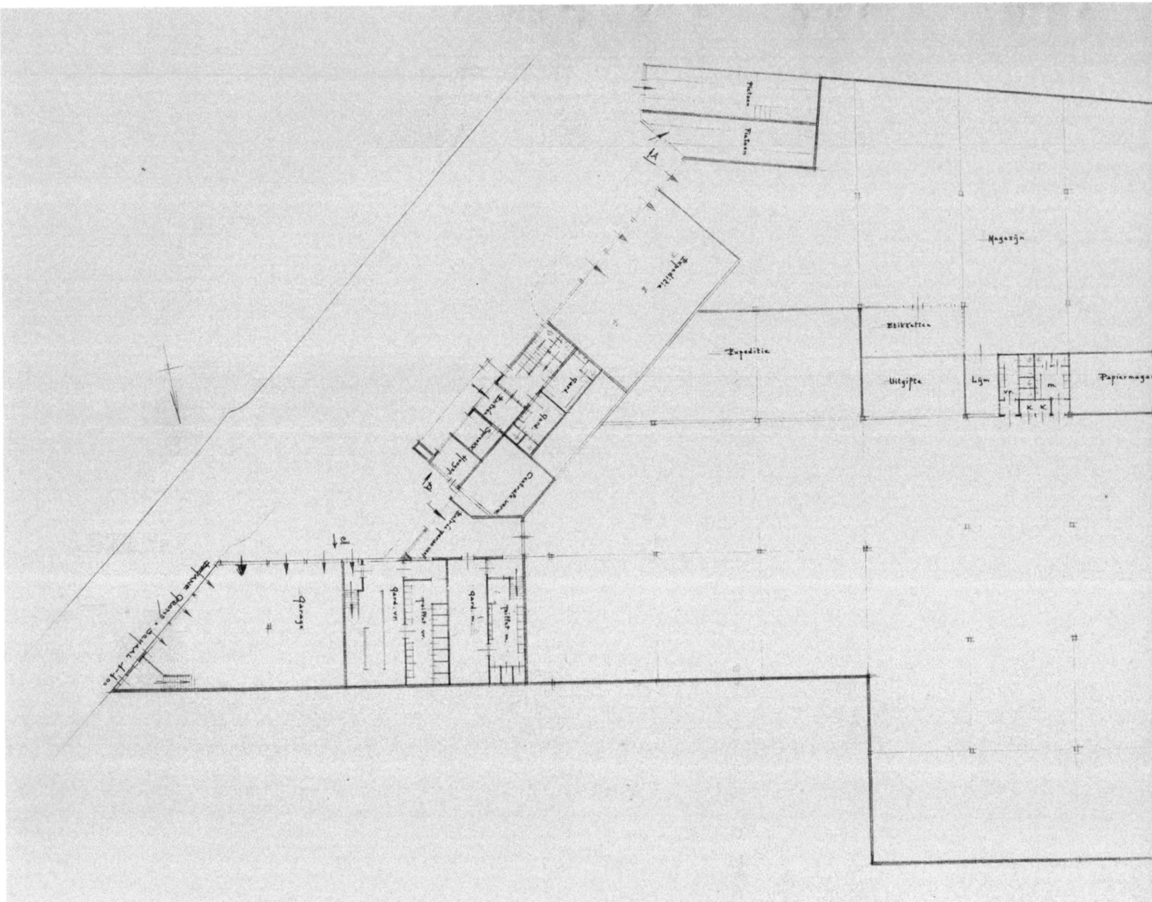

8a

8a Possibly the first (undated and unsigned) designs by Wil Jansen for the new cardboard packaging factory of her brother Tup. Floor plan of the ground floor.

8b Plan of the upper floors.

8c Front facade.

→

8d Side views and cross-sections.

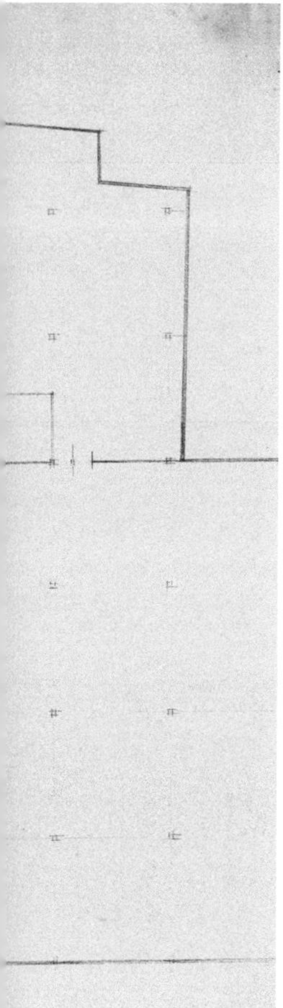

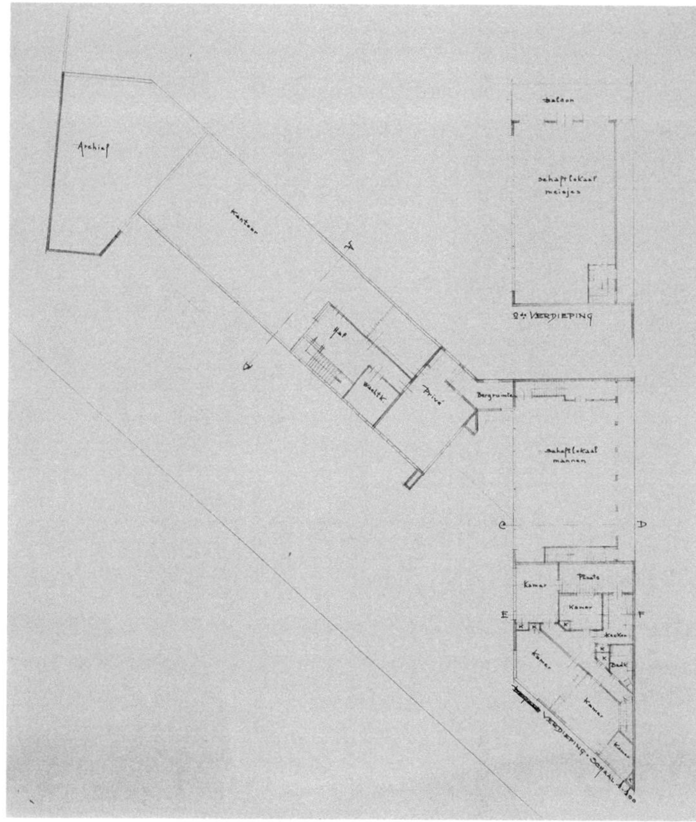
Archief
Kantoor
Privé
Bergruimte
Kamer
Keuken
8b

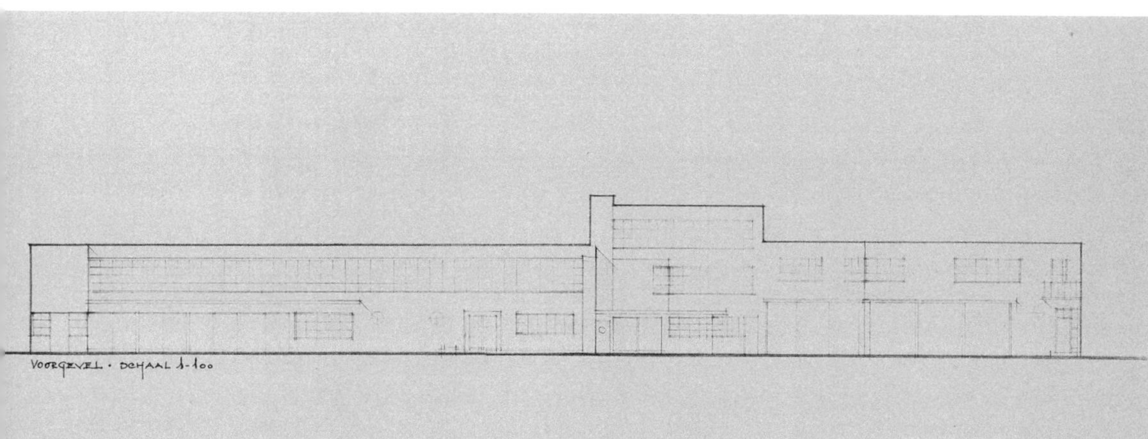
VOORGEVEL · SCHAAL 1-100
8c

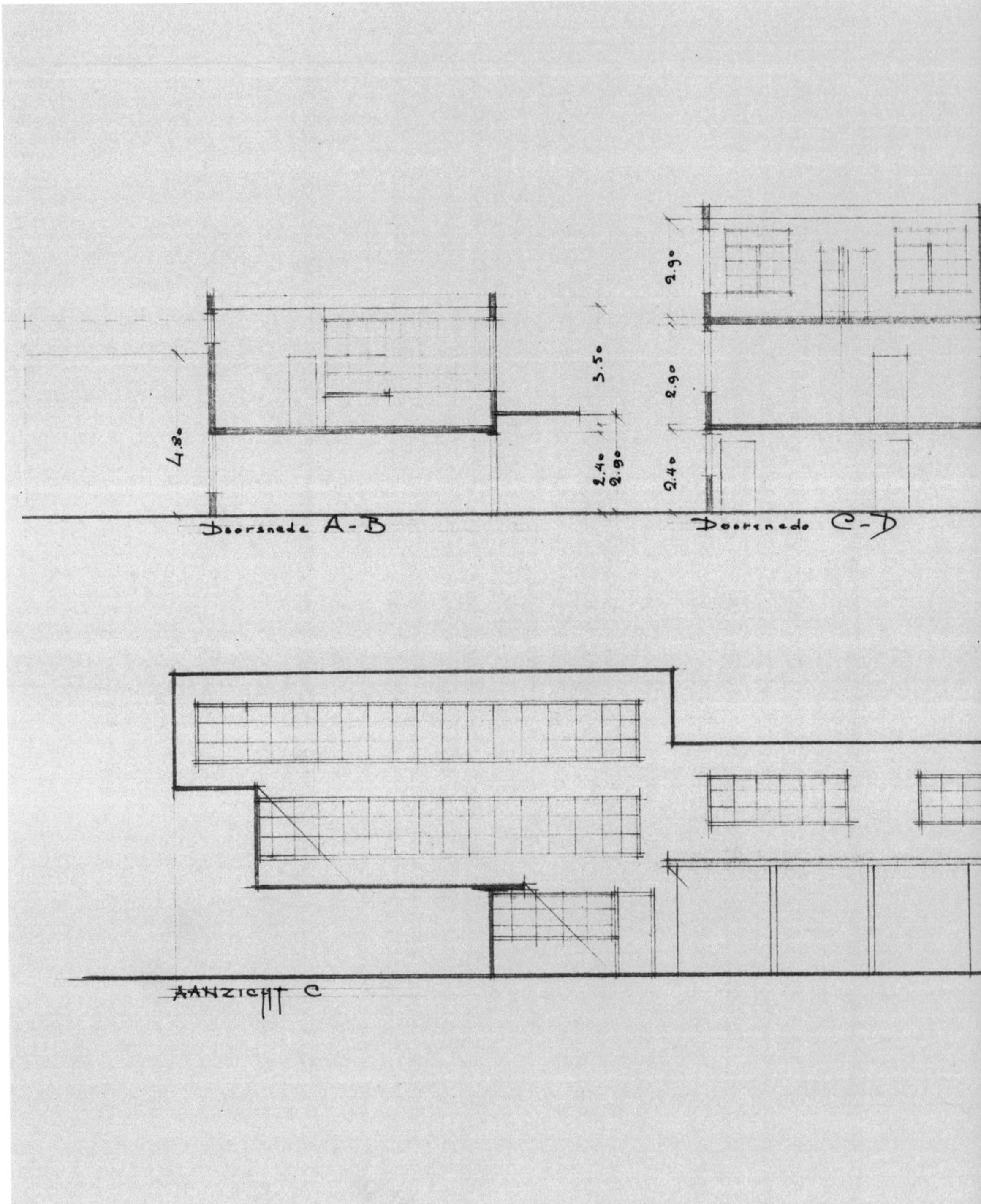
4.80
Doorsnede A-B
3.50
2.40
2.90
2.90
2.90
2.40
Doorsnede C-D
AANZICHT C

8d

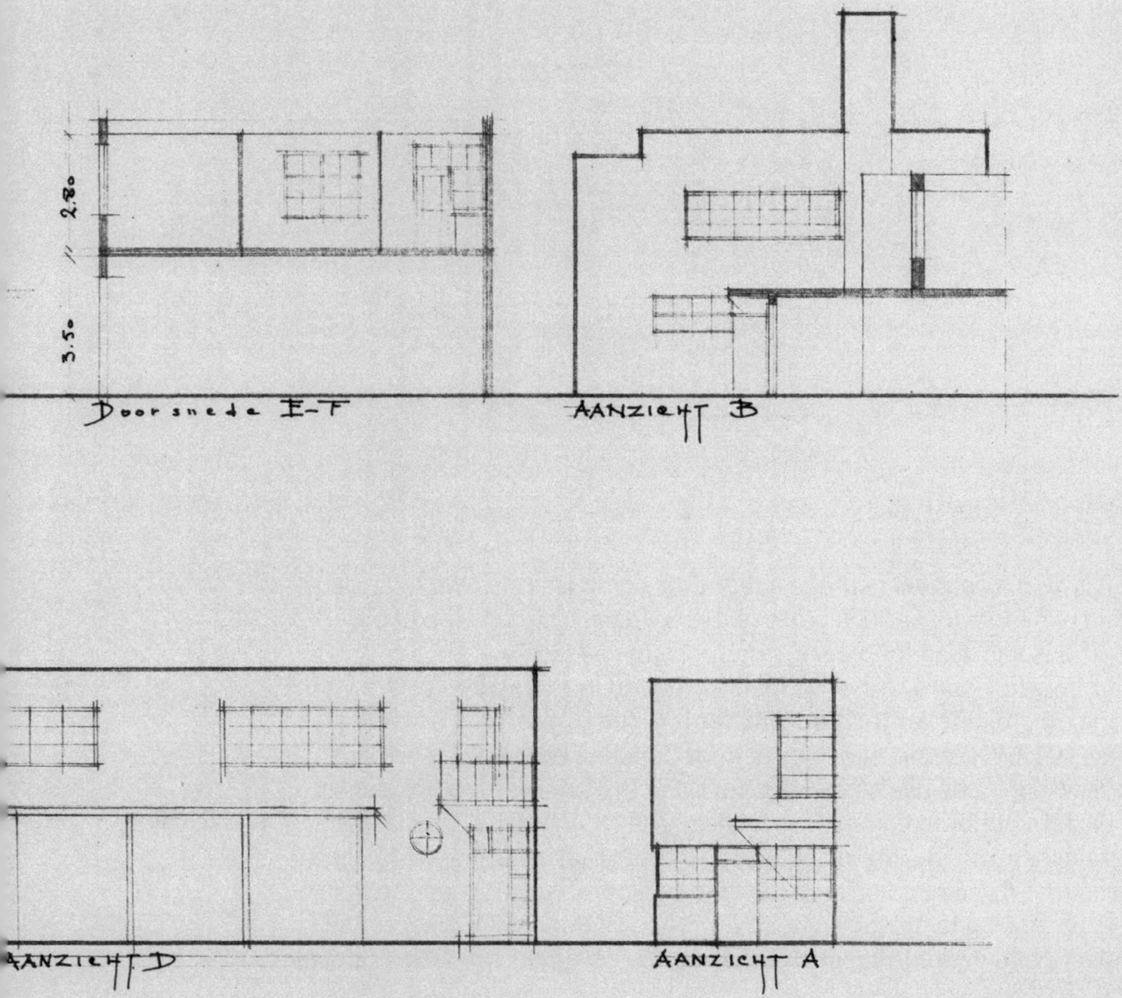
2.80
3.50
Doorsnede E-F
AANZICHT B
AANZICHT D
AANZICHT A

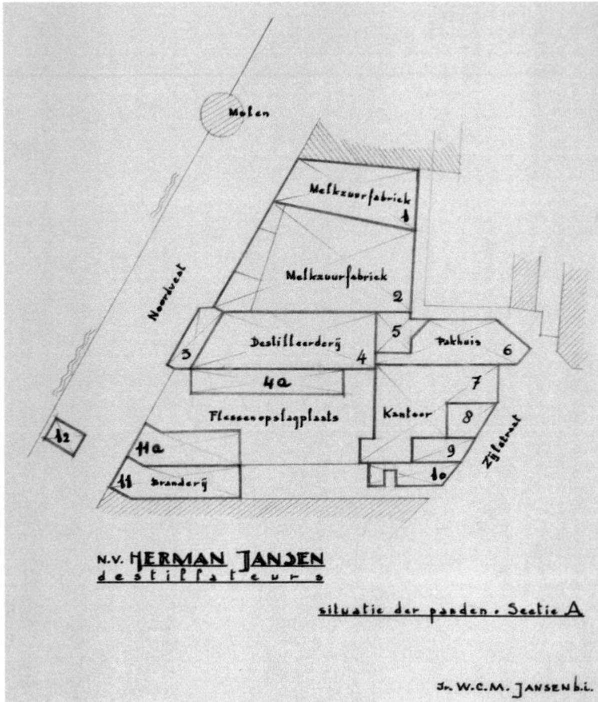

9

which is also a national heritage site.[67] Dick commissioned Wil to design interior elements for various parts of the building, including the boardroom.[68] It is still used for the same purpose by the family.

For over ten years, Wil was closely involved in renovation and expansion projects for the perfume factory run by her brother Guust (1895–1972).[69] For this son, too, Herman Jansen had come up with a company that made use of raw materials and byproducts from the distillery. The Valdelis perfume factory was originally based in the building at the Zijlstraat location, moving in 1943 to a former grain warehouse at Lange Nieuwstraat 47, located on a plot of land behind what was then the police office, continuing to the inner harbour of Nieuwe Haven. The successful company not only made various perfumes and colognes, but also a popular brand of aftershave called Fresh-up; it continued expanding from 1959 to 1968. Wil made various designs for these expansions, which also offer evidence of her modern tastes. For example, the facade of an expansion to the premises on the Nieuwe Haven side presents a sleek, coherent wall surface with square windows.[70] In 1968 she made the drawings for a factory expansion that included a warehouse, a packaging department and a storeroom **[fig. 10]**.[71] A strikingly large women's cloakroom with toilets was provided for these latter two areas.

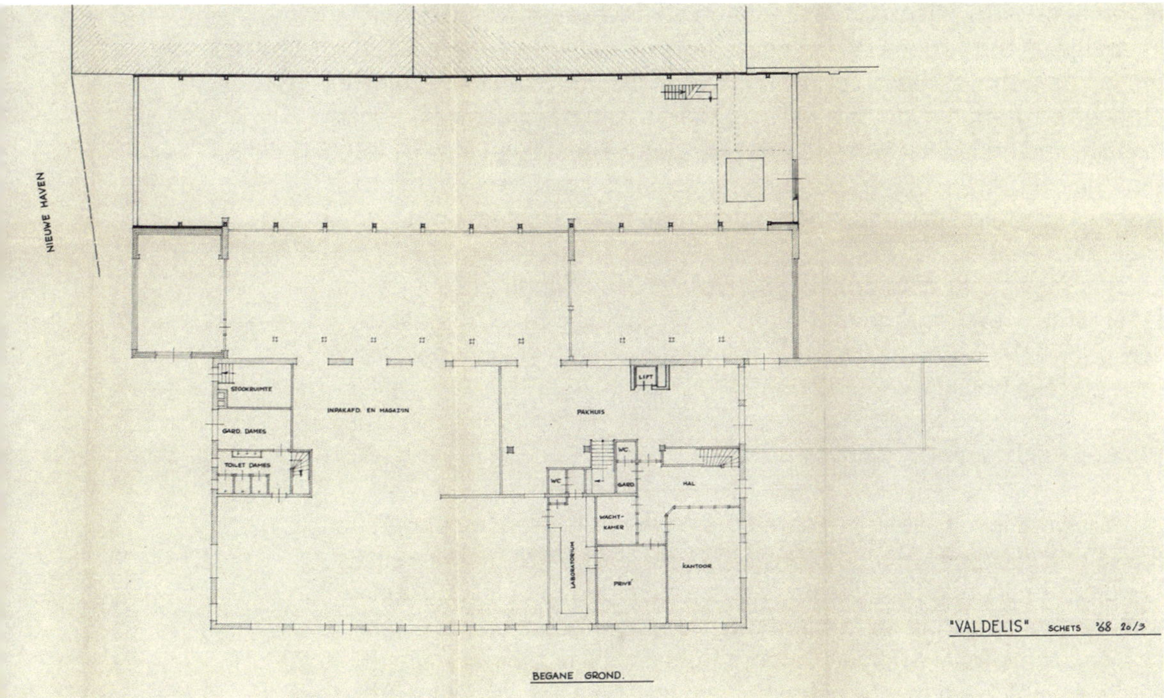

10

9 The factory and office complex of the Jansen family as surveyed by Wil Jansen, undated.

10 Unsigned design (1968) by Wil Jansen to extend the Valdelis perfume factory of her brother Guust. The packaging department/storeroom included a sizable women's cloakroom with toilets.

In the final years of her career, Jansen made several designs for Magneto Chemie, a joint initiative of her brothers Hans, Dick and Tup. The laboratories where experiments took place with anodes for the electrochemical industry were based in two former malting distilleries (1837–1874) owned by the family, located at Noordvestsingel 79-99. In addition to specific interior elements, such as rinsing tables, workboxes and acid cabinets, Wil designed a building volume consisting of two storeys that linked the two buildings.[72] She did not design a modern facade this time, but rather one that unified the two side buildings in an eclectic style. It is possible that the brothers did not want to invest significant sums on the exterior of the building, since it was used exclusively for experimentation for a long time. Since 2002, the complex has been a national heritage site.[73]

Jansen developed various interiors for off-licenses across the country. Some were owned by the family firm, others by its business relations or customers.[74] In 1950 Jansen obtained her distiller's certificate, and immediately used it to apply for a retail liquor license in Rotterdam for a building on Nieuwe Binnenweg where the family wanted to open an off-license.[75] Since she was the only person in the family who would be able to obtain that trade certificate, she was apparently willing to do so in the interests of the family firm.[76] The certificate may also have been useful to her in designing the various off-licenses. Jansen applied modern design principles in that context. For example, a design for three of the family's off-licenses features austere wall cupboards with open compartments in white, red and black Formica **[fig. 11a-11c]**.[77] The design also dictated that the countertop of the counters, from which customers could be served from various sides, should be made from the same modern, hygienic material.

This shows that Wil's brothers actively involved her in the flourishing family firm by awarding commissions to her for their various separate companies. However, her development as an architect would primarily take place in housing construction.

Women's Advisory Committee

From the earliest years of her career as an architect, Jansen played an active role in society. Her portfolio of orders, still slim at that time, gave her opportunity to do so; it is likely that she hoped to build up a network, with the aim of finding more clients. When she announced her eligibility as a candidate for the Roman Catholic State Party for the municipal council elections in Schiedam, she listed her occupation as architectural engineer and interior architect, an addition that may have been intended to achieve the same goal.[78] Jansen's civic activities were largely associated with her education and profession. Immediately after the Rotterdam branch was established in 1936, she joined the Vereniging van Vrouwen met een Academische Opleiding ('Association of Women with an Academic Education', VVAO).[79] This association was established in 1918 to represent the interests of academically educated women in society. Aletta Jacobs was one of the first members of the VVAO, which still exists today, under the name Vereniging van vrouwen met hogere opleiding ('Association of women with higher education'), and numbers approximately 4,000 members. One of its most significant activities back then was giving academic and professional advice. As president of the student society, Jansen had already encountered the more broadly oriented National Women's Council, with which the VVAO was affiliated.[80] It must have inspired her to spend time with other women in the same position, and to strive to improve social and societal conditions for women. She became a board member of the Rotterdam branch of the VVAO immediately after the war and sat on the executive board from 1947 to 1953. Her former classmate Ada Kuiper-Struyk was on the board at the same time.[81] This architectural engineer who had graduated in Delft in 1937 married her husband in that same year: Johannes Albertus Kuiper, who had also graduated in Delft, and was a partner at architecture firm Kuiper, Gouwetor, De Ranitz and Bleeker.

11a Wil Jansen designed interiors for off-licences owned by the Jansen family. Floor plan, 1962.

→
11b Wall of cupboards with countertop, 1962.

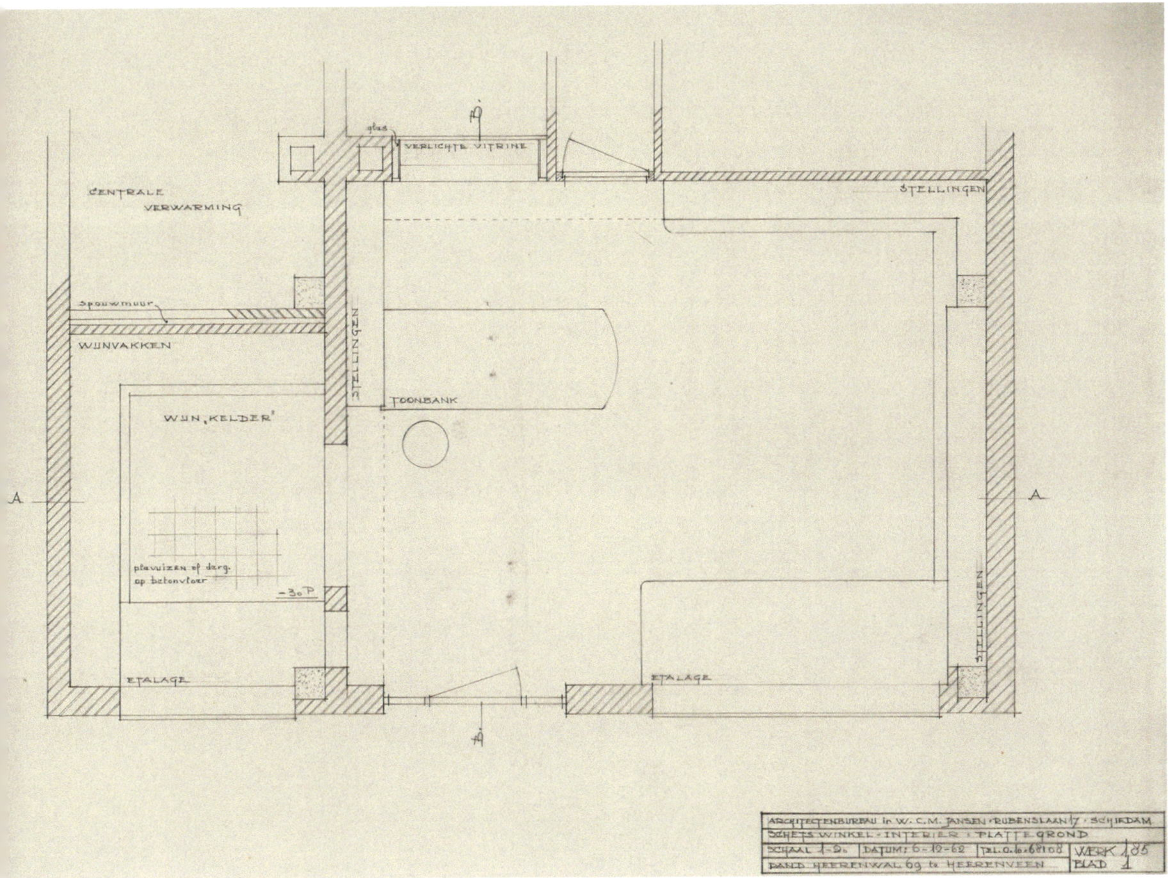
CENTRALE
VERWARMING
glas
VERLICHTE VITRINE
STELLINGEN
spouwmuur
WIJNVAKKEN
STELLINGEN
TOONBANK
WIJN „KELDER"
A
A
plavuizen of derg.
op betonvloer
-30 P
STELLINGEN
ETALAGE
ETALAGE
ARCHITECTENBUREAU ir W. C. M. JANSEN · RUBENSLAAN 17 · SCHIEDAM
SCHETS WINKEL - INTERIEUR : PLATTEGROND
DATUM: 6-12-62
TEL. 0.10.68108
WERK 185
BLAD 1
PAND HEERENWAL 69 te HEERENVEEN

11a

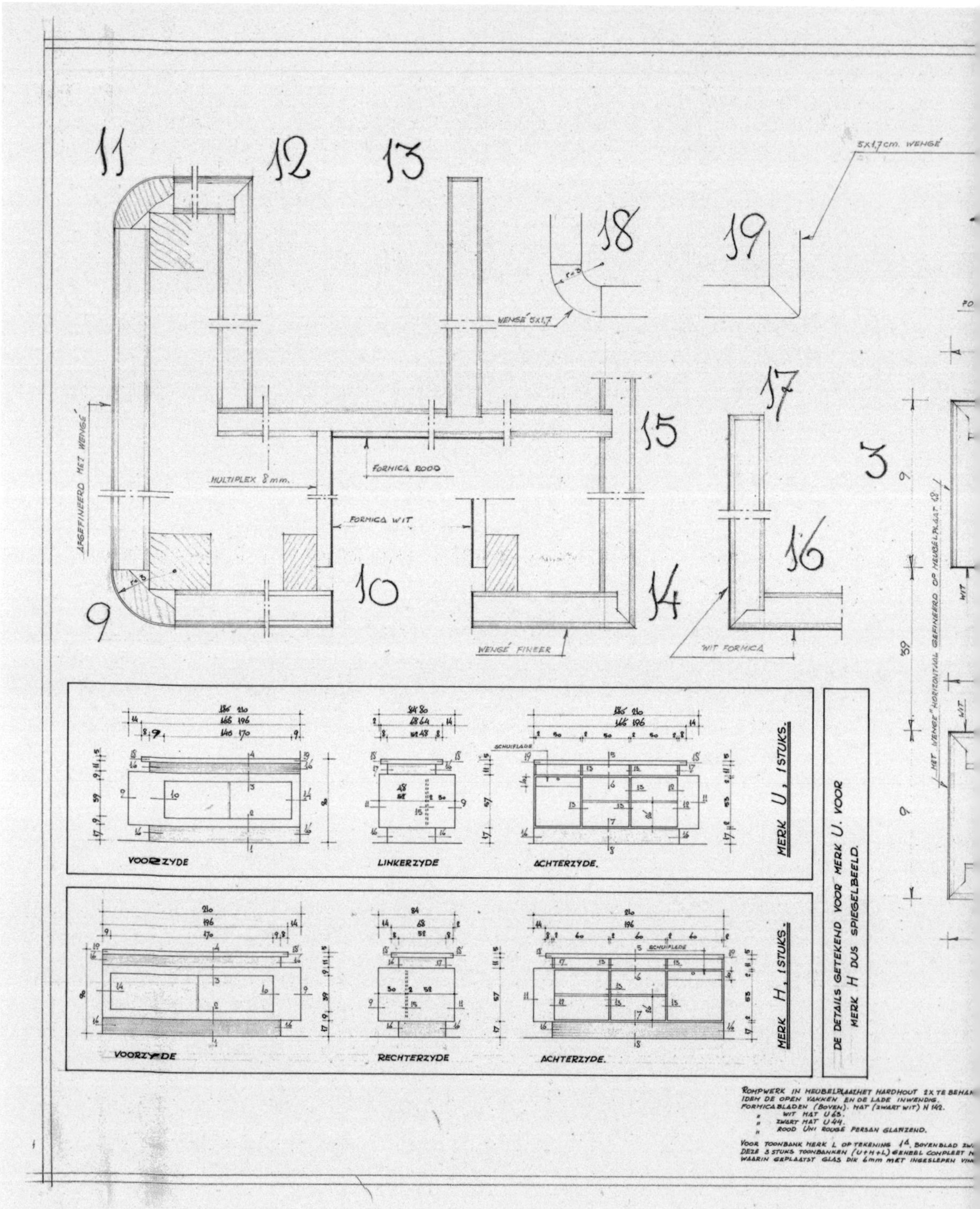
5x1,7cm. WENGÉ
WENGÉ 5x1,7
AFGEFINEERD MET WENGÉ
MULTIPLEX 8mm.
FORMICA ROOD
FORMICA WIT
WENGÉ FINEER
WIT FORMICA
VOORZYDE
LINKERZYDE
ACHTERZYDE.
SCHUIFLADE
MERK U, 1STUKS.
RECHTERZYDE
MERK H, 1STUKS.
DE DETAILS GETEKEND VOOR MERK U. VOOR
MERK H DUS SPIEGELBEELD.
ROMPWERK IN MEUBELPLAAT.HET HARDHOUT 2X TE BEHAN
IDEM DE OPEN VAKKEN EN DE LADE INWENDIG.
FORMICABLADEN (BOVEN). MAT (ZWART WIT) H 142.
" WIT MAT U 63.
" ZWART MAT U 44.
" ROOD UNI ROUGE PERSAN GLANZEND.
VOOR TOONBANK MERK L OP TEKENING 1A. BOVENBLAD ZW
DEZE 3 STUKS TOONBANKEN (U+H+L) GEHEEL COMPLEET M
WAARIN GEPLAATST GLAS DIK 6mm MET INGESLEPEN VIN

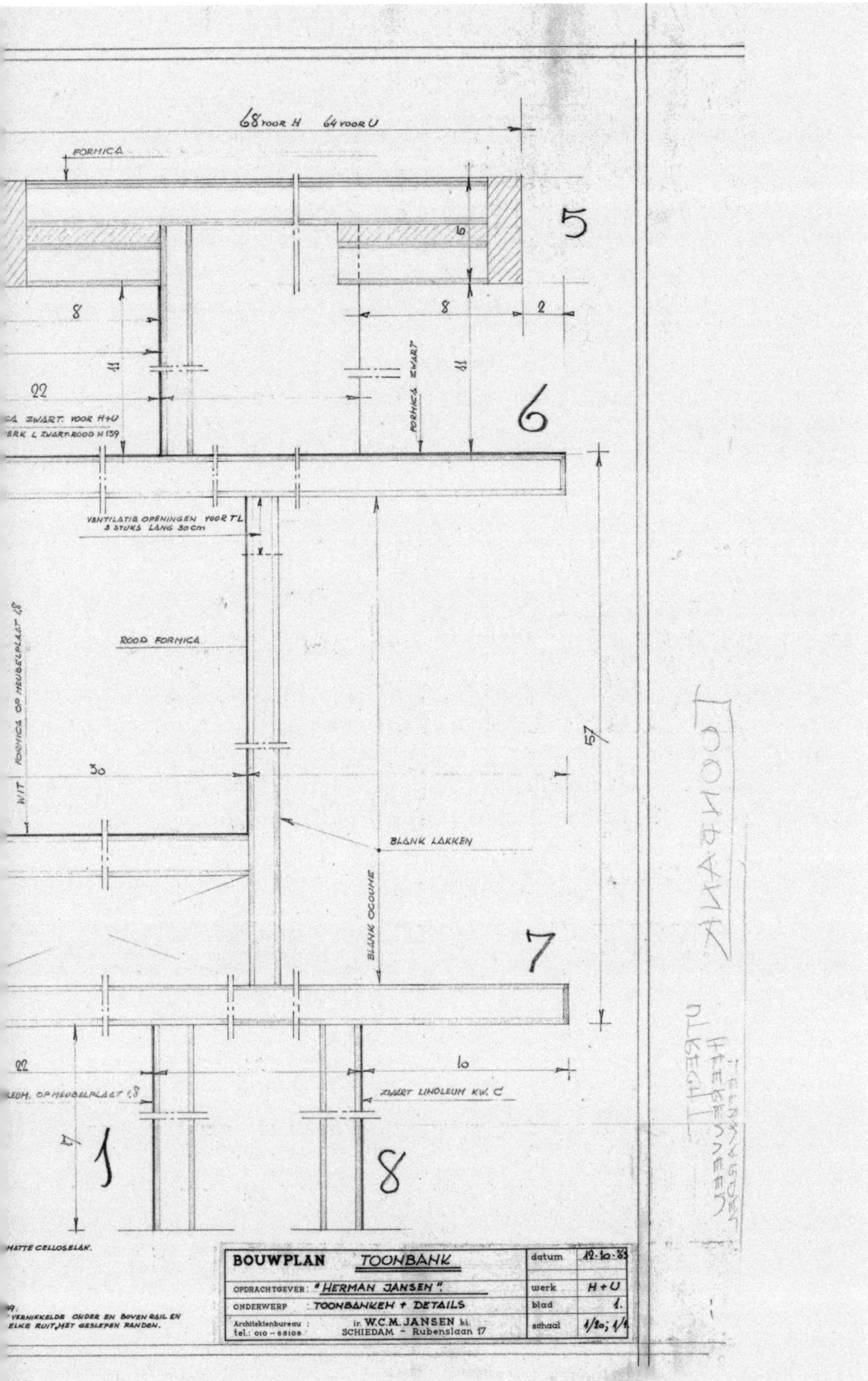
68 VOOR H 64 VOOR U
FORMICA
5
6
7
8
1
VENTILATIE OPENINGEN VOOR TL
3 STUKS LANG 30 cm
ROOD FORMICA
BLANK LAKKEN
BLANK OCOUME
ZWART LINOLEUM KW. C
MATTE CELLOSELAK.
BOUWPLAN TOONBANK
OPDRACHTGEVER: "HERMAN JANSEN".
ONDERWERP: TOONBANKEN + DETAILS
Architektenbureau : ir. W.C.M. JANSEN bi.
tel.: 010 – 68108 SCHIEDAM – Rubenslaan 17
datum 19-10-'65
werk H + U
blad 1.
schaal 1/20; 1/1

11b

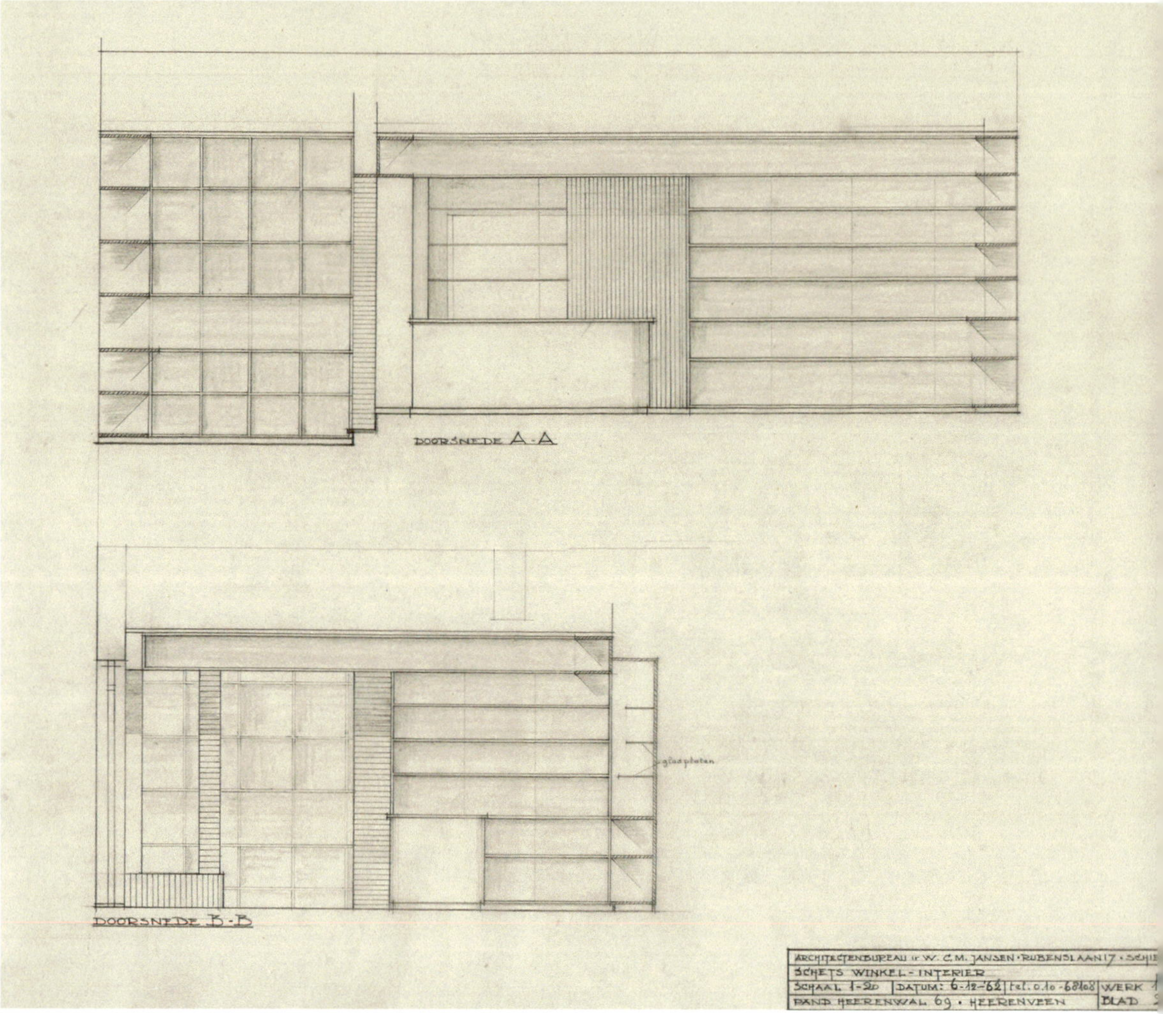
DOORSNEDE A-A
DOORSNEDE B-B
ARCHITECTENBUREAU ir W. C.M. JANSEN · RUBENSLAAN 17
SCHETS WINKEL-INTERIER
SCHAAL 1-20
DATUM: 6-12-'62
WERK
PAND HEERENWAL 69 · HEERENVEEN
BLAD

11c

That firm would later facilitate Jansen in designing the RVS apartment building.[82] During her time as a board member, Jansen gave various lectures to the VVAO members across the country, sometimes based on a recommendation from Kuiper-Struyk.[83] The topics of these lectures focused primarily on interior architecture and living in a modern home.

The post-WWII reconstruction prompted numerous women to speak up. Why not involve housewives in the design and construction of new homes? After all, these women spent most of their time at home and were ideally positioned to state the practical requirements that a home needed to meet. On the one hand, this remarkable claim seems to be at odds with women's vigorous efforts to distance themselves from that stereotype. On the other hand, this gave women the perfect opportunity to speak up and be heard in an area where they were the experts. The fact that this was popular may also have been related to the establishment – conceived entirely by men – of the Stichting Goed Wonen ('Good Living Foundation') in 1946.[84] The stated aim of this foundation, which was to foster a pleasant culture of living, was accompanied by recommendations for an efficient household – a topic that specifically concerned women.

The Nederlandse Vereniging van Huisvrouwen ('Dutch Association of Housewives', NVVH) published an article in *Bouw* magazine entitled 'Housewives speak out', presenting the results of a subscriber survey on criteria for a city home.[85] It included such topics as location, size and layout of the rooms, and various practical conveniences. The survey results were presented to the Director-General for Public Housing. The survey was criticized, mainly for lacking a representative overview: only 6 per cent of the over 3,300 members had completed and returned the survey form.[86] Margaret Staal-Kropholler, NVVH spokesperson, fiercely rejected the somewhat condescending commentary from economist Willem Somermeyer (1919–1982) regarding the survey methodology and what he referred to as the leading and unclear questions asked in the survey. In any case, the survey was a step toward giving a say to women as housing consumers.

11c Counter with details, 1963.

In the same year the foundation was established, the first women's advisory committee or Vrouwen Advies Commissie (VAC) was created in Rotterdam; this was a municipal advisory body for issues relating to housing construction, housing layout and the living environment.[87] The VAC gave solicited and unsolicited advice to the Public Housing Department. The committee members were women '(...) who had been schooled by practice and study to actually take part in the work (...)'.[88] As architectural engineers, Jansen and Kuiper-Struyk could make a useful contribution, but the same applied to housewives who 'had experience with housing – due to the household activities that they perform – that (...) is greater and more varied than that of any architect's'.[89] The advisory task performed by the VAC consisted largely of conducting surveys, inspired no doubt in part by the aforementioned NVH survey, which was also discussed and answered extensively within the VAC.[90]

Early in 1950, the VAC partnered with the Public Housing Department on a study of housewives, exploring their experiences and preferences with using their own home, so that these first-hand accounts could be considered in the construction of new housing. The target group was people living in various types of housing in ten residential complexes that were built after 1940, including Kralingen and Oud Mathenesse ('traditional construction', about 500 and 300 homes respectively), Bergpolder ('prefab', about 50 homes) and Overschie ('hollow concrete', about 100 homes).[91] The survey consisted of a detailed questionnaire asking about all the rooms in the home, their orientation, the routing, and the balcony and garden. Joined by a fellow member of the VAC, Jansen interviewed the women living in Oud Mathenesse, Rotterdam's westernmost neighbourhood, bordering on the adjacent town of Schiedam. Jansen's notes show that she spoke to a woman living 'in the white houses overlooking the communal gardens'.[92] These gardens were not at all to her liking, because they had been taken over by children from the start, so nothing could grow there. The woman also complained that children 'from all sorts of people' walked into her home uninvited and that her own children were unable to sleep because of noise in the gardens. The freestanding rows of housing built in one direction had 'an unpleasant feel', in this woman's opinion, and caused draughts. The white houses that this presumably refers to, which would later be known as the 'White Village', were built in 1922 based on a design by J.J.P. Oud and were intended to provide a healthy living environment for disadvantaged families. The freestanding rows of housing that were supposed to provide light, air and space were not entirely able to charm this local resident.[94] The VAC concluded in its final report that they had 'enjoyed' the survey – 'a formidable undertaking' – which gave housewives the opportunity to 'express themselves in their own setting for once'.[95]

Jansen's archive contains a design drawing from 1951 of a series of five types of senior housing for the Public Housing Department.[96] It appears to involve new construction. Jansen may have been approached about this project in the context of an extensive study that the VAC conducted on homes for the elderly.[97] The various types of housing featured in her design are plain but practical in layout, including enough cupboard space. There is no indication as to whether these homes were actually built.

Illustrating her rational, carefully considered floor plans, there is a design from 1958 for the room layout of an existing communal housing facility called 'Pluk den dag' ('Seize the day').[98] Jansen included the current floor plan, adding the label 'how not to do it', alongside the new variants that she came up with, in which she was able to merge the functions for living, eating, working, sleeping and cooking into a clear and functional concept in a single space **[fig. 12]**. Unfortunately, it was impossible to determine which housing facility this was.

Jansen was also involved in the laundry committee of the Rotterdam VAC, which researched housewives' experiences with the 'lavet', a large sink and counter combination used in small households in the 1950s for household and personal use.[99] She sent a letter to TNO inquiring about the suitability of various materials that might affect how fast the wash water cooled off, since rapid cooling could negatively affect how clean the laundry was.[100] The laundry committee also researched experiences with doing laundry inside the home or, for example, in a shared laundry room in a residential complex. Based on these research results, the committee drafted various advisory reports for the Public Housing Department.

Thanks to her VAC membership, Jansen was able to gain experience in topics related to living and housing; conversely, it is also clear that she showed from the start that she knew what she was talking about and contributed that knowledge in the committee. Her archival documents include her own comments added in red pencil. She received little notes that clearly show that she was soon considered an expert, with phrases like '(...) I would be so honoured if you could take a look at it [a recently published book about housing] and give us your opinion', and 'Get well soon, come help us out again with your practical knowledge!'[101] But in the end, it would be her VVAO membership that would lead to her most prominent commission.

The RVS apartment building

In 1938 there were plans to build a residential flat in Rotterdam for single women working in various professions.[102] Collective housing for unmarried women, living with parents or a landlady, had been seen before in the Netherlands on a very small scale, such as the 'residential home for Young Women' (1930) by the Stadswandelpark in Eindhoven.[103] Well into the post-war reconstruction period, there were hardly any options for unmarried working women to find independent living space. There are no known examples of collective housing of the type that some employers had built for their unmarried male workers, such as in the mining industry in Eygelshoven.[104] The Oranjehof (1942) in Amsterdam, designed by the architect couple Pot-Keegstra, was the first building for unmarried working women to be completed.[105]

Shortly after the Second World War, the plans for the apartment building in Rotterdam solidified thanks to the Rotterdam Women's Centre

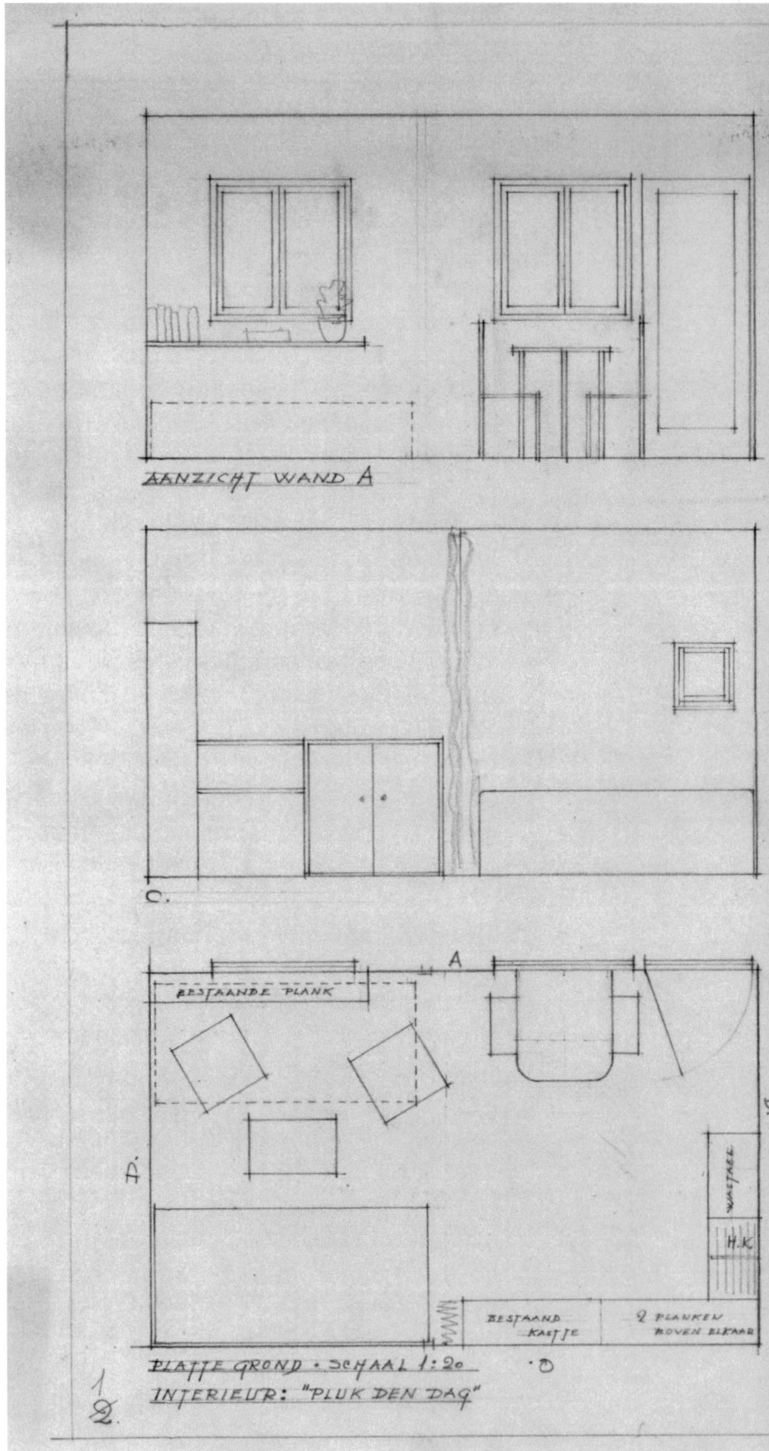
AANZICHT WAND A
C.
A
BESTAANDE PLANK
D.
WASTAFEL
H.K
BESTAAND KASTJE
2 PLANKEN BOVEN ELKAAR
PLATTE GROND · SCHAAL 1:20
INTERIEUR: "PLUK DEN DAG"
1/2

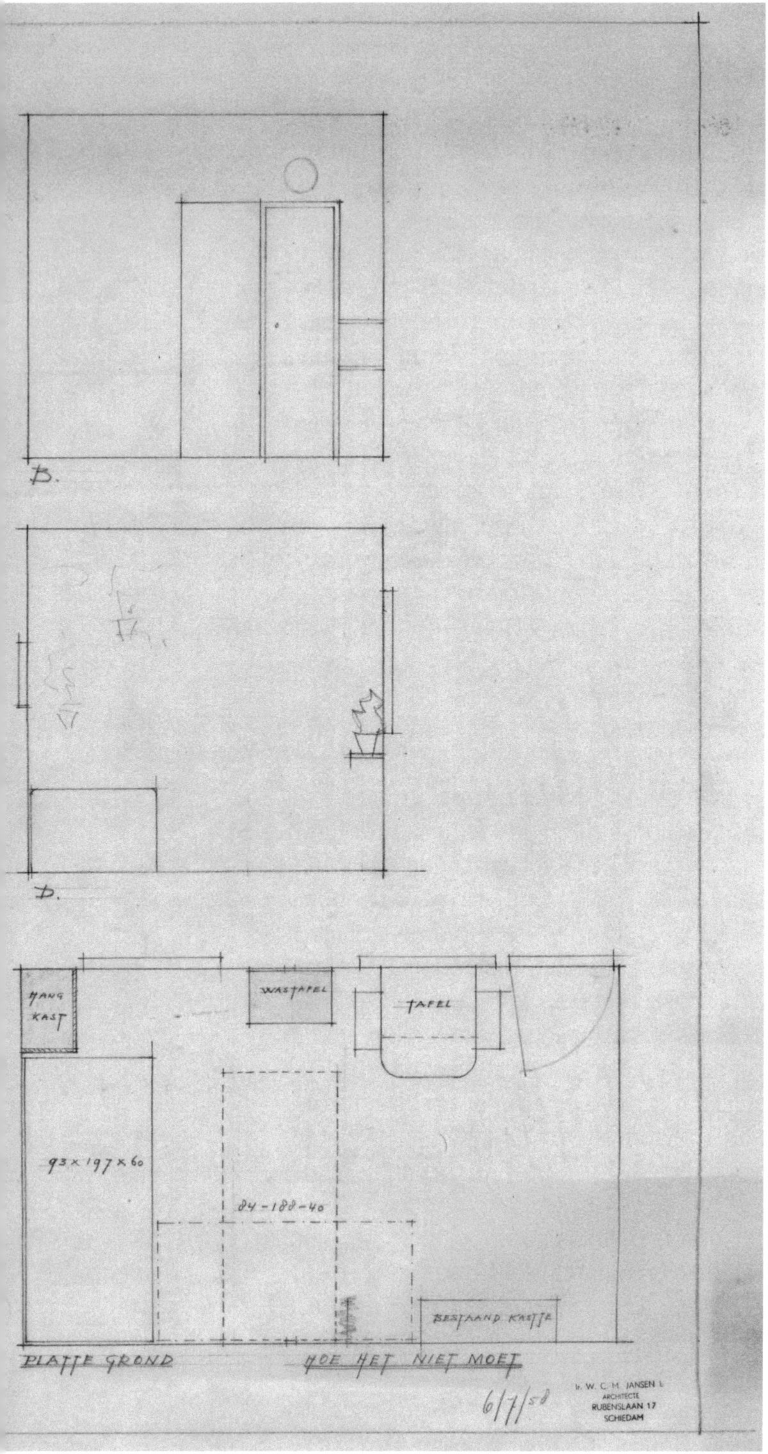

12

12 W.M.C. Jansen, interior design for the 'Pluk den dag' communal living facility, 1958.

Foundation, an alliance of seven women's associations, including the VVAO, where Jansen was a board member at the time.[106] The foundation surveyed its members in Rotterdam to explore the residential needs in such a building, and Jansen gave a talk for the members.[107] It would be considered a conflict of interest these days, but within the foundation it was a given from the start that she would design the building. Personally, as an unmarried working woman herself, she must have felt even more motivated by the stated aim of the apartment building. Moreover, it was an excellent opportunity to prove herself as a woman architect. It would be 1956 before the first pile was sunk. The plans had to be adapted more than once, because the municipal council repeatedly felt they cost too much. When it proved impossible to find funding in the context of the Housing Act, the public limited company Rotterdamsche Verzekering Sociëteiten (RVS) was willing to fund the project.

The authors of the publication *De RVS flat. Schone beloning voor vasthoudendheid in Rotterdam* ('The RVS Flat: beautiful reward for persistence in Rotterdam') attribute the design of the building entirely to Jansen.[108] The book indicates that she was supported by Rotterdam-based architecture firm Kuiper, Gouwetor De Ranitz & Bleeker (Kuiper was the husband of the aforementioned Ada Struyk). That support supposedly took the form of providing access to the drawing office and obtaining contacts with the building consortium. However, this is not corroborated by sources.

Most of the designs in Jansen's own archive are marked with both her name and the stamp of the architecture firm.[109] That would have been a very unusual expression of gratitude for providing access to their facilities. It is worth noting that Frits Gouwetor (1903–1972) was the main speaker when the building's first pile was sunk, which may indicate more significant involvement than providing the services listed above. His initials are also on various specification drawings.[110] These factors suggest that the firm was actively involved in the design, unless it was believed that jointly signing the design documents would increase the chances of approval by the municipal council. After all, Jansen did not have any major architectural works to her name, and was moreover a woman architect.

However, it is tempting to give Jansen full credit for all the designs of the apartment building. In view of her position, her experience on the Women's Advisory Committee, and her profession as a woman architect, she was an ideal choice for the foundation: she would understand the concepts envisioned for the building and be able to apply them in actual practice. Jansen herself wrote twice to Staal-Kropholler that she was working on an apartment building for working women (although she did not mention the other architecture firm).[111] It is very plausible that she needed a facilitator in the background for this first major commission – who could also serve as a sparring partner – and that Ada Struyk was an easy option.[112] Construction management, such as maintaining contact with the contractors, would have been a particularly difficult obstacle for Jansen to overcome, since it was uncommon for women to be in charge in the building sector. The fact is that publications about the RVS building do mention both Jansen and the Rotterdam-based architecture firm.[113]

The RVS building was built in 1958 on a plot designated by the municipality, at the corner of Heemraadssingel and Beukelsdijk **[fig. 13]**. The freestanding gallery-access building surrounded by greenery is a rectangular block, consisting of a ground floor with storage units and garages, and ten residential levels with 160 flats, each with between one and three rooms. The living room and small bedroom of the three-room flats are west-facing, while the large bedroom and kitchen are situated on the east side, along a gallery that provides access to the flats. The galleries are accessed from a main entrance that extends from the building on the east side, which includes stairs and a platform. The main entrance provides access to a stairwell and two lift shafts. A service stairwell and emergency access route on the north side of the building also opens onto the galleries. The two-room and one-room flats are located at the short ends of the building. All the flats have a balcony. The loadbearing walls were built in concrete up to the second residential level, in brick to the sixth residential level, and in sand-lime blocks to the tenth residential level. The floors and roof are made of reinforced concrete.

The efficiently structured flats were equipped with modern conveniences, such as central heating, a water heater, refrigerator, home phone, and a central TV antenna system. Jansen added practical details for the working residents, such as an order delivery cupboard that could be accessed from two sides, installed beside the front door, where deliverymen could drop off their goods.[114] The power company could check electricity and gas meters from the gallery when the women were at their work. There was a litterbin lift in the service stairwell.

In the original plans, the residential building was supposed to be equipped with all sorts of shared facilities, such as a restaurant, meeting room/lounge, shop, hair salon, guest room and a roof terrace with a winter garden and a small gym. Jansen was presumably inspired by Le Corbusier (1887–1965), one of the architects of the Modern Movement, who built similar shared spaces in his *Unité d'Habitation* (1947–1953) in Marseilles. The aim was to alleviate household burdens, as well as facilitate social interaction. When the RVS building was actually built, these facilities were limited to a roof garden and two shops on the ground floor. Besides financial considerations, this was prompted in part by lessons learned from such locations as the Oranjehof in Amsterdam, which had shown that such services were not cost-effective.

13

13 The RVS block of flats in Rotterdam designed by Wil Jansen, circa 1958.

14

14 The Bergpolder-flat residential building in Rotterdam designed by Willem van Tijen, 1935.

The RVS building is Jansen's most prominent architectural design, showing her modernist taste and views. The streamlined design of the building, in which residential functions and access determine the forms, created more air, light and space for the residents. It was with these functionalist principles of the Modern Movement that she stepped into the Rotterdam arena, where this architectural movement reigned supreme, and where renowned progressive colleagues like Willem van Tijen and Jo van den Broek (1898–1978) were actively working on the post-war reconstruction.[115] Van Tijen designed the first gallery-access apartment building, Bergpolder (1934) **[fig. 14]**, intended for small working-class families, and a gallery-access apartment building (1949) on Zuidplein. These residential buildings, which were similar in structure and architecture, must have inspired Jansen. It is very possible that she had already heard Van Tijen's theories in 1930, during the aforementioned international course, where Van Tijen lectured on homes and neighbourhoods at the TH.[116] He presented his vision on open rows of housing rather than perimeter blocks of housing, in which the front and back sides were replaced by east-facing and west-facing facades, creating a living and sleeping side to optimize daylight access. During the same course, Walter Gropius gave a talk on high-rise buildings, the orientation of residential blocks, and the usefulness of collective public facilities such as heating, waste disposal and laundrettes.

Notes in Jansen's archive show that she attended Van Tijen's lectures.[117] Van Tijen was part of a study group on post-war reconstruction headed by the Rotterdam Public Housing Department, the same municipal department that was advised by the Women's Advisory Committee (VAC). Jansen had contact with him through the VAC laundry committee that she sat on. The committee consulted with Van Tijen about laundry options in newly built residential complexes, basing their plans on the positive experiences with the shared laundry room in his Bergpolderflat.[118] It is interesting to note that Jansen had not included a shared laundry room in her original plans for the RVS building. The flats did not have a 'lavet'.

After the RVS building was completed, Van Tijen published an article in architectural weekly magazine *Bouwkundig Weekblad*, expanding his views on high-rise buildings. His article, illustrated with photos of the RVS building, was featured in a separate section, followed by a description of the RVS building that appeared to have been provided by the architect(s).[119] Van Tijen viewed high-rise buildings as a necessity, but under specific limiting conditions: as a single building or placed in small groups, situated on spacious grounds, *not* aiming to economize on building costs, and certainly not intended for children. With the exception of this final aspect, for which he generously forgave Le Corbusier, Van Tijen believed that the French architect's *Unité d'Habitation* fully met all these conditions – and implicitly, considering the layout in the magazine, suggested that the RVS building did as well. This must have felt like a meaningful acknowledgment of Jansen's work. In many ways, she was inspired by the Modern Movement, but her functionalist principles were also inspired by realizations that arose from the VAC surveys and other sources, which she managed to implement in actual practice.

The original purpose for which the RVS building was built – to provide housing for single working women who were members of the affiliated Rotterdam women's associations – was largely fulfilled. RVS and the municipality adopted a less restrictive application policy, allowing incomplete families to apply as well. This was formally defined as: two people consisting of a childless married couple, a parent and child, or two women sharing a home, which could include sisters or colleagues. Single women were required to be over the minimum age of 40 years, and did not necessarily have to be members of a women's association.[120] The apartment building clearly met an urgent need, since it had a long waiting list. Today the RVS building accommodates a wide range of tenants.

Bungalow in Meerssen

The bungalow became popular in the Netherlands in the 1950s.[121] This type of dwelling, which was brought over from America, was embraced by the more prosperous members of Dutch society. The freestanding, single-storey bungalow offered its occupants a sense of freedom. In 1955, Jansen made her first designs for a bungalow in Meerssen, intended for her oldest sister Ida (1891–1976) and brother-in-law Gerard (Gé) Edixhoven (1892–1980). Edixhoven, who was a member of the managing board of a mining company, came up with the building plans in anticipation of his pension in 1958. He and Ida – there were no children from their marriage – would continue living in the bungalow that Wil designed for them for the rest of their lives.

The spacious bungalow was built in 1957 on a large plot of land, situated on Korte Raarberg on the east side of Meerssen, about 20 km from Eygelshoven. Situated quite far from the road, the house is positioned with the back facing south, oriented towards the undulating landscape of south Limburg. The house is wide and has a slight jig in the basic shape at two points. The facades are made of brick. The rear facade has large glass windows **[fig. 15a]**. In contrast, the front facade is more closed in appearance, with smaller windows, but at the same time, because of the slight jig in the shape, it seems to embrace the semi-circular lane leading to the house. The bungalow has a single-pitched roof sloping towards the front. The slant of the roof takes on a playful effect because of the basic shape of the building. The bungalow has a concrete foundation with steel girders, and a cellar under part of the house.

In summer 1955, Jansen was still sketching compact, largely rectangular basic shapes for the bungalow, but her design gradually developed into the angled floor plan with clearly mapped functions **[fig. 15b]**.[122] Effectively, the house had three wings: the west side for living and working, the middle for sleeping, and a garage on the east side. This functional grouping of rooms is reinforced by variations in floor level, following the slight slope of the Raarberg hillside. The main entrance in the north facade opens onto a very spacious living room and study, separated by a half-open wall. Both rooms have a door to the garden on the south side. The higher middle wing is accessed from a short staircase in the living room. A central hallway gives access to four adjoining bedrooms at the back of the house and a shared bathroom. The front side of the middle wing houses various service rooms, including the kitchen, a room for the housekeeper, and a covered courtyard with a service entrance and a shed. A terrace along the entire south facade and part of the southwestern facade has a lovely view of the gently sloping garden and the landscape of meadows and orchards beyond it. The east wing, only half the depth of the rest

→
15a W.C.M. Jansen, specification drawings (1956) for the bungalow in Meerssen, intended for her sister Ida and brother-in-law Edixhoven.

→ →
15b Specification drawings (1956) of the floor plan.

of the house, holds a garage, which is also on a higher level. The cellar can be accessed through the kitchen and contains the central heating room, a storage space, a pantry and – probably prompted by the Cold War – a small bunker.

The bungalow as a new type of housing, the spacious plot and the trust placed in Jansen by her brother-in-law gave her the opportunity to elaborate on the many ideas she had developed during her time with the Women's Advisory Committee. The angled floor plan allowed for a supremely functional, practical layout, and allowed light to flood the house. The bungalow was a great example of the Modern Movement, in which function dictated form, superfluous decorative elements were eliminated, and light, air and space were key.

One notable feature is the housekeeper's room, which Jansen placed in a very central location in the middle wing, at the front of the bungalow. She added a service entrance here, which also gave access to the shed and garage via a covered courtyard. The housekeeper's room also had direct access to the kitchen. Since her room did not open onto the hallway of that wing, the bungalow's residents had complete privacy in their bedrooms.

Jansen designed various interior elements, such as a cupboard wall for the kitchen and living room with a practical 'pass-through' hatch **[fig. 16a and 16b]**.[123] Her design for the living room is modern and minimalist, giving it a spacious and restful appearance **[fig. 17]**.[124] The spacious feel is reinforced by the large windows in the south wall. Beside the fireplace, Jansen added a playful minimalist element in the form of three small square windows that offer a glimpse of the undulating landscape.

The bungalow was more than satisfactory in its position and floor plan, as evidenced by the fact that it still exists, and the subsequent occupants have largely limited their changes to modernizing the basic facilities and interior **[fig. 18a-18c]**.[125] An office extension was added on the east side.

It would probably be overstating the matter if we were to suggest that renowned architect Van Tijen had been inspired by Jansen's work when he built a bungalow (1961–1962) a few years later in Rotterdam, at Glazoenowlaan 3.[126] It was one of the few freestanding residences that he designed. However, it is interesting to note the similarities in the bungalows built in fairly quick succession by Jansen and Van Tijen, who knew each other by then. In the compact rectangular block, similar to what Jansen had initially envisioned for Meerssen, Van Tijen provided a functional separation between living, working and sleeping by means of a central hallway and entry hall. These separations were accentuated by differences in floor levels, similar to the house in Meerssen, but in this case not dictated by the sloping hillside. In Van Tijen's bungalow, too, the relatively closed

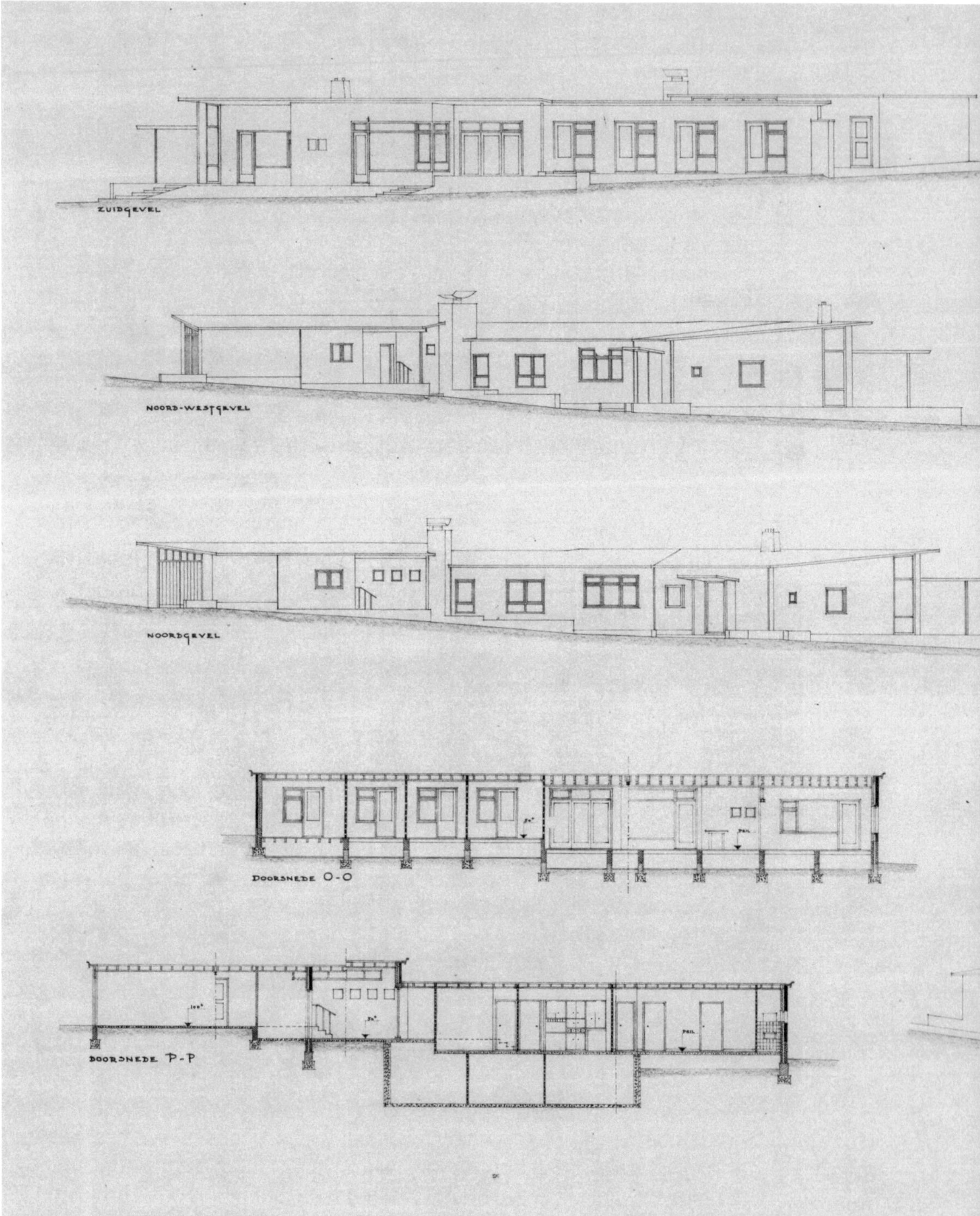
ZUIDGEVEL
NOORD-WESTGEVEL
NOORDGEVEL
DOORSNEDE O-O
DOORSNEDE P-P

15a

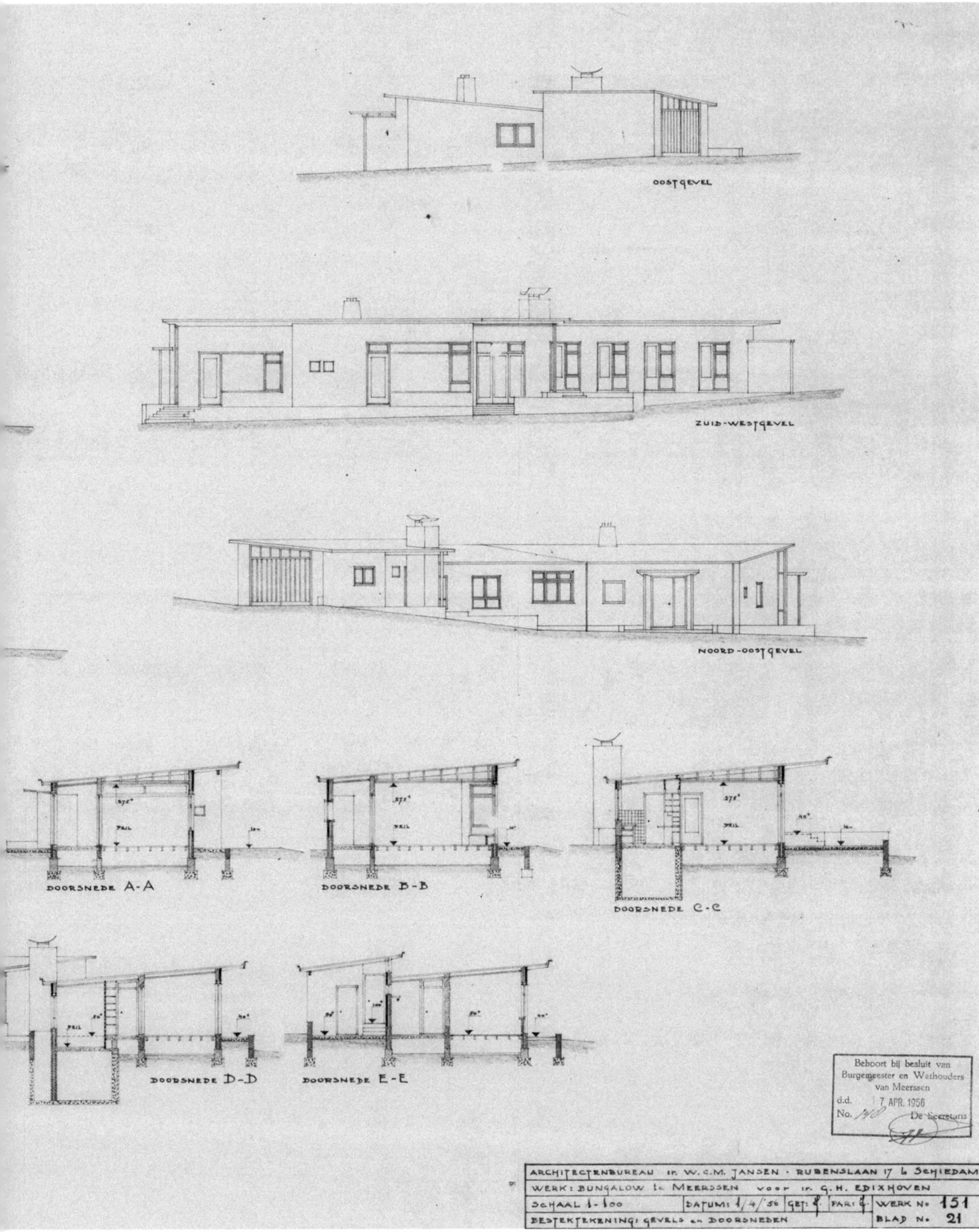
OOSTGEVEL
ZUID-WESTGEVEL
NOORD-OOSTGEVEL
DOORSNEDE A-A
DOORSNEDE B-B
DOORSNEDE C-C
DOORSNEDE D-D
DOORSNEDE E-E
Behoort bij besluit van
Burgemeester en Wethouders
van Meerssen
d.d. 17 APR. 1956
No.
De Secretaris
ARCHITECTENBUREAU ir. W.C.M. JANSEN · RUBENSLAAN 17 te SCHIEDAM
WERK: BUNGALOW te MEERSSEN voor ir. G.H. EDIXHOVEN
SCHAAL 1-100
DATUM: 1/4/'56
WERK No 151
BESTEKTEKENING: GEVELS en DOORSNEDEN
BLAD No 21

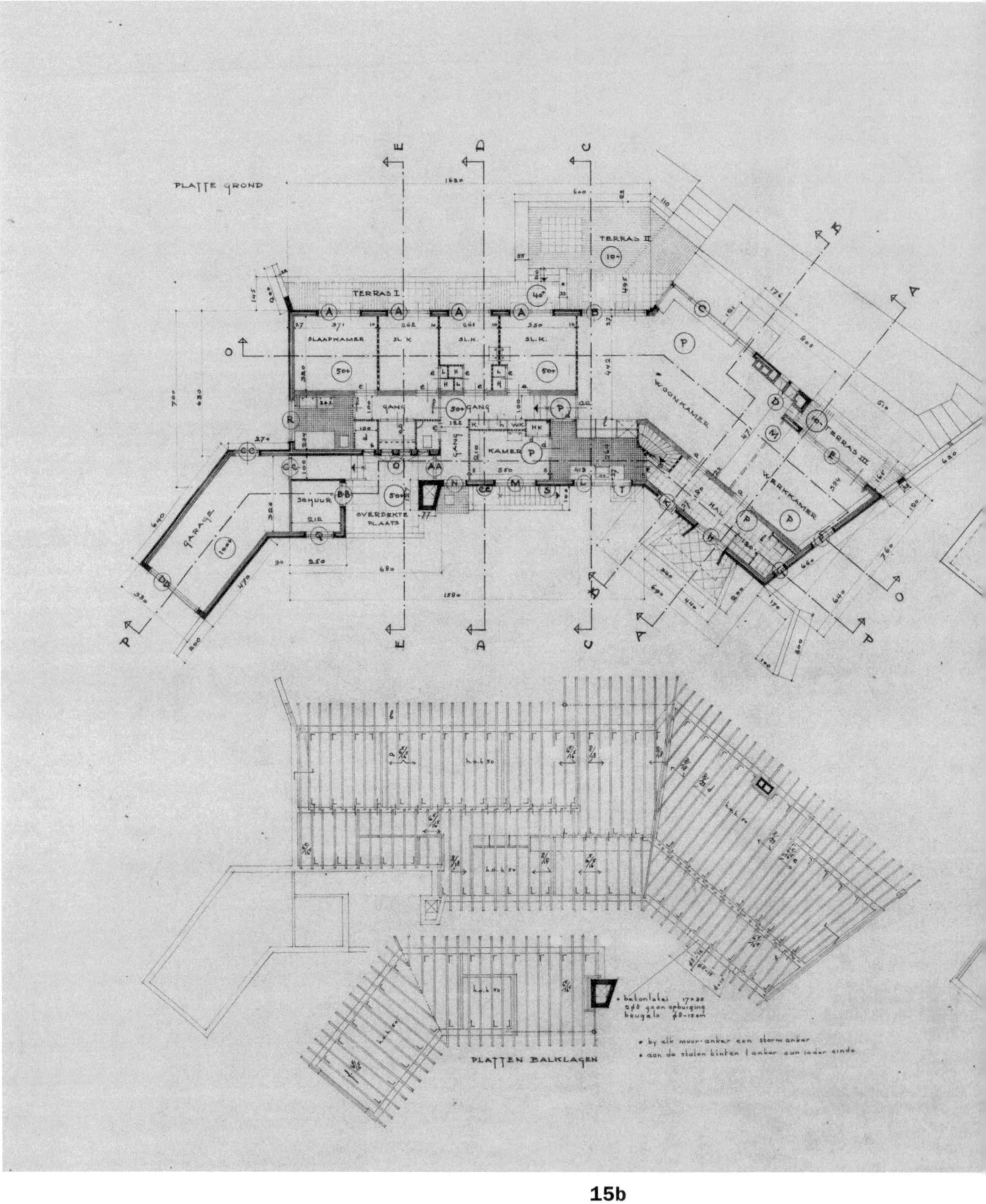
PLATTE GROND
TERRAS I
TERRAS II
TERRAS III
SLAAPKAMER
SL.K.
GANG
KAMER
WOONKAMER
WERKKAMER
HAL
SCHUUR
OVERDEKTE PLAATS
GARAGE
PLATTEN BALKLAGEN
• by elk muur-anker een stormanker
• aan de stalen binten 1 anker aan ieder einde

15b

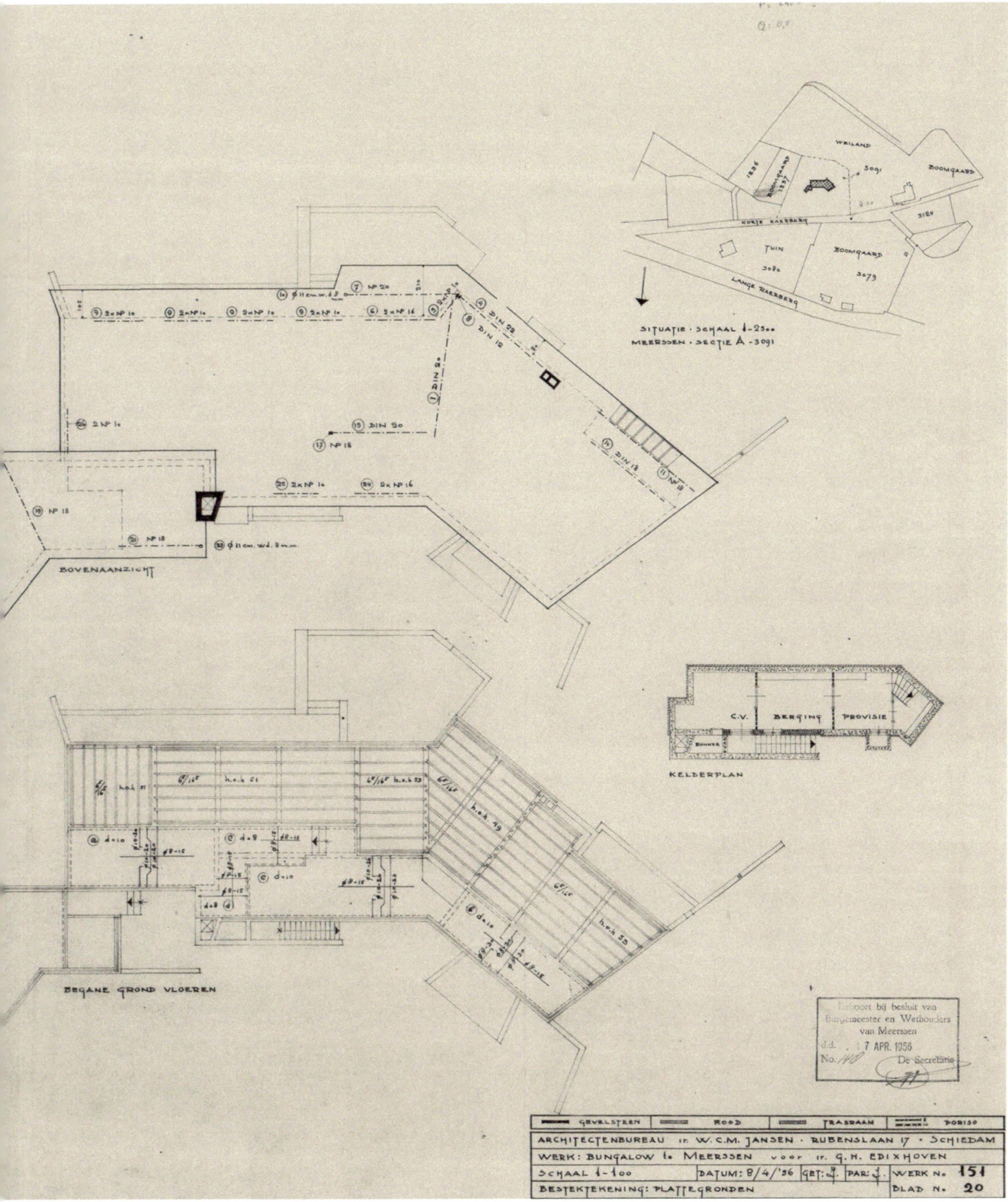
WEILAND
BOOMGAARD
3091
KORTE RAARBERG
TUIN
3080
BOOMGAARD
3079
LANGE RAARBERG
SITUATIE · SCHAAL 1-2500
MEERSSEN · SECTIE A-3091
BOVENAANZICHT
C.V.
BERGING
PROVISIE
KELDERPLAN
BEGANE GROND VLOEREN
Behoort bij besluit van
Burgemeester en Wethouders
van Meerssen
d.d. 17 APR. 1956
No. 148
De Secretaris
GEVELSTEEN
ROOD
TRASRAAM
DORISO
ARCHITECTENBUREAU ir. W. C.M. JANSEN · RUBENSLAAN 17 · SCHIEDAM
WERK: BUNGALOW te MEERSSEN voor ir. G.H. EDIXHOVEN
SCHAAL 1-100
DATUM: 8/4/'56
WERK No. 151
BESTEKTEKENING: PLATTEGRONDEN
BLAD No. 20

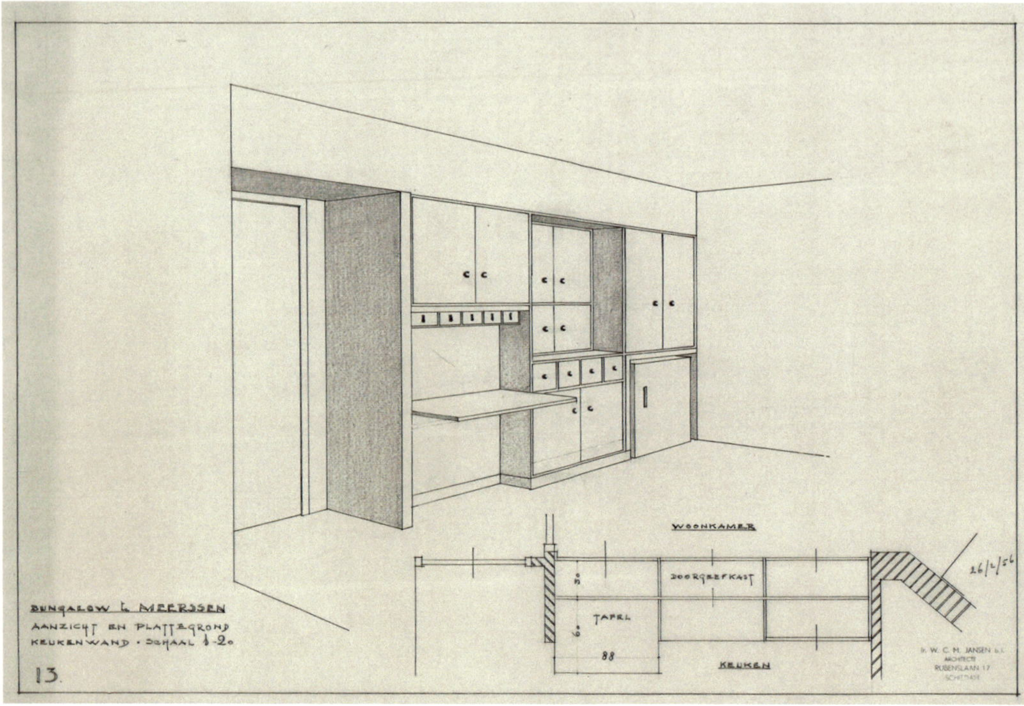

16a

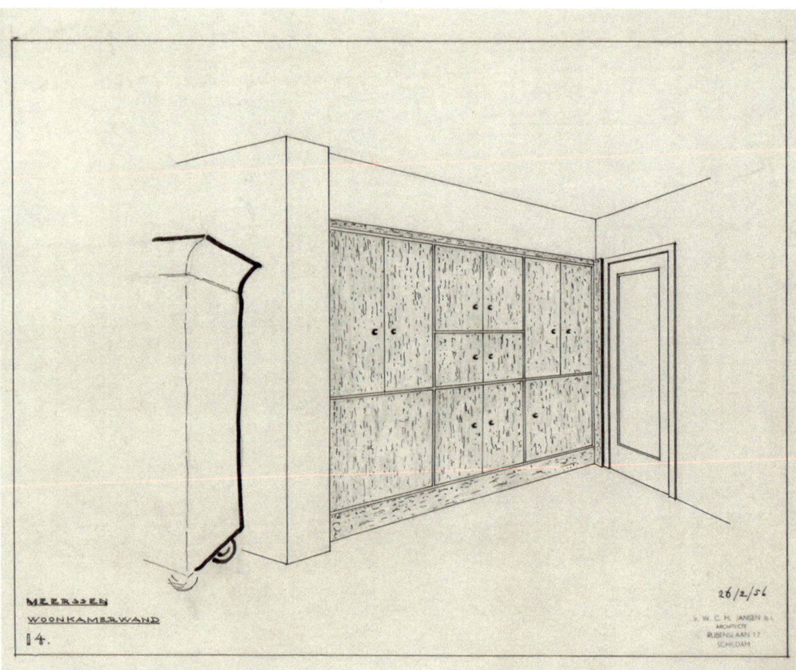

16b

16a W.C.M. Jansen, the kitchen side of the cupboard wall, showing the location of the 'pass-through' cupboard, 1956.

16b W.C.M. Jansen, living room cupboard wall, 1956.

17 The design of the living room by Wil Jansen with, next to the fireplace, three windows offering views of the undulating landscape, undated.

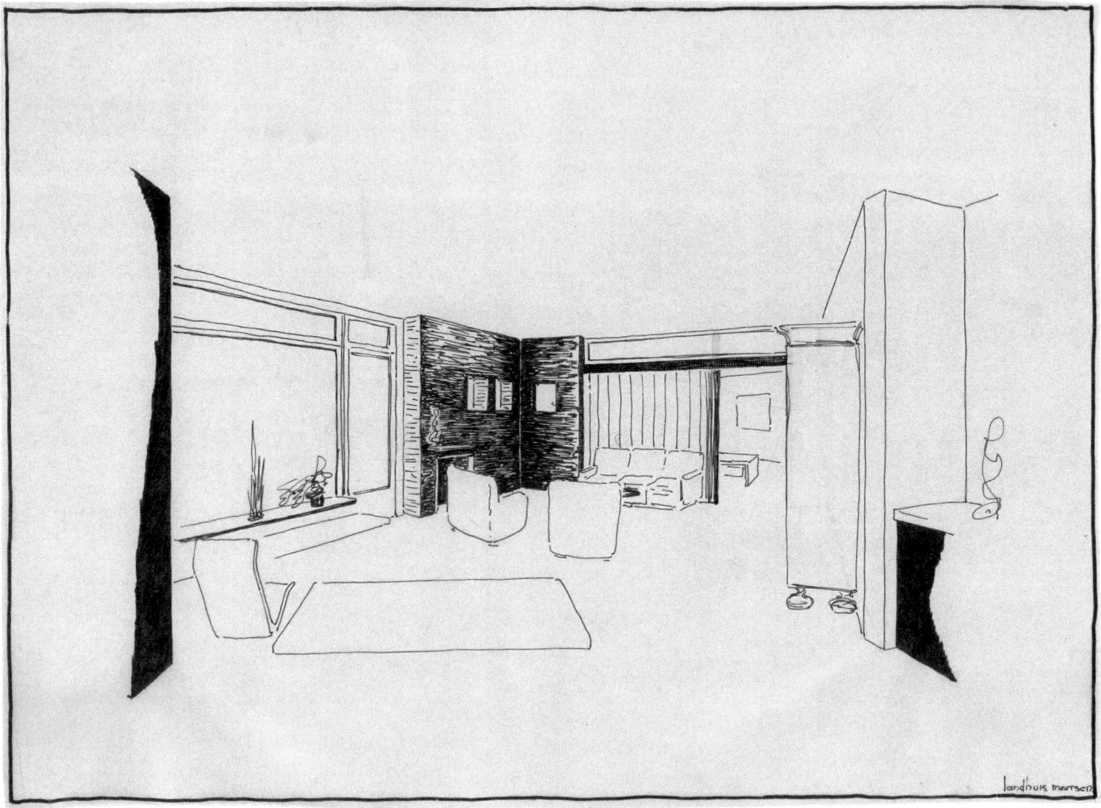

17

18a

18b

18a Front view of bungalow in Meerssen, 2019.

18b The back view overlooking the undulating landscape of Limburg.

18c The three little windows beside the fireplace have remained intact.

18c

19

appearance of the front facade stands in contrast to the glass walls at the back, providing optimal daylight access and a great view of the garden to the south.

Patronage from Limburg

Wil Jansen's commission from her brother-in-law to design a bungalow was not an isolated incident. Wil's oldest sister Ida married Edixhoven, a widower, on 15 January 1930.[127] A mining engineer by profession, he graduated from the TH in Delft and was immediately employed by the Laura en Vereeniging mining company in the town of Eygelshoven, in southern Limburg. In 1933, he was appointed chief engineer in charge of technical management.[128] (A street in Eygelshoven was later named after him: Edixhovenstraat.) In the early years of Wil's architecture practice, Edixhoven arranged various commissions for her. In 1937, based on his recommendation, she was commissioned to design the layout of the grounds around the Julia Mine that opened in 1926, the second coalmine following the Laura Mine. The coloured designs depict a large building complex surrounded entirely by greenery **[fig. 19]**.[129] Edixhoven had to defend the plan to the managing board, which objected to the plans

19 Design by Wil Jansen for the site layout of the Julia Mine in Eygelshoven, 1937.

for high trees that would block the view of the building complex.[130] The exchange of letters shows that Edixhoven had full confidence in his sister-in-law. Jansen herself was adamant that her design was complete as is, stating that the 'high trees (...) were an essential factor' and '[were] in a sense the building elements which achieved that spatial effect'.[131] Moreover, the planting scheme was designed to 'reinforce the architectural impact of the buildings'. This is one of the few remaining examples of Jansen's own views on her work. To put more pressure on the managing board, Edixhoven urged his sister-in-law to come up with the lists of plants for her design, so some of the planting could start already. These lists meant that the supplying plant grower had 'quite a lot to figure out'; he had to spend 'a Sunday afternoon on (...) puzzling the whole thing out'.[132] It has not been possible to confirm whether the design was implemented, but considering Edixhoven's determination to push the plan through, it does seem likely.

The project may not have been a dream job for Jansen, as an architectural engineer, but considering the challenging economic climate, she must have been happy to accept the work, and grateful that her brother-in-law had made the effort on her behalf. In those days, a number of women were starting to work in garden architecture. Girls from affluent families could pursue secondary education in garden design at the Middelbare Tuinbouwschool Voor Meisjes Huis te Lande, founded in 1907 in Rijswijk. Working with plants, flowers and the colour charts that often accompanied them seemed like a good occupation for women. In the period up to the Second World War, about twenty women were active in garden architecture. Although she had not been trained in the field, the topic did capture Jansen's interest. Her archive contained carefully filed cuttings, leaflets and notes on flowers, plants and gardens, as well as related topics such as 'colours and paints', birds and 'farming'.[133] Jansen's love of nature is also evidenced by her later membership of the executive board of the Stichting Natuurbescherming ('Nature Conservation Foundation') in Schiedam.[134] It was undoubtedly based on that background that she co-signed the objection to the plans to build a cultural centre in the Plantage, a historic city garden in Schiedam that had been redesigned in 1829 by Jan Zocher (1791–1870).[135]

In 1939 and 1940, Jansen received various commissions from the municipality of Eygelshoven for installing urban green spaces. She frequently met with the various municipal officials, including the mayor, to discuss these projects. Edixhoven must have played a role here, too. Jansen designed various city gardens, for instance on Schaesbergerweg, Bergeikstraat, Gulikstraat and the incline along Marialaan, as well as the gardens of the Mariakapel and the Roman Catholic housekeeping school.[136] The landscaping, which was carried out by unemployed youth, was delayed in some places by the installation of military reinforcements in view of the threat of impending war.[137] Jansen also provided planting schemes for the Roman Catholic cemetery on Rimburgerweg.[138] The various projects involved a wagonload of 13,000 kilos of 'living crops' delivered by the Nederlandsche Sierteelt Centrale, a horticultural supplier.[139] Some of these green spaces in Eygelshoven still exist: the garden of the Mariakapel, the slope along Marialaan and a small city garden on Bergeikstraat.

20 Unsigned design by Wil Jansen for twelve drive-in dwellings with gardens in Heerlen, 1938.

Jansen was also involved in plans for redesigning the grounds of the former 'Herman' lignite quarry located beside the cemetery. Herman Jansen (the names are coincidental) had previously held a concession to mine lignite from the quarry.[140] It was used as a raw material for the family's bottle factory in Schiedam. Jansen came up with sketches for the site as a recreational area with a rowing pond.[141] However, the municipality decided not to move forward with the project, for unknown reasons.[142] The area is now used as natural burial grounds.

In the period leading up to and in the early days of the Second World War, Jansen received various commissions from the southern parts of the Netherlands, including Heerlen. Her sister Ida, who had lived there before marrying Edixhoven, may have facilitated these contacts.[143] However, Jansen's family in Schiedam also linked her to Jos Klijnen (1887–1973),

Oct. 1938
SCHAESBERGERWEG · HEERLEN

21

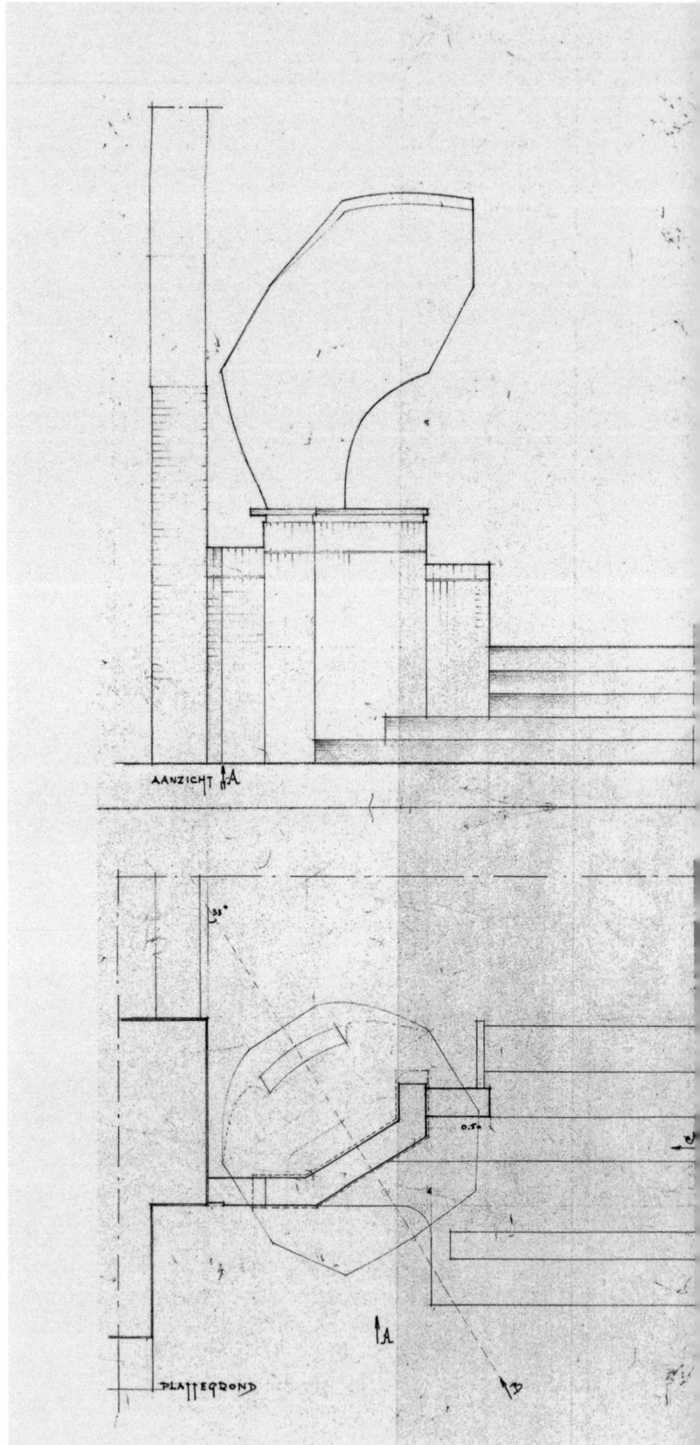

21 Design of a pulpit for the John the Baptist Church in Eygelshoven by Wil Jansen, 1936.

NZICHT B
AANZICHT C
1.50
1.00
1.00
0.85
DOORSNEDE over de AS
ONTWERP voor een PREEKSTOEL
voor de KERK te EYGELSHOVEN
SCHAAL 1-20

an architect and urban designer based in The Hague.[144] Klijnen had been commissioned to design an expansion plan for Heerlen. That was where Jansen built what was probably her first houses, in a series of twelve, with adjoining gardens **[fig. 20]**.[145] The houses were built 2.5 metres above street level, giving the owners access to a street-level garage placed under the living space. This new type of housing, also referred to as a drive-in dwelling, was designed to eliminate motor vehicles from the roadside.

Jansen came up with garden designs for various freestanding villas in Heerlen and Someren, and designed a series of seven gardens in Eindhoven.[146] The way she signed her designs shows her sense of growing professional renown. For the first time, we encounter not just her first and last names, but signatures including her titles, such as: 'Ir. W.C.M. Jansen, architectural engineer and architect'.[147]

Before Jansen was hired to design the grounds of the Julia Mine in 1937, and started focusing on landscape architecture, she designed a pulpit for the John the Baptist Church in Eygelshoven, with a particularly striking sounding board **[fig. 21]**.[148] She based her design on a sketch (presumably her own), based in turn on a photo of the parabolic reflector in the St. Egbert church in Almelo.[149] The church in Eygelshoven was built in 1922 to accommodate the huge population surge brought about by the coal industry. The church building was designed in expressionist style by architect duo Alphons Boosten (1893–1951) and Jos Ritzen (1896–1961) and unleashed furious criticism in the conservative congregation.[150]

When the church opened its doors, its interior was still incomplete. The organ could not be purchased until sufficient funds were raised from collection drives and jumble sales from the old 'Kleine Kerkje' (little church) that had previously served as the parish church.[151] The pulpit was also provided on temporary loan. In 1936, the year of Jansen's pulpit design, when the new church installed its stained-glass windows, Jansen's pulpit was probably also built. Ritzen and Boosten were no longer available for such projects. They had ended their partnership during the years of financial crisis, and Ritzen had had a busy practice in Antwerp for some time by that point.[152] Jansen's pulpit can be seen on old photos, but without the sounding board. This may have been because it obstructed the view of the preacher from the girls' chapel. Although Jansen's archive includes sketches of kneeling chairs, a prayer tool and a baptismal font, no information is available about their finished form **[fig. 22]**.[153]

Jansen's involvement in the church interior was presumably also arranged thanks to a recommendation by Edixhoven. It is very likely that he was living right next to the church at that time, in the chief engineer's residence at Sint Janstraat 15. The residence (1925), which is also a national heritage site, was part of a complex of official city houses, built on commission from Laura en Vereeniging.[154] Edixhoven also became

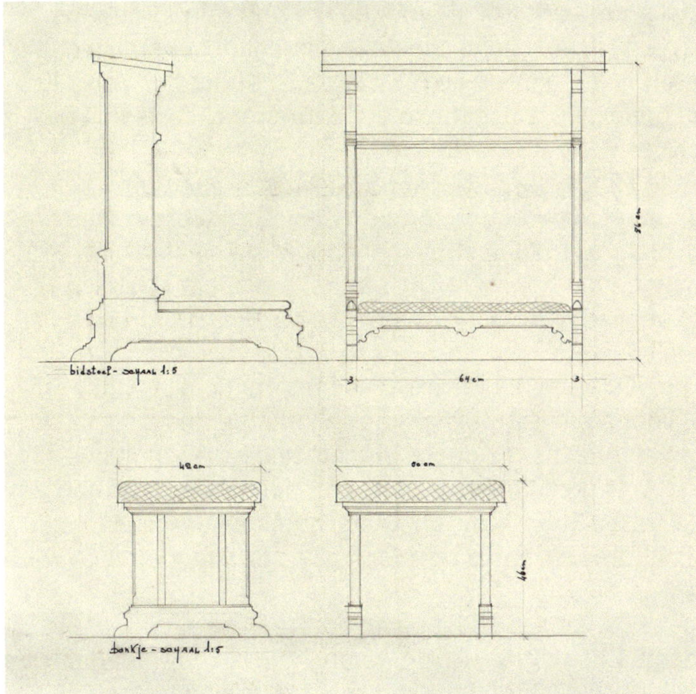

22

22 Design of a kneeling chair by Wil Jansen.

Jansen's direct client. She designed an interior and a bay window extension for him, for an unknown residence in Eygelshoven.[155] After his promotion in 1947 to managing director of Laura en Vereeniging, Edixhoven moved to a house on Rimburgerweg, beside the aforementioned cemetery, occupying the director's residence commissioned by his employer.[156] The floor plan found in Jansen's archive of this double director's villa, designed by Brussels-based architect Ernest Jaspar (1876–1940), includes several notes that could indicate a renovation for which Edixhoven consulted his sister-in-law.[157] Less than a decade later, he asked her to design the bungalow in Meerssen where he and Ida would live.

It is self-evident that Edixhoven had full confidence in his sister-in-law. Could this be because they had both studied in Delft? In any case, Edixhoven ensured that Wil was able to gain practical experience and build up a portfolio of orders. This would be foundational for her post-war career.

Developing an architectural style

The fact that Jansen was a modern woman in terms of personal development was already clear from her lifestyle. Her traditional family viewed her as a modern and progressive woman who knew what she wanted, not least because of her sense of independence and remarkable choice of profession.[158] In describing the development of her architectural style, we cannot rely in any way on her own writings about her views, perspectives and principles, since these are entirely lacking from her personal archive.

In any case, in the final year of her studies, Jansen must have encountered modernist architecture through the international course organized by architecture students. Her subsequent stay in Paris in 1931 undoubtedly expanded her horizons. The station project at Le Havre introduced her to applied knowledge of modern building materials, such as reinforced concrete.

Jansen soon proved her ability to express her practical insights in a functionalist floor plan. Early examples include the design competition for an architect's residence and study discussed above, and the design that was presumably intended for her brother's cardboard factory, its form dictated entirely by functional and logistical insights. These were her first forays towards developing her own modernist architectural style.

Starting in late 1933, Jansen spent some time in Groningen working with architect George Ros (1895–1956).[159] Very little is known about this architect. In 1929 he built the Ter Schouw-Van Sanen guesthouse.[160] Several blueprints were produced by Jansen in a series for the 'plan Geuzenkamp', a building project involving residential flats in the south-east of Groningen.[161] The designs show variations on floor plans and facades for an angled three-storey building block with five-room and six-room flats accessed through a shared entrance, located on the south side of Waldeck Pyrmontstraat. The block of flats looks like a cube without any decorative elements, with bold vertical and horizontal accents on the facade. The question is whether Ros gave her the room to create her own designs, or merely allowed her to produce design drawings.[162] If she did receive that room, her modernist facade designs were probably considered a step too far: the block of flats was built with a facade that included bay windows. Ros had used the same technique in a previous building block (1927) at Koninginnelaan 43, which is reminiscent of the Amsterdam School. Jansen's archive also contained a series of floor plans and facade designs for a housing and office complex at the corner of Gedempte Zuiderdiep and Herestraat in Groningen.[163] These facades also had a modern design, in the same style as the RVS building. In the end, Ros was not hired to build the complex.[164]

Utilitarian buildings, which comprised most of the projects that Jansen did for her brothers' factories, did not allow her to express her stylistic principles. These projects often involved renovations and structural adaptations that required her architectural insight. In the 1950s, she designed a modern look for several factory facades. For an external client, public limited company Nederlandsche Kantoorboekenfabriek Van 't Hoff & Jongepier, located at Westvest 38-40 in Schiedam, she designed a new facade, stripped of the roof decorations and countless arched windows and transformed into a sober front facade with horizontal and vertical accentuations **[fig. 23]**.[165] However, a different architect ended up building the new facade, using a more conservative design.[166]

Jansen's stylistic development took place mainly in residential construction, peaking in the 1950s with the construction of the RVS building in Rotterdam and the bungalow she designed for her sister and brother-in-law in Meerssen. Her modern architectural views and functionalist principles were expressed best in these projects, manifesting in her work as an architect of the Modern Movement. The early houses in Heerlen were applications of a modern typology: the drive-in dwelling. It is interesting to note that Jansen also designed several traditional country homes around the same time, presumably expressing the preferences and tastes of her commissioning clients. However, the designs were not built, for unknown reasons.[167]

Jansen continued designing renovations for the homes of family, friends, acquaintances and other commissioning clients all across the Netherlands until well into the 1960s, primarily utilizing her functionalist insights.[168] For example, she came up with several designs for home offices and private practices for doctors and other professionals. She also designed modern furniture and fireplaces.

Interestingly, Jansen also viewed her own professional practice as modernist. In a letter to clients who were personal friends of hers, regarding renovation of an attic room for their son, she wrote: 'As you have surely noticed, the structure of this plan is based on modern insights.'[169] She used terms like 'working and sleeping section', 'good spatial structure', 'spatial effect' and 'practical'.

Her professional life ended at the age of 67, when she decided to spend regular intervals with her sister Pop in the Spanish town of Altea, in a new bungalow that they commissioned. Interestingly, she hired an architect to build their bungalow in Spain.[170]

Did Jansen receive the professional renown that she deserved?

As one of the first woman architectural engineers in the Netherlands, Wil Jansen managed to develop a career as an independent architect. Initially, her portfolio of orders came in through her family. They not only gave her commissions in the early years of her professional practice, but continued to hire her throughout the course of her career. Her clientele gradually expanded to include friends and other clients.

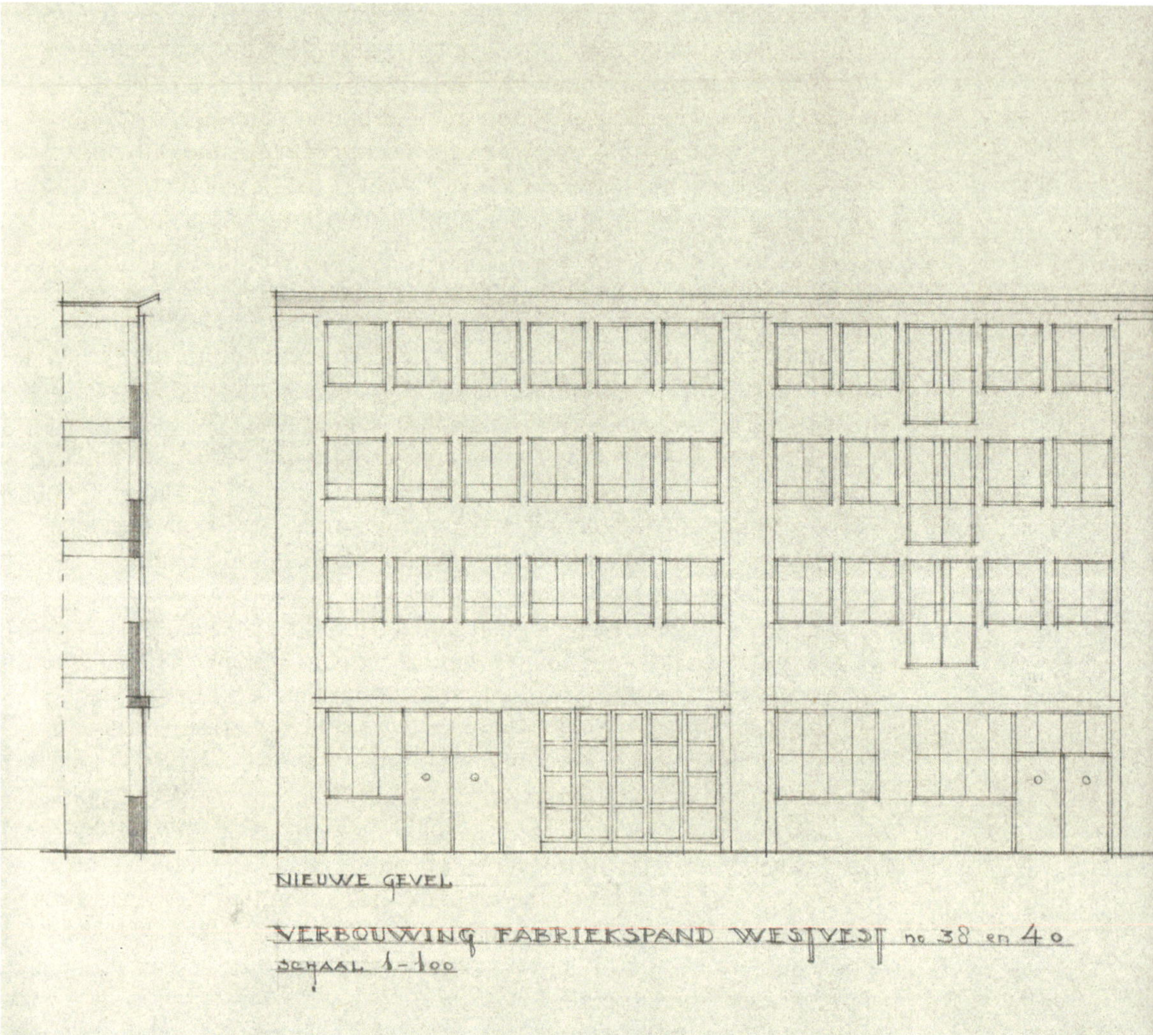
NIEUWE GEVEL
VERBOUWING FABRIEKSPAND WESTVEST no 38 en 40
SCHAAL 1-100

23

23 W.C.M. Jansen, design of a new facade for the Van 't Hoff & Jongepier office supply factory in Schiedam, 1954. The decorative elements on the roof and the arch windows have been replaced by a sleek, minimalist facade.

Jansen's studies at the Technische Hoogeschool (TH) gave her very limited exposure to modern architecture. During the post-WWII reconstruction period, through her membership of the Women's Advisory Committee (VAC) in Rotterdam, she encountered issues related to housing construction, public housing and architectural design; these years were highly formative. Jansen developed a building style based on the modernist, functionalist views of the Modern Movement, which was increasingly popular in the Netherlands. As a woman architect, she left her own marks on her designs by applying practical and housekeeping insights. Although her architectural insights took precedence in the projects she did for her brothers' companies, her stylistic development flourished in housing construction. In that line, the RVS building can be considered her most successful and prominent architectural accomplishment.

The fact that Jansen was a woman architect must have been at least partly why many of the commissions in her early years were limited to designing and structuring gardens, city squares and cemeteries. When she submitted an entry to a design competition, she did not mention her gender – and with good reason, since she might otherwise have been denied an honourable mention. Her interior designs were requested not only by private homeowners, but also by off-licenses. Her retail liquor certificate served her well on those projects. Designing the RVS building gave Jansen the ultimate chance, at the age of 54, to prove herself as a woman architect.

Although a limited number of newly built homes were based on her designs, her portfolio of orders remained well-filled until her pension in 1971, with various projects all across the Netherlands. It is surprising that the RVS building did not bring her the widespread renown that she may have hoped for. However, she must still have been proud of completing such a project, as one of the first woman architectural engineers in the Netherlands.

8 Architect couples

'So I'll have to make compromises; this will be demanding of course, with a family of 4 children.'
Jan Kammer-Kret

'He wanted to have me on the same level.'
Koos Pot-Keegstra

Of the 21 qualified architects in the Netherlands in the first half of the twentieth century, seven married an architect. They met their future husbands during their studies or married their employer. Joop (Johanna) Ferguson (1900–1982), who graduated from the Technische Hogeschool ('Technical College') in Delft in 1926, emigrated to Johannesburg, where she and her third husband ran an architecture firm, later called Ferguson, Stakesby-Lewis, & Sayce.[1] Ada Kuiper-Struyk, who graduated from Delft in 1937, became a politician.[2] Her husband was part of the architecture office Kuiper, Gouwetor and De Ranitz, which played an important role in the post-war reconstruction of Rotterdam. As the VVD (People's Party for Freedom and Democracy) spokesperson in parliament for policy on public housing, transport and water management, she campaigned to tackle the post-war housing shortage.

This chapter focuses on the five women who, together with their husbands, ran their own architecture offices in the Netherlands. These women architects, not all of them well-known, turn out to have produced a noteworthy and interesting body of work, both typologically and stylistically, especially during the years of post-war reconstruction. Non-residential construction was no less a part of their portfolio as, more obviously, housing. In that latter sector, they profited from their household insights and practical acumen by designing efficient floor plans and modern layouts with new, easy-to-clean materials.

In the area of private residences in particular – including their own houses –, retirement homes and schools, they applied the ideas of the Dutch modernist architecture movement known as 'het Nieuwe Bouwen'. This functionalist-oriented, sleek and sober architecture had nothing to do with female connotations such as elegant, graceful and decorative design. Nor did the new, rational style of building seem obvious in view of the education they had enjoyed. In the early 1930s, students at the faculty of architecture at the TH in Delft scarcely came into contact with the modern architecture views that were gaining currency at the time.[3]

The husbands of these five women were reputable architects. Were the qualified women architects successful in their own right or was that down to the name and fame of their husbands? If cooperation really was the case, on what model was it based?

Archives at Het Nieuwe Instituut (HNI) in Rotterdam were consulted in the cases of Koos Pot-Keegstra and Lotte Stam-Beese, both of whom completed their studies at the Voortgezet en Hooger Bouwkunst Onderricht ('Secondary and Higher Architectural Training', shortened to VHBO) in Amsterdam.[4] The publicity-oriented couple Pot-Keegstra not only gave interviews to daily newspaper but also wrote articles in professional journals.[5] Stam-Beese also did the latter. Two monographs about her appeared after her death.[6] To date, little was known about the three other women in the research group, all of whom graduated as architectural engineers from Delft.[7] In these cases, archival research and contact with surviving relatives formed part of the research. Thanks to a rare interview and personal accounts of her working activities, an impression could be formed of the oeuvre of Toki Lammers-Koeleman, whose work and that of her husband was always published under both of their names.[8]

This chapter is thematically organized. The first part presents a general overview of the architect couples and their shared practices and places them in time. Then their models of cooperation, along with the way in which the women architects were able form their own architectural views, are discussed. These are elaborated on the basis of a selection of their work.

Crisis and post-war reconstruction

While most of the architects in this study group were limited in the early phase of their careers by the poor economic conditions caused by the stock market crash of 1929, followed by uncertainty in the lead-up to the war, reconstruction plans were already being drawn up during the war years. These turned out to form the prelude to successful practices for the architect couples. Not only did heavily ravaged cities need reconstructing, but war damage throughout the country needed to be repaired, new buildings erected, and the housing shortage alleviated. Over the course of the 1950s and 1960s, cities grew, as did demand for homes as well as schools, churches, shops, banks and industrial buildings.

A year after graduating from the TH in 1931, Jan Kret married Harry Kammer (1902–1988). The couple settled in Schiebroek, with an architecture practice attached to their home.[9] Since graduating from Delft in 1929, Kammer had worked for the architecture firm

Brinkman and Van der Vlugt. That he and his wife set up their own practice during the crisis years was partly in response to the limited career opportunities for her at the time. Married women were excluded from government jobs, but opening an architecture practice together could enhance Jan's career. In the pre-war years in particular, she worked on her own projects as well as on projects jointly with her husband. During the war, their office was already involved in post-war reconstruction plans for Rotterdam. Over time, family matters demanded more and more attention, and Jan essentially became an advisor to her husband **[fig. 1]**.[10]

Shortly after graduating from Delft in 1940, Toki Koeleman married her employer, Hendrik Lammers (1909–1990), who had graduated as an architectural engineer in 1936 and ran his own practice in Arnhem, where she temporarily carried out work.[11] In 1944 the couple won a competition with their joint design for a canteen for the Koninklijke Stoomweverij (Royal Steam Weaving Mill) in Nijverdal. This weaving mill became a major client. Besides running his own practice at home after the war, Lammers took over at the helm of the Arnhem City Plan Office, charged with the reconstruction of the totally ravaged city.[12] The couple remained childless and Toki devoted her entire working life to her own commissions, consisting for the most part of housing.

Koos Keegstra and Joop Pot met during their studies at the VHBO in Amsterdam, where Koos became the first woman to complete the course in 1935.[13] They opened their own architecture office after marrying in 1938. During the war they were already working together on reconstruction projects. After the war the couple focused mainly on school and housing design, the latter varying from private residences to expansion districts in the form of residential neighbourhoods in, among others, Enschede, Diemen, Amersfoort and the western garden suburbs of Amsterdam. And for the last of those cities, the successful architect couple took on the task in 1967 of designing a penitentiary, later known as the Bijlmerbajes.

After graduating from Delft in 1934, Jeanne van Rijswijk spent half a year drawing at the Wassenaar office of Albert van Rood (1885–1947), whom she married that same year.[14] Van Rood, both a civil engineer and an architectural engineer, was a leading architect of industrial schemes.[15] He designed the entire industrial complex for Koninklijke Nederlandsche Hoogovens en Staalfabrieken (the steel producer currently called Tata Steel) in IJmuiden. Jeanne was only indirectly involved in the practice until Van Rood died. She kept the office going, initially with the current projects for Hoogovens, Mekog (Coke Oven Gas Exploitation Company) in Velsen and the rebuilding of the Noord-Brabant Leather Factory in Rijen. Jeanne died at the age of 55.[16]Lotte Beese occupies a somewhat different position among this group of women architects. She married the architect

1

Mart Stam in 1934. The couple opened the design office 'Stam en Beese architecten' in Amsterdam and entered into a temporary partnership with colleagues Willem van Tijen and Hugh Maaskant (1907–1977) for projects that included the construction of drive-in homes in Amsterdam.[17] Lotte and Mart separated after nine years. In 1945, Stam-Beese obtained her VHBO diploma in Architecture and developed into a respected urban designer.

Models of cooperation

It would be logical to assume that, after completing their studies in architecture, the women architectural engineers, if they wanted to work at an architecture office, would seek a full position there in the form of an association with architects already in employment. However, this was unthinkable in view of the prevailing social opinions and the male-dominated environment that architecture practice simply was at the time. But if a woman architect married a male architect, the possibility of opening a practice jointly did present itself. The unqualified Margaret Staal-Kropholler described it as follows: 'Before the competence of women can be recognized in architecture, they must first have an opportunity to demonstrate performance. A partnership with a man (who can provide that) offers just such an excellent opportunity.'[18] What exact the man could 'provide' is not clear, but her message does illustrate the views of the day.

1 Jan Kammer-Kret later became an advisor to her husband Harry.

Could these women develop a career within their own architecture practice? Was it a case of collaboration between partners based on equality? Can any specific division of tasks be discerned?

It comes as no surprise that the household affairs and upbringing tasks influenced the role of the women architects within the architecture practices. Most of the practices were attached to the home, making the mingling of family matters, household duties and work activities obvious. When the – unmarried! – architectural engineer Wil Jansen was asked whether she thought that the profession of architect was compatible with a family, she answered: 'Yes, certainly, unless you are in full employment somewhere, can't the drawing work be done at home?'[19] Although there was usually no shortage of household help or nannies, the care and attention for the family sometimes weighed heavier than the work, as in the previously-mentioned case of Jan Kammer-Kret. In response to a survey of the work of women architectural engineers, she wrote in 1951 to Staal-Kropholler: 'Unfortunately, I did less architecture than ever! Yet I'm extremely occupied trying to simplify my household to free up time! And by chance, I recently received a commission to design a doctor's residence by the sea! So I'll have to make compromises; this demands energy, with a family of 4 children (aged 15, 12, 5 and 2½).'[20]

Emancipated spouses

In the first year of their joint architectural careers, Harry and Jan Kammer-Kret took part in a design competition for a village church and rectory in Groningen. Such competitions offered starting and/or unemployed architects an opportunity to gain experience and, in the event of a good assessment, the chance to earn some money and a measure of fame. Jan and Harry each worked on their individual competition entries in separate spaces.[21] Jan took second prize and a sum of 75 guilders with her design entitled 'Rest', thanks to her practical floor plans and sober architecture, which, according to the jury, 'was distinguished in character' **[fig. 2]**.[22] That marked the start of an emancipated partnership.

A number of surviving design sketches for a Montessori school (1936) in Schiebroek give an interesting indication of the nature of their collaboration before there were any children. Most of the drawings bear the official signature 'Ir. H. Kammer b.i. Ir. J. Kammer-Kret b.i. Architecten Schiebroek', but the initials vary.[23] For example, some drawings are signed by an unknown individual and 'seen' by 'JKK' [Jan Kammer-Kret]; signed by 'JK' [Jan Kammer?] and signed by 'HK' [Harry Kammer]; signed by 'HK' and seen by 'JKK'. The last of these is interesting because it shows that drawings made by Harry were also reviewed and signed by Jan. This indicates an equal partnership. Architect Han van Loghem lauded in an article 'the collaboration of ingenuity and feeling of husband and wife Kammer-Kret'.[24]

The close collaboration between the couple also involved their joint visits to construction sites and evening discussions about design sketches at the dining table.[25] Despite household help and a live-in nanny, Kammer-Kret eventually chose for the upbringing of the four children in preference to operational tasks within the office.[26] She put this choice down in part to her individualist nature, which prevented her from working with others. By that she was referring to the assistants working in the office, whose number had increased after the war as a result of the growing portfolio of commissions. Kammer-Kret essentially became an advisor to her husband. In the evenings at the table she drew sketches as a way of offering advice and giving instructions about, for example, the positioning of windows.

2 The design, published in *Bouwkundig Weekblad Architectura*, for a village church with the motto 'Rest', with which Kammer-Kret won second prize.

The husband-and-wife Van Rood-van Rijswijk fled to London during the Second World War, where Van Rood became an advisor to the Dutch government in exile on the subject of military emergency homes.[27] Jeanne became Head of the Public Housing Division at the Department of the Interior, where she occupied herself with preparations for Dutch housing after the liberation.[28] Here she worked with her husband, who also acted as an advisor to the division. Immediately upon their return to the Netherlands after the end of the war, Jeanne became, as she herself

2

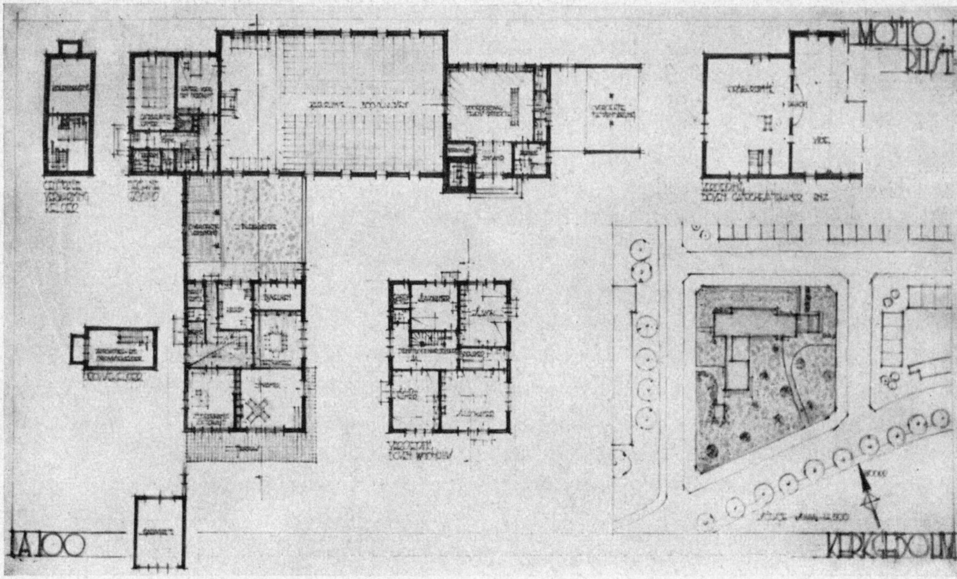

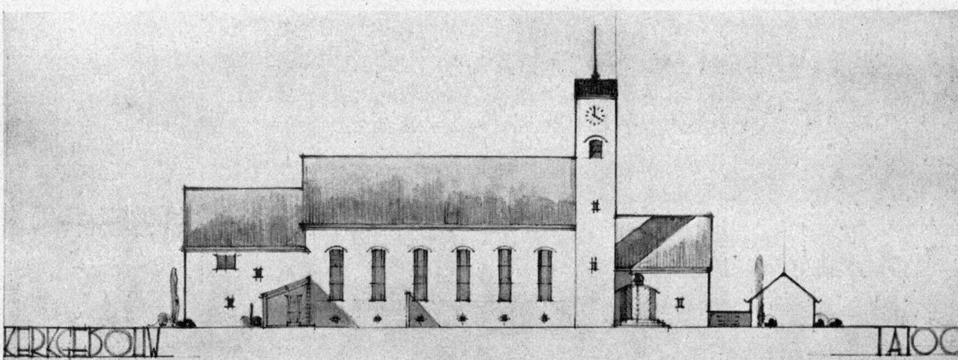

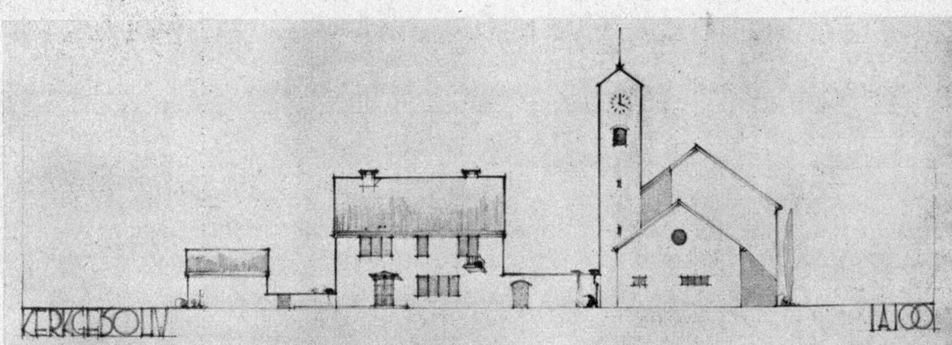

wrote, 'a housewife again'.[29] She limited herself to following Van Rood's work and lent a helping hand by drawing during busy periods. Ironically, her architecture career only flourished after the death of her husband, when she continued the practice.

Toki Lammers-Koeleman and Koos Pot-Keegstra were, like Jan Kammer-Kret, married to emancipated men. Toki and her husband viewed each other as colleagues and bore joint responsibility for the busy practice, which employed numerous draughtsmen, site foremen, secretaries and stenographers.[30] Toki was scarcely involved in management affairs. Much later, she defined her position on a questionnaire as 'Director partner office 1945–1979', with as activity 'Designing and building'.[31] In an interview in which she looked back on her career, she expressed the view that working alongside a husband did make it easier to practise the profession. She assumed, for example, that clients, contractors and construction workers with whom she conducted site meetings accepted her as a woman architect because they knew there was a man present somewhere in the background.[32]

The husband-and-wife Lammers-Koeleman never worked on the same design. The decision to attach both of their names to their projects in publications is striking. Within their emancipated collaboration, the professional field in which each of them specialized was less surprising: Hendrik concentrated on utility buildings, while Toki mostly dealt with housing. The reason she gave for this was that she did not feel drawn to 'that technical side'.[33] Retrospectively, she summarized her career and the collaboration with her husband as 'everything that a woman architectural engineer could wish for'.[34]In the case of Koos and Joop Pot-Keegstra, there was also no question of competition. Indeed, while Koos indicated that she enjoyed housekeeping and found the combination with work very tough, Joop wanted to continue involving her in the work. 'I was a support to him of course. He wanted to have me on the same level', she said in an interview.[35] An architecture practice attached to the home, designed by both of them in 1954, was a precondition for Joop: '(...) otherwise I'll never get my wife out of the kitchen.'[36] That resulted in an enduring collaboration and a large oeuvre, in which they went a step further than Lammers-Koeleman: they developed everything together, to such an extent that they could not say who had done what.

Thanks to the earlier collaboration with the architects Van Tijen and Maaskant, husband-and-wife Stam-Beese worked on a number of substantial projects during the crisis years, with Lotte focusing on interior design aspects.[37] The other activities of the couple consisted mainly of exhibition and competition designs. Details of the exact division of tasks are unknown. In an interview, Stam-Beese said of the collaboration with her husband that she sat at the drawing board while he conducted the meetings.[38] Hanneke Oosterhof's conclusion in her monograph that Stam-Beese's work was largely on the production side therefore seems hastily drawn. After all, it says nothing about the division of tasks. Stam-Beese could have been working creatively at the drawing board. In a letter to Lotte in 1935, when he spent some time in Germany, Mart wrote that he missed 'a schematic work rhythm' with her and that he wished she would take up her place *beside* him at the drawing board.[39] Moreover, he wanted their work not to be by either him or her exclusively. This, at least, indicates a desire for a closer and more equal cooperation with Lotte than had been the case.

Was she looking for a form of competition in order to develop herself? The designs that she completed under her own name during that period were mostly graphic and furniture designs, for which she had taken (but not completed) a course at the Bauhaus. It is even more interesting to note that an architectural design from 1939 for a residential building for working women in Amsterdam bears a different signature: 'Architekten Stam-Beese' instead of 'Stam en Beese architecten'.[40] It raises the question of whether it was Lotte who had taken control of this project on account of the specific target group of residents. In light of the previous remarks concerning their collaboration, could it be that Lotte did not allow her husband to work on this project with her? The design appears nowhere in the literature on Stam's work. The residential commission eventually went to husband- and-wife Pot-Keegstra. It is entirely possible that Stam-Beese, who has been described as a self-willed individual, sought ways like this to shape her own career path within the architecture practice.[41] It is noteworthy that she kept the name Stam-Beese after their divorce, even long after she had carved out her own career.

In summary, it can be concluded that the models of cooperation of most architect couples reveal a surprisingly emancipated picture in which the female partners enjoyed plenty of scope to develop. The collaboration was largely based on equality, and the division of tasks was often a response to personal preferences or practical considerations.

A selection from the repertoire

Now that we have an impression of the ways in which these architect couples cooperated with each other, it is interesting to consider which repertoire can be attributed to the women architects. What architectural principles underpinned their oeuvre? Did the partners mutually influence, strengthen and inspire each other within their architectural practices?

The answers to these questions are supported by a selection from their repertoire. This is divided into two categories: residential and utility buildings. In the case of housing, the homes of the architect couples themselves are

VACANTIE- EN WEEKEN

ARCHITECTE IR

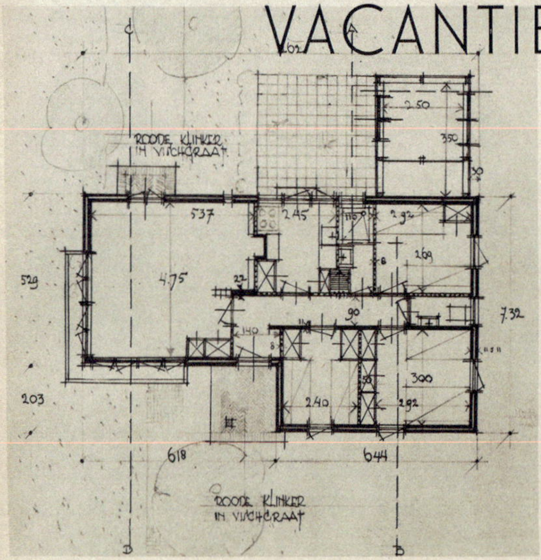

UITGEVOERD PLAN

Bijgaande foto's, plattegrond en situatie, geven een overzicht van een landhuisje te Oostvoorne, opgetrokken in het najaar 1934. Gelukkige omstandigheid was, dat op een zeer ruim bebosсht terrein met gunstige oriëntatie gebouwd moest worden. Het huis bevat: woonkamer met zitje bij de ingebouwde haard, boekenplanken, vast dressoir met glazen kastje, enz. – keuken met flinke berging – doucheruimte met vaste waschtafel, 3 slaapkamers, ieder voor 2 personen, met totaal 6 hang- en legkasten en met omtimmeringen voor de opklapbedden, toilet met waschhok, overdekte entrée, gang met trap naar ruime zolder, waarop een dienstbodenkamer met kast. Genoemde zolder biedt voldoende plaats voor eenige logeerbedden. Aan de noordzijde bevindt zich een aangebouwde houten schuur, op gemetselde fundeering en voorzien van betonvloer voor berging van fietsen, kolen, tuingereedschappen, waterdrukreservoir enz. Onder de geheele keuken bevindt zich een betonnen regenwaterbak, in de tuin een welwaterput.

Opdracht was, alle vertrekken gelijkvloers te maken.

Het huis is aan de buitenzijde over de baksteen

3a

HUIS TE OOSTVOORNE

AMMER-KRET B.I.

gekeimd in iets gebroken witte kleur en heeft een zwart plint. De dakpannen zijn zilvergrijs. De zinken goot is aluminium geschilderd. De luiken in de buitendeur veronesegroen, kozijnen en ramen wit. De ruwe gepotdekselde planken van gevels en schuurtje zijn gecarbolineerd. Hoewel de oplossing van de variantplattegrond beter is, werd door den principaal de voorkeur gegeven aan het uitgevoerde plan. Het toepassen van kant- of gevelpannen moest, hoewel degelijker en sierlijker, om financieele redenen achterwege blijven, zoodat gewone windveeren moesten worden gemaakt.

Alle binnenwanden zijn in duinzand geschuurd, plafonds zijn van donnacona. Het houtwerk in de kleur van duinzand, behalve in gang en keuken, waar de kleuren resp. terracotta en blauw zijn. De ramen zijn voorzien van raamdorpelsteenen en groote zwarte vensterbanktegels.

De totale bouwkosten, incl. electrische leidingen, sanitaires, waterdrukreservoir, gasleiding, waterput, losse houten luiken voor alle raamopeningen, (te gebruiken gedurende het niet bewoond zijn van het huis) enz. bedroeg f 3.593,– (exclusief honorarium en teekenonkosten).

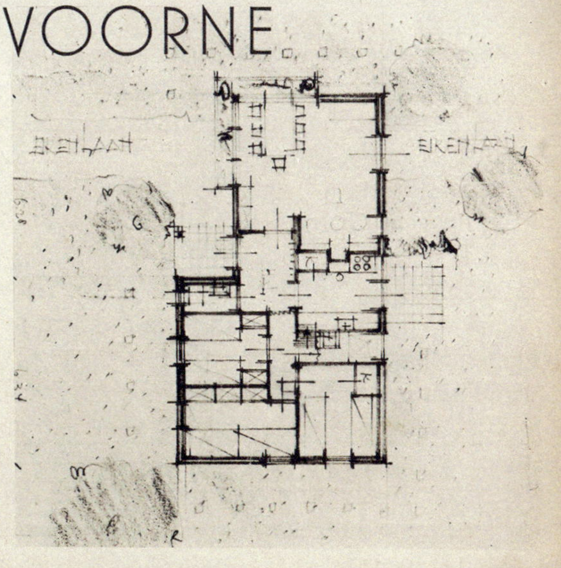

VOORPLAN

first taken as a revealing illustration of their ideas. Within the same category of housing, attention is then given to the application by women architects of new housing typologies, building materials and construction techniques. The final section examines residential projects for certain groups of residents. That the women architects also designed utility structures determined the choice for the theme of the final section devoted to their repertoire. Since the work of Jan Kammer-Kret falls somewhat outside the categories indicated, and was also completed in an earlier period, it is first examined in a separate section.

Achieving beauty through extreme simplicity

Jan Kammer-Kret recalled her 'very traditional' graduation assignment set by Professor Marinus Jan Granpré Molière to design a town hall out of stone.[42] She felt it was a pity that Granpré Molière was so opposed to concrete, a material he described as 'base'.[43] Granpré Molière represented the Delft School, commonly seen as traditionalist. The course at the TH offered students very little opportunity to familiarize themselves with emerging architecture opinions and construction methods. Kammer-Kret was negative about the atmosphere in the architecture faculty, the lack of attention for new ideas, and the uncritical imitation practiced by many fellow students.[44] Her work demonstrates a distinctively modern style. Given that she mostly worked with her husband, she must have been inspired by him, and vice versa. Although she has no extensive repertoire to her name, there are some interesting examples.

Kammer-Kret's first commission of her own concerned a holiday or week-end home (1934) for a family in Oostvoorne, a popular holiday destination for Rotterdammers in particular.[45] Willem van Tijen also designed a number of holiday homes there, including one for himself.[46] The photos of the holiday home designed by Kammer-Kret that were published in *Het Landhuis* magazine show a country home on a wooded site, with at first sight traditional features such as shutters and a pitched roof with a turret, fitted with a bell for calling the children home when playing outdoors **[fig. 3a and 3b]**.[47] But the house also displays modern aspects such as the glazed corner of the facade, as well as the efficient ground floor plan with its rational arrangement of living spaces and bedrooms. All manner of practical details had been considered, among them folding beds, numerous storage spaces and sanitary facilities such as a laundry room and a shower space with a fixed washbasin. A water borehole in the garden and a concrete rainwater container beneath the entire kitchen ensured a supply of water. It is very conceivable that the rustic elements of the exterior were added at the request of the client.[48] After all, in the previously mentioned competition for a village church, Kammer-Kret had already demonstrated her preference for sober architecture **[fig. 2]**.

3b

←
3a Holiday home in Oostvoorne (1934), designed by Kammer-Kret.

3b The sober and modern interior of the holiday home.

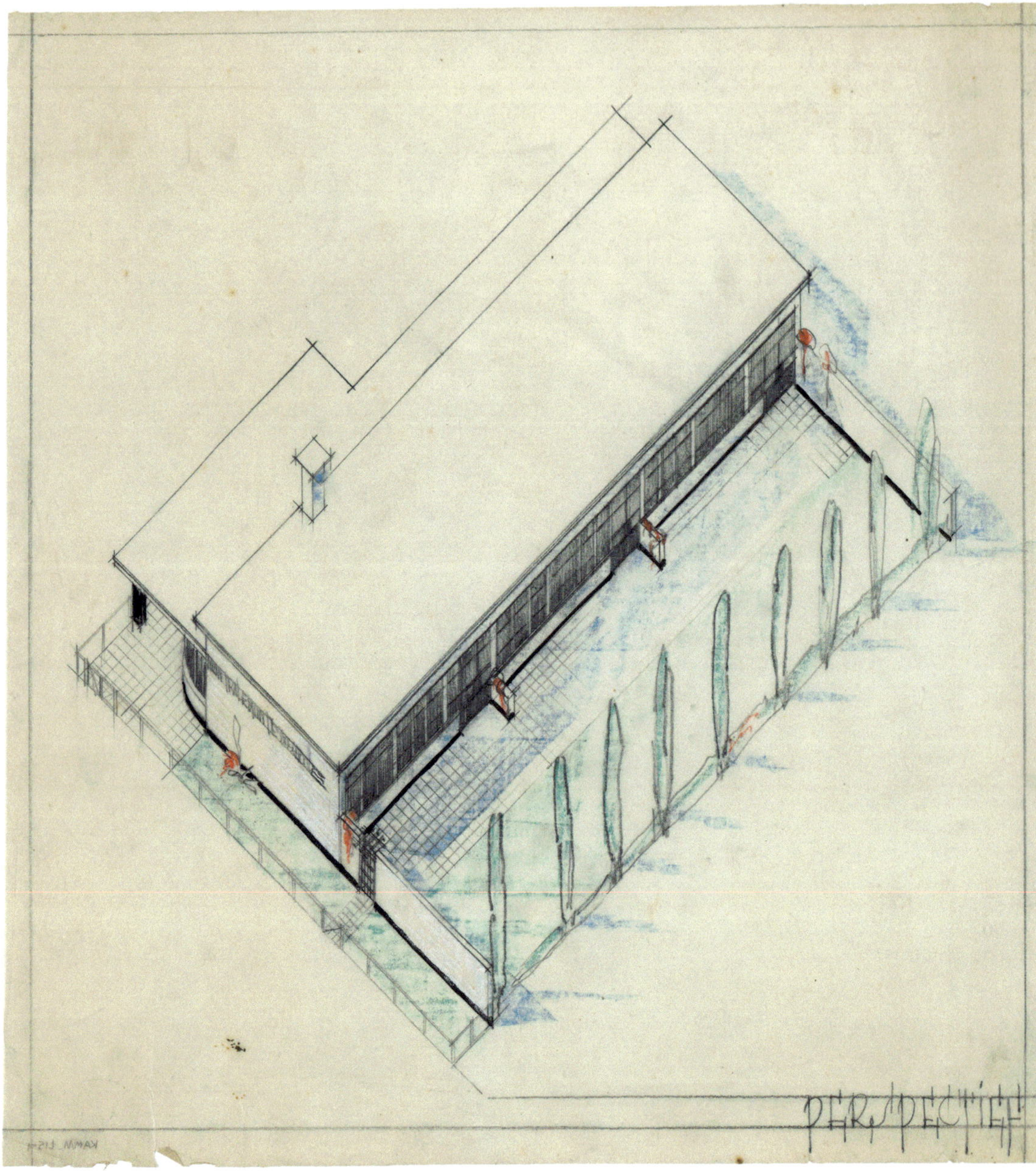

4a

4b

←
4a *Perspective*, undated design for Montessori kindergarten (1936) in Schiebroek by husband-and-wife Kammer-Kret.

4b The school entrance.

5

5 Front cover of *de 8 en Opbouw* with the Montessori kindergarten by husband-and-wife Kammer-Kret and the open-air school by Van Tijen.

6a The glazed wall of the south-east facade, circa 1936.

Two years later this was expressed more explicitly when the couple designed a Montessori kindergarten (1936) in Schiebroek, a stone's throw from their own home **[fig. 4a and 4b]**.[49] The school was prominently presented as an example of the Modern Movement style on the cover of *de 8 en Opbouw*, the organ of the architecture society of the same name, together with the Montessori school designed by Willem van Tijen on Albrecht Dürerstraat in Amsterdam, an open-air school featuring large expanses of glass wrapped around a concrete skeleton **[fig. 5]**.[50] According to reviewer Han van Loghem, for whom function and construction determined the success of a building, beauty could be achieved because of the extreme simplicity of the Schiebroek school. 'It is new because of the completely untraditional construction, but the newness does not impose itself anywhere, and the complex can be immediately accepted by any sensitive person without any change in their comprehension,' he contended.[51]The school could be built economically on a limited budget thanks to its modern construction methods and materials such as aerated concrete, steel and glass. Prefabrication made it possible to complete the one-floor school building in three months.[52] The south-east facade, a steel-frame construction consisting of three panels, each nine metres wide, drew light and air

6a

into the three spacious 63m2 classrooms **[fig. 6a]**. A protruding gutter protected the upper row of vertically pivoted windows from rainfall. Each classroom had double doors to its own outdoor play area with a grass strip and a flowerbed. The covered south-western entrance kept waiting parents dry during inclement weather. All four daughters of the couple, supporters of Montessori education, would attend school here.[53] Just like Van Loghem and Van Tijen, husband-and-wife Kammer-Kret were members of the architecture society Opbouw, which espoused the ideas of the Modern Movement.[54] It is clear that this environment inspired the couple. Kammer's experiences at the architecture office of Brinkman and Van der Vlugt, where he worked after graduating and during the construction of the Van Nelle Factory, must also have been influential. In an interview from the early 1980s, Kammer-Kret formulated her own view of architecture: above all, a building had to be functional, sound and also low-maintenance. That could certainly not be said of what she referred to as 'the new parochial style with all its pitched roofs', which to her was nothing but a 'fad'.[55] She would no doubt be happy that the enduring Montessori school building is still in use today. A new classroom and a music room were added to the building after 25 years **[fig. 6b]**.[56]

6b

6b A music room was added to the school 25 years after its completion.

6b

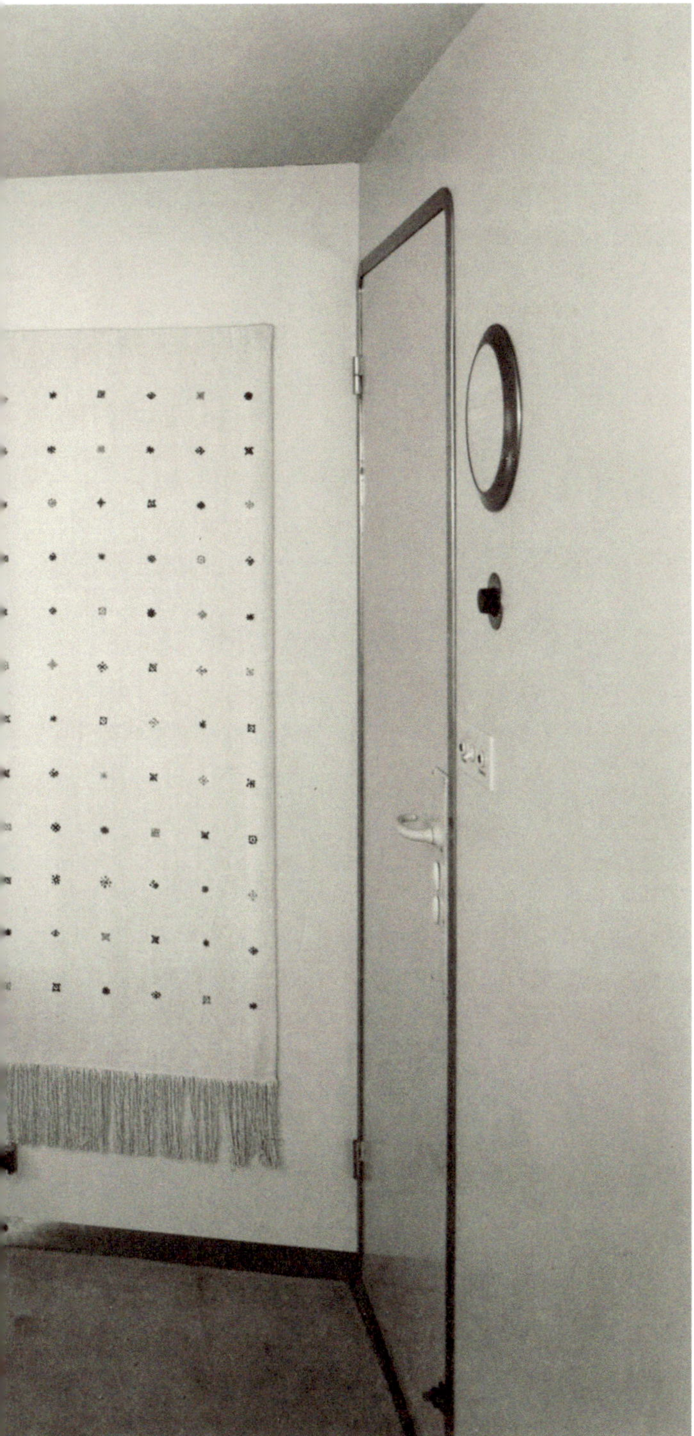

7

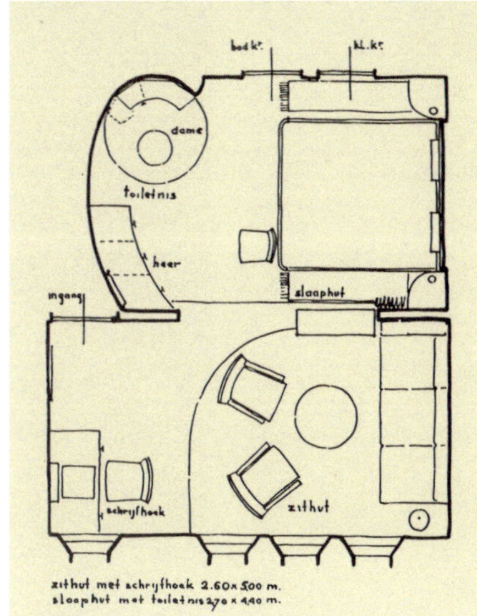

7

7 The luxury cabin (1937) designed by husband-and-wife Kammer-Kret for the *Nieuw Amsterdam* passenger liner, with its sleekly designed interior in shades of white and grey with metal accessories.

7

7

8

8 The private residence annex architecture office (1960) by husband-and-wife Kammer-Kret, Zuid-broekse Opweg 16, Berkenwoude, photo ca. 1970.

The Kammer-Kret couple were invited to design the interior of a luxury cabin on the *Nieuw Amsterdam* passenger liner (1937) operated by the Holland-Amerika Line. Numerous modernist designers, artists and architects worked on the project, among them Willem Gispen (1890–1981), J.J.P. Oud, Hendrik Wijdeveld (1885–1987) and the architecture partners Ben Merkelbach (1901–1961) and Charles Karsten (1904–1979).[57] The luxury cabin designed by the couple, which was also published in *de 8 en Opbouw*, features a modern, sleek interior with artificial leather and handwoven fabrics, all in shades of white and grey and with metal accessories **[fig. 7]**.[58]

Housing: the architect's home. An 'ugly shoe box'

The most obvious way to get an idea of the architectural views and the accompanying style of the women architects under consideration is to examine the houses (and attached studios) they and their husbands designed for their own use. After all, here they were free to realize their ideas without having to take into account the specific wishes of clients who may not have shared all their opinions. In this study, it could not be determined exactly who did what. Their own homes must therefore be considered the result of a close collaboration between both partners.

The first home in Schiebroek where husband-and-wife Kammer-Kret started their architecture practice in 1933 was designed in a similar style to that of the luxury cabin on the *Nieuw Amsterdam* passenger liner.[59] As soon as children arrived, however, the principles of the perfectly harmonious interior were abandoned, and elements such as white floor coverings and tubular steel tables with glass tops proved to be impractical. In 1960 the couple designed their own split-level dwelling, a reference in part to the previously discussed Schiebroek kindergarten.[60] Surrounded by plentiful greenery and water, the residence and architecture practice in Berkenwoude featured glazed sliding panels that offered light, air and space, with a panoramic view of the polder **[fig. 8]**.

Entirely in line with Kammer-Kret's views, the practical floor plan and materials ensure a minimum of maintenance **[fig. 9]**. The vestibule separates the sleeping quarters from the living and working areas. A similar grouping of functions was apparent in the earlier holiday home for a client in Oostvoorne. The large living room with a tall fireplace is placed perpendicular to and openly connected with a sitting room, elevated like a floating floor above the studio, located 1.5 metres below ground level in the basement. The spaces for living and working all face south-west. The couple created a house 'where everything was possible', with places for all sorts of activities.[61] The bike could be repaired beside the sofa, while drinks were enjoyed by the open hearth.

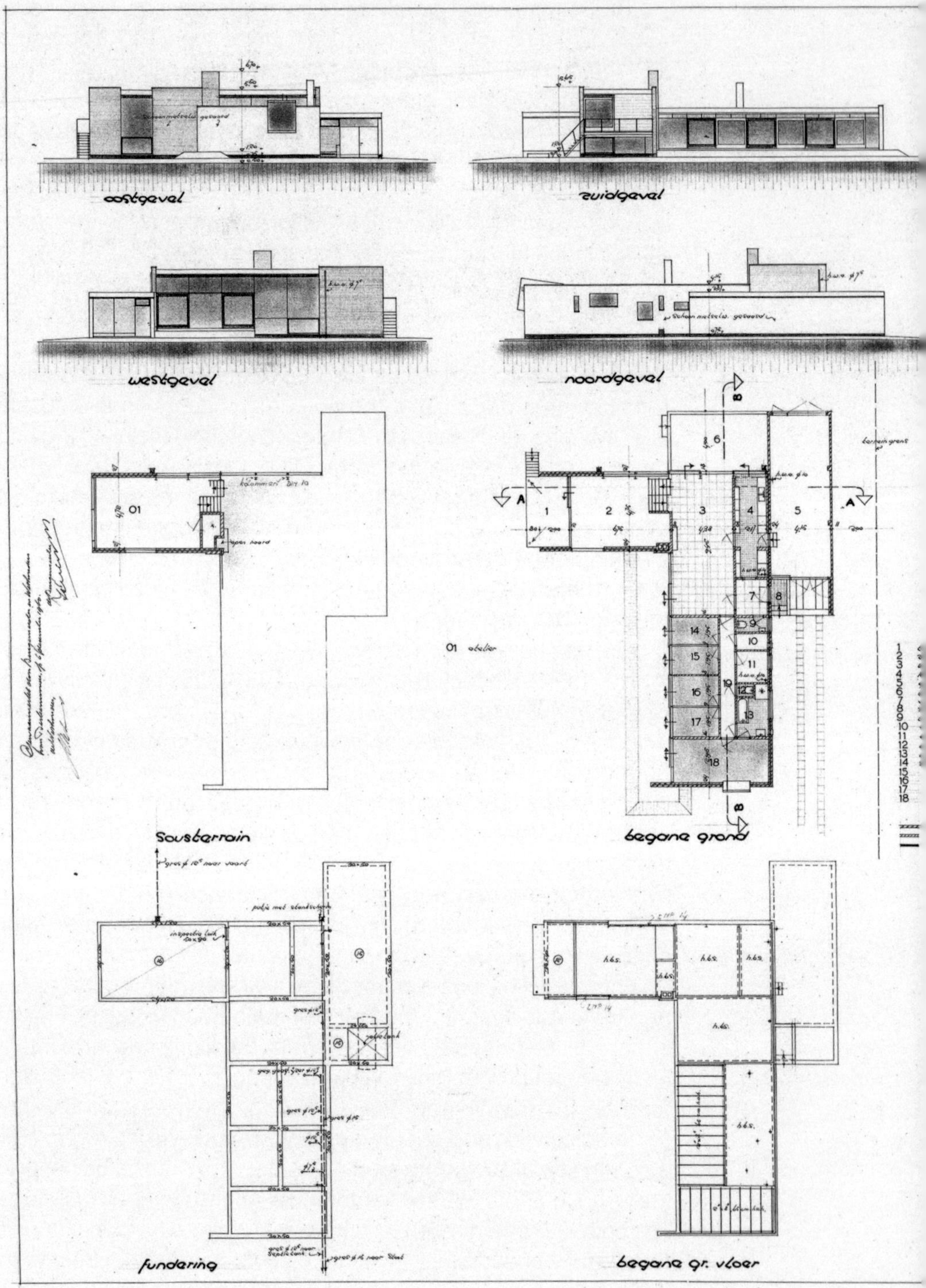
oostgevel
zuidgevel
westgevel
noordgevel
souterrain
begane grond
fundering
begane gr. vloer
01 atelier

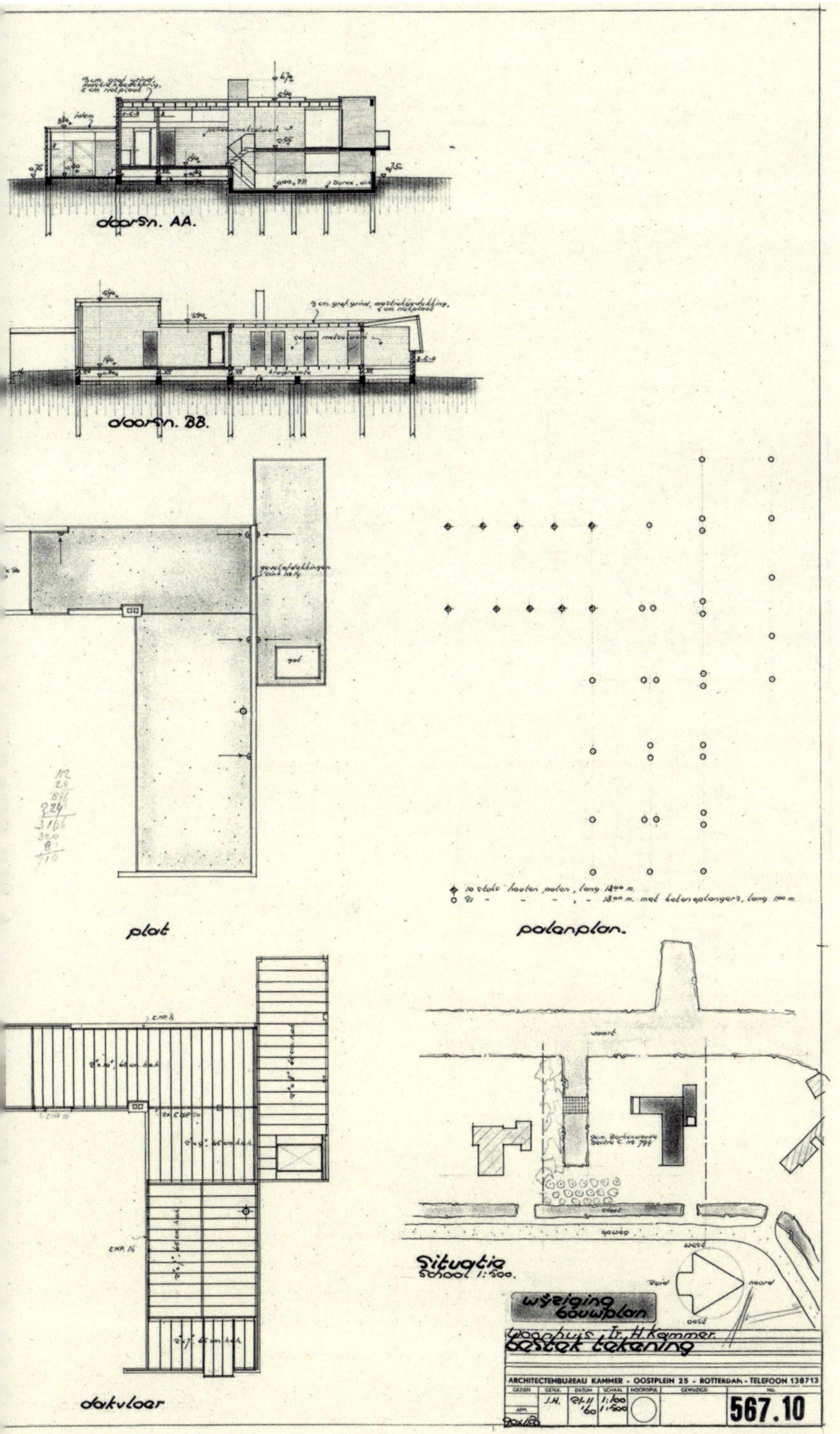

9

9 Specification drawing of the private residence annex architecture office by husband-and-wife Kammer-Kret, 1960.

10

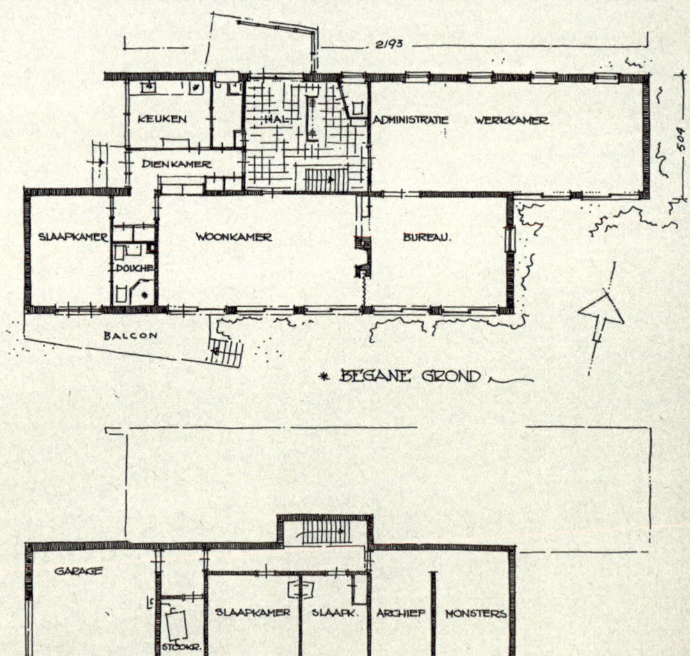

Eigen woonhuis Monnikensteeg (Monnikenhuizen), arch. ir H. Lammers en ir C. Ch. Lammers-Koeleman.

677

Husband-and-wife Lammers-Koeleman lived in a bungalow with an office attached, which they designed for themselves in Arnhem in 1954. The sober, rectilinear building has a flat roof and large expanses of facade glazing **[fig. 10]**.[62] An external stairs connects the main floor above the basement with the garden. Here, too, the floor plan shows a functional arrangement, with the working and living spaces grouped around a large hall on the main floor. The garage, guestrooms and archive spaces are located in the basement. Interestingly, Lammers-Koeleman also designed a bungalow in Arnhem for To Strumphler, a fellow student from Delft, who worked as an architectural engineer for the Gelderland Planning Department. The bungalow (1960) consisted of two apartments for the unmarried To and her mother.[63] It is the only known example of a residence designed and built for a fellow woman architect covered by this study.

In an interview in *De Telegraaf* newspaper, on the occasion of the presentation of her VHBO diploma in 1936 and long before her marriage to Joop Pot, Koos Keegstra expressed her support for the Modern Movement. She expected that, with new materials such as concrete and glass, beauty would 'return of its own accord'.[64] Pot shared this architectural point of view.[65] The pair knew each other from the VHBO college in Amsterdam, where they met like-minded fellow students such as Arthur Staal and Koen Limperg (1908–1943).[66] During the time that Koos Keegstra and Joop Pot studied there, the course tutors included representatives of the Modern Movement such as Leendert van der Vlugt (1894–1936) and Cornelis van Eesteren, as well as conservative architects like Frits Eschauzier (1889–1957), Koos's supervisor during her final year of study.[67] With its diligent search for a balanced composition among its faculty staff, the board of the VHBO sought to counter the criticism voiced by the progressive architecture groups De 8, Opbouw and Groep '32 that the ideas of the Modern Movement were insufficiently represented. It was therefore in the midst of this factional struggle that Koos Keegstra had charted her course.

10 The private residence annex architecture office (1954) by husband-and-wife Lammers-Koeleman, Monnikensteeg 20, Arnhem.

In 1954, Koos and Joop Pot-Keegstra seized the opportunity to apply their modern architecture opinions in the design of their own home and studio. They purchased a site on Haringvlietstraat in Amsterdam South, an urban expansion area that attracted young families. They invited the Amsterdam-based garden architect Mien Ruys to design the garden, which extended to the bank of the Boerenwetering waterway.[68] The architectural result provoked controversy: reactions varied from 'highlight of contemporary architecture' to 'ugly shoe box'.[69] The contrast between the home with attached practice and the neighbouring 1930s dwellings in late Amsterdam School style with English country house influences could not have been bigger. The facade composition of the flat-roofed rectilinear

11b

←
11a The private residence with architecture practice (left portion of the building) designed by husband- and-wife Pot-Keegstra, Haringvlietstraat 14, Amsterdam, 1955.

11b Living room of husband-and-wife Pot-Keegstra.

11c

building is articulated exclusively by the positioning of the deeply recessed windows **[fig. 10a]**. The only elements to subtly interrupt the symmetry are the small wall openings on both sides.

The architect couple wanted '(...) to place the most perfect structure (...) on this final vacant site, which has character because of its form. We want to build consciously and honestly, using architectural means only.'[70] They sought 'sleekness and pureness' rather than 'all sorts of nooks and crannies and lots of frills that serve no genuine purpose.'[71] They thought that the face of their residence was 'finished'; nothing could be added or removed without disturbing the balance. The couple had applied and refined their architectural ideals to the full in their own home. The interior of the house was a textbook example of Goed Wonen ('Good Living'), the foundation set up in 1946 that championed good living culture and propagated that in the periodical of the same name through advice and furnished model homes **[fig. 11b and 11c]**.

Housing: new types and construction methods

11c Staircase by husband-and-wife Pot-Keegstra.

Post-war reconstruction resulted in numerous housing commissions for the architecture practices discussed in this study. Even during the war years, husband-and-wife Pot-Keegstra were working on designs for new dwelling types in the form of split-level and drive-in houses. The use of half floor heights created more space in a split-level house. The couple realized such houses in Alkmaar (De Bergerhof, 1941–1942) as freestanding rows, a first for the city **[fig. 12a and 12b]**.[72] These houses were intended for refugees and evacuees from Den Helder and would later be occupied by inhabitants of Alkmaar. Drive-in houses are characterized by a built-in garage with part of the house above it. Although Pot-Keegstra gave the impression in a later interview that she and Pot had come up with these new forms, both housing types had been built before the war, for example in the drive-in houses in the previously mentioned collaboration project by architects Stam and Beese with Willem van Tijen.[73] Architectural engineer Wil Jansen had also completed such houses in Heerlen in 1938.[74]

Husband-and-wife Pot-Keegstra sought to create 'more space' with 'fairly revolutionary floor plans' to avoid any 'pokiness' and sought simple practical solutions such as a shed for bikes, a basement drying room for washing and a covered balcony.[75] Pot-Keegstra also stated that these household-related elements were developed by her and her husband together, just as the couple had consistently done in the media. Pot-Keegstra's comment in the same newspaper interview, long after the death of Pot, is therefore striking: 'My husband was knighted for that, before he had even turned 40.'[76] One cannot detect any displeasure from her concerning this honour bestowed upon her husband alone.

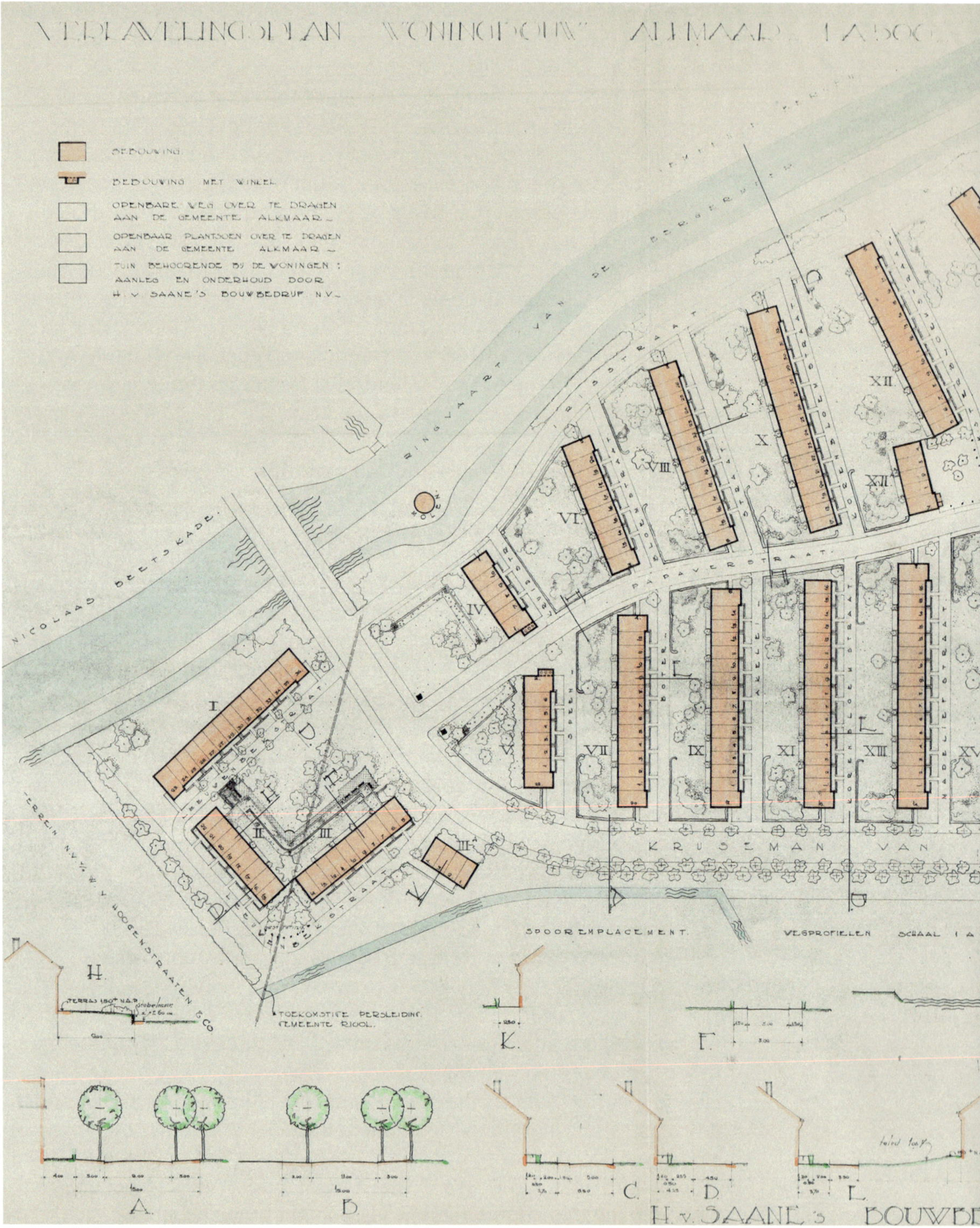

VERKAVELINGSPLAN WONINGBOUW ALKMAAR 1 A 500
BEBOUWING
BEBOUWING MET WINKEL
OPENBARE WEG OVER TE DRAGEN AAN DE GEMEENTE ALKMAAR
OPENBAAR PLANTSOEN OVER TE DRAGEN AAN DE GEMEENTE ALKMAAR
TUIN BEHOORENDE BIJ DE WONINGEN; AANLEG EN ONDERHOUD DOOR H. v. SAANE'S BOUWBEDRIJF N.V.
RINGVAART VAN DE
NICOLAAS BEETSKADE
MOLEN
IRISSTRAAT
PAPAVERSTRAAT
KRUSEMAN VAN
SPOOREMPLACEMENT
WEGPROFIELEN SCHAAL
TOEKOMSTIGE PERSLEIDING GEMEENTE RIOOL
A.
B.
C.
D.
E.
F.
H.
K.
H. v. SAANE'S BOUWBE

12a

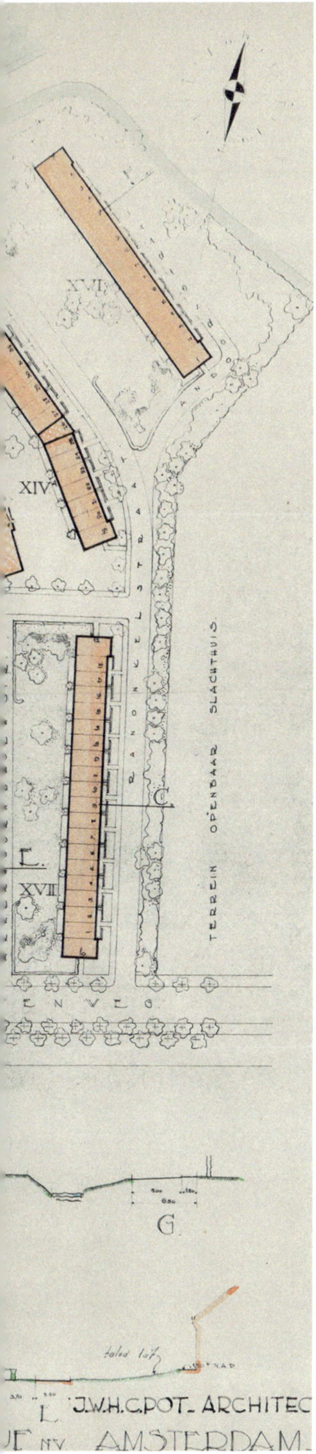

12a The Bergerhof (1941–1942) by husband-and-wife Pot-Keegstra. The first freestanding blocks of dwellings in Alkmaar.

→ **12b** Floor plans, section and facade composition of the Bergerhof split-level homes.

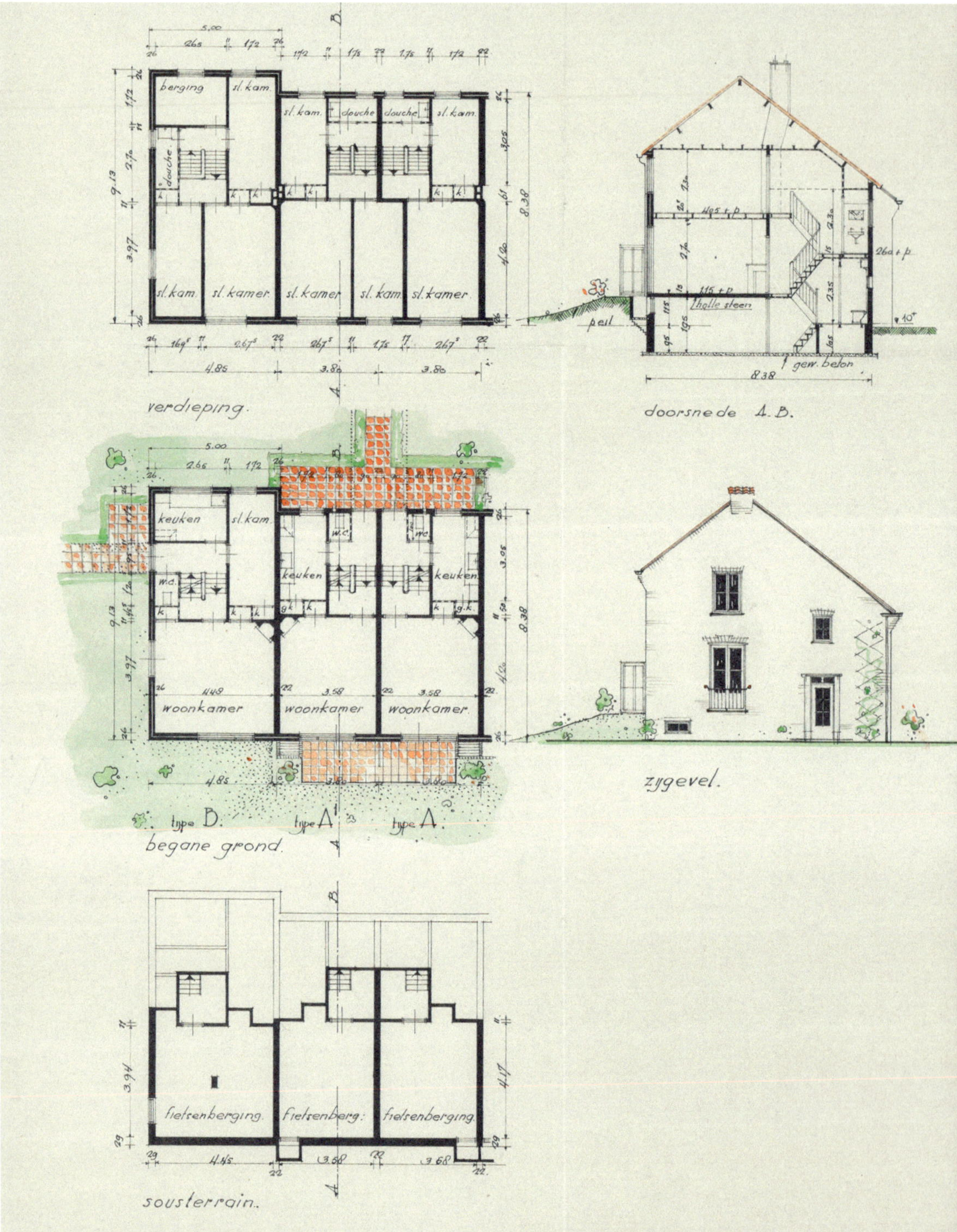
berging
sl. kam.
douche
keuken
w.c.
woonkamer
sl. kamer
verdieping.
doorsnede A.B.
holle steen
peil
gew. beton
begane grond.
type B.
type A'
type A.
zygevel.
fietsenberging.
fietsenberg:
sousterrain.

gevel woonkamerzyde.
gevel ingangzyde.
n.v. bouwbedryf H.v. Saane.
J.W.H.C. Pot. Arch. Sept. 1941.

12b

Toki Lammers-Koeleman focused largely on housing. While she initially built in what she herself referred to as 'traditionally in the Molière style', little by little her designs became more modern.[77] Toki and her husband received their post-war commissions from the Royal Steam Weaving Mill in Nijverdal, later renamed Ten Cate, on the strength of their previously mentioned competition design in a 'restrained Delft School style'.[78] The client did not care for the 'much too modern' entries by colleagues such as Ben Merkelbach and Jan Piet Kloos (1905–2001).[79] Lammers-Koeleman designed various housing schemes for working class and middle class employees at the weaving mill, and also for the Thomassen engine factory in De Steeg.

Housing for factory workers in so-called garden suburbs had already appeared in the Netherlands, among them Tuindorp 't Lansink (1911–1917) in Hengelo, commissioned by the Stork engineering works, which Thomassen partnered with in 1948.[80] Lammers-Koeleman possibly drew inspiration from this garden suburb. Granpré Molière and Pieter Verhagen designed Vreewijk, the 'First Rotterdam Garden Village', for a dry-dock company, the Rotterdamsche Droogdok Maatschappije, in 1920. It featured spacious workers homes set in green surroundings. The sites for the staff homes in Nijverdal were also spacious. Lammers-Koeleman positioned the rustic-style semi-detached houses (1949) for senior staff at the weaving mill in a staggered formation **[fig. 13]**.[81] Sheds placed perpendicularly to the houses created a domino-like arrangement that ensured privacy.

Lammers-Koeleman designed duplex homes (1948–1949) for Thomassen office employees.[82] This new housing type, consisting of separate lower and upper houses and intended to alleviate the post-war housing shortage, also proved to be an efficient model in De Steeg. The building blocks placed perpendicular to each other could be spaciously arranged along small gardens and drew sufficient air and light into the houses **[fig. 14]**. The favourably priced rental dwellings were a real boon, especially for young married employees at Thomassen.[83]

13 Staff homes (1949) in Nijverdal, designed by Lammers-Koeleman.

Husband-and-wife Lammers-Koeleman were closely involved in the post-war reconstruction of Arnhem. Hendrik was for a time head of the Arnhem City Plan Office set up by the city council and, possibly as a result, Toki received various housing commissions. In her reports to Staal-Kropholler, she wrote about various plans that 'had remained on paper because of the increasing cost of construction'.[84] Creative inventions also meant that some projects could proceed. Almost 400 flats (1950–1951) were constructed according to the hollow concrete construction system on the Meinerswijkseweg (now the Gelderse Rooslaan) in the affluent and quiet residential neighbourhood of Marlburgen-West in Arnhem South.[85] The scarcity of materials after the war meant that hollow concrete, made in this case of brick and mortar rubble from Arnhem, was a good alternative. The system was based on the normalization of

13

Ir. H. Lammers en Ir. C. Ch. Lammers-Koeleman, Middenstandswoningen, Nijverdal. 1949.

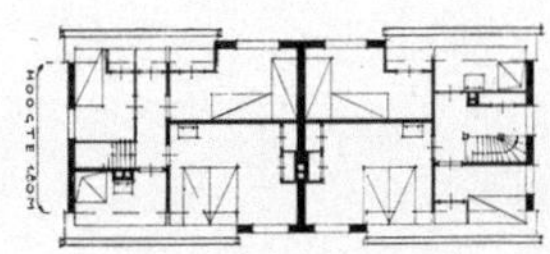

Verdieping.

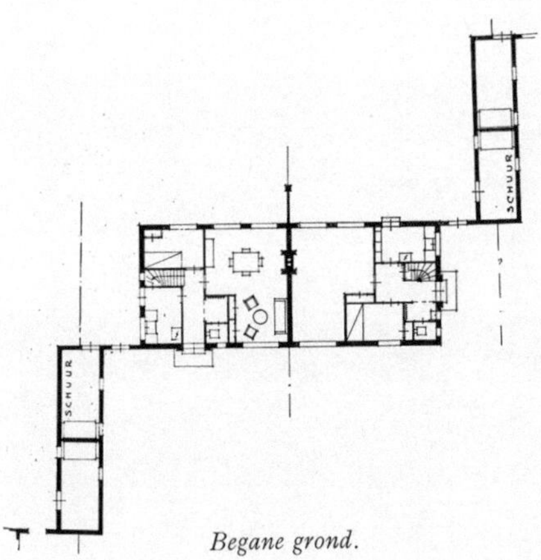

Begane grond.

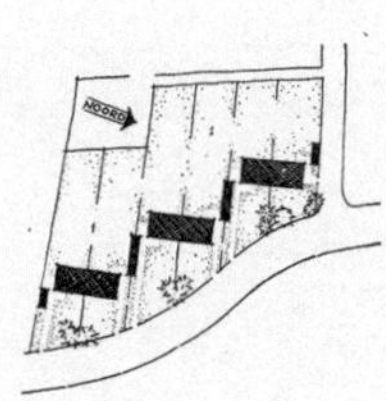

14

Ir. H. Lammers en Ir. C. Ch. Lammers-Koeleman, Duplexwoningen, De Steeg. 1949.

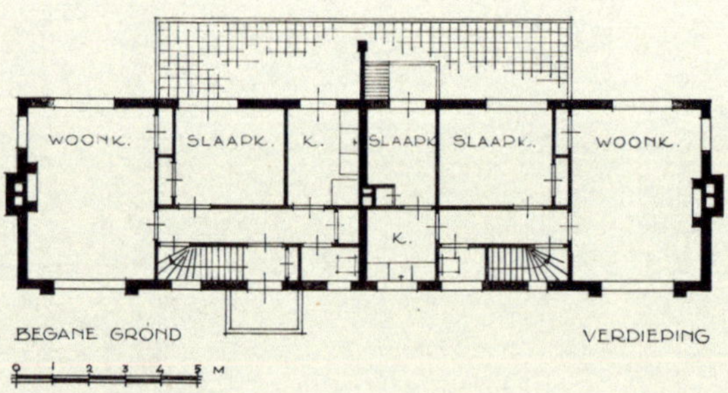

194

formwork in which the concrete was poured. That resulted not only in the insulation of walls and floors but also in a fast and efficient construction process. However, it limited the architects in their design, which had to be fully adapted to the system. Lammers-Koeleman could only determine the fenestration, balcony fencing and roof shape of the blocks of flats. The eight four-level hook-shaped blocks were grouped around courtyards designed as spaces for play and recreation **[fig. 15]**. This arrangement drew plenty of light and air into the homes. 'Upon entering, you are immediately struck by the calm atmosphere that pervades the staircase,' ran the report in the local press.[86] The flats feature a spacious hallway, a living room, two or three bedrooms, a Bruynzeel kitchen, a washbasin with a connection for a warm water appliance, and a balcony with a coal box. Storage units were contained in the base.[87]

Housing: new groups of residents

The demand for housing for specific and also new groups of residents offered Koos and Joop Pot-Keegstra opportunities to produce designs for them from an early stage. For example, even during the war-time occupation of the country, they carried out their first major commission, a block of flats for single women **[fig. 16a]**.[88] The close cooperation between the couple makes it impossible to determine which parts of the design can be attributed to Pot-Keegstra. The Oranjehof (1941–1942) – a name prompted by the war, just like the Schevening prison called Het Oranjehotel – is an eight-floor block of gallery-access flats on Korte Geuzenstraat in Amsterdam-West. Here the couple's penchant for sober and honest architecture is already apparent. The volume takes the form of an oblong block whose 'proportions (...) were such that corrections with contrived highlights or suchlike were deemed unnecessary,' Pot explained in a construction periodical.[89] 'Not a single addition was therefore made to the building programme to achieve a certain design (...)'.[90] Although the facade composition is fairly sober and flat, the segmental arched windows on the first and sixth floors of the rear facade, overlooking the Kostverlorenvaart waterway, are still traditional elements. Additions of this kind do not occur in the couple's later work.

14 Duplex homes (1948–1949) in De Steeg, designed by Lammers-Koeleman.

The block of flats, constructed partly of reinforced concrete, is symmetrically arranged, with the central section containing the staircase and lifts splitting the galleries on both sides in two.[91] This prevented the creation of long and instinctively unsafe access routes to the flats of the female occupants and kept the composition compact. The block features a rationally inspired floor plan. The first six floors contain 108 one- and two-room flats oriented east-west, the majority of which were intended for single working

15

15 The post-war reconstruction plan for Arnhem South. Visible to the west of De Monchyplein are the eight hook-shaped housing blocks by Lammers-Koeleman.

DE RIJN
HUISSENSE STRAAT
ARNHEM ZUID

16a

←
16a The Oranjehof (1941–1942) by husband-and-wife Pot-Keegstra, with the rear facade facing Kostverlorenvaart, Amsterdam, 1953.

16b

women and a small number on the lower floors for elderly women [fig. 16b]. Besides modern central amenities in the homes such as heating, warm water, radio distribution and telephone connections, there was a waste outlet on each floor. The ground floor with a porter's lodge contains numerous communal amenities such as bike storage and repair workshop, suitcase storage, a staffed laundry, restaurant, general store and ten guestrooms. The caretaker and the store manager each had their own homes. The seventh floor contained 28 semi-furnished boarding rooms for student girls, with a shared sitting and breakfast room where a live-in housekeeper served breakfast. She also took care of the 'weekly clean-up' of the rooms, 'the washing of windows and further services'.[92]

16b Interior of a flat in the Oranjehof, 1956.

That Pot-Keegstra – and not, as previously noted, Lotte Stam-Beese – landed the commission for this complex was probably down to the fact that Pot had worked for a period with the H. van Saane construction company, founder of the Oranjehof.[93] Although Stam-Beese's design was not that different in terms of layout, the fact that she was not a qualified architect – she had yet to start her VHBO course – may also have played a role.[94] As a flat complex for single women, the Oranjehof was replicated in The Hague, where the Elisabeth Brugsmaflat (1955–1959) was built, also to a design by Joop and Koos Pot-Keegstra.[95]

17a

17a Pot-Keegstra (in fur coat) in attendance as the first pile of the retirement home is driven into the ground, Cornelis Outshoornstraat, Amsterdam, 1966.

→
17b Geuzenveld with, left centre, the retirement home designed by husband-and-wife Pot-Keegstra, Amsterdam, 1975.

With housing commissions, Koos and Joop Pot-Keegstra always asked themselves whether they themselves would like to live in their design.[96] In a newspaper interview, we read a rare personal contribution from Pot-Keegstra in the otherwise inseparable collaboration between the pair. Her own fervent wish to provide the elderly with a private shower and toilet remained beyond reach in the 1960s: in the Maarten Lutherhuis Retirement Home (1959–1967) in Amsterdam-Osdorp, for example, the amenities in the homes were limited to a private lavatory and a hot plate.[97] 'Somewhat revolutionary' is how Pot-Keegstra described the positioning of the dining and recreation halls on the thirteenth floor at the top of the retirement home designed by the couple in Geuzenveld (1963–1967), a new district in the western garden suburbs of Amsterdam **[fig. 17a and 17b]**.[98] Apart from homes for the elderly, the couple designed other forms of communal housing for, among others, students and women nurses.

Starting in the 1960s, Toki Lammers-Koeleman realized twelve state-subsidized homes for the elderly in, among other places, Naarden, Bilthoven, Dieren, Hengelo and Lunteren.[99] In these projects she employed a functionalist arrangement of connected building blocks, each housing a different function such as living space, kitchen, sick bay and the work and office space for staff and management. One of these

18a

complexes was the Hoge Es Protestant Christian Retirement Home (1961–1963) on Bonteweg in Nijverdal **[fig. 18]**.[100] The construction of this centre was a response to the big demand for homes for the elderly, whose number at the time had passed the million mark in the Netherlands.[101] The demand consisted largely of seniors still living with family members, but also of residents of existing retirement homes that had failed to meet requirements in the area of health, safety and living comfort for some time. The complex contains not only living space for eighty able-bodied seniors, but also for the female director, her female deputy, and eight members of staff. Part of the complex could be isolated in the event of the outbreak of a contagious disease. Lammers-Koeleman designed homes on the basis of the view that residents, more than anything else, should feel at home in a building in which they themselves wanted to live in.[102] As we have seen, that view was shared by husband-and-wife Pot-Keegstra. For Lammers-Koeleman, what mattered was not so much a certain style of architecture. That is why the Hoge Es home reads essentially as functional architecture, based on the principle of letting residents retain their independence. They were free to move around, receive guests, and make contact with other residents. Hence the seats placed along the corridors and in the hall.

18a-c Exterior and hall with staircase of the Hoge Es Protestant Retirement Home (1961–1963) on Bonteweg in Nijverdal, designed by Lammers-Koeleman.

18b

18c

19a

Utility building

In 1949, two years after the death of her husband, Jeanne van Rood-van Rijswijk took on the commission to design a bottling plant for Coca-Cola. Besides finishing the projects of Van Rood, she appeared to want to take on new challenges, which she divided among the staff of the architecture office and herself.[103] The design for the factory and office building, she later wrote in her annual report to Staal-Kropholler, would be 'publishable'.[104] As far as we know, no such publication ever appeared. She did not publish work herself.

The bottling plant was built on a site located between Van Cleeffstraat and Van Deventerstraat in Schiedam-East **[fig. 19a]**. The structure, featuring a steel skeleton on reinforced concrete foundations and faced in brickwork facades, consisted of three connected building volumes that highlight the different functions of the spaces. Such a composition of building volumes, the horizontal roof lines, the use of roof overhangs and the minimal use of ornaments displays striking similarities to the work and views of Van Rood, such as the Transformer and Switching Station (1932) in Gasselte and the Provincial Electric Power Station (1930) in Helpman near Groningen **[fig. 20]**.[105] Van Rood sought to create utility buildings with an appropriately

19a Coca-Cola bottling plant (1949) designed by Van Rood-van Rijswijk on Van Deventerstraat in Schiedam, photo 1957. The composition of building volumes with horizontal roof lines is strongly reminiscent of the work of Van Rood **[fig. 20]**.

19b Garage of the Coca-Cola bottling plant, photo 1950–1956.

19b

sleek and objective character, with respect for commercial requirements.[106] Van Rood-van Rijswijk was thus adhering to the style of architecture of her husband. What was striking, however, were the pitched roofs with roof lights above the garage, which could house 65 trucks, and above the canteens and staff changing rooms **[fig. 19b]**. While Van Rood was a proponent of flat roofs, she added her own personal touch.[107]

It is understandable that Van Rood-van Rijswijk stayed largely faithful to the architectural style of her husband. After all, she took little part in the office until after his death. Van Rood's name alone graced the letterheads and signatures on design drawings for a number of years.[108] Perhaps she did this to honour Van Rood, but probably because of the reputation that he had built up and which the office could continue to build on. Industrial clients would not, in all likelihood, be keen on securing the services of a woman architect.

In 1950, Van Rood-van Rijswijk received commissions from Mekog and from Hoogovens, both of which were regular clients of Van Rood. For Hoogovens she designed the extension to the Central Laboratory that her husband had designed. In terms of style, the new building, the total construction cost of which amounted to 850,000 guilders, blended harmoniously with the original laboratory. She gave

20

21

20 Gasselte transformer station designed by Van Rood, 1935.

21 Extension to Hoogovens Central Laboratory (1951–1952), IJmuiden, designed by Van Rood-van Rijswijk.

a horizontal top to the saw-tooth roofs that ensured the required daylight conditions in the laboratory **[fig. 21]**.

All that is known about the brief period up to her death in 1960 is that Van Rood-van Rijswijk designed another new factory for concrete products (1950) in Lisse ontwierp.[109] It would be interesting to know whether she moved further away from the style employed by Van Rood by applying her own inventions, but insufficient information about the concrete factory and about her later work could be found unfortunately.[110] A highly specific commission landed by Joop and Koos Pot-Keegstra concerned the design of a penal institution in Amsterdam, better known as the Bijlmerbajes prison. The project was still at the design stage when Pot died in 1972. Pot-Keegstra continued the design work together with the fifteen people employed at the office.[111] After the tendering procedure in 1974, she supervised construction up until completion in 1978. This generated the necessary publicity.[112] In an interview in *Het Parool* she emphasized that the architectural profession was particularly suited to women, 'because it concerns the problems of life'.[113] She viewed the design of a prison more as a form of communal housing. As already stated, the couple had gained plenty of experience with housing designs for specific groups of residents, though not for prisoners. The cells of

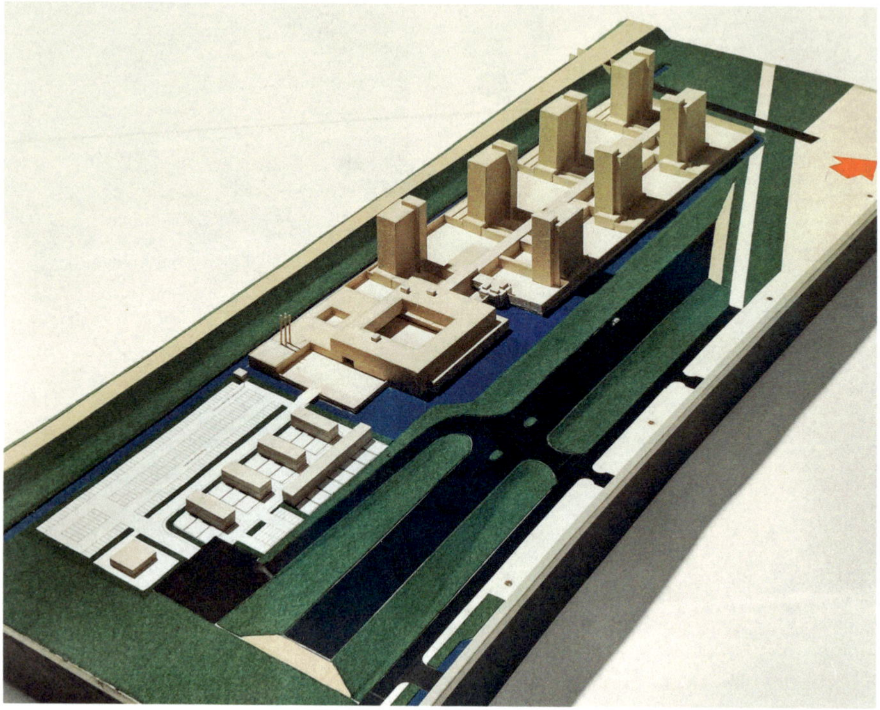

22

the Amsterdam Over-Amstel Penal Institution, as the Bijlmerbajes was officially called, were denoted on the floor plans of the design as 'living units'.[114]

The complex, located on an elongated site in Amsterdam-East, consisted of a two-level main building and six so-called residential towers, thirteen floors tall, one of which was reserved for women inmates **[fig. 22]**.[115] The concrete towers, faced in smooth white prefabricated facade panels, housed some 600 inmates **[fig. 23]**. The upper ten floors of each tower were divided into 24 living units and extended over two levels, with a shared double-height space for sports and relaxation, the so-called living space **[fig. 24]**. The unprecedented approach stemmed from the design brief drawn up by the Ministry of Justice, which focused fully on creating a humane environment for the inmates in order to speed up their rehabilitation into society. The windows were not barred and offered unimpeded views of the city. Each prefabricated living unit had its own sanitary facilities and was laid out in such a way that freed up more space, a motto that the architect couple also embraced in housing developments, as we have already seen.[116] Warm materials such as wood, used as finishes in the corridors, as well as various colours, were deployed to make the living environment more pleasant **[fig. 25]**.[117]

22 Model of the Over-Amstel Penal Institution.

Stepping up to city design

As already noted, Lotte Stam-Beese occupies a special position among this group of architect couples. Her marriage and professional collaboration with Mart Stam ended in a fiasco. After obtaining her VHBO diploma in 1945, Stam-Beese could start working for the Department of City Development in Rotterdam as an – inexperienced – urban design architect. She would be the first and only woman in this position, and remained so until her retirement in 1968.[118] She owed her appointment in part to a recommendation from Willem van Tijen, who was active on many fronts in the post-war reconstruction effort. Stam-Beese knew Van Tijen from their earlier collaboration in Amsterdam when she and Stam were starting their architecture office, and from the VHBO academy, where Van Tijen tutored graduating students. Stam-Beese developed into a reputable urban designer, creating neighbourhoods such as Kleinpolder (1946–1952), Pendrecht (1948–1952, in collaboration with the architecture society Opbouw) and Het Lage Land (1961–1962).[119] She applied the phenomenon of the neighbourhood idea that emerged during the period of reconstruction to promote a sense of community. Stam-Beese combined the neighbourhood idea with living units intended to provide housing for four stages of life: from young singles, to small and large families to seniors. To this end, she deployed repeated blocks of dwellings to ensure light, air and space, alternating with strips of greenery that serve as communal gardens. Mart Stam had already designed this form of development in 1929 for the Hellerhofsiedlung in Frankfurt am Main. Lotte's marriage and collaboration with Stam, as well as the circles in which both of them moved, such as De 8, and the views they shared concerning the Modern Movement, did establish the basis for her urban design career.

Koos Keegstra had a strong wish to become an urban designer. But her father did not agree to her studying in Paris, which had been recommended to her by the architect and urban designer Cor van Eesteren.[120] Almost thirty years later she wrote a one-off urban design article in the *Bouwkundig Weekblad* about the negative influence of holiday customs on nature and the landscape. Pot-Keegstra made a case for government planning intervention in what she saw as the tasteless and unbridled allotment gardens – she even went so far as to describe certain complexes of allotment garden as 'no more cheerful than a concentration camp' –, unsightly camping sites with permanent motorhomes, low rows of houseboats and the cafés appearing everywhere.[121] She praised the pristine quality of the Amsterdamse Bos landscape plan, without 'commercial park furniture'.[122] Perhaps this was a subtle tribute to Van Eesteren, under whose leadership this plan had been developed and who at the time was leaving the Department of City Development in Amsterdam.[123] While it may not have

22

23 The Over-Amstel Penal Institution under construction, a design by husband-and-wife Pot-Keegstra, H.J.E. Wenckebach-weg 48, Amsterdam, ca. 1976.

24

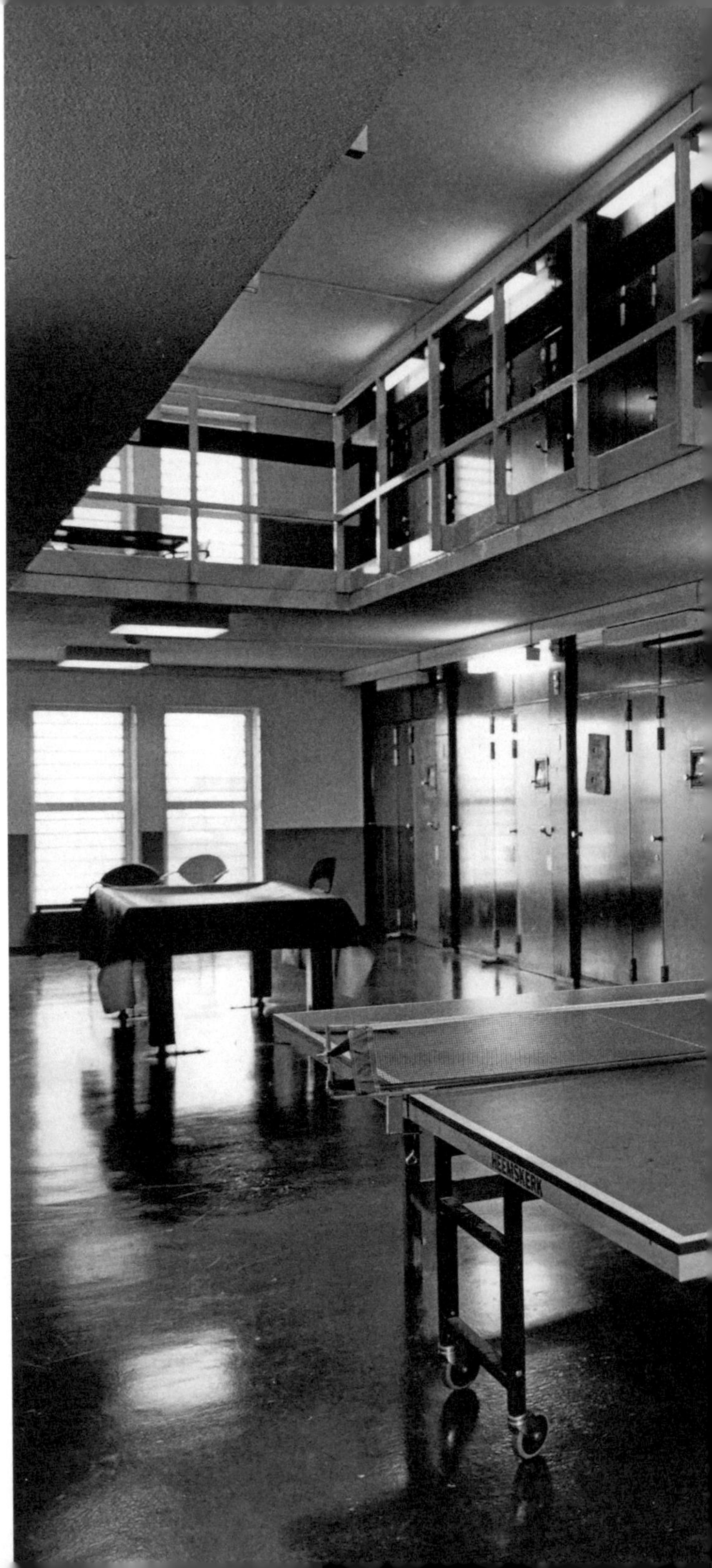

24 A pavilion in the Over-Amstel Penal Institution with an activity supervisor, 2000.

AMSTEL

25

25 The walls were finished in warm materials such as wood.

been as an urban designer but as an architect, Pot-Keegstra was able to make her contribution to the garden suburbs of Amsterdam with her designs for various housing schemes that formed part of Van Eesteren's General Expansion Plan.

Who inspired whom?

The five women architects discussed here, who together with their husbands ran architecture practices for shorter or longer periods, managed to develop successfully within their profession. In the case of most of the architect couples, the models of cooperation display a surprisingly emancipated picture within which the female partners enjoyed ample scope to develop. Based on equality, collaboration took various forms. In the case of husband-and-wife Lammers-Koeleman, each partner worked on his or her own projects, even for the same client, while both of their names appeared beside all their work in publications. Kammer-Kret worked on commissions both together and individually. Husband-and-wife Pot-Keegstra operated at the very opposite end of the spectrum. They tackled every assignment in very close cooperation and acted jointly in their dealings with the media. Although having the practice attached to the home meant that the mixing of office affairs with household duties and family matters was more obvious for the woman, in the case of Pot-Keegstra it was the husband who pressed for the joint working practice. When children entered the picture, Kammer-Kret became an advisor to Kammer. Stam also sought closer collaboration with Stam-Beese.

The models of cooperation reveal that the women architects did not lean on the name and fame of their husbands but were, instead, very capable of forging their own careers. Conversely, one could ask whether, and to what extent, the husbands benefitted from the knowledge and expertise of their wives. The advisory role of Kammer-Kret is a good example of that. In the work of the women architects we can discern the ideas of the Modern Movement in the application of a restrained design language and rationalist, practical floor plans. Their repertoire reveals a surprising degree of variation. They responded to the spirit of the times and the occasionally difficult economic conditions by deploying new types of dwellings, construction materials and techniques, by designing buildings for new groups of residents, and by examining in depth the latest requirements set by industrial clients and government bodies. That the architect couples largely espoused the same modernist architectural views, prompted in part by the circles in which they moved, must have contributed to their mutual inspiring and possibly also their influencing of each other's work.

9 The 21 women architects

Lotte Beese

Charlotte Ida Anna Beese (Reisicht [now Rokitki, Poland], 1903 – Krimpen aan den IJssel, 1988), daughter of a railway employee, attended secondary school in Breslau and studied from 1926 to 1929 at the Bauhaus in Dessau.[1] Two years before the end of the course, however, she had to abandon her studies on account of her relationship with the married architecture teacher and later director Hannes Meyer (1889–1954). As a student at the Bauhaus, Beese focused initially on interior architecture, specializing in weaving. From 1927 on, this department fell under the responsibility of Hannes Meyer, and she also became acquainted with architecture as well as photography.

From 1934 to 1943, Beese was married to the architect Mart Stam and they ran an architecture office together (see Chapter 8). In 1940, Stam-Beese enrolled at the Voortgezet en Hooger Bouwkunst Onderricht (Secondary and Higher Architectural Training, or VHBO), from which she was the second woman to graduate. Stam-Beese, who retained that surname after her divorce, developed into a reputable urban designer at the Department of City Development in Rotterdam, where she continued to work until her retirement. Stam-Beese had two children: one from her relationship with Meyer, and one from her marriage to Stam.

1 Lotte Beese during her time as a student at the Bauhaus, Dessau, circa 1929. In the background Hartmut Schulze.

Riné Boerée

Chatthariné Heripsimé Marie Boerée (Naarden, 1898 – Oegstgeest, 1995), whose father had a military career, attended secondary school in The Hague. After obtaining her school diploma in 1916, she studied architecture at the TH in Delft, graduating in 1929. She contributed to the Delftsche Vrouwelijke Studenten Vereeniging as second secretary of the board in the period 1918–1919.

Boerée, who never married, became a highly respected concrete expert with the armed forces, where she worked until her pension in 1964.

For more information, see Chapter 6.

2 Riné Boerée a year before her graduation, 1928.

Wil van den Broek d'Obrenan

Wilhelmina van den Broek d'Obrenan (Batavia, 1905 – Groningen, 1966) was the daughter of an engineer employed by the Department of Water Management in the Dutch East Indies.[2] After attending secondary school in Utrecht, she began to study architecture in 1924 at the Technische Hogeschool Delft (Technical College of Delft, or TH). In the 1925–1926 academic year she was a board member of the Delftsche Vrouwelijke Studenten Vereeniging ('Delft Female Student Society', or DVSV).[3]

After graduating in 1934, Van den Broek d'Obrenan worked for a short period at the Institute for City and Landscape in the province of Zuid-Holland.[4] In the years that followed she was registered as an architect, residing in The Hague and Voorburg. Probably owing to a lack of employment, she returned in 1938 to Batavia, where she worked as an engineer for the Department of City Development and Public Housing. More than ten years later, she was registered in Haarlem as chief engineer at the Planning Department of the Noord-Holland Provincial Water Management Agency.[5] There she worked closely with civil engineer Els van den Ban (1894–1973).[6] In 1956, Van den Broek d'Obrenan became head of the new urban design division at the Public Works Department in Hilversum.[7] As far as is known, Van den Broek d'Obrenan never married.

3 Wil van den Broek d'Obrenan, 1928.

Joop Ferguson

Johanna Eleanor Ferguson (Shanghai, 1900 – Camberley [UK], 1982), daughter of a customs official, attended secondary school in The Hague and completed her studies in architecture at the TH in Delft in 1926.[8] A year before her graduation, *De Vrouw en haar Huis* published an article by her about 'small practical tables' that she had designed and made.[9] In that same year she married Ewoud van Everdingen (1900–1978), a chemical engineer in Breda, with whom she had two children. Her professional ambitions were still clearly present after her marriage, as shown by her listing on the *Register of Dutch Architects*.[10]

In 1934 she married Paul Boswinkel in Naarden, and had one child with him. Four years later she married for the third time in Johannesburg, and from then on she used her second name, Eleanor. She opened an architecture office with her husband Stakesby-Lewis (1906–1997), later known as Ferguson, Stakesby-Lewis, & Sayce.[11] In 1953 the family moved to Salisbury, Rhodesia (now Harare, Zimbabwe) where the architect couple opened a new office. In 1961 the family relocated to Camberley near London.

4 Joop Ferguson, circa 1925.

Ina Groenevelt

As the daughter of a Higher Civil School teacher, Josina Cornelia Groenevelt (The Hague, 1898 – Charlotte [US], 1977) attended secondary school in The Hague. After finishing school she enrolled at the faculty of architecture at the TH in Delft, graduating in 1923.[12] Soon thereafter she married Jan Heijkoop (1895–1973). Ina Heijkoop-Groenevelt was registered annually as an architectural engineer with the Society of Delft Engineers without a position until after the Second World War.[13] Husband-and-wife Heijkoop-Groenevelt relocated definitively to the United States when Heijkoop was sent to North Carolina in 1929 to build the first Enka textile factory there. The couple had three children.

5 Regrettably there is no known portrait of Ina Groenevelt.

Sophie (Dé) Heyting

Suzanne Sophia Heyting (The Hague, 1894 – Utrecht, 1988) attended secondary school in The Hague for a few years.[14] On 24 September 1910, she and her sister boarded the SS *Tambora* in Rotterdam and set sail for the Dutch East Indies, where her father Henri Heyting (1863–1916) was a high-ranking public administrator.[15] Heyting completed secondary school in Surabaya and returned to the Netherlands to study architecture at the TH in Delft. In the 1920–1921 academic year she chaired the Delftsche Vrouwelijke Studenten Vereeniging.[16] After nine years she graduated in 1923 together with, among others, Henry Zwiers, who in 1938 would become professor of architecture at the TH.[17]

For a number of years she was registered as an 'Architect' in The Hague, and in 1937 briefly as a 'Teacher at a Girls Secondary School', most likely owing to a lack of employment in her profession.[18] Little is known about her work as an independent architect. In 1928 she designed a villa in Wassenaar an expressionist style for her mother Anna Elisabeth Heyting-Mullemeister (1869–1957).[19] As a member of the Building Committee of the Dutch Society of Housewives, Heyting wrote the booklet *Waar moet men bij het kiezen van een huis op letten?*.[20]

At the age of 56, her career took 'a completely unexpected turn' when she became 'Municipal Architect' in Hoogeveen.[21] According to Heyting, she owed her appointment to the house that she had designed for her sister, a teacher at the Christelijk Lyceum in Hoogeveen, for which she had also supervised construction. Heyting, along with her mother, moved in with her sister.[22] She designed a police station, a health centre and a gymnasium, among other things, for the municipality of Hoogeveen. However, construction of these utility buildings was shelved in favour of public housing 'after Korea and everything connected with it'.[23] As a member of the Housing Committee of the Dutch Household Advisory Board, Heyting helped to draw up of standard floorplans for efficient housing construction.[24]

6 Dé Heyting as chairwoman of the board of the DVSV, 1920–1921.

In 1964, the Good Shepherd Dutch Reformed Church in Hoogeveen was built to a design by the then 70-year-old Heyting.[25] There is no sign of the expressionistic style evident in the previously mentioned Wassenaar villa. Without the freestanding bell tower, the sober building might be mistaken for a factory structure.

Wil Jansen

Wilhelmina Catharina Maria Jansen (Schiedam, 1904 – Schiedam, 1989) was the daughter of a Schiedam businessman who successfully expanded the old family distillery into an industrial empire in which his five sons were active. Wil was the youngest of eight children and the only one to go on to further education. After secondary school she began to study architecture in Delft, graduating in 1931. She was president of the Delftsche Vrouwelijke Studenten Vereeniging in the 1927–1928 academic year. Jansen was a very active member of the first Advisory Commission for Women (VAC) set up in Rotterdam. Jansen managed to establish a successful architecture practice, with a substantial portfolio of commissions. For more information, see Chapter 7.

7 Wil Jansen, 1927.

Koos Keegstra

Jacoba Froukje Keegstra (Amsterdam, 1908 – Amsterdam, 1997), whose mother was a teacher and whose father was a director of the Municipal Giro System, spent her secondary school years at the Amsterdams Lyceum.[26] Her interest in architecture was stimulated by visits with her father, chairman of a housing association, to building projects. She studied building construction at the Secondary Technical School in Haarlem – where she was the first woman student – and graduated in 1930.

Keegstra worked as a draughtswoman for the Public Works Department in Amsterdam but was made redundant owing to the crisis. She then enrolled at the VHBO evening academy in Amsterdam, from which she was the first woman to graduate in 1935. While a student, she worked as a writer for the Municipal Housing and Building Control Department in Amsterdam. From 1936 to 1938, Keegstra again worked for Public Works, first as a draughtswoman and then as a technical supervisor. In 1938 she married Joop Pot (1909–1972), whom she had met during her VHBO studies. The couple opened their own architecture office (see Chapter 8) and had one daughter.

In 1941, the couple followed a course in architecture under the auspices of the society Architectura et Amicitia, with teachers that included Marinus Jan Granpré Molière, Gerrit Rietveld and Willem van Tijen.[27] Keegstra chaired the editorial committee of the periodical *Bouwkundig Weekblad* from about 1959 to 1965.

8 Koos Keegstra, date unknown.

Co van der Kloet

Jacoba van der Kloet (Dordrecht, 1896 – Rijswijk, 1959), daughter of a shopkeeper on Voorstraat in Dordrecht, completed secondary school in 1914, and two years later she began to study architecture in Delft.[28] There she met Pieter Stempels (1898–1979), whom she married a few months after graduating in 1926.[29] The couple had one son.

Stempels, a civil engineer, worked as a volunteer at the Public Works Department in The Hague, charged with the daily supervision of the construction of a dock, the Tweede Binnenhaven, in Scheveningen.[30] In 1928, he took a job as an engineer with a contracting firm, the NV Nederlandsche Aannemingsmaatschappij, in The Hague. In 1953 he was forced to step down as director of the Hawoma home construction company in The Hague, set up by the municipality to build homes out of hollow concrete.[31] Stempels had stored reinforcement bars unprofessionally and was responsible for company overspending. For many years he was a member of the Rijswijk municipal council for the VVD party and an alderman responsible for public works.

It could not be ascertained whether Co Stempels-van der Kloet had a career as an architectural engineer. She did, however, join the registry as an 'Architecte B.N.A.', residing in Rijswijk.[32] In 1934 she designed a folding bicycle whereby a men's bicycle could be turned into one for ladies by folding down the crossbar.[33] It is not known if the design was ever produced.

9 Co van der Kloet on the day of her wedding to Pieter Stempels, 1 December 1926.

Toki Koeleman

Cato Christine Koeleman (Karlsbad [Bohemia, now Czech Republic] 1911 – Wageningen, 2000), daughter of a mine director, completed secondary school in her native country.[34] Although she actually wanted to become a sculptor, her parents advised against it because she would not be able to earn a living. [35] Immediately after obtaining her leaving certificate in 1931, Koeleman started to study architecture at the TH in Delft. She graduated ten years later, during the Second World War. During her student years, she chaired the Delftsche Vrouwelijke Studenten Vereeniging from 1935 to 1937.[36]

After graduating, Koeleman was approached by another Delft graduate, Hendrik Lammers (1909–1990), to join his office and manage the current projects of a Jewish architect who had fled to England. After a few months, Koeleman and Lammers married and ran the architecture office together (see Chapter 8). The couple remained childless.

In the 1950s, Koeleman was a member of the Housing Committee of the Dutch Household Council of the Royal Institute of Dutch Architects (BNA), whose members included Willem van Tijen and Hugh Maaskant.

10 Toki Koeleman, ca. 1935.

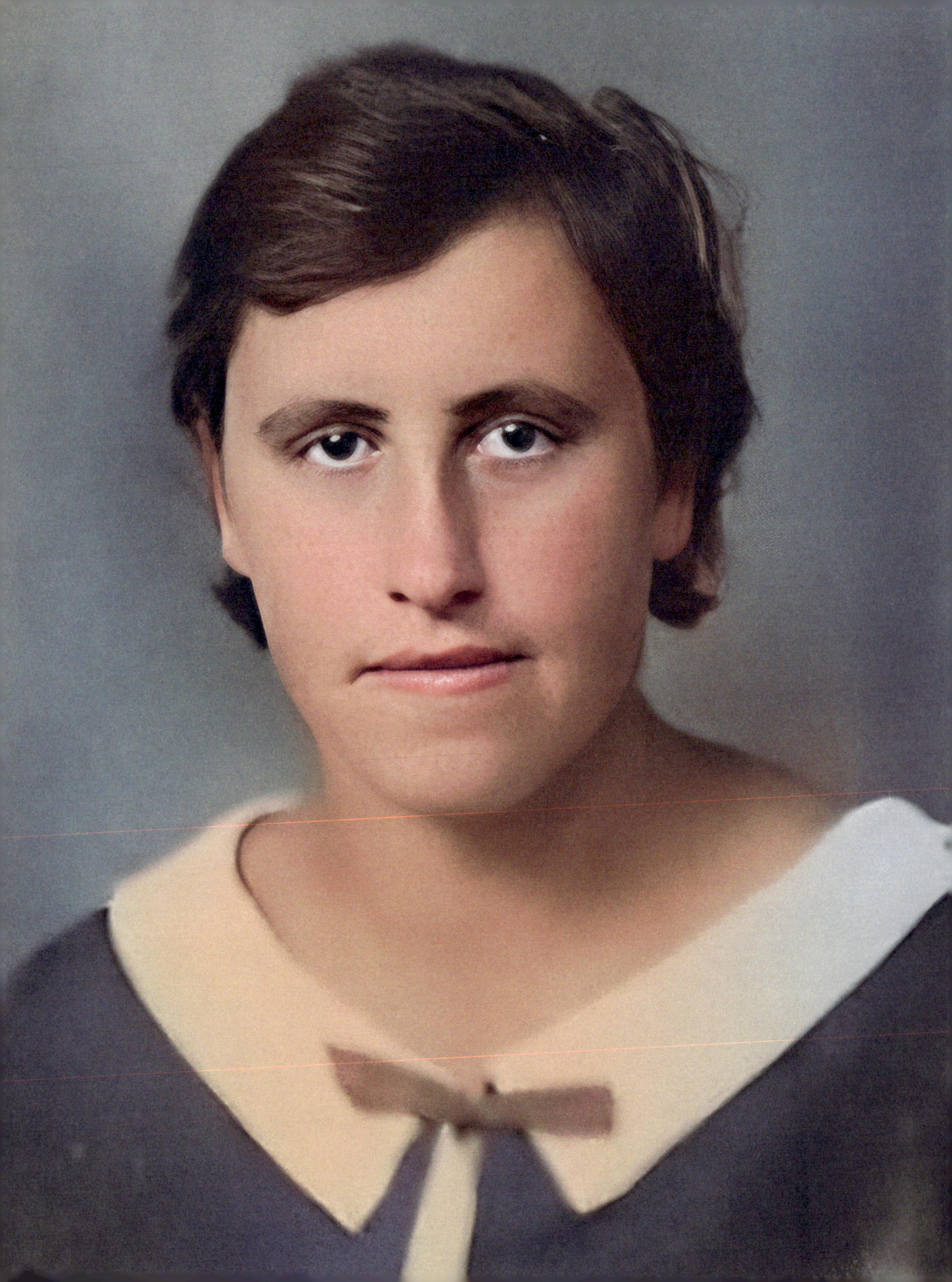

Jan Kret

Janne Johanna Kret (Rotterdam, 1906 – Gouda, 1984), whose father was a trading clerk, attended the '2nd HBS secondary school in Rotterdam' from 1918 to 1923.[37] Mathematics was her favourite subject.[38] When she turned out to be the only student of architecture at the TH in Delft, she initially opted to study chemistry.[39] After half a year, however, she switched to architecture, the course that continued to attract her and to which six women students had by then been admitted. Kret graduated in 1931 and a year later married her fellow student Harry Kammer (1902–1988), who at the time was working for the architecture office of Brinkman and Van der Vlugt, the designers of the Van Nelle Factory. The couple opened their own practice in Schiebroek (see Chapter 8) and had four daughters, the two youngest of whom followed in their parents footsteps by becoming architectural engineers.

11 Jan Kret, 1928.

Ko Mulder

Jakoba Helena Mulder (Breda, 1900 – Amsterdam, 1988) was the daughter of an army officer stationed in the Dutch East Indies, where she attended primary school.[40] She returned to the Netherlands with her sister and went to secondary school in Zutphen and then Assen – as the only girl to do so – where she obtained her leaving certificate in 1918. She was good in science subjects, and her father, by then a teacher of mathematics and physics at a secondary school in Java supported her in her decision to study architecture at the TH in Delft. In the 1924–1925 academic year, Mulder chaired the Delftsche Vrouwelijke Studenten Vereeniging.[41] She graduated in 1926.[42]

Mulder found a job as a draughtswoman in The Hague at the architecture office of Gerretsen and Wegerif, friends of hers, where she mostly elaborated sketch designs. In 1928, she became deputy architect at the urban design department in Delft, where she worked on an expansion plan for the town. Thanks to her unmarried status, she could continue to work for the city government, and in 1930 she was appointed deputy architect at the urban development division of the Public Works Department of the City of Amsterdam. Here she worked closely with civil engineer Theodoor van Lohuizen (1890–1956) and architect Cornelis van Eesteren, who were responsible for the General Expansion Plan that would shape the city's growth to the west. Mulder was entrusted with the layout of a large park, the later Amsterdamse Bos, where she became involved in early landscape architecture. In elaborating this park design, she travelled to numerous European cities. With an eye for the social environment, Mulder made a name for herself with the construction of many children's playgrounds, designed by architect Aldo van Eyck (1918–1999), both in existing Amsterdam neighbourhoods and in the new garden suburbs. She developed the idea of courtyard development: building blocks grouped around a green court, which were built in Slotermeer. In 1958, Mulder who was by then chief architect, succeeded Van Eesteren as head of the urban development division, a position that she retained until her retirement. After that she continued to act as an advisor to the municipality for some time.

12 Ko Mulder, date unknown.

She was a lecturer in planning at the University of Amsterdam until the age of seventy. During her career, Mulder held many other positions and published numerous articles (see Chapter 4).

Greet van der Poest Clement

Margaretha van der Poest Clement (Hattem, 1912 – Rotterdam, 1976), daughter of a patent assessor, went to secondary school in The Hague. Achieving high scores in subjects such as 'Straight Drawing', 'Algebra and Trigonometry' and 'Stereometry and Descriptive Geometry', she quickly chose to study architecture.[43] She was an active member of the Delftsche Vrouwelijke Studenten Vereeniging, holding positions that included secretary of the board when Toki Koeleman was chairwoman.[44] Van der Poest Clement completed her studies in architecture after six years in 1938, after which she took up a temporary position at the Government Buildings Agency.[45] Shortly after the Second Word War she was registered as an engineer at the Rotterdam City Plan Advisory Office (ASRO), set up by the government, which worked on the reconstruction of the city. It is not known how long she worked here. Van der Poest Clement was married to Hendrik (Henk) Christoffel Milius (1919–1983), an urban designer employed by the Department of City Development in Rotterdam and a direct colleague of Lotte Stam-Beese.

13 Greet van der Poest Clement at the start of her studies at the TH in Delft, 1932.

Loes Pomes

Louise Maria Pomes (Rotterdam, 1905 – The Hague, 1964), daughter of a 'teacher in Schiedam', obtained her secondary school certificate in 1922.[46] That same year she enrolled for the course in architecture at the TH in Delft, where she graduated nine years later. From that time on, she was registered without a position and resident in Schiedam.[47] She got married in 1934 to Jan Willem Christiaan Dommerholt (1905–1984), an inspector at the Ministry of Justice. The couple had an unknown number of children. As far as is known, Pomes did not practice her profession actively.

14 Loes Pomes, 1928.

Jeanne van Rijswijk

Adriana Petronella van Rijswijk (The Hague, 1904 – Wassenaar, 1960) attended secondary school in The Hague and obtained her leaving certificate in 1924. Her final result, with failing grades in mathematics and physics, among others, did not prevent her from choosing to study architecture at the TH in Delft. Van Rijswijk was apparently under the charge of a certain P. Visser in Utrecht, and was listed in the student administration as a 'pupil'.[48] After a ten-year period of study, she graduated in 1934.

Van Rijswijk worked for half a year as a draughtswoman at the Wassenaar architecture office of civil and architectural engineer Albert van Rood (1885–1947), whom she married in the same year as her graduation. The couple probably had one child; Van Rood had six children from two previous marriages. After the death of her husband, Van Rijswijk continued the architecture practice (see Chapter 8). As a member of Housing Committee of the Dutch Household Advisory Council, she helped to draw up standard floor plans for efficient housing construction.

15 Jeanne van Rijswijk, 1928.

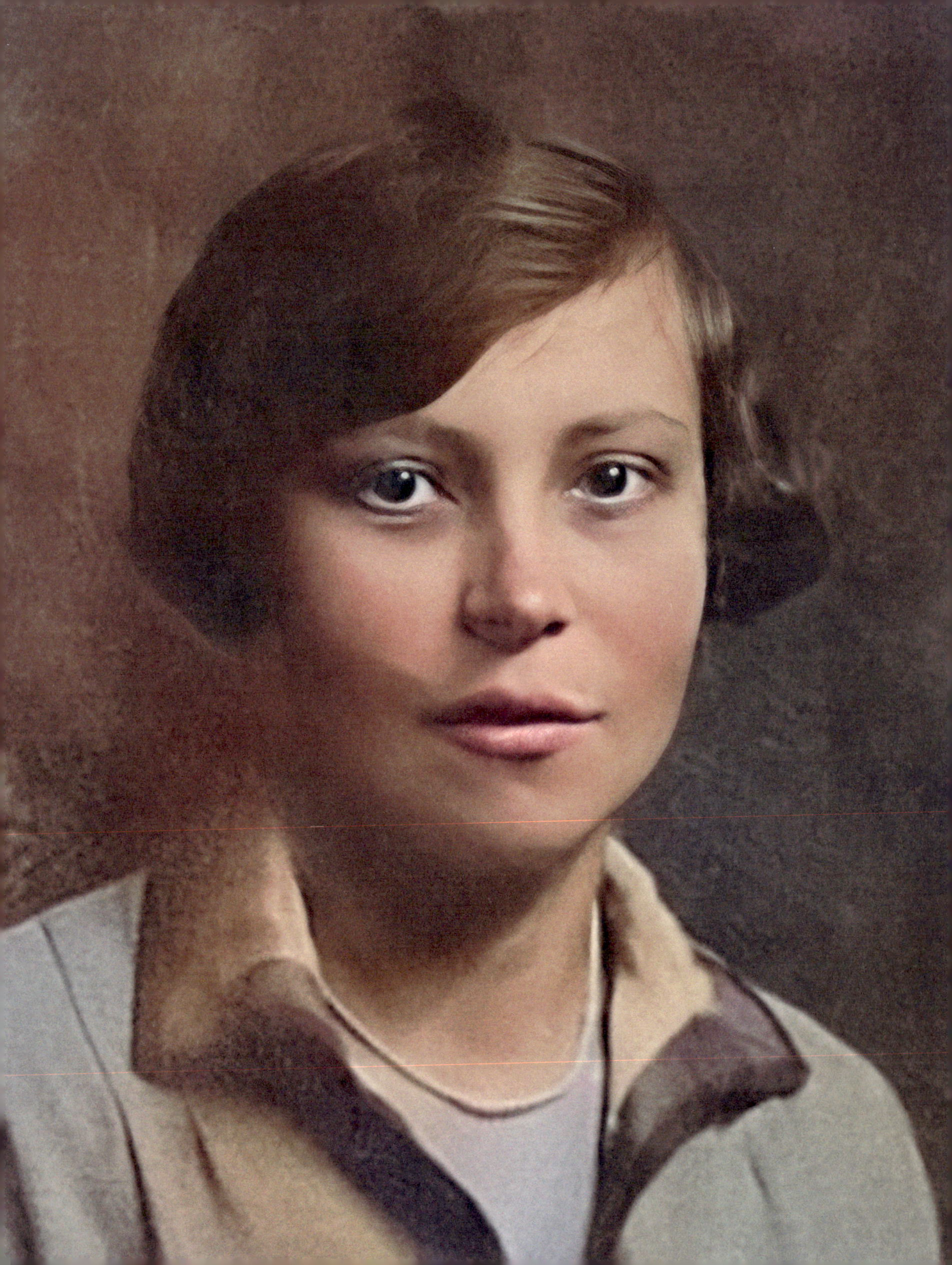

Paula Rooseboom

Pauline Willemine Rooseboom (Batavia, 1899 – Laren, 1975) studied at a lyceum secondary school in The Hague.[49] Her father, an employee of a business that imported Indian products, died when she was 11 years old.[50] In 1918, a year after receiving her leaving certificate, Paula Rooseboom began to study architecture at the TH in Delft, graduating in 1931. During her studies, she was the only woman active as 'treasurer' and 'archivist' of the Civil and Architectural Students Society for Practical Study.[51] She was also a board member of the Delftsche Vrouwelijke Studenten Vereeniging.[52]

After graduating, Rooseboom was a member of the Building Committee of the Dutch Society of Housewives. Owing to illness, she could not complete the publication *Waar moet men bij het kiezen van een huis op letten?*, which she had prepared (see Heyting).[53] From 1937 on, Rooseboom was registered as 'Partner architect' in The Hague and Scheveningen.[54] No works by her could be traced. Paula Rooseboom remained unmarried. She died at the age of 75 after a long illness. Her death notice was signed by, among others, Ko Mulder.[55]

16 Paula Rooseboom, 1928.

Marie Snethlage

Marie Felicia Henriëtte Snethlage (Werkendam, 1893 – The Hague, 1998), daughter of an inheritance tax official, attended secondary school in Rotterdam, which she completed in 1911.[56] A year later she enrolled as a student of architecture at the TH in Delft, graduating in 1921. As 'treasurer', she sat on the board of the Delftsche Vrouwelijke Studenten Vereeniging.[57] In the year she graduated, she worked for three months at the architecture office of Abel Kok (1881–1951) in Amsterdam. Kok focused on the restoration of churches and residences, and a main client of his was the Hendrick de Keyser Society.[58]

Possibly to build up a professional network, Snethlage sought election to the Architectura et Amicitia Society, where she was installed in 1922 and which she remained a member of for ten years.[59] From 1926 on she was forced to work as a correspondent at the banking house Hope & Co in Amsterdam.[60] Snethlage did not lack any ambition to work as an architectural engineer. A striking note in the student administration at the TH in Delft tells us that, eight years after graduating, she attended 'all classes' for a whole academic year.[61] She may have been uncertain about her further career possibilities as an architectural engineer and wanted to update her knowledge in this way.

17 Marie Snethlage, 1929.

Snethlage did not find work in her profession. From 1937 to about 1947, she was a librarian at the Academy of Fine Arts in The Hague.[62] She then worked for the archives of the Government Architect up until her retirement in 1958. A source lists her as 'processor/editor'.[63] Snethlage remained unmarried.

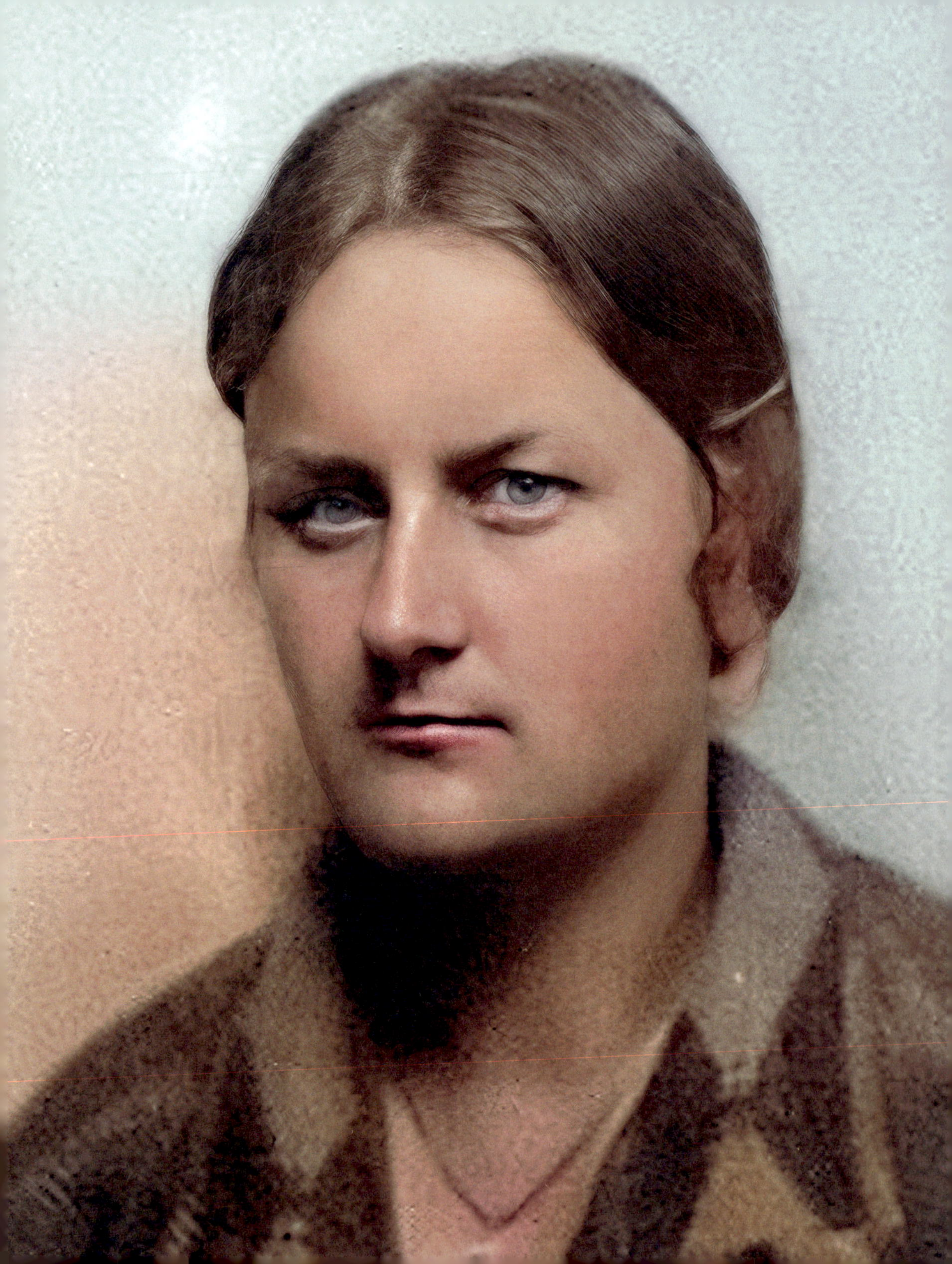

To (Toot) Strumphler

Catharina Strumphler (Oldenzaal, 1911 – Arnhem, 1981), daughter of a chemical engineer, was a pupil at secondary school for girls before starting to study architecture at the TH in Delft in 1931.[64] In the 1934–1935 academic year she was a board member of the Delftsche Vrouwelijke Studenten Vereeniging.[65] After graduating in 1941, she was registered as a 'Consultant Engineer' in Delft, where she worked with architect and urban designer Sam van Embden (1904–2000).[66] During the war years she followed the new course in urban design at the TH, under the auspices of the architecture department. However, she could not complete the course owing to the closure of the TH. From 1943 to 1945, Strumphler worked as a draughtswoman at the architecture office of Kees Elffers (1898–1987) in Rotterdam.

After the war, she worked as an engineer for the Gelderland Provincial Plan Office in Arnhem, a challenging position after the complete destruction of the provincial hall and the archives held there. In 1949, Strumphler described her work as the design of regional plans.[67] These were not in her name, but in that of the Plan Office or of the Provincial Water Management Department, under which the office fell. Alongside her government position, Strumphler worked on private commissions about which nothing is known. In the 1950s her work shifted towards an advisory role as chief engineer at what was then called the Provincial Planning Department, with a focus on the Achterhoek region. In this capacity, she was a member of the Provincial Monuments Committee. She highlighted the profession of planning in newspaper interviews.[68] She also wrote articles about subjects related to her work.[69] These could not be traced, however.

18 To Strumphler, 1931.

The unmarried Strumphler commissioned Toki Lammers-Koeleman to design a bungalow for her and her mother. This was completed in 1960.[70] It is the only known example within this study of a private residence designed and built by and for a woman architect.

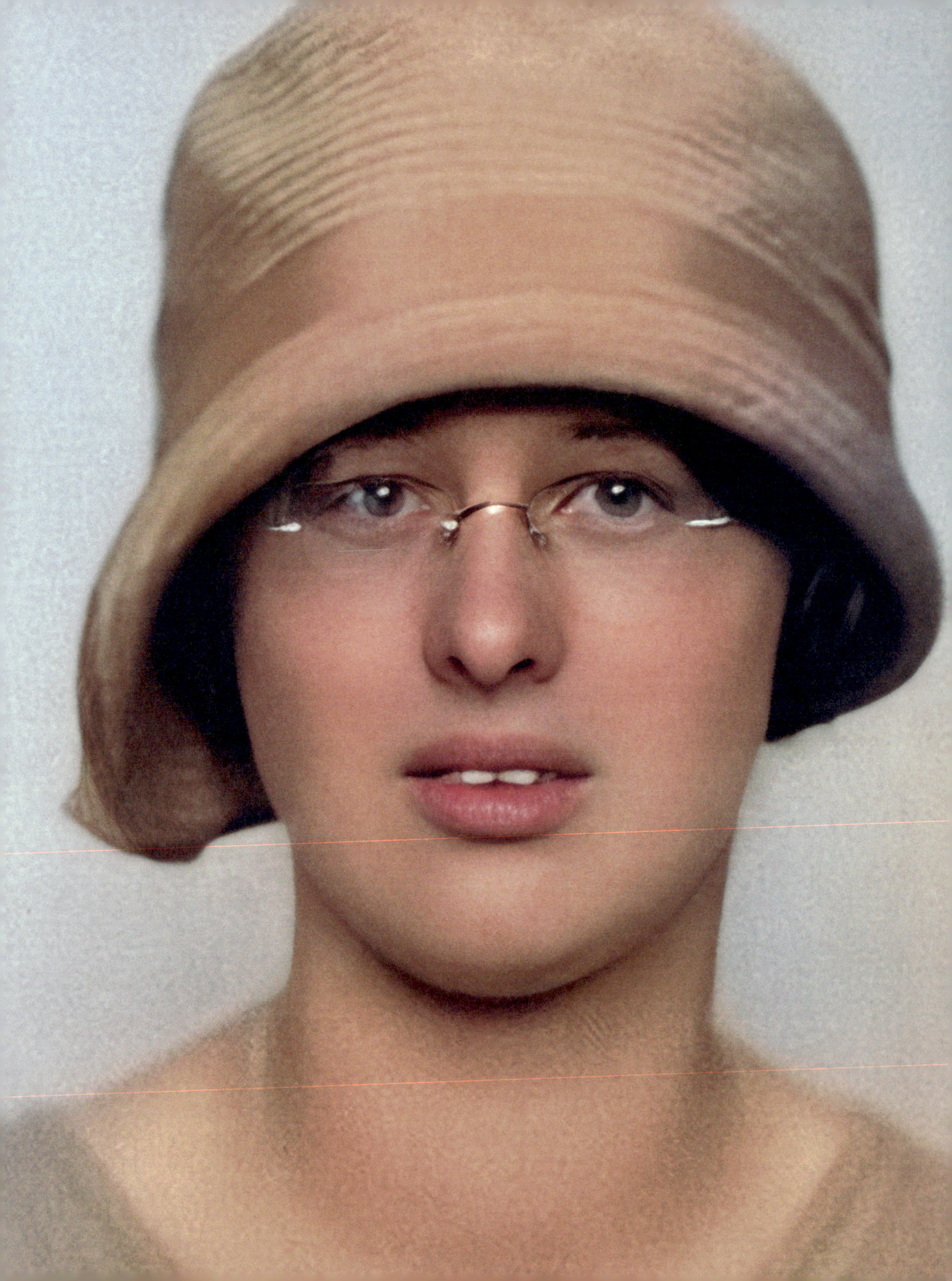

Ada Struyk

Ada Struyk (Delft, 1908 – Epe, 1985), daughter of an accountant, attended the Marnix Gymnasium secondary school in Rotterdam from 1920 to 1928.[71] In 1928 she began to study architecture at the TH in Delft, graduating in 1937. In that same year she married the architectural engineer Johannes Albertus Kuiper (1907–2003), a partner at the architecture office that later became known under the name Kuiper, Gouwetor and De Ranitz, and which played an important role in the post-war reconstruction of Rotterdam.

Kuiper-Struyk was not active as an architectural engineer but as a politician. As a member of the People's Party for Freedom (VVD), she was a Rotterdam city councillor from 1953 to 1966, and from 1959 to 1966 a member of parliament, where she was a spokeswoman on public housing, transport and waterworks, and scientific education.[72] Kuiper-Struyk campaigned for humane post-war public housing for families with open spaces and plenty of greenery, as well as for homes for single women.[73] She advocated a more generous allocation of public housing units and subsidized owner-occupied homes outside the Randstad.[74] To solve the housing crisis, she proposed the construction of extremely cheap homes, without any luxury, for the healthy and harmonious development of family life and with a layout that ensured the smooth functioning of the household. In addition, she fought against the impoverishment of vocational education for girls. In 1960, she participated in discussions concerning the proposed Monuments and Historic Buildings Act.[75] She stepped back from politics owing to the threat of a heart attack caused by too much work in combination with the care of a family of four children.

19 Ada Struyk, 1928.

Kuiper-Struyk held numerous positions in social organizations and was active in professional societies. For example, she was a member of the Council for Public Housing, vice-chair of the Housing Committee of the Dutch Household Council, board member of the Rotterdam division of the Society of Women with an Academic Education, and vice-chair of the Women's Advice Committee.

Grada Wolffensperger

Gerarda Wilhelmina Elisabeth Wolffensperger (The Hague, 1887 – The Hague, 1965), daughter of a mortgage official, completed secondary school in 1908. That same year she started studying architecture at the TH in Delft. She became the first woman architectural engineer in the Netherlands when she graduated in 1917.

Wolffensperger did not enjoy an illustrious career. She worked as deputy architect for the Public Works Department in Haarlem from 1920 to 1922.

For more information, see Chapter 5.

20 Grada Wolffensperger after her graduation, 1918.

Beb (Bep) Zeeman

Elisabeth Cornelia Zeeman (Vrijenban, Delft 1895 – Haarlem, 1990), daughter of a mathematics professor at the University of Leiden, the town where she attended secondary school from 1907 to 1912.[76] The following year she was the only woman to begin to study architecture at the TH in Delft, from which she graduated in 1920. That made her the second woman architectural engineer in the Netherlands. As a student, she chaired the Delftsche Vrouwelijke Studenten Vereeniging from 1916 to 1918.[77] Just after graduation, she wrote an article about timber country homes for *De Vrouw en haar Huis*.[78] She also offered her views on the role of women in architecture in an article for the periodical *Bouwkundig Weekblad*.[79]

In the year she graduated, Zeeman began work as an engineer – the only woman – at the small architecture office of Willem Leliman (1878–1921) in Baarn.[80] After his death, she worked for three years as deputy architect for the Public Works Department in Amsterdam, where Ko Mulder would later make her career. In both positions, Zeeman's work was limited to elaborating sketch designs.[81]

In 1925 she married Willem Frederik Einthoven (1893–1945), an electro-technical engineer and son of the doctor and Nobel Prize winner Willem Einthoven, with whom she moved to Bandoeng, where Einthoven was appointed head of the PTT Laboratory.[82] During the Second World War the family with four children was deported to Tokyo, where Einthoven died of exhaustion and illness.

21 Beb Zeeman during her tenure as chairwoman of the board of the DVSV, 1916–1917.

Einthoven-Zeeman returned to the Netherlands in 1945. Although she was offered a number of jobs in architecture offices, she started to teach mathematics – the subject at which she excelled – at the Kennemerlyceum school in Haarlem. This position, supplemented with remedial lessons for children from Indonesia, was easy to combine with her family life. Professionally, she remained involved as a member of the Women's Advisory Committee in Haarlem. In that role she interviewed women in new housing developments about the functioning of their kitchens.

Conclusion

How did professionally educated women make their entry into the field of architecture in the Netherlands? Who were these women? These were the primary research questions that led to this publication. I focused on the period from 1905 until the end of the Second World War. This publication showcased 21 women architects who graduated from university and held a degree. They deserve a place in the history books. In actual fact, their progressive parents do too. They supported their daughters in this choice of profession – remarkable for that time – that flouted all social conventions and cautionary recommendations.

The women sometimes encountered blatant pushback during and after their studies, which sometimes had major consequences for them. Rather than a fully fledged position at an architecture firm or their own independent architecture practice, many of them ended up working in jobs that they were overqualified for, or were unrelated to the architect's profession – or, worse yet, became unemployed. A job in government service was an option, but only for women who were unmarried and remained single.

It is hard to imagine now that several women later said in interviews that they had never experienced such forms of discrimination. They were satisfied with what they had achieved, simply because their expectations had not been very high to begin with. They gave reasons like 'there wasn't anything else' and 'we were happy with what we could get'; that says it all. Another remarkable aspect is the very modest position that most of these women held in the media. They received little or no media coverage.

During the course of my research, I also observed that these women had a certain pragmatic resignation, feeling no urgent need to claim the spotlight. Where did that sense of modesty come from? They built not only homes, but also laboratories, factories and runways. To our modern eyes, this seems like a fairly amazing accomplishment. Were they more emancipated back then than we are now?

In any case, I hope that this book has filled in a number of gaps, although I realize that we will never have a comprehensive overview. History is constantly in flux.

Notes

1 introduction

1 Website: *Musée d'Orsay*.
2 Metz 2019.
3 De Klerck 2019.
4 Websites: *Rijksmuseum Twenthe* and *National Gallery*. For media attention, see (for example): Branbergen 2020.
5 Website: *Rijksmuseum Twenthe* b.
6 Website: *Kunsthal Rotterdam*.
7 Website: *RKD*.
8 Website: *Rijksmuseum*.
9 Snoodijk 2023, 28-30.
10 Website: *Het Nieuwe Instituut – Collecting Otherwise*.
11 For example, the research underlying this publication led to the recent transfer to Het Nieuwe Instituut of the complete archive of Mr and Mrs Kammer-Kret.
12 Website: *See All This*.
13 Website: *Registry of Architects – Annual Report 2021*.
14 Website: *A.Zine*.
15 Doumato 1988.
16 Martin/Sparke 2003, x-xv.
17 Cole 1973, vii.
18 Torre 1977.
19 The Women in Architecture Archive of the American Institute of Architects in Washington D.C. was established in 1984. The International Archive of Women in Architecture (IAWA), founded by the Virginia Polytechnic Institute and State University, Blacksburg, has been in existence since 1985. Simpson 1991, 44-48.
20 Wright 1977, 280-308.
21 Allaback 2008.
22 Website: *Paul Mellon Centre*.
23 Singha 2019.
24 The editors are L. Brown (Syracuse University) and K. Burns (University of Melbourne). Website: *Experts of Syracuse University*. The publication was delayed by the COVID-19 pandemic, and is currently listed as "Unpublished".
25 Hall 2019, 122.
26 Schwitalla 2021, 22-23.
27 See e.g.: website: *Huygens Institute for Dutch History – Royal Netherlands Academy of Arts and Sciences (KNAW) – Kropholler, Margaret*; website: Het Nieuwe Instituut – Staal-Kropholler, M.
28 Wijdeveld 1918, 2-20, citation p. 8.
29 Van Kessel/Kuperus, undated [1991], 87.
30 The other two women were approached in their capacities as civil engineer and interior architect, respectively.
31 The only other architect included as furniture and interior designer is Lotte Stam-Beese. Groot 2007, 400, 401-406, 458, 500.
32 It is interesting to note the entry of architect/architectural engineer Jacoba Mulder in the lexicon as member of the Soroptimist Club. Groot 2007, 401 (citation), 511.
33 Groot 2007, 399.
34 Van Agtmaal 1978.
35 Website: *Utrecht University*; website: *Royal Library of the Netherlands – Exceptional women, exceptional books*.
36 Website: *Wikipedia – Aletta Jacobs*.
37 Couvée/Boswijk 1962, 190.
38 This statement is attributed to Hendrik Willem Bakhuis Roozenboom (1854–1907). Couvée and Boswijk 1962, 159.
39 Website: *Atria, Archive of the National Exhibition of Women's Labour 1898*, citation: Introduction. Het doel van de Vereeniging Nationale Tentoonstellling van Vrouwenarbeid, under b).
40 Groot 2007, 122.
41 Heinen 1914, 407-417.
42 Linders 2003, 246-252.
43 Linders 2003, 246.
44 One effect of the abolishment of the legal incapacity of women was that married women could independently open their own bank accounts.
45 Buikema/Plate 2015, 393.
46 In this chapter the comparison is only directed towards garden architecture, rather than landscape architecture, because the option to earn a degree in landscape architecture was only available starting in 1945. Until that time, it was generally the architect who would be in charge of the landscape architecture on any given project.
47 The initial results of the research were published in *Bulletin KNOB*. Smeets-Klokgieters 2017, 43-57.
48 Haslinghuis/Janse 2001, 12.
49 The Technische Hogeschool Eindhoven was founded in 1956, and its department of structural engineering and design was opened in 1967.
50 Wendt 2008; Het Nieuwe Instituut, Rotterdam (HNI), archive of the Academie van Bouwkunst, Amsterdam (ABAM).
51 Van Kessel/Kuperus 1982.
52 The research results were published in the *Jaarboek Haerlem*. Smeets-Klokgieters 2019, 153-177.
53 M. Staal-Kropholler, *List of women architectural engineers*, typescript, undated, HNI, Rotterdam, archives of Staal J.F., Kropholler A.J. and Staal-Kropholler, M. (STAX), inv.no. 110339037.
54 On Riné Boerée's career, there is a recent article in the armed forces journal *Militaire Spectator*. See: Smeets-Klokgieters 2019, 252-271.
55 Heijkoop/Bakker 2010.
56 See also: Smeets[-Klokgieters] 2020 a, 32-36; 2020 b, 62-67; 2020 c, 84-89.
57 Damen/Devolder 1993; Oosterhof 2018.
58 Oosterhof 2018, 95.
59 For example, Kammer-Kret. Van Kessel/Kuperus 1982, 104.
60 Architecte 1946.
61 Roos 1978.

2 The rise of women in furniture design, interior design and garden architecture

1 Groot 2007, 15-22, 64, 398-401.
2 Strijland 1999, 30.
3 Fuhring/Eggink 1981, 38-46.
4 Website: *Kenniscentrum voor de Nederlandse Architecten Praktijk*.
5 Fuhring/Eggink 1981, 39.
6 Fuhring/Eggink 1981, 40.
7 Fuhring/Eggink 1981, 40-41.
8 Fuhring/Eggink 1981, 41-43.
9 Fuhring/Eggink 1981, 41.
10 Fuhring/Eggink 1981, 41.
11 Fuhring/Eggink 1981, 41.
12 Fuhring/Eggink 1981, 42.
13 Fuhring/Eggink 1981, 42.
14 Fuhring/Eggink 1981, 45.
15 Groot 2007, 398-417.
16 Fuhring/Eggink 1981, 42.
17 Website: *Registry of Architects – Annual Report 2021*.
18 Groot 2007, 400.
19 Wendt 2008, 56; Van Kessel/Kuperus [1991], 9-10. In the latter publication, the name given for the Dagteeken- en Ambachtschool voor Meisjes is not correct.
20 Wendt 2008, 56; Van Kessel/Kuperus [1991], 13. In both of these publications the name given for the School voor Bouwkunde, Versierende Kunsten en Ambachten is not correct. The School voor Kunstnijverheid only took on a different name in 1918: School voor Bouwkunde, Versierende Kunsten en Kunstambachten. Groot 2007, 451.
21 Van Kessel/Kuperus [1991], 11-13; Groot 2007, 401-403.
22 Groot 2007, 211, 406-412, 522-523. How long Jo van Regteren Altena studied at the School voor Kunstnijverheid is not clear.
23 Van Oven 1939, 11-14.
24 Groot 2007, 412-417, 505.
25 Fuhring/Eggink 1981, 40.
26 Schilt 1982, 139-157.
27 Oosterhof 2018, 93, 101.

28 Liefrinck 1932, 220-222, citation: 222.
29 Groot 2007, 510-511.
30 Strijland 1999, 5.
31 Strijland 1999, 19-21.
32 In accordance with a revision of the Dutch University Education Act, the name was changed to Landbouwuniversiteit in 1986. Its current name is Wageningen University and Research. Website *Wageningen University and Research (WUR)*.
33 Backer 2016, 429.
34 Strijland 1999, 21.
35 Strijland 1999, 32.
36 Backer 2016, 458.
37 Strijland 1999, 21; Backer 2016, 429-434; Holtkamp 2020.
38 Strijland 1999, 28.
39 Backer 2016, 432.
40 Strijland 1999, 21.
41 Backer 2016, 432.
42 Strijland 1999, 30.
43 Backer 2016, 412-421.
44 Strijland 1999, 31-32.
45 Strijland 1999, 29-30.
46 Strijland 1999, 36.
47 Backer 2016, 415.
48 Strijland 1999, 30-31.
49 Strijland 1999, 31.
50 Blok 1992, 101-118; Website: *Wageningen University & Research – E. Blok, Jongere Tuinkunst 1900–1940*.
51 For Cool's bibliography, see: Blok 1992, 163-166.
52 Backer 2016, 441-444; Strijland, 21.
53 Backer 2016, 436-441.
54 Ruys studied at the Institut für Gartengestaltung at the Landwirtschaftliche Hochschule in Berlin-Dahlem. Backer 2016, 472-481.
55 Backer 2016, 477.
56 Of Jo Bouwens it is known that in 1914 she earned her diploma from the Middelbare Tuinbouwschool Voor Meisjes Huis te Lande. Strijland 1999, 21.
57 Strijland 1999, 8. This organization's current name is the Nederlandse Vereniging voor Tuin- en Landschapsarchitectuur (NVTL).
58 Roeters van Lennep 1933, 17-18, citation 17.
59 Fokker 1933, 18-19, citation 18.
60 Faber 1928, 199.
61 Strijland 1999, 31.
62 Blok 1992, 119-143.

3 The pioneering women architects

1 Geerts/Den Boon 1999, 225.
2 Krabbe 1997, 13.
3 Bosma 2007, 460-467; Krabbe 1997, 136-138.
4 Krabbe 1997, 104-107, 123-125.
5 Koninklijk 1897, XVII-XVIII; Kamp 1955, 27; Krabbe 1997, 167-168.
6 Kamp 1955, 9-20; Zwiers 1955, 213-227.
7 Van Damme-van Weele/Ressing-Wolfert, 1995, 15.
8 Zwiers 1955, 226.
9 Study 1914, 16-22.
10 Aalbers et al. 1994, 35-36.
11 Van Kessel/Kuperus 1982, 101.
12 Study 1914, 17.
13 Study 1914, 17.
14 Study 1914, 21.
15 Kamp 1955, Lists of names, charts, X-XV.
16 Van Kessel/Kuperus 1982, 92-93, 102, 110.
17 Van Kessel/Kuperus 1982, 93.
18 Study 1914, 21.
19 Kooijman 1995, 20.
20 Kamp 1955, Lists of names, charts, X-XV.
21 Study 1914, 20.
22 Van Kessel/Kuperus 1982, 109-110.
23 De Jong 1997, 227-242.
24 Kamp 1955, 21-22; Van Damme-van Weele/Ressing-Wolfert 1995, 13.
25 Vereeniging van Delftsche Ingenieurs 1905.
26 Vereeniging van Delftsche Ingenieurs 1905; Van Damme-van Weele/Ressing-Wolfert 1995, 15, 97, 101.
27 Vereeniging van Delftsche Ingenieurs 1947.
28 Polak 1928, 118.
29 Van Kessel/Kuperus 1982, 88, 92.
30 Van der Weide 1918, 3-13.
31 Van der Weide 1918, 9.
32 Polak 1928, 118.
33 Everts 1910, 30.
34 Van Kessel/Kuperus 1982, 102.
35 F.J.H.P. 1932, 7.
36 Van Kessel/Kuperus 1982, 88-108.
37 Interview with nephew of H.T.F. Jansen, 4 March 2019.
38 Kirejczyk 1993, 234-247.
39 *List of all Female Students in Delft*, undated [1877–1945], unpaginated, City Archive of Delft (SAD), archive of Delftsche Vrouwelijke Studenten Vereeniging (DVSV), archive number 357, inv.no. 180; Delftsche undated [1905], 403-452; Yearbook 1917, 22; National Archives, The Hague (NA), archive of Technische Hogeschool Delft (THD), Student Administration, access no. 3.12.08.04, inv.nos. 86, 130, 248.
40 Everts 1910, 29.
41 Heinen 1914, 60.
42 National Archives, The Hague (NA), archive of Technische Hoogeschool Delft, Student administration, access no. 3.12.08.04, inv.no. 292.
43 Yearbook 1918, 60.
44 Yearbook 1922, 71.
45 Yearbook 1941, 59.
46 De Jong 1997, 232.
47 De Jong 1997, 231.
48 Van Kessel/Kuperus 1982, 88-115.
49 Van Kessel/Kuperus 1982, 92.
50 Van Kessel/Kuperus 1982, 92.
51 Van Kessel/Kuperus 1982, 92.
52 Van Kessel/Kuperus 1982, 110.
53 Van Kessel/Kuperus 1982, 102.
54 Van Zomeren 1984, 24-29, citation 26.
55 v. T. 1917, 5.
56 Van Kessel/Kuperus 1982, 109-110.
57 Van Kessel/Kuperus 1982, 88-89.
58 Vereeniging van Delftsche Ingenieurs 1947; Van Kessel/Kuperus 1982, 201. The group of 81 women registered as students does not include the women who audited the courses.
59 Van Damme-van Weele/Ressing-Wolfert 1995, 167, 182.
60 Cardinaal 1913, 10; Vereeniging van Delftsche Ingenieurs 1947.
61 For information on the DVSV, see: Kristinsson-Reitsema, undated [1994].
62 Van Kessel/Kuperus 1982, 88.
63 Almanac, undated [1913], 54.
64 Van der Weide 1918, 11. The report is dated 23 May 1914.
65 Van der Weide 1918, 12.
66 Wendt 2008, 12-33; Schilt/Van der Werf 1992, 92-94.
67 Schilt/Van der Werf 1992, 28.
68 Genootschap 1908, 114-115. Summary of the prerequisite education deemed suitable, with corresponding required practical experience.
69 Architectura 1908, 118.
70 In 1915 the Genootschap placed the VHBO in an association, under the protection of the Genootschap and other institutions, including the BNA. In 1946 the programme was given its own accommodations in the Oudezijds Huiszittenhuis on Waterlooplein in Amsterdam, where it is still located. From then on, it was known as the Academie van Bouwkunst, but that name only became official in 1965. Schilt/Van der Werf 1992, 104; Wendt 2008, 30-37, 118, 127.
71 Wendt 2008, 38.
72 Genootschap 1908, 114-115.
73 Wendt 2008, 40.
74 Heinen 1914, 340.
75 Wendt 2008, 56.
76 Wendt 2008, 49, 77.
77 Wendt 2008, 9, 74-76, 89.
78 Cursus 1938, 73-77, citation: 73.
79 Wendt 2008, 67, 85.

80 Moussault-Veegens 1936; B. 1956; Roos 1978.
81 B. 1956.
82 Eschauzier 1936, 99-104, citation: 99.
83 Wendt 2008, 84-91.
84 Wendt 2008, 88. Annual numbers and breakdown of students by gender are incomplete. Het Nieuwe Instituut, Rotterdam, archive of the Academie van Bouwkunst, Amsterdam (ABAM), 614-615.
85 Damen/Devolder 1993, 25-29.
86 Wendt 2008, 100.
87 Damen/Devolder 1993, 25.
88 Wendt 2008, 100.
89 Wendt 2008, 128.

4 The professional practice of the first women architects in the Netherlands

1 Krabbe 1997, 136-137, 159-160.
2 Bosma et al. 2007, 540-541.
3 Website: *Het Nieuwe Instituut – Bond van Nederlandse Architecten.*
4 Since 1957 this organization has been called the Koninklijke Maatschappij tot Bevordering der Bouwkunst, Bond van Nederlandse Architecten BNA. Website: *Koninklijke Maatschappij tot Bevordering der Bouwkunst, Bond van Nederlandse Architecten BNA.*
5 Bosma et al. 2007, 539-541.
6 Central Committee for Academic Interests of the Technische Hoogeschool 1932, 16-17.
7 Moussault-Veegens 1936.
8 Roos 1978.
9 Groot 2007, 354 (citation), 511.
10 National Women's Council of the Netherlands 1951, typescript, 46; Staal-Kropholler 1951, unpaginated typed manuscript, Het Nieuwe Instituut, archive of STAX, inv.no. 31.
11 Married couple of architects 1964.
12 Later this became the architecture firm of Kuiper, Gouwetor and De Ranitz, which would play an important role in Rotterdam's reconstruction. In that work, the firm worked closely with independent architect Wil Jansen. Heijkoop/Bakker 2010, 34.
13 Van Zomeren 1984, 24-29.
14 Woman architect 1946.
15 Van Kessel/Kuperus 1982, 89.
16 Website: *Het Nieuwe Instituut – Kok, A.A.*
17 De Jong 1997, 235; Van Damme-van Weele/Ressing-Wolfert 1995, 18; Kamp 1955, 27, III-XXIII.
18 Van Kessel/Kuperus 1982, 93 (citation); Van Zomeren 1984, 24-29.
19 Schilt/Van der Werf, 1992, 229.
20 Website: *Vereniging van vrouwen met hogere opleiding*; website: *Atria – Archive of the Vereniging van vrouwen met hogere opleiding (VVAO)*; Atria Kennisinstituut voor Emancipatie en Vrouwengeschiedenis, Amsterdam (Atria), archive of the Vereniging van vrouwen met hogere opleiding (VVAO), IIAV00000539, inv.no. 191.
21 Website: *Nederlandse VrouwenRaad*; Heinen 1914, 123-125.
22 There are no architect associations on the member list of 1949. No previous member lists are available. Atria, archive of Nationale Vrouwenraad van Nederland, member list of November 1949.
23 *Reports of the forty-third and forty-fourth annual meetings held 28 and 29 November 1948 in the Beursgebouw in Rotterdam (also 50th anniversary celebration) and on 24 and 25 May 1949 in "Esplanade" in Utrecht*, The Hague 1949, Atria, archive of Nationale Vrouwenraad van Nederland, IIAV00000111, inv.no. 62.
24 Het Nieuwe Instituut, archive of STAX, inv.no. 31.
25 Vereeniging van Delftsche Ingenieurs 1905 (series up to and including 1921); Vereeniging van Delftsche Ingenieurs, 1922 (series up to and including 1939); Vereeniging van Delftsche Ingenieurs, 1940 (series up to and including 1942); Vereeniging van Delftsche Ingenieurs 1947.
26 Officieele 1939, unpaginated.
27 Website: *Het Nieuwe Instituut – Bond van Nederlandse Architecten.*
28 Officieele 1931, unpaginated.
29 Het Nederlandsch Instituut van Architecten (NIVA), founded in 1929 as the commercially oriented counterpart of the more 'artistic' BNA, has no women among the approximately 300 members listed on its member list of 1939. In 1941 the NIVA was absorbed into the BNA. Member lists 1913–1939 and 1940–1950, Het Nieuwe Instituut, archive of the Bond van Nederlandse Architecten (BNA) and of the legal persons affiliated with the BNA (BNAR), inv.no. 1846/a5141-a5142.
30 Schilt/Van der Werf 1992, 218.
31 Schilt/Van der Werf 1992, 28 and 216.
32 Kristinsson-Reitsema, undated [1994], 32-62.
33 Housing Committee 1953, 839, 844.
34 Website: *VACpunt Wonen.*
35 v. T. 1917, 5.
36 Zeeman 1920a, 203-205.
37 Zeeman 1920a, 204.
38 Zeeman 1920a, 204.
39 Moussault-Veegens 1936.
40 Roos 1978.
41 Schilt/Van der Werf 1992, 233-235; De Reus 2011, 123-142.
42 For a list of all articles published by Stam-Beese: Oosterhof 2018, 332-333.
43 Oosterhof 2018, 101, 108; Liefrinck 1932, 220-222; Schilt 1982, 139-157.
44 Minutes of the combined meeting of the executive board and the institute committee, The Hague 10 December 1936, unpaginated typescript, Atria, archive of the Nederlandse Vereniging van Huisvrouwen (NVVH), IIAV00000116, inv.no. 0033.
45 Van den Ban/Mulder, undated [1947], 54-59; publications on city planning such as: Mulder/Bakker/Van Heesch 1960; Mulder 1973, 100.
46 Kuiper-Struyk 1946, 6-7.
47 Example: Pot/Pot-Keegstra 1951 361-365. See also Chapter 8.
48 Pot-Keegstra 1959, 309-320.
49 Pot-Keegstra held this position until at least 1964.

5 Grada Wolffensperger, the first women architectural engineer in the Netherlands

1 National Archives, The Hague (NA), archive of Technische Hoogeschool Delft, Student administration, access no. 3.12.08.04, inv.no. 292.
2 SAD, DVSV archives, archive no. 357, inv.no. 180; National Archives, The Hague (NA), archive of Technische Hoogeschool Delft, Student administration, access no. 3.12.08.04, inv.no. 69.
3 v. T. 1917, 5. The same article was published in newspaper *Bataviaasch Nieuwsblad*: v. T. 1917.
4 A. 1918, 68; cutting from unknown source, website: *Geheugen van Nederland.*
5 Laatste 1908; National Archives, The Hague (NA), archive of Technische Hoogeschool Delft, Student administration, access no. 3.12.08.04, inv.no. 292.
6 National Archives, The Hague (NA), archive of Technische Hoogeschool Delft, Student administration, access no. 3.12.08.04, inv.no. 292.
7 Van der Meer van Kuffeler 1913, 83.
8 Everts 1910, 29-30.
9 SAD, DVSV archives, archive no. 357, inv.no. 180; National Archives, The Hague (NA), archive of Technische Hoogeschool Delft, Student administration, access no. 3.12.08.04, inv.no. 69.

10 National Archives, The Hague (NA), archive of Technische Hoogeschool Delft, Student administration, access no. 3.12.08.04, inv.no. 292. The male students who completed their propaedeutic year as architectural engineers along with Wolffensperger were H. van Halewijn, W.A. Molengraaff, M.B. Tideman and P.J. Willekes MacDonald. The passing exam results were published in various regional and local newspapers, including: Binnenland 1910.

11 National Archives, The Hague (NA), archive of Technische Hoogeschool Delft, Student administration, access no. 3.12.08.04, inv.no. 292. The male students who completed their candidate examinations along with Wolffensperger were M.Th. Elout, J.A. Hijner and M.B. Tideman. The passing exam results were published in various regional and local newspapers, including: Exams 1915.

12 Delftsche 1914, 337. First year in which the almanac published an overview of student enrolment numbers per academic year, without any distinction between women and men.

13 Family Advertisements 1915.

14 Kristinsson-Reitsema s.a. [1994], 10.

15 Kristinsson-Reitsema s.a. [1994], 8.

16 Website: *Stylos.*

17 The men studying at the TH who graduated with Wolffensperger were M.Th. Elout, J. Gerber, H.J. van der Heijden, W. Lemei, M.C.A. Meischke and M.B. Tideman. NA, archive of Technische Hoogeschool Delft, Student administration, access no. 3.12.08.04, inv.no. 292. The passing exam results were published in various media, including: Binnenland 1917; 'Ingenieurs-Examens 1917', 217; Uitslag 1917, 522.

18 Scheffer 1967, 9-27.

19 A. 1918, 68.

20 Woman 1917, 1. The same photo appeared in an unspecified reference. Only this source attributed the photo to Berssenbrugge. That would mean that the photographer also took photos of Grada in her own home. Website: *Geheugen van Nederland.*

21 v. T. 1917, 5.

22 Website: *Digital Women's Lexicon of the Netherlands – Catharina van Tussenbroek.* Another author working for *De Amsterdammer* was Otto van Tussenbroek. His articles included art-related topics and his byline was O.v.T.

23 v. T. 1917, 5.

24 The photo appeared a week later. Amsterdammer 1917, 5.

25 Study 1914, 1-22, cited quote 20.

26 It concerns final diplomas for civil, mechanical, naval, electrical, chemical and mining engineers.

27 Heinen 1917, 134.

28 Study 1914, 18.

29 Van der Weide 1918, 8-9.

30 Van der Weide 1918, 9.

31 Website: *Royal Library of the Netherlands – World War I – Women at work.*

32 Vereeniging van Delftsche Ingenieurs 1919, unpaginated.

33 Van Voorst Vader 1919, 1; Vereeniging van Delftsche Ingenieurs 1919, unpaginated.

34 *Verslagen van het verhandelde in de vergaderingen van den Raad der gemeente Haarlem* ('Meeting minutes of the Council assemblies of the municipality of Haarlem'), Haarlem 1919, 140-142, North Holland Archives, Haarlem (NHA), Haarlem City Council archives, access no. 2295.

35 *Verslagen van het verhandelde in de vergaderingen van den Raad der gemeente Haarlem*, Haarlem 1919, 141, NHA, Haarlem City Council archives, access no. 2295.

36 *Verslagen van het verhandelde in de vergaderingen van den Raad der gemeente Haarlem*, Haarlem 1919, 1302, NHA, Haarlem City Council archives, access no. 2295.

37 NHA, Haarlem City Council archives, access no. 2295, inv.no. 14940 1919, 1/B-1/E.

38 Stenvert et al. 2006, 313.

39 NHA, Haarlem City Council archives, access no. 2295, inv.no. 14953 1920, 1/A-101-1/A-173.

40 Letter by L.C. Dumont to Municipal Executive, 14 March 1920, NHA, Haarlem City Council archives, access no. 2295, inv.no. 14985 1920, 1/B-1/E.

41 Bylaw of 15 December 1917, *Verslagen van het verhandelde in de vergaderingen van den Raad der gemeente Haarlem*, Haarlem 1917, 765-766, NHA, Haarlem City Council archives, access no 116.

42 Letter from Director of Public Works, 12 March 1920, recorded in correspondence log, NHA, Haarlem City Council archives, access no. 2295, inv.no. 15878. The associated letter is not present in the file, access no. 2295, inv.no. 14953 1920, 1/A-101-1/A-173.

43 Her colleague Jan Buijs is listed in the correspondence log of the Municipal Executive as one of the five civil servants hired on 15 March 1920. NHA, Haarlem City Council archives, access no. 2295, inv.no. 14953 1920, 1/A-101-1/A-173. As it turned out, however, he had already been hired as an 'unattached civil servant' in 1919. List of unattached civil servants, 30 October 1919, NHA, Haarlem City Council archives, access no. 2295, inv.no. 14940 1919, 1/B-1/E. Authorization to appoint a temporary assistant architect had already been granted on 9 July 1919. Letter from Dumont to Municipal Executive, 24 June 1919, NHA, Haarlem City Council archives, access no. 2295, inv.no. 15877.

44 Website: *Biographical Dictionary of the Netherlands.*

45 Website: *Address Book of Haarlem*, Haarlem 1921, 11.

46 Website: *Genealogy of Pareau & Dumont.*

47 Letter from Dumont to Municipal Executive, 1 June 1921, NHA, Haarlem City Council archives, access no. 2295, inv.no. 14971 1921, 1/B-1/M.

48 NHA, Haarlem City Council archives, access no. 2295, inv.no. 14971 1921, 1/B-1/M.

49 Letter from Dumont to Municipal Executive, 13 December 1921, NHA, Haarlem City Council archives, access no. 2295, inv.no. 14971 1921, 1/B-1/M.

50 Kurtz 1942, 49; Groote 1922, 389-391.

51 Groote 1922, 390. Interestingly, Dumont had been a long-standing board member of Vereniging Haerlem, almost since its establishment in 1901. Annual Reports and Yearbooks of Vereniging Haerlem, 1 January 1935, 1, website: *newspaper viewer of the Noord-Hollands Archive.*

52 Letter from Dumont to Municipal Executive, 13 December 1921, NHA, Haarlem City Council archives, access no. 2295, inv.no. 14971 1921, 1/B-1/M. This presumably regarded a redevelopment plan for the old trade school on Kamperstraat.

53 Handwritten letter, stamped 'Sent 19 April 1922', NHA, Haarlem City Council archives, access no. 2295, inv.no. 14986 1922, A/23-A/29.

54 Letter from Dumont to Municipal Executive, 21 April 1922, NHA, Haarlem City Council archives, access no. 2295, inv.no. 14986 1922, A/23-A/29.

55 Commemorative album compiled on the occasion of the 25th anniversary in civil service of L.C. Dumont as Director of Public Works, 1 November 1927, NHA, Image Collection of the city of Haarlem, access no. 1100, inv.no. 54-999051 U. This album includes typed lists of all the civil servants who were hired and dismissed during Dumont's term in office. These overviews also report that Wolffensperger had already been hired as a temporary employee as of 1 December 1919. No other evidence was found of her 'honourable discharge from service' and her possible previous appointment.

56 The letter confirming this was not found, but it is a confirmed fact, as evidenced by the incoming correspondence log of the Municipal Executive. NHA, Haarlem City Council archives, access no. 2295, inv.no. 15880.

57 Website: *Het Nieuwe Instituut – Buijs, J.W.E.* According to Dumont's commemorative album, Buijs received his honourable discharge from service on 1 September 1924. Commemorative album compiled on the occasion of the 25th anniversary in civil service of L.C. Dumont as Director of Public Works, 1 November 1927, NHA, Image Collection of the city of Haarlem, access no. 1100, inv.no. 54-999051 U.

58 Vereeniging van Delftsche Ingenieurs 1921 and 1922, unpaginated.

59 Vereeniging van Delftsche Ingenieurs 1923–1939, 1940–1942 and 1947, unpaginated.

60 *Haagsche* 1923 and 1924.

61 Diecke 1934, unpaginated.

62 The civil registry in Utrecht, the city where she died, lists her given names as Barbera Johanna, which would mean that she had been given exactly the same names as her mother. Website: *The Utrecht Archives – Searching for Persons*. The newspaper obituary lists her name as Barbara Johanna Wolffensperger. Vaderland 1921, 4. For the purposes of this chapter, the name Barbera has been used.

63 With thanks to Mrs Y. Houtsmuller-Noë, a close friend of the family. Telephone call, 28 July 2017.

6 Riné Boerée, concrete specialist with the Army Corps of Engineers (Genie)

1 This interview was conducted in February 1995 for the publication by Van Damme-van Weele/Ressing-Wolfert 1995, 34. The notes from this interview have been deposited in the City Archive of Delft, Collection J.H.M. Ressing-Wolfert/90 jaar Delftse vrouwelijke ingenieurs, archive 606, inv.no. 7.

2 With thanks to Ir. G.W.O. Boissevain, advisor on military cultural heritage for Rijksvastgoedbedrijf (Central Government Real Estate Agency), and emeritus professor Dr M.C. Kuipers, Rijksdienst voor het Cultureel Erfgoed (Cultural Heritage Agency – RCE). Research in the personal archives of Riné Boerée that were donated in 1998 by her half-brother Pieter Reinier Boerée (1926–2004) to Het Nieuwe Instituut (HNI) in Rotterdam, as well as the small archive still held by the widow of Mr Boerée. With thanks to Ms A.M. Boerée-de Groote and her daughter Ms J.C. Boerée.

3 With thanks to Dr P.E. van Loo, head of the Operational Services department, and R.E. Koedijk MA, Operational Action researcher, both working at the Netherlands Institute of Military History (NIMH) / Ministry of Defence, The Hague.

4 With thanks to S.R. Maaskant, Operational Action researcher, NIMH / Ministry of Defence, The Hague. The original drawing is in the Municipal Archives of The Hague, Balie Inzage Bouwtekeningen, CR5950, 1519. Maaskant also confirmed that the personnel file of Riné Boerée was destroyed a long time ago, in accordance with standard practice at that time.

5 Van den Aardweg/Hüllstrung et al., Amsterdam 1938, 174.

6 Appointments 1887, 268; Personalia 1902, 890 and 1903, 854.

7 Website: *Huygens Institute for Dutch History – Royal Netherlands Academy of Arts and Sciences (KNAW) – Boerée, Theodoor Alexander.* T.A. Boerée later made a name for himself as a military historian, for example with his in-depth research on the British defeat at Arnhem (September 1944).

8 [Ressing-Wolfert], notes from an interview with Boerée, February 1995, City Archive of Delft, Collection J.H.M. Ressing-Wolfert/90 jaar Delftse vrouwelijke ingenieurs, archive 606, inv.no. 7.

9 Yearbook 1917, 110-120. One of the first-year students was Louis Kalff (1897–1976). After graduating, he went on to work for Philips, specializing in integrating artificial lighting into architecture. Kalff designed buildings for Philips, such as the Evoluon, as well as light shows and exhibitions. Website: *Louis Kalff Instituut*. Another student who started studying architecture at the same time as Riné was Willebrordus Cornelis Wouters (1897–1960). He would later design various churches and schools in The Hague. Website: *Archiwijzer Stichting Bonas*.

10 National Archives, The Hague (NA), archive of the Technische Hoogeschool Delft (THD), student records, access no. 3.12.08.04, inv.no. 88.

11 Study 1914, 18.

12 NA, student records of the Technische Hoogeschool Delft, access no. 3.12.08.04, inv.no. 88.

13 Vereniging Oud Oegstgeest (website) 1987, 5, 31.

14 Study 1914, 16-22.

15 [Ressing-Wolfert], notes of study results provided by telephone by Mr Smeenk, library of architecture at Delft University of Technology, February 1995, Delft city archive, Collection J.H.M. Ressing-Wolfert/ 90 jaar Delftse vrouwelijke ingenieurs, archive 606, inv.no. 7. All official information regarding study results were lost in a 2008 fire in the architecture faculty of Delft University of Technology in 2008.

16 HNI, archive Boerée, C.H.M. (BOER), inv.no. 2; Delftsche 1921, 149.

17 Aalbers et al. 1994, 35-36.

18 Van Kessel/Kuperus 1982, 92.

19 Notebook on *History of Architecture by Prof. Evers*, 1919, HNI, archive BOER, inv.no. 2.

20 Untitled notebook, undated, HNI, archive BOER, inv.no. 2.

21 Untitled notebook, undated, HNI, archive BOER, inv.no. 2.

22 Numbered series of drawings 1917–1921, HNI, archive BOER, inv.no. 3. These drawings are initialled by J.H.G.P. de Rouw, architecture lecturer.

23 Notebook on *Dutch Architecture. Prof. v/d Steur*, 1925, HNI, archive BOER, inv.no. 2.

24 Notebook on *Dutch Architecture. Prof. v/d Steur*, 192, HNI, archive BOER, inv.no. 2. Van der Steur also discussed this topic in his lecture as rector magnificus on the occasion of the Gedenkdag (Memorial Day) at the Technische Hoogeschool, 8 (10) January 1922. Yearbook 1922, 8.

25 It concerns the following works: Weissman 1912 (Riné wrote 'Mysman' in her class notes, but must have misunderstood the name Weissman); Kalf s.a. [1914]; Vermeulen 1928–1941.

26 Regarding Vermeulen's membership in the National Socialist Movement in the Netherlands (NSB), see e.g.: Wendt 2008, 93; Schulte 1995, 92; Bosman 2018, 169-171.

27 Communication with the publishers was extremely difficult, due to Vermeulen's repeated failure to keep his promises. Vermeulen 1941, part 3, unpaginated [1].
28 Molema/Leemans 2010, 77.
29 Van Kessel/Kuperus 1982, 92.
30 Study 1914, 17-21.
31 NA, student records of the Technische Hoogeschool Delft, access no. 3.12.08.04, inv.no. 88.
32 Kristinsson-Reitsema, undated [1994], 30.
33 The two merged in 1976.
34 Almanac 1916, 24.
35 Almanac 1915, 20. Zeeman and Snethlage graduated, after Wolffensperger, in 1920 and 1921 respectively.
36 Almanac, undated [1919], 18.
37 Van Kessel/Kuperus 1982, 88.
38 Almanac 1916, 27.
39 Almanac 1924, 81. Henri Boerée proved to be a loyal donor until 1932.
40 HNI, archive BOER, inv.no. 4.
41 Local 1929. The Korteweg-Dorsman family lived in the house. With thanks to P. in 't Veld, Ooltgensplaat and M. Bos, Regional Archives of Goeree-Overflakkee, Middelharnis.
42 Work camps 1937. Henri Boerée co-founded the Vrijwillige Burgerwacht (volunteer civil defence force) in the Netherlands in 1918. Van den Aardweg/Hüllstrung et al. 1938, 174. Questions were raised in Parliament regarding the possible 'fascist hazard' posed by the civil defence forces. Boerée openly distanced himself from this. Fascist 1933.
43 The work camps were not uncontroversial and were seen as militaristic re-education camps. Work camps 1936; Camp work 1938; Graalfort 1937. Henri Boerée later co-founded the Nederlandse Bond voor Lichamelijke Opvoeding ('Dutch League for Physical Education') and the Scouting Organization, and was instrumental in the launch of the Vierdaagse, known internationally as the Four-Day Marches. Colonel 1949.
44 Fort 1940. Even before the Germans invaded, people were imprisoned 'on the grounds of their conduct', including Meinoud Marinus Rost van Tonningen LL M (1894–1945). During the war, the fort had no strategic significance and served as a leisure resort for German soldiers serving at the front. After the war, it was used as a prison for collaborators and NSB members. Remus 1991, 86.
45 Polak 1928, 151-152.
46 Personalia [graduation announcement for Boerée] and Open 1929, 277-278; entire year 45 (1930) consulted.
47 [Ressing-Wolfert] notes from an interview with Boerée, February 1995, City Archive of Delft, Collection J.H.M. Ressing-Wolfert/90 jaar Delftse vrouwelijke ingenieurs, archive 606, inv.no. 7. The name of the architecture firm could not be identified.
48 HNI, archive BOER, inv.no. 4.
49 Bauduin 1950, 53-55; Kooij 2011, 60-65; Lobbezoo 2000, 23-25, 59 (aerial photo from 1979: the fuel station still seems to be present).
50 [Ressing-Wolfert], notes from an interview with Boerée, February 1995, City Archive of Delft, Collection J.H.M. Ressing-Wolfert/90 jaar Delftse vrouwelijke ingenieurs, archive 606, inv.no. 7.
51 Bak 1982, 74-81; Bergeijk 2016, 94-99, 108-127, 230-237; Bullhorst/Van Harmelen/Jager 1999, 65-143; Molema/Bak 1987, 22-25, 75-77.
52 Letter of 19 September 1928 quoted in: Molema/1987, 77.
53 A less plausible explanation is a possible shared network of Delft students and alumni. Wiebenga graduated in 1912, Duiker in 1913 (under Evers). Riné had not yet started her studies at that time.
54 According to the publication *Vrouwen in techniek. 90 Jaar Delftse Vrouwelijke Ingenieurs*, basing its claims on the interview with Boerée, her drawings and calculations for the Nirwana block of flats were added to the HNI archives some time later (Van Damme-van Weele/Ressing-Wolfert 1995, p. 34). This is not the case, however. Nor were any drawings that could be attributed to Boerée found in the Wiebenga archive (HNI, inv. no. 681).
55 Boerée was said to have completed a number of small projects independently. Van Damme-van Weele/Ressing-Wolfert 1995, 34.
56 Written statement by P.R. Boerée, drafted as part of the transfer of the personal archives of Riné Boerée to HNI in 1998. Archive management records reviewed by the HNI on 25 January 2018, with thanks to curator Suzanne Mulder. Boerée is also listed in this job in: Vereeniging van Delftsche Ingenieurs 1930, unpaginated.
57 [Ressing-Wolfert], notes from an interview with Boerée, February 1995, City Archive of Delft, Collection J.H.M. Ressing-Wolfert/90 jaar Delftse vrouwelijke ingenieurs, archive 606, inv.no. 7.
58 Almanac 1931, 126. The name 'Rijksgebouwendienst' was used for the Government Buildings Agency from 1946 on.
59 Van der Peet/Steenmeijer 1995, 449-455, 481-496, 640-641; Van Nieuwpoort 1992, 145-155; website: *Het Nieuwe Instituut – Bremer, G.C.*
60 The blueprints are undated, but the HNI estimated the date around 1930–1933. HNI, archive BOER, inv.no. 4.
61 The complex consisted of two connected buildings. The caretaker's residence was on the third floor of the auxiliary building (1917–1920), Kortenaerkade 11, and covered the entire side wing on Bazarlaan. Havelaar 1993, 5-7. According to the undated design schemes that are available, a staircase was not initially envisioned there. Other design schemes have a residence on the second floor of the same auxiliary building, but on the side facing De Ruijterstraat, or on the second floor of the main building (Kortenaerkade 12, 1923), facing Bazarlaan. Website: *Het Nieuwe Instituut – Bremer, G.C.*, BREXpf1. The Boerée archive also contains a series of specification drawings of the main building, although it is unclear how these ended up in Boerée's personal archives. One explanation might be that she had to work from these (copied?) drawings, which is how they entered into her possession. Website: *Het Nieuwe Instituut- Boerée, C.H.M.*
62 The staff complement of the department can be found in: State Almanac 1931, 497-498.
63 Van den Aardweg/Hüllstrung et al. 1938, 174. It is interesting to note that the Government Buildings Agency and the Army Corps of Engineers had been mentioned in combination in a discussion several years earlier about temporary placement of young engineering officers – without previous experience in new buildings – in the Government Buildings Agency. However, this did not happen. Van den Beemt/Boekema/Thijssens 1988, 40-43.
64 Rengers taught the course alongside engineer J.A. Zwolsman. Rengers was a board member of the Betonvereniging ('Concrete Association') for years and received honorary membership in 1963. Website: *Cement*.
65 Website: *Kunstbus*.
66 HNI, archive BOER, inv.no. 1.
67 Announcements 1935, 94; Van Damme-van Weele/Ressing-Wolfert 1995, 34.

68 Vereeniging van Delftsche Ingenieurs 1937, unpaginated.

69 *Kazernebouw Den Haag* ('Barracks Construction in The Hague') 1934–1935, typescript and manuscript, unpaginated, Geniemuseum, Vught, no. D09447. With thanks to F. van Bavel.

70 During the Second World War, J. Kok was an active member of the Resistance after spending some time as a prisoner of war. In the 1960, Major-General Kok was once again involved in construction work at the Frederikkazerne in his capacity as Inspector of the Army Corps of Engineers. Van Hoof 2018, 9-45.

71 *Kazernebouw Den Haag* ('Barracks Construction in The Hague') 1934–1935, typescript and manuscript, unpaginated, Geniemuseum, Vught, no. D09447.

72 Building plans were found for the following, among others: 'P. v. Broekhuizen', 'E. Smit', 'Jan Bos', 'G. Jansen' and 'v.d. Beld' (Van den Beld). NA, First Engineer of the Army Corps of Engineers in The Hague, Alexanderkazerne 1938–1939, access no. 3.09.44.05, inv.no. 16. Other building plans that were viewed had been initialled by people other than Boerée. NIMH, Access 406 Barracks, army sites, buildings, inv.no. 277-334 and 811.

73 *Kazernebouw Den Haag* ('Barracks Construction in The Hague') 1934–1935, typescript and manuscript, unpaginated, Geniemuseum, Vught, no. D09447.

74 *Design for the construction of barracks for the army equestrian unit in The Hague*, or the design scheme for the Alexander barracks and the Frederik barracks, 1933, NIMH. With thanks to S.R. Maaskant.

75 *Kazernebouw Den Haag* ('Barracks Construction in The Hague') 1934–1935, typescript and manuscript, unpaginated, Geniemuseum, Vught, no. D09447.

76 Van den Beemt/Boekema/Thijssens 1988, 40.

77 Bosma et al. 2007, 496-498.

78 New 1938.

79 *Kazernebouw Den Haag* ('Barracks Construction in The Hague') 1934–1935, typescript and manuscript, unpaginated, Geniemuseum, Vught, no. D09447.

80 Municipal archives of The Hague, Balie Inzage Bouwtekeningen, CR5950, 1519.

81 The Alexander barracks took heavy damage from a German air offensive in 1940. Dozens were killed or injured and 110 horses died. The barracks were demolished in 2012 to make way for the International Court of Justice.

82 Van den Beemt/Boekema/Thijssens 1988, 43.

83 Written statement by P.R. Boerée 1998, archive management records C.H.M. Boerée HNI.

84 It is uncertain exactly when Boerée was head of the concrete department.

85 [Ressing-Wolfert], notes from an interview with Boerée, February 1995, City Archive of Delft, Collection J.H.M. Ressing-Wolfert/90 jaar Delftse vrouwelijke ingenieurs, archive 606, inv.no. 7.

86 Written statement by P.R. Boerée 1998, archive management records C.H.M. Boerée HNI.

87 HNI, archive BOER, inv.no. 5.

88 [Ressing-Wolfert], notes from an interview with Boerée, February 1995, City Archive of Delft, Collection J.H.M. Ressing-Wolfert/90 jaar Delftse vrouwelijke ingenieurs, archive 606, inv.no. 7.

89 Vereeniging van Delftsche Ingenieurs 1940, unpaginated.

90 Naam 1964.

91 For example, the company had a thriving business in building tennis courts. Driemaal 1964.

92 Website: *Cultural heritage of Leiden and surroundings* a.

93 Interesting 1942.

94 Diary of Mia Boerée 1945, unpaginated, Atria institute on gender equality and women's history, Amsterdam (Atria), archive Boerée, Mia, IAV1000164. Struyk Verwo Infra, the company that absorbed Wernink Concrete, unfortunately no longer has its predecessor's archives. Written correspondence from J. Ploeg, 6 October 2017.

95 Disassembly 1984. For the contextual situation of the grounds, see the website: *Cultural heritage of Leiden and surroundings* b.

96 Interview with Mrs N. Nagel from Leiden, 18 November 2018, website: *Cultural heritage of Leiden and surroundings* c.

97 Diary of Mia Boerée 1945, unpaginated, Atria, archive Boerée, Mia, IAV1000164. Mia was joint director of the publishing house N.V. Uitgeverij 'De Nationale Gedachte', Amsterdam. Henri Boerée was on the supervisory board of the publishing house. Untitled 1935, 949. Mia also spent time typing out a book for 'Uncle Jo' Boasson. Dr Johan Jozef Boasson LL M (1882–1967) was municipal secretary of The Hague and published various titles under his own name. His book entitled *De bestemming van de mens* ('Man's Destination') was published in 1949; this may have been what Mia was working on. Boasson was married to Helena Gerardina Scholten (1882–1968), who had exactly the same given names as Mia's mother, who had died in 1918. It is very likely that this woman was a younger sister, and therefore Mia's aunt.

98 Written statement by P.R. Boerée 1998, archive management records C.H.M. Boerée HNI. Boerée also devoted herself to learning the Armenian language spoken by her grandmother. Her estate included various reference books, dictionaries and notebooks filled with exercises.

99 Written statement by P.R. Boerée 1998, archive management records C.H.M. Boerée HNI. It was not until June 1941 that all departments of the Army Corps of Engineers were disbanded and their tasks were transferred to the Germans. Van den Beemt/Boekema/Thijssens 1988, 44. In 1946, Boerée is listed as 'Engineer at the department responsible for construction, management and maintenance of airfields (BABOV)' in Amsterdam. Vereeniging van Delftsche Ingenieurs 1947, unpaginated.

100 Written statement by P.R. Boerée 1998, archive management records C.H.M. Boerée HNI.

101 Van den Beemt/Boekema/Thijssens 1988, 46.

102 Website: *National Archives, Archives of the Ministry of Defence/Department of Buildings, Works and Grounds*.

103 HNI, archive BOER, inv.no. 5.

104 Goed 1946, 23.

105 With thanks to G. Tornij, Deelen airbase museum.

106 An example of a tender from BABOV Leiden: Soldier 1959.

107 HNI, archive BOER, inv.no. 5. The new hangar was made possible by the US-funded Mutual Defense Assistance Programme (MDAP), which supported countries in rebuilding their armed forces after the Second World War. Since the hangar foundation was already laid and an assembly contract had already been signed, they had to purchase a steel structure in the Netherlands, for which 650,000 guilders had to be found in the Navy's budget. Ondeugdelijk 1956; Van Alphen/Geneste/Staal 2007, 46-49.

108 Van Alphen/Geneste/Staal 2007, 49.
109 Feminine 1938.
110 Van Damme-van Weele/Ressing-Wolfert 1995, 34.
111 M. Staal-Kropholler, *National Women's Council of the Netherlands. Data for the report on Dutch Art*, typescript 18 March 1949, 27 March 1950 and 22 March 1951, HNI, archive Staal J.F., Kropholler A.J. and Staal-Kropholler, M. (STAX), inv.no. 110339037.
112 M. Staal-Kropholler, *List of women architectural engineers*, typescript, undated, HNI, archive STAX., inv.no. 110339037.

7 Wil Jansen, an enterprising women architect from Schiedam

1 Eleven women preceded Jansen.
2 Heijkoop/Bakker 2010.
3 Municipal Archives of Schiedam (GAS), archive no. 608 Ir. W.C.M. Jansen (Jansen), inv.nos. 1-10. These are preliminary inventory numbers, since a full inventory of the archive has not yet been completed. With thanks to Nita Friedel.
4 Abma undated [ca. 1956], 156.
5 Van der Sloot 2015, 20-33; interview Jansen 2019.
6 The homes were built on Fabristraat by Schiedam-based architect Piet(er) Sanders (1882–1937) and are also considered a national heritage site. Websites *Municipality of Schiedam – Pieter Sanders* and *Image Bank of the Municipality of Schiedam – Pieter Sanders*.
7 The building was demolished in 1939 to create breakthrough access to Westvest (Griffioenstraat). Website: *Image Bank of the Municipal Archives of Schiedam – Volksbadhuis*.
8 National Archives, The Hague (NA), archive of Technische Hoogeschool Delft, Student administration, access no. 3.12.08.04, inv.no. 156.
9 Nieuwe 1920 and 1921.
10 Jansen's archive contains one rejection in response to a job application to an architecture firm. Letter from L. van der Laan & Ir. Jan A. van der Laan Architects in Leiden, 15 October 1934. Archive owned by H.Th.F. Jansen. During that period, Wil Jansen received her first commissions from the family.
11 Pop ('doll') was Anna Maria's nickname. Interview with Jansen 2019. Various design drawings signed by Jansen for the renovation of Rubenslaan 17, 1956–1968, GAS, archive no. 608 Jansen, inv.no. 8f.
12 Various documents such as business operation overviews, archive owned by H.Th.F. Jansen.
13 Architecture firm Ir. W.C.M. Jansen, architectural engineer, *Summer cottage in Reeuwijk. WC, hall and washroom, 2 February 1965* and *Building plan for Reeuwijk. Counter and Tabletop*, 15 March 1965, GAS, archive no. 608 Jansen, inv.no. 8b. The summer cottage was torn down at some point.
14 Yearbook 1925, 66-73; Almanac 1924, 78.
15 Delftsche 1925 through 1932.
16 Yearbook 1925, 78. Willy van den Broek d'Obrenan and Jeanne van Rijswijk were active as board members and committee members from the second year of their studies. Almanac 1925, 20-22.
17 Almanac 1928, 20-21, 31.
18 Almanac 1928, 41.
19 National Archives, The Hague (NA), archive of Technische Hoogeschool Delft, Student administration, access no. 3.12.08.04, inv.no. 156.
20 The group also included two women who were studying architecture: Willy van den Broek d'Obrenan and Jeanne van Rijswijk. Technische Hoogeschool, architectural department, *Excursion to Normandy, Brittany, Loire and Champagne from 28 August to 18 September 1929*, 3, archive owned by H.Th.F. Jansen.
21 Technische Hoogeschool, architectural department, *Excursion to Normandy, Brittany, Loire and Champagne from 28 August to 18 September 1929*, 12, archive owned by H.Th.F. Jansen.
22 Van Rosse/Kammer 1945, 2-5.
23 Letter by M.J. Granpré Molière to W. Jansen, 17 October 1931, archive owned by H.Th.F. Jansen.
24 National Archives, The Hague (NA), archive of Technische Hoogeschool Delft, Student administration, access no. 3.12.08.04, inv.no. 368; Yearbook 1931, 95.
25 Molema/Leemans 2010, particularly 6-7, 68-82, 120-133.
26 Study 1930, 1.
27 Websites: *Wikipedia – Urbain Cassan* and *Wikipedia – Louis Plousey*.
28 Letter from Wil Jansen to her father, 8 August 1931, GAS, archive no. 608 Jansen, inv.no. 5.
29 Letter from Wil Jansen to her father, 8 August 1931, GAS, archive no. 608 Jansen, inv.no. 5.
30 Zwiers 1932, 99.
31 Zwiers 1932, 99.
32 Bruin/Smits/Zwiers 1932, 193-204, cited quote 193.
33 The ten best submissions included designs by architects Joop Pot, who would later marry Koos Keegstra, and Arthur Staal (1907–1993), both of whom were also at the start of their careers and working in Amsterdam. All submissions were displayed on 20 June 1932 in the great hall of the Heystee building, Heerengracht 545-549 in Amsterdam. Blaauw/Zwiers 1932, 228.
34 Yearbook 1939, 129.
35 Various unsigned and undated sketches of floor plans and facades, GAS, archive no. 608 Jansen, inv.no. 8a; for the final design as submitted, see: Bruin/Smits/Zwiers 1932, 198 (design no. 130).
36 Bruin/Smits/Zwiers 1932, 204 (design no. 130).
37 Bruin/Smits/Zwiers 1932, 195.
38 Bruin/Smits/Zwiers 1932, 204 (design no. 147).
39 Bruin/Smits/Zwiers 1932, 193.
40 Bruin/Smits/Zwiers 1932, 195.
41 Vierde undated [ca. 2010], 166-167. The typescript, owned by H.Th.F. Jansen, is a more detailed version of the typescript by Abma undated [ca. 1956].
42 Hinderwet ('Nuisance Act') 1923.
43 Unsigned design, *Schiedam Cardboard Factory, Lange Haven no. 17*, undated, blueprint, GAS, archive no. 608 Jansen, inv.no. 8e. The factory building and the parental home were demolished in 1939.
44 Various sketches, including several signed 'W.C.M. Jansen' and dated 5 December 1931, GAS, archive no. 608 Jansen, inv.no. 8e. An office was later added on the southwest side of the building, but no designs were found for that. In 1976 all the buildings were torn down to make way for apartments, although the facades of the factory building were constructed in the same style. Website: *Image Bank of the Municipal Archives of Schiedam – Oranjestraat*.
45 Unsigned design, *Advertising in evening light*, undated, GAS, archive no. 608 Jansen, inv.no. 8e.
46 Oranjebrug 1935.
47 Municipal Works Department, *Plan for new Oranjebrug. Improvement of surrounding streets*, 1935; W.C.M.J. [Jansen], *Variant to the plan for the new Oranjebrug*, location unspecified [Schiedam] 7 March 1936; various unsigned and undated [1936] floor plans and drawings in bird's eye perspective, GAS, archive no. 608 Jansen, inv.no. 8e.

48 Oranjebrug 1936.
49 GAS, archive no. 346, Archives of the city council and later municipal council of Schiedam (1798) 1816–1953 (1973), inv.nos. 57-58, 159-160, 174; archive no. 61 Archives of the Municipal Public Works Department (1759–1837) 1848–1991 (1999), inv.no. 510.
50 Bosma et al. 2007, 541-542.
51 Dettingmeijer 1988, 69-73.
52 Website: *Bouwdossiers online* a.
53 The stepped gables are still clearly visible on an aerial photo from 1925. Website: *Image Bank of the Municipal Archives of Schiedam – Noordvestsingel*.
54 Mayor 12 July 1956.
55 Cardboard Factory 1956. It is striking that this article refers to relocating from the building on Oranjestraat.
56 News 1956.
57 Modern 1958. The building was demolished in 2004 to make way for housing.
58 Schiedamsche 1956, quoted in: Vierde undated [ca. 2010], 166-167.
59 Unsigned and undated floor plans and facades, GAS, archive no. 608 Jansen, inv.no. 8e.
60 The cardboard industry employed a substantial number of women. Nearly 400 women worked in the factory on Burgemeester Honnerlage Gretelaan. Their changing room was larger than the men's counterpart. Interview with H.Th.F. Jansen, 5 August 2020.
61 Vierde undated [ca. 2010], 163-164.
62 *Schiedam Lactic Acid Plant. Static calculations*, typescript, undated and various drawings dated 1952, GAS, archive no. 608 Jansen, inv.no. 7c.
63 Website: *Bouwdossiers online* b. The drawings that were submitted, which are also in the archive, were dated April and May 1952. GAS, archive no. 608 Jansen, inv.no. 7c.
64 Interview Jansen 2019. Coen Kramers, scion of a distilling family, wrote books about the malt wine industry and was a municipal council member and alderman in Schiedam.
65 Parts of this industrial complex remain standing to this day. There are plans to demolish the building that once housed the lactic acid plant at Noordvest 97. Interview with Jansen 2019.
66 Ir. W.C.M. Jansen, architectural engineer, *Situation of the buildings. Section A. N.V. Herman Jansen destillateurs*, undated, GAS, archive no. 608 Jansen, inv.no. 8d.
67 Website: *Registry of National Heritage Sites – 528815*.
68 Various unsigned designs for cupboard walls, 1959, GAS, archive no. 608 Jansen, inv.no. 7c.
69 Vierde undated [ca. 2010], 164; various sets of signed designs (1954–1968), GAS, archive no. 608 Jansen, inv.no. 3a, 3b and 8b.
70 Architecture firm Ir. W.C.M. Jansen, *Expansion of parfumerie Valdelis. Lange Nieuwstraat 47*, 12 August 1959, GAS, archive no. 608 Jansen, inv.no. 7c.
71 Architecture firm Ir. W.C.M. Jansen, architectural engineer, *New building for Valdelis. Lange Nieuwstraat 47*, 17 October 1967 and unsigned, *"Valdelis" sketch*, 1968, GAS, archive no. 608 Jansen, inv.no. 3b and 3b. Following the sale of Valdelis in 1974, the buildings were demolished in 1996. It was not possible to determine whether Jansen's designs were implemented.
72 Architecture firm Ir. W.C.M. Jansen, architectural engineer, *"Magneto-Chemie" Noordvestsingel 79 Schiedam. Linking structure, buildings 77 and 79*, January 1969, GAS, archive no. 608 Jansen, inv.no. 8b.
73 Website of the *Registry of National Heritage Sites – 525416*. Magneto Chemie now uses the name Magneto Special Anodes BV.
74 Jansen created designs for liquor retailers in The Hague, Rotterdam, Utrecht, Leeuwarden and more. GAS, archive no. 608 Jansen, inv.nos. 7c, 8b and 8f.
75 Statement by the Instituut voor Middenstandsvakonderwijs in Nederland (senior vocational school), 23 October 1950; correspondence between W.C.M. Jansen and the Municipal Executive of Rotterdam, 1950, archive owned by H.Th.F. Jansen.
76 Interview with Jansen 2020. In 1960 Jansen renovated the interior of the liquor shop on Nieuwe Binnenweg.
77 Various signed designs for liquor shops in Heerenveen, Utrecht and Rotterdam, dated 1962 and 1963, commissioned by "Herman Jansen", GAS, archive no. 608 Jansen, inv.no. 8b.
78 State Party 1939. Jansen was not listed very low on the electoral list, but ended up in an ineligible position. Heijkoop/Bakker 2010, 88, nt. 13.
79 Website: *Atria – Archief VVAO Vereniging van vrouwen met hogere opleiding*; Atria, archives VVAO, IIAV00000539, inv.no. 191.
80 Jansen attended the conference of the Nationale Vrouwenraad (National Women's Council, NVR) on 18 April 1929 in her capacity as the DVSV president. Almanac 1928, 29. The NVR was founded in 1878 during the National Exhibition of Women's Labour, with the goal of pooling women's knowledge and expertise in various areas. De VVAO was affiliated with the NVR as a sector-based association. In the 1950s, Jansen sat on the NVR as a deputy representative for the VVAO. Letter from VVAO to Jansen, 17 July 1953, GAS, archive no. 608 Jansen, inv.no. 1b.
81 Ada Struyk joined DVSV during her first year in 1928, when Wil Jansen was president. Almanac 1928, 71.
82 Heijkoop/Bakker 2010, 34.
83 Various meeting minutes and convocations of the VVAO chapters in The Hague, Rotterdam, Breda and Utrecht; recommendation by Kuiper-Struyk in: letter from Breda chapter to Jansen, 11 September 1950, GAS, archive no. 608 Jansen, inv.no. 1b. The lectures themselves are no longer available. As a member of the Travel Committee, responsible for receiving foreign colleagues, mainly in Rotterdam, Jansen went to the 10th Conference of the International Federation of University Women in Zürich. While there, she met her fellow member Marga Klompé (1912–1986), who was an MP in the Dutch House of Representatives at the time. GAS, archive no. 608 Jansen, inv.no. 1b.
84 The foundation published the *Goed Wonen* housing magazine and decorated show homes in new neighbourhoods. Krabbe/Broekhuizen/Smit 2018, 159. The editorial staff of the magazine and the foundation board consisted largely of men. Van Moorsel 1992, 76-83. From about 1952 on, interior design architect Cora Nicolaï-Chaillet (1919–1975) played an active role in the foundation. Website: *Het Nieuwe Instituut – Nicolaï-Chaillet, C.*
85 The survey consisted of 60 questions. Huisvrouw 1947, 367-370. The first results appeared in April. Staal-Kropholler 1947, 5.
86 Schreuder-Gratama et al. 1947, 403-406.
87 After Rotterdam, women began forming VACs in other municipalities. These local committees can still be found today, in their previous forms or as housing advisory committees known as a WoonAdviesCommissie (WAC). Website: *VACpunt Wonen*.
88 *Memorandum on Aim, Composition, Methods and Contacts of the Committee*, Rotterdam 26 February

1953, typescript, 1, GAS, archive no. 608 Jansen, inv.no. 1b.

89 Quoted in: Heijkoop/Bakker 2010, 53. Jansen and Kuiper-Struyk were listed as members from 1951 on, while the latter was vice-chair from 1953–1957. Heijkoop/Bakker 2010, 89, nt. 22. The authors do not list any sources. Jansen's archive shows that she was a member right away, from 1946 on. GAS, archive no. 608 Jansen, inv.no. 1a.

90 Minutes VAC, 11 November 1946, GAS, archive no. 608 Jansen, inv.no. 1a.

91 VAC survey report, *Het oordeel van de huisvrouw over haar woning*, Rotterdam 9 February 1950, typescript, 1, GAS, archive no. 608 Jansen, inv.no. 1a.

92 Report of 16 March 1950, handwritten sheet of paper, GAS, archive no. 608 Jansen, inv.no. 1a.

93 VAC survey report, *Het oordeel van de huisvrouw over haar woning*, Rotterdam 9 February 1950, typescript, 1, GAS, archive no. 608 Jansen, inv.no. 1a.

94 The workers homes, originally intended as temporary housing, were not demolished until the 1980s.

95 *Memorandum on the Women's Advisory Committee (VAC)*, Rotterdam 14 December 1950, typescript, 2, GAS, archive no. 608 Jansen, inv.no. 1a.

96 Unsigned design, *The elderly*, 17 March 1951, GAS, archive no. 608 Jansen, inv.no. 7c.

97 Survey on *Housing for the elderly*, 1950, reports and list of senior homes to visit, GAS, archive no. 608 Jansen, inv.no. 1a.

98 Signed designs of *Interior "Pluk den dag"*, 1958, GAS, archive no. 608 Jansen, inv.no. 7c.

99 In the context of researching Wil Jansen for this study, Marlous Heikamp (currently studying architecture at Delft University of Technology) surveyed the activities of the washing committee. Heikamp 2019.

100 Letter by W.C.M. Jansen to TNO, 1 September 1955, GAS, archive no. 608 Jansen, inv.no. 1a.

101 The book was *Die Behausungsfrage* (1947), by Austrian architect Roland Rainer (1910–2004). Typescript, 5 July 1949, signed 'your Jeanne' (probably former classmate and colleague Jeanne van Rood-van Rijswijk); meeting minutes VAC, 28 January 1947, typescript with handwritten note, signature partly illegible (Bep?), GAS, archive no. 608 Jansen, inv.no. 1a.

102 Heijkoop/Bakker 2010, 19-29.

103 The building was designed by A.U. Ingwersen (1882–1959). Krabbe/Broekhuizen/Smit 2018, 98.

104 Laura en Vereeniging built a 'gezellenhuis' (guesthouse) on Laurastraat in Eygelshoven. Website: *De Nederlandse mijnstreek in het heden*.

105 See Chapter 8 for more on this. In 1926 Jan Buijs designed an apartment building for single women, with the envisioned location on Benoordenhoutseweg in The Hague. The project did not move forward. De Hoog 1926, 83-86.

106 The foundation consists of the following women's associations: VVAO, Nederlandse Bond van Vrouwen werkzaam in Bedrijf en Beroep, NVVH, Nederlandse Vereniging voor Vrouwenbelangen en Gelijk Staatsburgerschap, Nederlandse Vrouwen Electriciteitsvereniging, Unie van Nederlandse Soroptimistclubs, Unie van Vrouwelijke Vrijwilligers. Jansen was a member of the first two associations.

107 Appeal by A. Kuiper-Struyk, *Vereeniging van Vrouwen met Academische Opleiding. Rotterdam branch*, undated [spring 1946], typescript, GAS, archive no. 608 Jansen, 1b (the survey itself is not present); appeal by the Board, *Vereeniging van Vrouwen met Academische Opleiding. Rotterdam chapter*, undated [lecture of 23 September 1946], typescript, GAS, archive no. 608 Jansen, 1b. There is no text still available of the lecture, entitled *The Block of Flats*.

108 Heijkoop/Bakker 2010, 24, 27, 31, 34-35.

109 Designs from 1946 state: 'W.C.M. Jansen, architectural engineer, and architecture firm Verhagen, Kuiper and Gouwetor'; designs from 1956 state: 'W.C.M. Jansen and architecture firm Kuiper, Gouwetor, de Ranitz and Bleeker, Rotterdam', alternating between handwritten, or handwritten (Jansen) in combination with an inked stamp (architecture firm). During the construction in 1957 and 1958, she made designs for the walls of the hall which she signed as an independent architect in Schiedam, GAS, archive no. 608 Jansen, inv.no. 10.

110 For example: Ir. W.C.M. Jansen and architecture firm Kuiper, Gouwetor, de Ranitz and Bleeker, *Residential building on Heemraadssingel in Rotterdam for the account of the public limited company R.V.S. in Rotterdam*, specification drawing no. 5445, page 12, with at the bottom right the signature of Jansen and Gouwetor, GAS, archive no. 608 Jansen, inv.no. 10.

111 Letters by W.C.M. Jansen to M. Staal-Kropholler, 2 March 1949 and 12 March 1951, HNI, archives of Staal J.F., Kropholler A.J. and Staal-Kropholler M. (STAX), inv.no. 31. In that period, Staal-Kropholler (who was not university-educated) conducted three surveys about the activities of the small group of women architectural engineers and reported the results in the National Women's Council. In her 1951 letter, Jansen asks Staal-Kropholler how her apartment building is doing. Staal-Kropholler made her first designs for the building in 1937. It was not until 1963 that the Louise Went House for single women on Prins Bernhardplein in Amsterdam was built, based on a design by Staal-Kropholler.

112 Jan de Ranitz (1903–1972), who was similar in age, must also have been an appealing sparring partner for Jansen. In 1930, he was actively involved in the international course on international architecture, held at the TH and discussed previously in this chapter. Rede 1930, 3.

113 See for more on this: De Ridder 1958, 252-255; residential building 1958, 498-502; residential building 1959, 1280-1283.

114 Heijkoop/Bakker 2010, 25, 67, 73.

115 Van den Broek designed the De Eendracht housing complex (1935), among others.

116 Summaries of the course lectures were published. Internationale 1930, 506-507.

117 In his capacity as chairman of the study group on the Functional Principles of the Home, Van Tijen gave a speech at a study day on 3 July 1955 entitled *Ieders Huis* ('Each person's house'), which was about the floor plan of the residence. It became a permanent exhibition in Bouwcentrum Rotterdam. Lecture announcement and handwritten notes by Jansen, GAS, archive no. 608 Jansen, inv.no. 1a.

118 Minutes VAC, 25 February 1947, typescript, GAS, archive no. 608 Jansen, inv.no. 1a.

119 Van Tijen 1958, 497. The article is followed by a description of the apartment building by 'the architects' themselves, 498-502, quote 499.

120 Heijkoop/Bakker 2010, 24-29, 74-78.

121 Krabbe/Broekhuizen/Smit 2018, 148-150.

122 Various designs, including: Ir. W.C.M. Jansen architectural engineer, *Residence in Meersen* [sic], 13 July 1955 (rectangular building block), GAS, archive no. 608 Jansen, inv.no. 7c; architecture firm of Ir. W.C.M. Jansen, *Bungalow in Meerssen for Ir. G.H. Edixhoven*, 1 April 1956,

Meerssen city archive, building permits 1933–1981, annex to approved building permit dated 17 April 1956, inv.no. 1663. With thanks to Dan Peerenbooms, Documentaire Informatievoorziening.

123 Various designs, including: Ir. W.C.M. Jansen, architectural engineer, *Bungalow in Meerssen. View and floor plan of kitchen wall*, 26 February 1956 and Ir. W.C.M. Jansen, architectural engineer, *Meerssen. Living room wall*, 26 February 1956, GAS, archive no. 608 Jansen, inv.no. 7c.

124 Unsigned and undated design [ca. 1957], *Country house in Meersen*, GAS, archive no. 608 Jansen, inv.no. 7c.

125 With thanks to Henri Marres, later occupant, and Désirée van der Heijde, current occupant. The current address of the bungalow is Korte Raarberg 46.

126 Krabbe/Broekhuizen/Smit 2018, 417-421.

127 Vierde undated [ca. 2010], 162.

128 Website: *Rijckheyt centre for regional history.*

129 W.J.[ansen], *Overview of the site layout of the Julia mine'*, 5 March 1937, GAS, archive no. 608 Jansen, inv.no. 3a; W.J.[ansen], *Design for the layout of the grounds of the Julia mine*, 5 March 1937, GAS, archive no. 608 Jansen, inv.no. 8e.

130 Letters by G.H. Edixhoven to W.C.M. Jansen, 7 and 9 March 1937, GAS, archive no. 608 Jansen, inv.no. 3a.

131 Letter by W.C.M. Jansen to G.H. Edixhoven, 10 March 1937, GAS, archive no. 608 Jansen, inv.no. 3a.

132 Unsigned and undated design [1937], *Planting scheme of the Julia mine*, GAS, archive no. 608 Jansen, inv.no. 8e; letter from Firma Jan G. van der Bom Boomkwekerijen Oudenbosch to W.C.M. Jansen, 23 March 1937, GAS, archive no. 608 Jansen, inv.no. 3a.

133 Various covers, GAS, archive no. 608 Jansen, inv.no. 5. According to her list of final marks at the Higher Civic School, Jansen's highest mark was an 8/10 in 'Botany and Zoology'.

134 News 1948.

135 Address 1949. The plans were shot down by the municipal council. Cultural 1949.

136 Various correspondence with the municipality of Eygelshoven and the Municipal Housing Company in 1939 and 1940, for example a letter from the municipality of Eygelshoven to W.C.M. Jansen, 3 April 1939, GAS, archive no. 608 Jansen, inv.no. 3a. No designs were found. The housekeeping school no longer exists.

137 Woman architect 1946.

138 Various letters by W.C.M. Jansen to the municipality of Eygelshoven, such as on 13 and 21 April 1939, GAS, archive no. 608 Jansen, inv.no. 3a. The planting schemes are not included.

139 Letters from the municipality of Eygelshoven to W.C.M. Jansen, 31 March and 1 April 1939, GAS, archive no. 608 Jansen, inv.no. 3a.

140 Van der Sloot 2015, 132-133.

141 Various unsigned and undated [1939] sketches, GAS, archive no. 608 Jansen, inv.no. 8d.

142 Letter from the municipality of Eygelshoven to W.C.M. Jansen, 3 April 1939, GAS, archive no. 608 Jansen, inv.no. 3a.

143 Vierde undated [ca. 2010], 162.

144 Unsigned letter, presumably from Pop when she was still living in their parental home, to Wil Jansen, 2 May 1934, archive held by H.Th.F. Jansen. The letter mentions one Frits Beukers (name difficult to decipher) who is willing to introduce Jansen to Klijnen. For M.P.J.H. Klijnen, see: website: *Heerlen Vertelt.*

145 Architect 1946; unsigned and undated [1938], *Design for the landscaping of 12 gardens on Schaasbergerweg in Heerlen*; unsigned, *Schaesbergerweg, Heerlen*, Oct. 1938, axonometric drawing with several gardens and houses, GAS, archive no. 608 Jansen, inv.no. 8a. No other designs of the houses were found in the archive.

146 Ir. W.C.M. Jansen, architectural engineer and architect, *Design for the landscaping of a garden in Heerlen on the corner of Akerstraat – Molenberglaan*, in a cover labelled 'Heerlen Garden Mr Meyers 1939'; Ir. W.C.M. Jansen, architectural engineer and architect, *Design for the landscaping of a garden in Heerlen*, May 1939; Ir. W.C.M. Jansen, architectural engineer in Schiedam, *Design for the landscaping of a garden in Heerlen at Franciscusweg 37*, March 1943, blueprint in cover labelled 'Heerlen 1941 garden landscaping Mr H. Anten'; Ir. W.C.M. Jansen in Schiedam, *Design for a garden in Someren*, undated [1941], GAS, archive no. 608 Jansen, inv.no. 3a and 8a; Ir. W.C.M. Jansen, architect, *Design for the landscaping of 7 gardens in Eindhoven. St. Jorislaan*, March 1939, blueprint, GAS, archive no. 608 Jansen, inv.no. 8a. There may have been contact between Jansen and the Eindhoven-based architecture and engineering firm Th.P. v.d. Boomen and F.W.M. v.d. Berg that designed several of the villas. Jansen had their building plans.

147 See note 146.

148 W.J.[ansen], *Design for a pulpit for the church in Eygelshoven*, 16 December 1936, blueprint, GAS, archive no. 608 Jansen, inv.no. 8a.

149 Unsigned and undated sketch, *Sound reflection in the St. Egbert Church, Almelo. Front view. Side view*, with the note: 'from photo', GAS, archive no. 608 Jansen, inv.no. 3a.

150 Website: *Rijckheyt centre for regional history.* The church has been a national heritage site since 2001. Website: *Registry of National Heritage Sites – 513744.*

151 The Late Gothic church was in poor condition; it was purchased by the municipality in 1932 and renovated in 1939. Website: *Stichting "Eygelshoven door de eeuwen heen".*

152 Schiphorst 2006, 79-91.

153 Unsigned and undated sketches of kneeling chairs, prayer stools and baptismal font, GAS, archive no. 608 Jansen, inv.no. 8a. Both the 'old' and the 'new' church still serve as the parish church. With thanks to the reverend Mr M. Heemels and B. Nols, Parish of St. John the Baptist, Eygelshoven.

154 The home was designed by Anton Bartels (1879–1966) from Heerlen. Website: *Registry of National Heritage Sites – 513736.*

155 Arch. Ir. W.M.C. [the front letters are switched here] Jansen, *Bay window extension for Dr Edixhoven*, March 1938, blueprint, GAS, archive no. 608 Jansen, inv.no. 3a; W.C.M. Jansen, *Bay window extension for Dr Edixhoven*, March 1938; unsigned and undated [1938] interior design, GAS, archive no. 608 Jansen, inv.no. 8a.

156 In 1950 Edixhoven lived at Rimburgerweg 1, which is now Rimburgerweg 3. List of names 1950, unpaginated; decision by Municipal Executive to renumber, 7 May 1952, municipality of Kerkrade, archive Eygelshoven 1938 through 1981, file no. 989.

157 The notes in red pencil include a change to the ceiling in the salon. Unsigned [Jaspar], *Laura en Vereeniging. The Julia mine. Construction of two Engineers' Homes. Plan of the ground floor. Technical specification no. 1A*, undated [1925], GAS, archive no. 608 Jansen, inv.no. 8e. The double director's residence is a national heritage site. The layout of the left side has remained virtually intact.

Website: *Registry of National Heritage Sites – 513743*.

158 Interview with Jansen 2019.

159 Interview with Jansen 2019. Wil Jansen stayed in Groningen until May 1934, when she returned to the house on Lange Haven. An exchange of letters with her brother Tup shows that Ros, who was facing creditors, was no longer able to pay her allowance. Tup sent Wil 50 guilders. She was staying at Emmasingel 9 with the Van der Werff family, who were the in-laws of Ros. Letter from Tup Jansen to his sister Wil, undated, GAS, archive no. 608 Jansen, inv.no. 5.

160 Websites: *Beeldbank Groningen* and *Staat in Groningen. Architectuur in stad – Ter Schouw-Van Sanen Foundation*.

161 'Signed by W.C.M. J.'[ansen], *Plan for 16 flats "Geuzenkamp" Groningen*, 18 December 1933 and 'signed W.C.M. J', *Plan for 19 flats "Geuzenkamp" Groningen*, no. 14 March 1934, GAS, archive no. 608 Jansen, inv.no. 8e.

162 A colleague and draughtsman also worked on the project. 'signed RJO', *Plan for 19 flats "Geuzenkamp" Groningen*, 12 March 1934, GAS, archive no. 608 Jansen, inv.no. 8e.

163 Unsigned and undated floor plans and facade views of the plot on Gedempte Zuiderdiep at the corner of Herestraat in Groningen, GAS, archive no. 608 Jansen, inv.no. 8e.

164 In 1935 the 'De Faun' complex was erected here, designed by Adriaan Wittop Koning (1878–1961) and Antonius Theodorus van Elmpt (1866–1953) and commissioned by De Utrecht life insurance company. The building is characteristic of Delft School architecture. Website: *Staat in Groningen. Architectuur in stad – De Faun*.

165 Ir. W.C.M. Jansen, architectural engineer and architect, *Renovation of factory building at Westvest no 38 and 40*, 2 September 1954, GAS, archive no. 608 Jansen, inv.no. 7c.

166 The architect of the existing facade was M.A.H. van de Laarschot. Website: *Bouwdossiers online – Westvest 38-40*.

167 Signed and dated (1971) designs for a residence intended for brother Tup in Meer (Belgium), GAS, archive no. 608 Jansen, inv.no. 8b/8f. The house was presumably built by a local architect. Interview with Jansen 2019. Signed and dated (1963–1964) designs for a doctor's home in Ossendrecht, commissioned by Dr J.L. Edixhoven, presumably related to her brother-in-law Edixhoven. GAS, archive no. 608 Jansen, inv.no. 8b/8f.

168 Retained correspondence with various clients shows that relations were either professional or friendly. In the latter cases, the letters used informal language and sometimes exchanged personal trivia.

169 Letter from W.C.M. Jansen, 19 July 1962, to Jules and Joop Boots-Beukers in 's-Hertogenbosch. GAS, archive no. 608 Jansen, inv.no. 3b. It concerns the renovation of their new home, Rondeweg 5 in Vught.

170 The architect was Reyer Schaatsbergen (1912–1981) from Soest, GAS, archive no. 608, inv.no. 4 and 8b.

8 Architect couples

1 Joop Stakesby-Lewis-Ferguson was registered with the Institute of South African Architects (Instituut van Suid-Afrikaanse Argitekte en Bourekenaars) from 1937 to 1967. Website: *Artefacts. Southern African Built Environment*. Marieke Kuipers has recently carried out research into Ferguson. Kuipers 2022, 34-54.

2 See: website *Parlement – Ada Kuiper-Struik*.

3 See: Molema/Leemans 2010.

4 The archives of Koos Pot-Keegstra and Lotte Stam-Beese were consulted at Het Nieuwe Instituut (HNI)

5 For an overview of publications, see: Website Het Nieuwe Instituut – Keegstra, J.F., publications

6 Damen/Devolder 1993; Oosterhof 2018.

7 For them, archival research and contact with relatives formed part of the research.

8 The architecture office was acquired by ZZDP Architects in Amsterdam. This office no longer possesses the archives of husband-and-wife Lammers-Koeleman.

9 The house annex workspace was located on Plataanweg 24 in Schiebroek.

10 Van Kessel/Kuperus 1982, 103.

11 Toki Koeleman was recruited to handle the business affairs of a Jewish architect who had fled to England. Van Kessel/Kuperus 1982, 108-117.

12 Website: *Het Nieuwe Instituut – Stadsplan Arnhem*.

13 Wendt 2008, 67; Website: *Het Nieuwe Instituut – Pot J.W.H.C. and Pot-Keegstra, J.F.*

14 Letter from A.P. van Rood-van Rijswijk to M. Staal-Kropholler, 17 February 1949, HNI, archive STAX, inv. no. 31.

15 Website: *Het Nieuwe Instituut – Rood, A.H. van*.

16 The office was acquired by R.L. de Vries (1924–1986) in Wassenaar. It is not known if the practice was continued.

17 Oosterhof 2018, 86-91.

18 Staal-Kropholler was using 'man' here to refer to 'husband'. Memo by M. Staal-Kropholler, *National Women's Council of the Netherlands. Details for the report on Dutch Art: Architecture*, typescript, 27 March 1950, HNI, archive STAX, inv. no. 31.

19 Architecte 1946.

20 Staal-Kropholler reported to the National Women's Council on the activities of a small group of active female architectural engineers. Postcard from J. Kammer-Kret to M. Staal-Kropholler, 8 March 1951, HNI, archive STAX, inv. no. 32. This possibly concerns the 'Villa Egmond, 1951', which appears on the list of works by Harry Kammer, but, according to the HNI, 'no material of which exists in the archive'. Website: *Het Nieuwe Instituut – Kammer, H.* Until recently, the archive of Harry Kammer contained none of Jan's own designs, apart from drawings done while she was a student. In late 2022 the family handed over to the HNI the private archive of husband-and-wife Kammer-Kret, which does contain designs by Kammer-Kret. In April 2023 this archive had not yet been processed.

21 Van Kessel/Kuperus 1982, 102-103.

22 Result 1934, 120-122, quote 121. The winner of the first prize was later disqualified for plagiarizing a design by M.J. Granpré Molière.

23 HNI, archive Kammer, H. (KAMM), inv. no. t15.

24 Van Loghem 1936, 66-69, quote 66.

25 With thanks to daughter K.J. van Manen-Kammer. Written correspondence, 2 October 2020.

26 Van Kessel/Kuperus 1982, 102-105.

27 Bosma/Wagenaar 1995, 239-241.

28 As part of her duties, Van Rood-van Rijswijk was delegated to the United Nations Works and Building Committee, set up by the Ministry of Works, and to the Inter-Allied Committee for Physical Planning and Reconstruction, set up by the Ministry of Town and Country Planning. Letter from A.P. van Rood-van Rijswijk to M. Staal-Kropholler, 17 February 1949, HNI, archive STAX, inv. no. 31.

29 Letter from A.P. van Rood-van Rijswijk to M. Staal-Kropholler, 17 February 1949, HNI, archive STAX, inv. no. 31. There was no big family to look after.

Jeanne and Albert probably had just one child. Albert had six children from two previous marriages, both of which ended in divorce. It is unlikely that Jeanne looked after these children.
30 Van Kessel/Kuperus 1982, 114-115.
31 Questionnaire undated [ca. 1994] for the book Van Damme-Van Weele/ Ressing Wolfert 1995, City Archive of Delft, Ressing collection, archive no. 606, inv. no. 2.
32 Van Kessel/Kuperus 1982, 114.
33 Van Kessel/Kuperus 1982, 114.
34 Van Kessel/Kuperus 1982, 114.
35 Roos 1978. The couple had one daughter.
36 B. 1956.
37 Oosterhof 2018, 85-100.
38 Oosterhof 2018, 96. The remarks were not published but noted during the interview.
39 Oosterhof 2018, 96.
40 HNI, archive Stam-Beese, Ch.I.A. (STAB), inv. no. t55.
41 See, for example, Oosterhof 2018, 44-45, 99, 156. Stam-Beese had two children: one from her relationship with the then director of the Bauhaus, Hannes Meyer, and one from her marriage to Mart Stam.
42 Van Kessel/Kuperus 1982, 101-102, quote 102.
43 Van Tijen 1972, 21. Granpré Molière later withdrew his critical comments on the matter in education. Discussie 1972, 24-37.
44 Written correspondence from K.J. van Manen-Kammer, 2 October 2020. K.J. van Manen-Kammer, as well as a sister, also studied to be an architectural engineer at Delft.
45 J.K. [Jan Kammer], *Plan for a country residence on a cadastral site in Oostvoorne for Mr Westerveld from Hillegersberg*, 20 September 1934, HNI, inventory not yet processed, archive of husband-and-wife Kammer-Kret handed over by the family in late 2022.
46 Website: *Het Nieuwe Instituut – Tijen, W. van*; Wissing 1974, 299-305.
47 Vacantie- 1935, 649, 660-662.
48 The periodical *Bouwkundig Weekblad*, for example, contended that 'the architect of private residents (...) deals with personalities, for the client is not simply an individual with various wishes – so many rooms, kitchen, pantry, boudoir and view of the copse of birch trees on the left and the beech tree on the right, (...) that, for example, demands a low riser on the steps flanked by tall handrails – but also a personality who can also assert himself.' M. [Mieras] 1924, 365.
49 HNI, archive KAMM, inv. no. t15.
50 Opbouw 1936, unpaginated, front page.
51 Van Loghem 1936, 67.
52 Van Kessel/Kuperus 1982, 103.
53 Daughter K.J. van Manen-Kammer recalls that she thought it was the most normal thing in the world to attend a school that her parents had built. Telephone conversation 27 February 2020 and written correspondence 2 October 2020.
54 Website: *Het Nieuwe Instituut – de 8 en Opbouw.*
55 Van Kessel/Kuperus 1982, 104.
56 Van Kessel/Kuperus 1982, 103, 106. The school building is located on Sleedoornlaan 25 in Rotterdam today and houses an out-of-school care centre.
57 Website: *Wikipedia – Nieuw Amsterdam.*
58 Luxury cabin 1940, 132-133. The designs themselves are not present. HNI, archive KAMM 110512146.
59 Telephone conversation with K.J. van Manen-Kammer, 27 February 2020; Van Kessel/Kuperus 1982, 104.
60 Van Kessel/Kuperus 1982, 103-104. The design is known as a supplement to the application for a building permit dated 6 December 1960, Midden-Holland Regional Archive, Gouda, access and inventory number. 0780.304. The HNI contains just one drawing of the foundations. HNI, archive KAMM, inv. no. t109. The bungalow is located on Zuidbroekse Opweg 16, Berkenwoude.
61 Written correspondence from K.J. van Manen-Kammer, 2 October 2020.
62 Heuvelink 1955, 677. The bungalow is located on Monnikensteeg 20 in Arnhem.
63 Van Kessel/Kuperus 1982, 112. The bungalow is located on Joris van der Haagenlaan 52.
64 Moussault-Veegens 1936.
65 See, for example: Emeis 1955.
66 Architects couple 1964. Both Staal and Limperg left the course for Secondary and Higher Architecture Training (VHBO) after just one year, very likely as a result of dissatisfaction with what they saw as the traditional direction of the course. Wendt 2008, 76-77.
67 Wendt 2008, 84-90; B. 1956.
68 Website: *Wederopbouw Amsterdam.* The project, now a municipal monument, concerned a double residence. Husband-and-wife Pot-Keegstra lived and worked at number 14; house number 12 was occupied by a certain Hola. A connection between the couple and this person is unknown. For Mien Ruys, see: Backer 2016, 472-481.
69 Emeis 1955.
70 Emeis 1955.
71 Emeis 1955.
72 HNI, archive Pot, J.W.H.C. and Pot-Keegstra, J.F. (POTK), inv. no. a16t2. The designs still bore the signature of J.W.H.C. Pot alone, who at the time, alongside his architecture practice, worked for the private contractor Huibert van Saane (1903–1981), who built the Bergerhof. Website: *Het Nieuwe Instituut – Pot J.W.H.C. and Pot-Keegstra, J.F.*; Van Rosse 1944, 9-15; Zietsma 1947, 245-249.
73 Roos 1978; Krabbe/Broekhuizen/ Smit 2018, 131, 143. The location of the drive-in dwellings (1945) mentioned in the interview could not be traced. The drive-in dwellings (1935–1937) by Stam and Beese are located on Anthonie van Dijckstraat in Amsterdam. Oosterhof 2018, 86-87.
74 Architecte 1946.
75 Roos 1978.
76 Roos 1978.
77 Van Kessel/Kuperus 1982, 111.
78 Van Kessel/Kuperus 1982, 111.
79 Van Kessel/Kuperus 1982, 111.
80 Krabbe/Broekhuizen/Smit 2018, 92-96.
81 Van den Broek/Friedhoff/Vereniging van Delftse Ingenieurs 1956, 193.
82 Van den Broek/Friedhoff /Vereniging van Delftse Ingenieurs 1956, 194.
83 Written correspondence from C. Westhoven, 10 May 2020. With thanks to De Schakels Thomassen Foundation in Doesburg. The existing dwellings on Havelandseweg were later sold to the current municipality of Rheden.
84 Letter from C.Ch. Lammers-Koeleman to M. Staal-Kropholler, 8 March 1952, HNI, archive STAX, inv. no. 31.
85 C.Ch. Lammers-Koeleman, *List of buildings completed or under construction*, undated [25 January 1950]; letter from C.Ch. Lammers-Koeleman to M. Staal-Kropholler, 8 March 1951, HNI, archive STAX, inv. no. 31; Website: *Stedenbouw.*
86 Nieuwe 1951.
87 The dwellings were renovated in 2015. Lammers-Koeleman also completed housing schemes constructed using hollow concrete in the Presikhaaf neighbourhood in Arnhem-East. They were demolished in the 1990s.
88 HNI, archive POTK 110452414; Architect couple 1964.
89 Pot 1943, 69-74, quote 71. Although the design was published under both of their names, like all the couple's designs, Pot alone was noted as the author of this article.

90 Pot 1943, 71.
91 HNI, archive POTK, inv. no. 37t1-t7.
92 Van Saane 1943, 18-24, quote 23.
93 Pot was employed by the private building contractor Huibert van Saane as head of the drawing office from 1932 to 1936 and in 1941. Website: *Het Nieuwe Instituut – Pot J.W.H.C. and Pot-Keegstra, J.F.* See also note 70. To safeguard the interests of the residents, a foundation that included representatives of a number of women's organizations was to have been set up. However, this never materialized owing to conflicting interests between this foundation and the operating company. The foundation eventually set up only contained representatives of operator Van Saane and of the city council. Van Saane 1943, 20.
94 The archive contains just a site sketch, some floor plans and an accompanying explanatory text. HNI, archive STAB, inv. no. t55.
95 The project was a collaboration with the architect Gart Westerhout (1893–1976); the garden was designed by Mien Ruys. HNI, archive POTK, inv. no. 175.
96 Architect couple 1964.
97 HNI, archive POTK 110454438.
98 Architect couple 1964; HNI, archive POTK, inv. no. 145. The retirement home, now demolished, was located on a site between Cornelis Outshoornstraat and Adriaan Dorsmanstraat.
99 Van Kessel/Kuperus 1982, 113.
100 Lammers/Lammers-Koeleman 1965, 372-374.
101 Retirement home 1963.
102 Van Kessel/Kuperus 1982, 113-114.
103 Letters from A.P. van Rood-van Rijswijk to M. Staal-Kropholler, 17 February 1949 and 22 January 1950, HNI, archive STAX, inv. no. 31.
104 Letter from A.P. van Rood-van Rijswijk to M. Staal-Kropholler, 22 January 1950, HNI, archive STAX, inv. no. 31.
105 See: website *Archiwijzer Stichting Bonas*.
106 Website: *Het Nieuwe Instituut – Rood, A.H. van*.
107 Parts of the complex have been preserved and are occupied by another owner.
108 The letters to Staal-Kropholler (note 101) bear the letterhead: 'Ir. A.H. van Rood, civil and architectural engineer – architect B.N.A.' The designs for the bottling plant bear the signature: 'Former office of ir. A.H. van Rood c. and b.i. – arch. B.N.A.', website *Bouwdossiers online – Van Rood-van Rijswijk bottling plant*. In 1953 we see another letterhead: 'Ir. A.P. van Rood-van Rijswijk b.i. arch. B.N.A., formerly Bureau Ir. A.H. van Rood c.b.i.'. Letter from A.P. van Rood-van Rijswijk to M. Staal-Kropholler, 4 June 1953, HNI, archive STAX, inv. no. 31.
109 Letter from A.P. van Rood-van Rijswijk to M. Staal-Kropholler, 10 March 1951, HNI, archive STAX, inv. no. 31. This letter was her final annual report.
110 Written correspondence by H. Schaap, 29 September 2020. With thanks to the 'Oud Lisse' Cultural-Historical Society.
111 Roos 1978.
112 See, for example: Roos 1978; Vrouw 1983.
113 Roos 1978.
114 HNI, archive POTK 110454511; Kuperus/Meinsma 1990, 85.
115 Leistra/Van Ulden 2016.
116 Roos 1978.
117 Website: *Andere Tijden*. Bijlmerbajes prison closed in 2016 and was briefly used as an asylum seekers' centre. Demolition of the complex started in 2019 to make way for a residential development.
118 Oosterhof 2018, 145.
119 Oosterhof 2018, 163-233.
120 Roos 1978.
121 Pot-Keegstra 1959, 309-320, quote 312.
122 Pot-Keegstra 1959, 313.
123 Van Eesteren was succeeded by Ko Mulder.

9 The 21 women architects

1 Damen/Devolder 1993; Oosterhof 2018.
2 National Archives, The Hague (NA), archive of Technische Hoogeschool Delft, Student administration, access nr. 3.12.08.04, inv. no. 96.
3 Kristinsson-Reitsema undated [1994], 46.
4 Vereeniging van Delftsche Ingenieurs 1935 (series up to 1939), 1940 (series up to 1942) and 1947, unpaginated.
5 Website: *Noord-Hollandsarchief*.
6 Elizabeth Frederika van den Ban (1894–1973) graduated as one of the first female civil engineers from the TH in Delft in 1918. She worked from 1926 to 1950 as chief engineer for the planning division of the Noord-Holland Provincial Water Management Agency, and from 1950 to 1959 for the department of Zuiderzee Works. City Archive of Delft, Collection J.H.M. Ressing-Wolfert/90 jaar Delftse vrouwelijke ingenieurs, archive 606, inv. no. 7; website: *Het Nieuwe Instituut – Ban, E.F. van den*. On the collaboration with Van den Broek d'Obrenan: letter from E.F. van den Ban to M. Staal-Kropholler, 5 February 1950, HNI, archive STAX, inv. no. 31.
7 Mej. 1956.
8 National Archives, The Hague (NA), archive of Technische Hoogeschool Delft, Student administration, access nr. 3.12.08.04, inv. no. 122.
9 Ferguson 1925, 450-452.
10 Diecke 1934, unpaginated.
11 From 1937 to 1967, Joop Stakesby-Lewis-Ferguson was registered with the Institute of South African Architects (Instituut van Suid-Afrikaanse Argitekte en Bourekenaars). Website: *Artefacts. Southern African Built Environment*. See also: Kuipers 2022, 34-54.
12 National Archives, The Hague (NA), archive of Technische Hoogeschool Delft, Student administration, access nr. 3.12.08.04, inv. no. 131.
13 Vereeniging van Delftsche Ingenieurs 1922–1942 and 1947, unpaginated.
14 National Archives, The Hague (NA), archive of Technische Hoogeschool Delft, Student administration, access nr. 3.12.08.04, inv. no. 144.
15 Passagiers 1910.
16 Almanak 1921, 20; Kristinsson-Reitsema undated [1994], 38.
17 School 1923.
18 Vereeniging van Delftsche Ingenieurs 1923–1942 and 1947, unpaginated.
19 The villa is located at Duinlustweg 11.
20 Minutes of the joint meeting of the central board and the institute committee, The Hague, 10 December 1936, unpaginated typescript, Atria, archive NVVH, access nr. IIAV00000116, inv. no. 0033. The publication could not be traced.
21 Letter from S.S. Heyting to M. Staal-Kropholler, 18 March 1951, HNI, archive STAX, inv. no. 31.
22 The house, now demolished, was located at Van Limburg Stirumstraat 4 in Hoogeveen.
23 Letter from S.S. Heyting to M. Staal-Kropholler, 18 March 1951, HNI, archive STAX, inv. no. 31.
24 Housing Committee 1953, 839, 844.
25 Website: *Reliwiki*.
26 Website: *Het Nieuwe Instituut – Keegstra, J.F.*
27 *Lijst der deelnemers aan den tweeden Leergang 1941 onder auspiciën van het Genootschap Architectura et Amicitia*, HNI, STAX, inv. no. 31.
28 National Archives, The Hague (NA), archive of Technische Hoogeschool Delft, Student administration, access nr. 3.12.08.04, inv. no. 167.

29 Advertisements 1926.
30 City Archive of Delft, Collection Pieter Stempels and Jacoba van der Kloet, access 743.
31 See, for example: Fiasco 1954; Fiasco-Hawoma 1954.
32 Vereeniging van Delftsche Ingenieurs 1926–1942 and 1947, unpaginated.
33 Website: *Rijwielindustrie*.
34 National Archives, The Hague (NA), archive of Technische Hoogeschool Delft, Student administration, access nr. 3.12.08.04, inv. no. 169.
35 Van Kessel/Kuperus 1982, 108-115.
36 Kristinsson-Reitsema undated [1994], 59, 62.
37 National Archives, The Hague (NA), archive of Technische Hoogeschool Delft, Student administration, access nr. 3.12.08.04, inv. no. 175.
38 With thanks to daughter K.J. van Manen-Kammer. Telephone conversation 27 February 2020.
39 Van Kessel/Kuperus 1982, 101-105.
40 Van Kessel /Palstra 1994; website: *Digitaal Vrouwenlexicon van Nederland – Ko Mulder*; Teijmant 2013, 51-67; Van Zomeren 1984, 24-29; Van Kessel/Kuperus 1982, 91-100.
41 Kristinsson-Reitsema undated [1994], 45.
42 National Archives, The Hague (NA), archive of Technische Hoogeschool Delft, Student administration, access nr. 3.12.08.04, inv. no. 200.
43 National Archives, The Hague (NA), archive of Technische Hoogeschool Delft, Student administration, access nr. 3.12.08.04, inv. no. 214.
44 Kristinsson-Reitsema undated [1994], 62.
45 Vereeniging van Delftsche Ingenieurs 1938–1942 and 1947.
46 National Archives, The Hague (NA), archive of Technische Hoogeschool Delft, Student administration, access nr. 3.12.08.04, inv. no. 215.
47 Vereeniging van Delftsche Ingenieurs 1922–1942 and 1947.
48 National Archives, The Hague (NA), archive of Technische Hoogeschool Delft, Student administration, access nr. 3.12.08.04, inv. no. 231.
49 National Archives, The Hague (NA), archive of Technische Hoogeschool Delft, Student administration, access nr. 3.12.08.04, inv. no. 227.
50 Website: *Nederland's Patriciaat*.
51 Onderwijs 1924 and 1925; Kristinsson-Reitsema undated [1994], 45.
52 Kristinsson-Reitsema undated [1994], 45.
53 Minutes of the joint meeting of the central board and the institute committee, The Hague 10 December 1936, unpaginated typescript, Atria, archive NVVH, access nr. IIAV00000116, inv. no. 0033. The publication could not be traced.
54 Vereeniging van Delftsche Ingenieurs 1937–1942 and 1947, unpaginated.
55 NRC 1975.
56 National Archives, The Hague (NA), archive of Technische Hoogeschool Delft, Student administration, access nr. 3.12.08.04, inv. no. 246.
57 Almanak 1916, 19.
58 Website: *Het Nieuwe Instituut – Kok, A.A. and Kok, Y.*
59 Wijdeveld/Boterenbrood 1922, 1. Snethlage is listed here as: Mej. N.[M.]F.H. Snethlage, B.I.; Schilt/Van der Werf 1992, 218.
60 Vereeniging van Delftsche Ingenieurs 1926–1939.
61 National Archives, The Hague (NA), archive of Technische Hoogeschool Delft, Student administration, access nr. 3.12.08.04, inv. no. 246. It is not clear exactly which academic year or which lectures this concerns.
62 Website: *Municipal Archives of The Hague*.
63 Website: *Wikidata*.
64 National Archives, The Hague (NA), archive of Technische Hoogeschool Delft, Student administration, access nr. 3.12.08.04, inv. no. 255.
65 Kristinsson-Reitsema undated [1994], 57.
66 Vereeniging van Delftsche Ingenieurs 1941; signature illegible, 'Gegevens Ir. C. Strumphler (Catharina, roepnaam Toot)', 5 October 1994, typescript, City Archive of Delft, Collection J.H.M. Ressing-Wolfert/90 jaar Delftse vrouwelijke ingenieurs, archive 606, inv. no. 7; Van Damme-van Weele/Ressing-Wolfert 1995, 35.
67 Letter from C. Strumphler to M. Staal-Kropholler, 18 February 1949, HNI, archive STAX, inv. no. 31.
68 R-F 1955; 'Ms C. Strumphler, engineer. As a planner you must not be sentimental', name of newspaper missing and undated [ca. 1965], City Archive of Delft, Collection J.H.M. Ressing-Wolfert/90 jaar Delftse vrouwelijke ingenieurs, archive nr. 606, inv. no. 7.
69 In her letter to Staal-Kropholler she announces an article about country estates in *De Toeristenkampioen*. The date of publication is unknown. Letter from C. Strumphler to M. Staal-Kropholler, 18 February 1949, HNI, archive STAX, inv. no. 31.
70 The bungalow is located at Joris van der Haagenlaan 52 in Arnhem.
71 National Archives, The Hague (NA), archive of Technische Hoogeschool Delft, Student administration, access nr. 3.12.08.04, inv. no. 255.
72 Website: *Parlement – Ada Kuiper-Struyk*.
73 Kuiper-Struyk 1946, 6-7.
74 Proceedings of Second Chamber of the States-General 1960–1961, Establishment of chapter IX A (Public Housing and Construction Sector) of the state budget for the year 1961, 34rd meeting – 21 December 1960. Website: *Government* a.
75 See, for example: Proceedings of Second Chamber of the States-General 1960–1961, Proceedings of draft legislation on measures to preserve monuments of history and art (Law on Historical Buildings), 23rd meeting – 29 November 1960. Website: *Government* b.
76 National Archives, The Hague (NA), archive of Technische Hoogeschool Delft, Student administration, access nr. 3.12.08.04, inv. no. 295.
77 Kristinsson-Reitsema undated [1994], 2, 34.
78 Zeeman 1920b, 212-218.
79 Zeeman 1920a, 203-205.
80 Vereeniging van Delftsche Ingenieurs 1920–1922.
81 Van Kessel/Kuperus 1982, 88-90.
82 Website: *Comité Herdenken en Vieren Oegstgeest*.

Archives

Atria Research Institute on Gender Equality and Women's History, Amsterdam (Atria)
- IAV1000164 archive Boeree, Mia
- IIAV0000011 archive National Women's Council
- IIAV00000116 archive Dutch Association of Housewives (NVVH)
- IIAV00000539 archive VVAO Association of women with a higher education

Meerssen municipal archives
- 1663 building permits 1933–1981

Schiedam municipal archives (GAS)
- 61 archive of Department of Public Works (1759–1837) 1848–1991 (1999)
- 346 archive of Schiedam city and municipal council (1798) 1816–1953 (1973)
- 608 archive Ir. W.C.M. Jansen

Geniemuseum, Vught
- D09447 archive without name

Municipal archives of The Hague
- CR5950 Construction drawings archive

Het Nieuwe Instituut, Rotterdam (HNI)
- ABAM archive Academy of Architecture, Amsterdam
- BNAR archive of the Royal Institute of Dutch Architects (BNA) and of its affiliates
- BOER archive Boerée, C.H.M.
- KAMM archive Kammer, H.
- POTK archive Pot, J.W.H.C. and Pot-Keegstra, J.F.
- STAB archive Stam-Beese, Ch.I.A.
- STAX archive Staal J.F., Kropholler A.J. and Staal-Kropholler, M.
- WIEB archive Wiebenga, J.G.

National Archives, The Hague (NA)
- 3.09.44.05 archive of Executive Engineer for Military Structures in The Hague, Alexanderkazerne 1938–1939
- 3.12.08.04 Technical College Delft (THD) archives, Student administration

Netherlands Institute of Military History, The Hague (NIMH)
- 406 archive of barracks, military sites, buildings

Noord-Hollands Archives, Haarlem (NHA)
- Provinciale Atlas collection
- 1100 Image collection of the municipality of Haarlem
- 2295 Haarlem City Council archives

Private archives of the Boerée, Ferguson, Jansen and Kammer-Kret families

Dordrecht Regional Archives
- Collection H.G. Beerman
- Cultural Heritage Agency, Amersfoort (RCE)
- beeldbank

City Archive of Delft (SAD)
- 357 archive Delftsche Vrouwelijke Studenten Vereeniging (DVSV)
- 606 collection J.H.M. Ressing-Wolfert/90 jaar Delftse vrouwelijke ingenieurs
- 743 collection Pieter Stempels and Jacoba van der Kloet

Rotterdam City Archives (SAR)
- 4121 collection Ary Groeneveld

Goeree-Overflakkee Regional Archives, Middelharnis

Midden-Holland Regional Archives, Gouda
- 0780 collection of building permits Berkenwoude 1906–1984

Literature

A

A., M., 'Mlle G.W.E. Wolffensperger, la première architecte en Hollande', *De Kroniek, geïllustreerd maandblad voor Nederland en België* 4 (1918) No. 3 (March), 68.

Aalbers, K. et al., *Honderd jaar fin-de-siècle 1894–1994. PS : Stylos*, Delft 1994.

Aardweg, H.P. van den, J.P.J.C. Hüllstrung (ed.) et al., *Persoonlijkheden in het Koninkrijk der Nederlanden in woord en beeld. Nederlanders en hun werk*, Amsterdam 1938.

Abma, L.A., *De Schiedamse familie Jansen*, Schiedam s.a. [ca. 1956], typescript.

Agtmaal, W. van (ed.) et al., *Een tipje van de sluier. Vrouwengeschiedenis in Nederland*, Amsterdam 1978.

Allaback, S., *The First American Women Architects*, Urbana/Chicago 2008.

Almanak der Delftsche Vrouwelijke Studentenvereeniging 1914, s.l. [Delft] s.a. [1913].

Almanak der D.V.S.V. 1916, Delft 1915.

Almanak der D.V.S.V. 1917, Delft 1916.

Almanak der D.V.S.V. 1920, Delft s.a. [1919].

Almanak der D.V.S.V. 1922, Delft 1921.

Almanak der D.V.S.V. 1925, Delft 1924.

Almanak der D.V.S.V. 1926, Delft 1925.

Almanak der D.V.S.V. 1929, Delft 1928.

Almanak D.V.S.V. 1932, Delft 1931.

Alphen, M.A. van, W.J.J. Geneste and P. Staal, *'Terg mij niet'. De geschiedenis van marinevliegkamp Valkenburg*, Franeker 2007.

De Amsterdammer, weekblad voor Nederland 41 (1917) No. 2094 (11 August), 5.

'"Architectura et Amicitia", afdeeling "Voortgezet en Hooger Bouwkunst-Onderricht". Meeting of teachers and members of the "Architectura et Amicitia" society, held on Saturday 28 March 1908', *Architectura. Orgaan van het genootschap Architectura et Amicitia* 16 (1908) No. 14 (4 April), 118.

B

Backer, A.M., *Er stond een vrouw in de tuin. Over de rol van vrouwen in het Nederlandse landschap*, Rotterdam 2016.

Bak, P. et al. (ed.), *J. Duiker. Bouwkundig Ingenieur. Constructeur in stuc en staal*, Rotterdam 1982.

Ban, E.F. van den and J.H. Mulder, 'Ingenieur', in: *Vrouwenberoepen. De weg naar de toekomst*, s.l., s.a. [1947], 54-59.

Bauduin (ed.), J., *Het begon in een smidse. De geschiedenis van een Nederlandse onderneming 1850–1920–1950*, Maarssen 1950.

Beemt, F.H. van den, D. Boekema and K.K. Thijssens (ed.), *300 Jaar bouwen voor de landsverdediging*, The Hague 1988.

'Benoemingen, verplaatsingen, enz.', *De Ingenieur* 2 (1887) No. 31 (30 July), 268.

Bergeijk, H. van, *Jan Duiker, bouwkundig ingenieur (1890–1935). Van warm naar koud*, Nijmegen 2016.

Blaauw, C.J. and H.T. Zwiers, 'Tentoonstelling van inzendingen op studieprijsvraag A. et A. No. 1, 1932', *Bouwkundig Weekblad Architectura* 53 (1932) 25 (18 June), 228.

Blok, E., *Jongere Tuinkunst 1900–1940*, Wageningen 1992 (Nederlandse Tuinarchitectuur III), 101-118.

Bosma, K. and C. Wagenaar (ed.), *Een geruisloze doorbraak. De geschiedenis van architectuur en stedebouw tijdens de bezetting en de wederopbouw van Nederland*, Rotterdam 1995.

Bosma, K. et al. (ed.), *Bouwen in Nederland 600-2000*, Amsterdam/Zwolle 2007.

Bosman, L., 'Vereniging Hendrick de Keyser in oorlogstijd. Beleid en bestuur gedurende de Duitse bezetting 1940-1945', *Bulletin KNOB* 117 (2018) No. 3, 169-171.

Branbergen, A., 'Artemisia Gentileschi. De geniale uitzondering', *De Groene Amsterdammer* 144 (2020) No. 12 (18 March), <https://www.groene.nl/artikel/de-geniale-uitzondering> (retrieved 2 February 2021).

Broek, J.H. van den, G. Friedhoff en Vereniging van Delftse Ingenieurs, *Nederlandse architectuur. Uitgevoerde werken van bouwkundige ingenieurs*, Amsterdam 1956.

Bruin, W., A.P. Smits and H.T. Zwiers, 'Rapport betreffende de eerste korte studieprijsvraag, uitgeschreven door het Genootschap Architectura et Amicitia', *Bouwkundig Weekblad Architectura* 53 (1932) 23 (4 June), 193-204.

Buikema, R. and L. Plate (ed.), *Handboek genderstudies in media, kunst en cultuur*, Bussum 2015.

Bullhorst, R., K. van Harmelen and I. Jager, *Duiker in Den Haag*, The Hague 1999.

C

Cardinaal, J., *Verslag van de lotgevallen der Technische Hoogeschool gedurende den cursus 1911–1912*, Delft 1913.

Central Committee for Study Interests of the TH (ed.), *Studie, werkkring en vooruitzichten van den ingenieur*, Delft 1932.

Cole, D., *From Tipi to Skyscraper. A History of Women in Architecture*, Boston 1973.

Couvée, D.H. and A.H. Boswijk, *Vrouwen vooruit! De weg naar gelijke rechten*, The Hague 1962.

'Cursus voor voortgezet en hooger bouwkunstonderricht', *Bouwkundig Weekblad Architectura* 59 (1938) No. 10 (5 March), 73-77.

D

Damen, H. and A. Devolder (ed.), *Lotte Stam-Beese, 1903–1988. Dessau, Brno, Charkow, Moskou, Amsterdam, Rotterdam*, Rotterdam 1993.

Damme-van Weele, M.A. van and J.H.M. Ressing-Wolfert, *Vrouwen in techniek. 90 Jaar Delftse Vrouwelijke Ingenieurs*, Delft 1995.

de 8 en Opbouw 7 (1936) No. 6 (21 March), unpaginated, front page.

De Studie te Delft. Inlichtingen voor den student en toekomstigen student aan de Technische Hoogeschool, Delft 1914.

Delftsche Studentenalmanak voor het jaar negentien-honderd-zes, Delft s.a. [1905].

Delftsche Studentenalmanak voor het jaar negentien-honderd-vijftien, Delft 1914.

Delftsche Studenten Almanak 1922, Delft 1921.

Delftsche Studenten Almanak, Delft 1925 to 1932.

Dettingmeijer, R., *Open Stad. Planontwikkeling, stedebouw, volkshuisvesting en architektuur in Rotterdam tussen de twee Wereldoorlogen*, Rotterdam 1988.

Diecke, J., *Register van alle Nederlandsche Architecten, Rijks- & Gemeente-Architecten, Directeuren van Gemeente-Werken, Directeuren of Inspecteurs van Bouw- & Woning Toezicht, alle Bouwkundige Ingenieurs, de Bouwkundigen of Timmerlieden in kleine plaatsen, die soms als Architect optreden, van de Directiën van den Rijks- & Provincialen-Waterstaat, van de voornaamste Firma's in Gewapend-Beton, enz., alles met vele aantekeningen, alsmede van de Hoogleeraren en Leeraren bij het Technisch Onderwijs, benevens van de Binnenhuis-Architecten en van vele Waterbouwkundigen*, The Hague 1934.

'Discussie over de betekenis van granpré molière', *Plan. Maandblad voor ontwerp en omgeving* 3 (1972) No. 6 (June), 24-37.

Doumato, L., *Architecture and women: a bibliography documenting women architects, landscape architects, designers, architectural critics and writers and women in related fields working in the United States*, New York 1988.

E

[editorial], 'Is de studie aan de T.H. academisch?', *De Spiegel. Officieel orgaan van het Delftsch Studenten-*

corps en van de Centrale Commissie voor Studiebelangen 7 (1930) No. 11 (5 December), 1.

Eschauzier, F.A., 'Werk der gediplomeerden van den cursus H.B.O. 1935', *Bouwkundig Weekblad Architectura* 57 (1936) No. 9 (29 February), 99-104.

Everts, S.G., *Verslag van de lotgevallen der Technische Hoogeschool gedurende den cursus 1908–1909*, Delft 1910.

F

F.J.H.P., 'Boekbespreking. Studie, werkkring en vooruitzichten van den Ingenieur. Samengesteld door de C.C. voor Studiebelangen. Publication: J. Waltman Jr., Delft', *De spiegel* 8 (1932) No. 33 (2 July), 7.

Faber, M., 'Tuinarchitectuur', *Onze Tuinen* 23 (1928) No. 14 (6 April), 199.

Ferguson, J.E., Cand. bouwk. ir., 'Drie practische tafeltjes', *De Vrouw en haar Huis*, 19 (1925) No. 11 (March), 450-452.

Fokker, J.P., 'De positie van den tuinarchitect', *Bouwkundig Weekblad Architectura* 54 (1933) No. 3 (21 January), 18-19.

Fuhring, P. and R. Eggink, *Binnenhuisarchitektuur in Nederland 1900–1981. Een geschiedenis van de interieurarchitekt(uur)*, The Hague 1981.

G

Geerts, G. and T. den Boon, *van Dale groot woordenboek der Nederlandse taal*, Utrecht/Antwerp 1999.

'Genootschap "Architectura et Amicitia" te Amsterdam. Afdeeling: Voortgezet en Hooger Bouwkunst-Onderricht', *Architectura. Orgaan van het genootschap Architectura et Amicitia* 16 (1908) No. 14 (4 April), 114-115.

'Goed nieuws voor aspirant-vliegers', *Vliegwereld* 12 (1946) 2 (15 January), 23.

Groot, M., *Vrouwen in de vormgeving in Nederland 1880–1940*, Rotterdam 2007.

'De Groote Houtbrug te Haarlem', *De Bouwwereld* 50 (1922) 6 (13 December), 389-391.

H

Hall, J., *Breaking ground. Architecture by women*, London/New York 2019.

Haslinghuis, E.J. and H. Janse (ed.), *Bouwkundige termen. Verklarend woordenboek van de westerse architectuur- en bouwhistorie*, Leiden 2001.

Havelaar, J.J. et al., *Kortenaerkade 11 en 12. Van directiekantoor tot internationaal onderwijsinstituut*, Den Haag 1993.

Heijkoop, A.C. and J. Bakker, *De RVS flat. Schone beloning voor vasthoudendheid in Rotterdam*, s.l. [Rotterdam] 2010.

Heikamp, M., *Switching the program. How the female advice committee in Rotterdam introduced the voice of the woman in housing*, Delft 2019, unpublished thesis.

Heinen, M., *Vrouwenjaarboekje voor Nederland 1915*, The Hague 1914.

Heinen, M., 'Technisch onderwijs aan meisjes', *De vrouw en haar huis* 12 (1917) No. 4 (August), 134.

Heuvelink, H.J., 'Woningen en woningblokken', *Bouw* 10 (1955) No. 33, 677.

Holtkamp, F., *Huis te Lande, vrouwen in de tuinbouw. Middelbare tuinbouwschool voor meisjes, uniek in Nederland*, Rijswijk 2020.

Hoof, J. van, *Gelegerd in Den Haag. De geschiedenis van de Alexanderkazerne en Frederikkazerne*, The Hague 2018.

Hoog, G.J. de, 'Het Wilhelminahuis. Het eerste gebouw voor vrouwen, van vrouwen in Nederland', *De Vrouw en haar Huis* (1926) No. 2 (June), 83-86.

I

'Ingenieurs-Examens vóór de Zomervacantie 1917', *Studenten Weekblad* 19 (1917) No. 31 (7 July), 217.

'Internationale Leergang voor Nieuwe Architectuur', *Het Bouwbedrijf. Maandblad voor bouwkunde, techniek en handel* 7 (1930) No. 25 (5 December), 506-507.

J

Jaarboek van de Technische Hoogeschool te Delft 1916–1917, Delft 1917.

Jaarboek van de Technische Hoogeschool te Delft, Delft 1918.

Jaarboek van de Technische Hoogeschool te Delft, Delft 1922.

Jaarboek van de Technische Hoogeschool te Delft, Delft 1925.

Jaarboek van de Technische Hoogeschool te Delft, Delft 1931.

Jaarboek van de Technische Hoogeschool te Delft, Delft 1939.

Jaarboek van de Technische Hoogeschool te Delft, Delft 1941.

Jong, F. de, 'Standhouden in Delft', *Gewina* 20 (1997) No. 4 (April), 227-242.

K

Kalf, J., *Een geschiedenis der Nederlandsche bouwkunst*, s.l. s.a. [1914].

Kamp, A.F. (ed.), *De Technische Hogeschool te Delft 1905–1955*, The Hague 1955.

Kessel, E. van en M. Kuperus, *Vrouwen in de (stede)bouw wat doen jullie nou? Over werk en werkervaringen van vrouwelijke bouwkundig ingenieurs in Nederland*, VU art history doctoral thesis, Amsterdam 1982.

Kessel, E. van and M. Kuperus, *Margaret Staal-Kropholler, architect 1891–1966*, Rotterdam s.a. [1991].

Kessel, E. van and F. Palstra, *Ir Jakoba Mulder (1900–1988) stedebouwkundige en landschapsarchitecte*, Amsterdam 1994.

Kirejczyk, M., 'Vrouwen kozen exact; studie en beroepsuitoefening rond de eeuwwisseling', *Gewina* 16 (1993) No. 3, 234-247.

Koninklijk Instituut van Ingenieurs. Gedenkboek 1847–1897, The Hague 1897.

Kooij, B., 'Nederlands oudste verzinkerijen Bammens B.V. uit Maarssen en Johan Vis & Co. te Amsterdam', *Stichting Bouwhistorie Nederland. Nieuwsbrief* (2011) No. 51 (November), 60-65.

Kooijman, D., *Wortels van het architectuuronderwijs*, Delft 1995 (Architectuuronderwijs in Nederland, 1).

Krabbe, C.P., *Ambacht. Kunst. Wetenschap. De bevordering van de bouwkunst in Nederland (1775–1880)*, Amsterdam 1997.

Krabbe, C.P., D. Broekhuizen and N. Smit, *Huizen in Nederland. De negentiende en twintigste eeuw. Architectuurhistorische verkenningen aan de hand van het bezit van Vereniging Hendrick de Keyser*, Amsterdam 2018.

Kristinsson-Reitsema, F.L. (ed.), *Delfts Studenten Corps, 1904–1994. Ter gelegenheid van het 90-jarig jubileum van de Delftsche Vrouwelijke Studenten Vereniging*, s.l. s.a. [1994].

Kuiper-Struyk, A., 'De menschwaardige huisvesting van het Nederlandse volk', *Vrouwenbelangen* 11 (1946) No. 4 (1 August), 6-7.

Kuipers, M., 'Ir. Johanna Eleanor Ferguson. Internationale vrouw in de bouw en de theosofie', *Bulletin KNOB* 121 (2022) No. 2, 34-54.

Kuperus, M.S. and H.C. Meinsma, *Architectes*, Amsterdam 1990.

Kurtz, G.H., *Beknopte geschiedenis van Haarlem*, Haarlem 1942.

L

Lammers, H. en C.Ch. Lammers-Koeleman, 'Bejaardencentrum "De Hoge Es" te Nijverdal', *Bouwkundig Weekblad* 83 (1965) No. 20, 372-374.

Leistra, G. and A. van Ulden, *Biografie van de bajes. De roerige geschiedenis van de Bijlmerbajes*, s.l. 2016.

Liefrinck, I., 'Binnenarchitekt en woninginrichting', *de 8 en Opbouw* 3 (1932) No. 22 (27 October), 220-222.

Linders, A., *'Frappez, frappez toujours!' N.C. Corry Tendeloo (1897–1956) en het feminisme in haar tijd*, Hilversum 2003.

Lobbezoo, N., *Als het tij verloopt verzet men de bakens, anderhalve eeuw Dammens 1850-2000*, Amsterdam 2000.
Loghem, J.B. van, 'Sch[oo]l van de Neutrale Montessorischool-Vereeniging voor Voorbereidend Lager Onderwijs te Schiebroek', *de 8 en Opbouw* 7 (1936) No. 6 (21 March), 66-69.
'Luxe-hut s.s. "Nieuw-Amsterdam"', *de 8 en Opbouw* 11 (1940) No. 13/14 (28 June), 132-133.

M
M. [Mieras], J.P., 'Landhuizen en villa-tjes', *Bouwkundig Weekblad* 45 (1924) No. 38 (20 September), 365.
Martin, B. and P. Sparke (ed.), *Women's places: architecture and design 1860–1960*, London/New York 2003.
'Mededeelingen der Betonvereeniging. Nieuwe Leden', *Beton* 3 (1935) No. 12 (6 December) (Bijlage van *De Ingenieur* 50 (1935) No. 49), 94.
Meer van Kuffeler, V.C. van der, 'De veranderde maatschappelijke en politieke verhouding van de Vrouw in Nederland', in: A. van Hogendorp et al., *Van Vrouwenleven 1813–1913. Ontwikkelingsgang van het leven en werken der vrouw in Nederland en de Koloniën*, Groningen 1913, 83.
Molema, J. and P. Bak, *Jan Gerko Wiebenga. Apostel van het Nieuwe Bouwen*, Rotterdam 1987.
Molema, J. and S. Leemans, *Moderniteit in een behoudende omgeving. Jan Albarda en De Groep van Delft*, Heijningen 2010.
Moorsel, L.H.M van, *Contact en controle. Over het vrouwbeeld van de stichting goed wonen*, Amsterdam 1992, academic dissertation.
Mulder, J.H., G. Bakker and C. van Heesch, *Het Amsterdamse Bos*, Amsterdam 1960.
Mulder, J.H., 'Schaalveranderingen en markante keerpunten in de Stedebouw in de afgelopen 40 jaar', *Stedebouw en Volkshuisvesting* 54 (1973) No. 3, 100.

N
Naamlijst voor de interlocale telefoondienst. Deel I, The Hague 1950.
'Naamlooze Vennootschap', *Nieuwsblad voor den boekhandel* 102 (1935) No. 97 (31 December), 949.
Nieuwpoort, M.-A.D. van, 'De architectuur van Gustav Cornelis Bremer', *Bulletin KNOB* 91 (1992) No. 5-6, 145-155.

O
'Officieele mededeelingen aan de vereenigingen no. 28 behorend bij', *Bouwkundig Weekblad Architectura* 52 (1931) No. 29 (18 July), unpaginated.
'Officieele mededeelingen aan de leden van de vereenigingen no. 7 behorend bij', *Bouwkundig Weekblad Architectura* 60 (1939) No. 9 (4 March), unpaginated.
Oosterhof, H. *'Want de grond behoort ons allen toe'. Leven en werk van stedenbouwkundig architecte Lotte Stam-Beese*, Nijmegen 2018.
Oven, R. van, 'Het Binnenhuis en Johanna van Regteren Altena', *Binnenhuis en Buitenwereld* 21 (1939) No. 2 (February), 11-14.

P
Peet, C. van der and G. Steenmeijer (ed.), *De Rijksbouwmeesters. Twee eeuwen architectuur van de Rijksgebouwendienst en zijn voorlopers*, Rotterdam 1995.
'Personalia', *De Ingenieur* 17 (1902) No. 50 (13 December), 890.
'Personalia', *De Ingenieur* 18 (1903) No. 49 (5 December), 854.
'Personalia' and 'Open betrekkingen', *De Ingenieur* 44 (1929) No. 27 (6 July), 277, 278.
Polak, A., *Leidraad voor Nederlandsche meisjes bij de keuze van een beroep*, The Hague 1928.
Pot, J.W.H.C., 'Gebouw voor alleenwonende werkende vrouwen te Amsterdam', *Bouwbedrijf en openbare werken* 20 (1943) No. 10 (7 May), 69-74.
Pot, J.W.H.C., and J.F. Pot-Keegstra, '20 Woningen te Zandvoort', *Bouwkundig Weekblad* 69 (1951) nrs. 41-42 (9-16 October), 361-365.
Pot-Keegstra, J.F., 'Marchse gedachten over vakantie', *Bouwkundig Weekblad* 77 (1959) No. 26 (27 June), 309-320.

R
'Rede uitgesproken door den Heer J. de Ranitz, President van den Senaat van het Delftsch Studenten Corps ter gelegenheid van den ontvangst van de deelnemers aan het Congres voor Nieuwe Architectuur', *De Spiegel. Officieel orgaan van het Delftsch Studentencorps en van de Centrale Commissie voor Studiebelangen* 7 (1930) No. 11 (5 December), 3.
Remus, A.M., *Ooltgensplaat zoals het was*, s.l. 1991.
Reus, A. de, 'Vrouwen in *Wendingen*' in: M. Groot et al. (ed.), *Design en gender. Van object tot representatie. Jaarboek voor Vrouwengeschiedenis*, Amsterdam 2011 (31), 123-142.
Ridder, K. de, 'Woongebouw voor alleenwonenden', *De Vrouw en haar Huis* 52 (1958) No. 6 (June), 252-255.
Roeters van Lennep, H., 'Het bestaansrecht van den tuinarchitect', *Bouwkundig Weekblad Architectura* 54 (1933) No. 3 (21 January), 17-18.
Rosse, I.Th. van, 'Woningcomplex "De Bergerhof" bij Alkmaar', *Bouwbedrijf en Openbare Werken* 21 (1944) No. 2 (28 January), 9-15.
Rosse, I.Th. van and H. Kammer, 'In memoriam Prof.Ir. R.L.A. Schoemaker', *Bouwbedrijf en Openbare Werken* 22 (1945) No. 1 (4 October), 2-5.

S
Saane, H. van, 'Gebouw voor alleenwonenden te Amsterdam', *Tijdschrift voor volkshuisvesting en Stedebouw* 24 (1943) No. 2 (February), 18-24.
Scheffer, H.J., *Portret van een fotograaf: Henri Berssenbrugge 1873–1959*, Leiden 1967.
Schilt, J., '1947-1957: tien jaar "Opbouw"' in: W. Beeren et al. (ed.), *Het Nieuwe Bouwen in Rotterdam 1920–1960*, published to accompany an exhibition in Rotterdam (Museum Boymans-van Beuningen) 1982, 139-157.
Schilt, J. and J. van der Werf, *Genootschap Architectura et Amicitia 1855–1990*, Rotterdam 1992.
Schiphorst, L., '"Klaarheid moet heersen". Architect Jos Ritzen, compagnon van Alphons Boosten 1920-1923', *Het Land van Herle* 56 (2006) No. 3, 79-91.
Schreuder-Gratama, A.E.F. et al., 'De huisvrouw spreekt zich uit. Enkele beschouwingen naar aanleiding van de enquête van de Nederlandse Vereniging van Huisvrouwen', *Bouw* 2 (1947) No. 49 (6 December), 403-406.
Schulte, A.G. et al. (ed.), *Jaarboek Monumentenzorg 1995. Monumenten en oorlogstijd*, Zwolle/Zeist 1995.
Schwitalla, U. (ed.), *Women in Architecture. Past, Present, and Future*, Berlin 2021.
Simpson, P.H., 'Book Review', *Woman's Art Journal* 11 (Autumn, 1990–Winter, 1991) 2, 44-48.
Singha, S. (ed.), *Women in Architecture: Critical Concepts in Architecture*, London/New York 2019.
Sloot, H. van der, *Herman Jansen, een bevlogen brander-distillateur 1859–1935*, s.l. [Schiedam] 2015 (Schiedamse Vertellingen, IV).
Smeets-Klokgieters, E., 'Vrouw in de bouw. De eerste vrouwelijke afgestudeerde architecten in Nederland', *Bulletin KNOB* 116 (2017) No. 1, 43-57.
Smeets-Klokgieters, E.M., 'Grada Wolffensperger, de eerste vrouwelijke bouwkundig ingenieur van Nederland', in: P. de Rooij et al. (ed.), *Jaarboek Haerlem 2018*, Haarlem 2019, 153-177.

Smeets-Klokgieters, E.M., 'Riné Boerée, betonspecialist bij de Genie', *Militaire Spectator* 188 (2019) No. 5 (May), 252-271.
Smeets[-Klokgieters], E.[M.], 'Wil Jansen, een ondernemende architecte. Eén van de eerste vrouwelijke bouwkundig ingenieurs in Nederland', *Scyedam* 46 (2020 a) No. 1 (March), 32-36.
Smeets[-Klokgieters], E.[M.], 'Wil Jansen, een ondernemende architecte. Volop aandacht voor stenen en stadsgroen', *Scyedam* 46 (2020 b) No. 2 (June), 62-67.
Smeets[-Klokgieters], E.[M.], 'Willy Jansen, een ondernemende architecte uit Schiedam', *Scyedam* 46 (2020 c) No. 3 (September), 84-89.
Snoodijk, D., 'Zalen vol vrouwen', *Tijdschrift van de Rijksdienst voor het Cultureel Erfgoed* 15 (2023) No. 1 (February), 28-30.
Staal-Kropholler, M., 'Onze woning enquête', *De Huisvrouw. Maandblad der Nederlandse Vereniging van Huisvrouwen* 31 (1947) No. 1 (April), 5.
[Staal-Kropholler, M.], 'De huisvrouw spreekt zich uit. Uitslag van een enquête van de Nederlandse Vereniging van Huisvrouwen', *Bouw* 2 (1947) No. 45 (8 November), 367-370.
Staatsalmanak voor het Koninkrijk der Nederlanden 1932, The Hague 1931.
Stenvert, R. et al., *Monumenten in Nederland. Noord-Holland*, Zwolle 2006, 313.
Strijland, A., *Vrouwelijke tuin- en landschapsarchitecten in Nederland 1898-1998: een geannoteerde bibliografie met inleidend essay over de positie van vrouwen in onderwijs en beroep*, Haarlem 1999.

T

T., v., 'De eerste vrouwelijke Bouwkundige', *De Amsterdammer, weekblad voor Nederland* 41 (1917) No. 2093 (4 August), 5.
Teijmant, I., 'Ko Mulder (1900-1988): stedenbouw op ooghoogte', *Amstelodamum* 100 (2013) No. 2 (April-June), 51-67.
Tijen, W. van, 'Hoogbouw - het verlossende woord?', *Bouwkundig Weekblad* 76 (1958) No. 43 (25 October), 497.
Tijen, W. van, 'Prof.ir. M.J. Granpré Molière', *Plan. Maandblad voor ontwerp en omgeving* 3 (1972) No. 6 (June), 21.
Torre, S., *Women in american architecture: a historic and contemporary perspective*, New York 1977.

U

'Uitslag der examens aan de Technische Hoogeschool', *De Ingenieur* 32 (1917) No. 27 (7 July), 522.
'Uitslag van de prijsvragen uitgeschreven door de Vereeniging tot Bevordering der Bouwkunst te Groningen, ter gelegenheid van haar 50-jarig jubileum in 1933', *Bouwkundig Weekblad Architectura* 55 (1934) No. 13 (31 March), 120-122.

V

'Vacantie- en weekendhuis te Oostvoorne', *Het Landhuis* 30 (1935) No. 19 (9 October), 649, 660-662.
Vereeniging van Delftsche Ingenieurs, *Alphabetische Naamlijst van Ingenieurs gediplomeerd aan de Delftsche Academie en van Ingenieurs en Technologen gediplomeerd aan de Polytechnische School 1846-1905*, The Hague 1905 (series up to and including 1921).
Vereeniging van Delftsche Ingenieurs, *Alphabetische Naamlijst van de Ingenieurs en Technologen gediplomeerd aan de Koninklijke Akademie 1846-1864 Polytechnische School 1865-1905 Technische Hoogeschool 1906-1917*, The Hague 1922 (series up to and including 1939).
Vereeniging van Delftsche Ingenieurs, *Adresboek 1940 van de Ingenieurs en Technologen gediplomeerd aan de Polytechnische School 1865-1905 en de Technische Hoogeschool 1906-1940*, The Hague 1940 (series up to and including 1942).
Vereeniging van Delftsche Ingenieurs, *Naamlijst 1946-1947 van de Ingenieurs en Technologen gediplomeerd aan de Polytechnische School 1865-1905 en de Technische Hoogeschool 1906-1947*, The Hague 1947.
Vermeulen, F.A.J., *Handboek tot de geschiedenis der Nederlandsche bouwkunst*, The Hague 1928-1941, 6 parts, part 3.
Vierde stamreeks Hermanus Johannes Jansen 1859-1935, s.l. [Schiedam] s.a. [ca. 2010], typescript.
Voorst Vader, P.J. van, 'Alphabetische naamlijst', *De Ingenieur* 34 (1919) nrs. 3, 4 and 5 (18 January, 25 January, 1 February), 1.
De Vrouw en haar huis 12 (1917) No. 5 (September), 1.

W

Weide, O.B. van der, 'De studie der vrouw aan de Technische Hoogeschool', in: C.M. Werker-Beaujon, C. Wichmann en W.H.M. Werker (ed.), *De Vrouw, de vrouwenbeweging en het vrouwenvraagstuk. Encyclopaedisch Handboek* (deel II), Amsterdam 1918, 3-13.
Weissman, A.W., *Geschiedenis der Nederlandsche bouwkunst; met 185 afbeeldingen naar schilderijen, teekeningen, prenten en fotografien* [sic], Amsterdam 1912.
Wendt, D., *Academie van Bouwkunst Amsterdam 1908-2008*, Rotterdam 2008.
Wijdeveld, H.Th., 'Het park Meerwijk te Bergen-Binnen', *Wendingen* 1 (1918) No. 8 (30 August), 2-20.
Wijdeveld, H.Th. and J. Boterenbrood, 'Mededeelingen van het Genootschap', *Architectura* 26 (1922) No. 38 (23 September), 1.
Wissing, W., 'In Memoriam dr.Ir. W. van Tijen', *Stedebouw en Volkshuisvesting* 55 (1974) No. 7/8 (July/August), 299-305.
De Woningcommissie, 'Huisvrouwen spreken haar oordeel uit. Over de standaard plattegronden van de Studiegroep Efficiënte Woningbouw', *Bouw* 8 (1953) No. 43 (24 October), 839, 844.
['Toelichting door de architecten'], 'Woongebouw voor alleenwonenden en onvolledige gezinnen te Rotterdam', *Bouwkundig Weekblad* 76 (1958) No. 43 (25 October), 498-502.
[toelichting door de architecten], 'Woongebouw voor alleenwonenden en onvolledige gezinnen te Rotterdam', *Bouw* 14 (1959) No. 45 (7 November), 1280-1283.
Wright, G., 'On the fringe of the profession: women in American architecture', in: S. Kostof (ed.), *The Architect: Chapters in the History of the Profession*, Berkeley and Los Angeles (California)/ London 1977, 280-308.

Z

Zeeman, B., 'De taak van de vrouw in de architectuur', *Bouwkundig Weekblad* 41 (1920a) No. 34 (August), 203-205.
Zeeman, B., 'Houten landhuisjes', *De vrouw en haar huis* 15 (1920b), No. 7 (November), 212-218.
Zietsma, J., 'Woningcomplex "De Bergerhof" te Alkmaar', *Bouwkundig Weekblad* 65 (1947) No. 31 (28 October), 245-249.
Zomeren, P.J. van, 'Mej.Ir. Ko Mulder. 2 March 1900, Breda. "Stedebouw was mijn houvast"', in: P.J. van Zomeren, *Een gegeven moment. Interviews met mensen van 1900*, Amsterdam 1984, 24-29.
Zwiers, H.T., 'Mededeelingen over prijsvragen, uit te schrijven door het Genootschap "Architectura et Amicitia"', *Bouwkundig Weekblad Architectura* 53 (1932) 12 (19 March), 99.
Zwiers, H.T., 'De techniek in het bouwvak' in: A.F. Kamp (ed.), *De Technische Hogeschool te Delft 1905-1955*, The Hague 1955, 213-227.

Newspapers

A

'Adres aan de Raad', *Nieuwe Schiedamsche Courant* 28 May 1949.

'Advertentiën', *Haagsche Courant* 1 December 1926.

'Een architecte aan het woord', *Het Parool. De Schiedammer* 14 November 1946.

'Architecten-echtpaar Pot-Keegstra: bijna 30 jaar samen bouwen', *Trouw* 13 November 1964.

B

B., G., 'De architecte J.F. Pot-Keegstra: Iedereen heeft recht op een goede woning', *Het Vrije Volk* 22 September 1956.

'Bejaardencentrum "De Hoge Es". Nijverdal krijgt een zeer modern bejaarden-tehuis', *Holtens Nieuwsblad* 7 September 1963.

'Binnenland', *Rotterdamsch Nieuwsblad* 21 June 1910.

'Binnenland', *Rotterdamsch Nieuwsblad* 2 July 1917.

'Burgemeester Peek slaat de eerste paal', *Rotterdamsch Parool/De Schiedammer* 12 July 1956.

C

'De Cartonnagefabriek verhuist', *Rotterdamsch Parool/De Schiedammer* 17 March 1956.

'Er komt geen Cultureel Centrum!', *Nieuwe Schiedamsche Courant* 29 October 1949.

D

'Demonteren bom Morssingel wordt gigantisch karwei. Omvangrijke voorbereidingen nodig', *Leidsch Dagblad* 8 December 1984.

'Driemaal gouden jubileum Van Wernink's Beton- en Aanneming-Mij. luisterrijk gevierd. Schenkingen aan personeel en wetenschappelijke fondsen', *De Leidse Courant* 17 August 1964.

E

Emeis jr., M.G., 'Joop en Koosje bouwden niet à la Hans en Grietje', *De Telegraaf* 19 February 1955.

'Examens Technische Hoogeschool', *Haagsche Courant* 5 July 1915.

F

'Familie-Advertentiën', *Nieuwe Rotterdamsche Courant* 17 February 1915.

'Fascistisch gevaar in de Burgerwacht. Een onderhoud met den commandant van de Amsterdamsche burgerwacht', *Algemeen Handelsblad* 25 November 1933.

'Fiasco in Haagse Gemeentebedrijf. Strop van 1 ¼ millioen. Slappe leiding, slecht beheer', *De Telegraaf* 7 January 1954.

'Het fiasco-Hawoma. Voormalige directeur geeft een geheel andere lezing', *Trouw* 11 January 1954.

'Fort "Prins Hendrik". Teruggevorderd van de Graal', *De Zuid-Willemsvaart* 8 January 1940.

G

'Het Graalfort te Ooltgensplaat', *De Tijd: godsdienstig-staatkundig dagblad* 25 December 1937.

H

Haagsche Courant [job ads] 13 October 1923, first page, 3; 17 November 1923, third page, 3; 11 November 1924, fourth page, 4.

'Hinderwet', *Nieuwe Schiedamsche Courant* 16 August 1923.

I

'Een interessante brandproef', *Leidsch Dagblad* 30 May 1942.

K

'Kampwerk Ver. voor Nationale Volks-opvoeding', *Algemeen Handelsblad* 9 February 1938.

Klerck, B. de, 'Speuren naar vergeten schilderessen. Stichting Advancing Women Artists restaureert in Florence kunstwerken van onbekende vrouwen, zoals Plautilla Nelli', *NRC Handelsblad* 5 February 2019.

'Kolonel Boerée overleden', *Algemeen Handelsblad* 10 January 1949.

L

'Laatste berichten', *Haagsche Courant* 13 August 1908.

M

'Mej. v.d. Broek d'Obrenan benoemd te Hilversum', *Haarlems Dagblad* 19 May 1956.

Metz, T., 'Charlotte Perriand geloofde in de kunst van het wonen', *NRC Handelsblad* 24 October 2019.

'Militaire aanbesteding', *De Leidse Courant* 19 November 1959.

'Aan modern en stijlvol pand wordt laatste hand gelegd. "Zwevend gebouw"', *Rotterdamsch Parool/De Schiedammer* 29 January 1958.

Moussault-Veegens, M., 'Plannen en idealen van mej. Keegstra, architecte. "Op de nieuwe zakelijkheid moet worden voortgegaan"', *De Telegraaf* 5 April 1936.

N

'Naam van Wernink 150 jaar verbonden aan bouwwereld', *De Leidse Courant* 14 August 1964.

'De nieuwe kazernes der cavalerie te 's-Gravenhage. Rondgang door het gebouwencomplex aan de Van Alkemadelaan. Licht, lucht, hygiëne', *Algemeen Handelsblad*, 17 August 1938.

Nieuwe Schiedamsche Courant [advertisements] 14 October 1920 and 9 March 1921.

'Nieuwe woningen in Arnhem-Zuid', *Arnhemsche Courant* 2 August 1951.

'Nieuws uit Stad en Omtrek. Natuur-bescherming', *Nieuwe Schiedamsche Courant* 10 April 1948.

'Nieuws uit Stad en Omtrek', *Nieuwe Schiedamsche Courant* 5 April 1956.

[death announcement], *NRC Handelsblad* 4 April 1975.

O

'Onderwijs', *Het Vaderland* 14 October 1924 and 19 February 1925.

'Ondeugdelijk materiaal voor hangar. Staalconstructie wordt nu in ons land aangekocht', *Algemeen Handelsblad* 9 January 1956.

'De Oranjebrug', *Schiedamsche Courant* 6 November 1935.

P

'Passagiers', *Algemeen Handelsblad* 25 September 1910.

'Plaatselijk nieuws', *Maas- en Scheldebode* 15 May 1929.

R

R-F, E., 'In gesprek met: Mejuffrouw Ir. C. Strumphler', *NRC Handelsblad* 4 June 1955.

'Rond de Oranjebrug', *Nieuwe Schiedamsche Courant* 7 March 1936.

Roos, J., 'Praten met Koos Pot-Keegstra', *Het Parool* 9 March 1978.

S

'De Schiedamsche Cartonnagefabriek bouwt ... en hoe?', *Het Nieuwe Stadsblad* 18 July 1956.

'School en Opvoeding. Academische Examens', *Algemeen Handelsblad* 29 June 1923.

'R.k. Staatspartij. Candidaatstelling voor den gemeenteraad', *Nieuwe Schiedamsche Courant* 6 February 1939.

T

T., v., 'De eerste vrouwelijke Bouwkundige', *Bataviaasch Nieuwsblad* 32 (1917) No. 509 (24 November).

V

Het Vaderland: staat- en letterkundig nieuwsblad [death announcement], 15 January 1921, 4.

'Vrouw nog uitzondering in wereld van architectuur. Expositie "Van Boschplan tot Bijlmerbajes" om toegankelijkheid te vergroten', *De Telegraaf* 25 April 1983.

'Vrouwelijk vrijwilligerskorps te 's-Hertogenbosch', *Het Vaderland: staat- en letterkundig nieuwsblad* 26 October 1938.

W

'De werkkampen in forten. Een uiteenzetting maar geen bevrediging', *De Tribune. Dagblad voor de arbeiders* 22 December 1936.

'Werkkampen bij Willemstad. Bisschoppelijke instemming', *De Tijd: godsdienstig-staatkundig dagblad* 18 March 1937.

Other sources

Interviews

– Ms K.J. van Manen-Kammer, 27 February 2020 (telephone).
– Ms Y. Houtsmuller-Noë, 28 July 2017 (telephone).
– H.Th.F. Jansen, Schiedam, 4 March 2019 and 5 August 2020.

Websites

A

– *Adresboek van Haarlem*, Haarlem 1921, 11
<http://nha.courant.nu/issue/ABH/1921-01-01/edition/null/page/17?query=adres-boek%20haarlem%201921&sort=relevance>
(consulted 27 November 2017).
– *Andere Tijden*
<https://anderetijden.nl/aflevering/87/Bajes-zonder-tralies>
(retrieved 24 September 2020).
– *Architectenregister – Jaarverslag 2021*
<https://www.architectenregister.nl/media/1176/jaarverslag-architecten-register-2021-definitief.pdf>
(retrieved 7 February 2023).
– *Archiwijzer Stichting Bonas*
<https://www.bonas.nl/archiwijzer/architecten.php>
(retrieved 5 October 2020).
– *Artefacts. Southern African Built Environment*
<http://www.artefacts.co.za/main/Buildings/archframes.php?archid=496&countadd=1>
(retrieved 6 May 2020).
– *Atria – Archief Nationale Tentoonstelling van Vrouwenarbeid 1898*
<https://atria.nl/bibliotheek-archief/collectie/archief/IIAV00000110/>
(retrieved 1 February 2021).
– *Atria – Archief VVAO Vereniging van vrouwen met hogere opleiding*
<https://atria.nl/bibliotheek-archief/collectie/archief/IIAV00000539/>
(retrieved 5 January 2021).
– *A.Zine*
<https://a-zine.nl/2021/01/19/26-January-lancering-mevr-de-architect/>
(retrieved 26 January 2021).

B

– *Beeldbank Gemeentearchief Schiedam – Pieter Sanders*
<https://beeldbank.schiedam.nl/beeld/?mode=gallery&view=horizontal&q=fabristraat%20sanders&rows=1&page=1>
(retrieved 5 June 2019).
– *Beeldbank Gemeentearchief Schiedam – Volksbadhuis*
<https://beeldbank.schiedam.nl/beeld/detail/38f749f8-f6de-2c4e-bd74-3abb7de0fc8d/media/0ee8e98d-d0a0-3e7c-2659-d5fd5a4f7e0c?mode=detail&view=horizontal&q=volksbadhuis&rows=1&page=21>
(retrieved 16 April 2020).
– *Beeldbank Gemeentearchief Schiedam – Oranjestraat*
<https://beeldbank.schiedam.nl/beeld/?mode=gallery&view=horizontal&q=oranjestraat&rows=25&page=9>
(retrieved 14 May 2019).
– *Beeldbank Gemeentearchief Schiedam – Noordvestsingel*
<https://beeldbank.schiedam.nl/beeld/detail/8690e7a9-f6ae-2d46-2503-e35c941723e2/media/42278c1c-3a47-a817-15aa-b3e4970d7546?mode=detail&view=horizontal&q=noordvestsingel&rows=1&page=71&fq%5B%5D=search_i_period:%5B18800000%20TO%2019530000%5D>
(retrieved 18 May 2020).
– *Beeldbank Groningen*
<https://www.beeldbankgroningen.nl/beelden/detail/b33aa16f-503a-38b5-69a2-ab0517830479/media/40f1ef35-7326-038c-3c93-36ff0f9bcc81?mode=detail&view=horizontal&q=george%20ros&rows=1&page=1>
(retrieved 23 September 2019).
– *Biografisch Woordenboek van Nederland*
<http://resources.huygens.knaw.nl/bwn/BWN/lemmata/bwn1/buijs>
(retrieved 12 November 2017).
– *Bouwdossiers online* a
<http://mijnadrespubliek.hosting.deventit.net/detail.php?nav_id=4-1&id=20618769&index=2&volgnummer=8>
(retrieved 6 June 2019).
– *Bouwdossiers online* b
<://mijnadrespubliek.hosting.deventit.net/detail.php?nav_id=0-1&index=2&id=20617546>
(retrieved 2 September 2019).
– *Bouwdossiers online – Westvest 38-40*
<https://mijnadrespubliek.hosting.deventit.net/detail.php?nav_id=0-1&id=22512729&index=0&volgnummer=11>
(retrieved 3 September 2019).
– *Bouwdossiers online – bottelarij Van Rood-van Rijswijk*
<https://mijnadrespubliek.hosting.deventit.net/detail.php?nav_id=8-1&id=19559723&index=0&volgnummer=0>
(retrieved 22 September 2020).

C

– *Cement*
<https://www.cementonline.nl/artikel/in-memoriam-ir-nj-rengers> en <https://www.cementonline.nl/artikel/ir-nj-rengers>
(retrieved 1 August 2018).
– *Centrum voor regionale geschiedenis Rijckheyt*
<http://www.rijckheyt.nl/sites/rijckheyt/files/pdf/persoonsdocumentatie/Edixhoven,G.H.ir.pdf>
(retrieved 18 June 2019).
– *Comité Herdenken en Vieren Oegstgeest*
<https://www.oorlogsgravenoegstgeest.nl/nl/verzetstrijders/einthoven>
(retrieved 10 November 2020).

D

– *Digitaal Vrouwenlexicon van Nederland – Ko Mulder*
<http://resources.huygens.knaw.nl/vrouwenlexicon/lemmata/data/MulderKo>
(retrieved 14 January 2021).
– *Digitaal Vrouwenlexicon van Nederland – Catharina van Tussenbroek*
<http://resources.huygens.knaw.nl/vrouwenlexicon/lemmata/data/Tussenbroek>
(retrieved 13 February 2018).

E

– *Erfgoed Leiden en omstreken* a
<https://www.erfgoedleiden.nl/collecties/beeldmateriaal/zoeken-in-beeldmateriaal/detail/3d90fc81-3dd3-7c02-1c8b-b86e767e2947/media/331e419d-b539-0ebd-80a7-576ace93f7f1?mode=detail&view=horizontal&q=Wernink&rows=1&page=29>
(retrieved 19 June 2018).
– *Erfgoed Leiden en omstreken* b
<https://www.erfgoedleiden.nl/collecties/beeldmateriaal/zoeken-in-beeldmateriaal/detail/195b30e0-4af7-bc41-ae7c-62140e9506ff/media/3bc252f4-b6c6-e739-dec4-bf5aa28a67ef?mode=detail&view=horizontal&q=genie&rows=1&page=2>
(retrieved 20 June 2018).
– *Erfgoed Leiden en omstreken* c
<https://www.erfgoedleiden.nl/collecties/uw-verhalen/uw-verhalen?search=Wernink>
(retrieved 19 June 2018).
– *Experts of Syracuse University*
<https://experts.syr.edu/en/publications/the-bloomsbury-global-encyclopedia-of-women-in-architecture>
(retrieved 20 April 2023).

G

– *Geheugen van Nederland*
<http://www.geheugenvannederland.nl/nl/geheugen/view?coll=ngvn&identifier=CBG01%3A24397>
(retrieved 27 February 2018).
– *Gemeente Schiedam – Pieter Sanders*
<https://archief.schiedam.nl/nieuws/architect-sanders-zettte-stempel-op-schiedam>
(retrieved 5 June 2019).
– *Genealogie Pareau & Dumont*
<http://pareau.nl/dumonts/dumonts-1850-1900/lc-dumont-1865/lc-dumont-im/>,
(retrieved 7 March 2018).

H

– *Haags Gemeentearchief*
<https://haagsgemeentearchief.nl/archieven-mais/overzicht?mivast=59&mizig=210&miadt=59&micode=0058-01&milang=nl&mizk_alle=m.f.h.%20snethlage&miview=inv2>
(retrieved 10 november 2020).

– *Heerlen Vertelt*
<http://www.heerlenvertelt.nl/2016/12/acht-keer-over-het-spoor-deel-38/>
(retrieved 8 augustus 2020).

– *Het Nieuwe Instituut – Ban, E.F. van den*
<https://zoeken.hetnieuweinstituut.nl/nl/personen/detail/?q=e.f.%20van%20den%20ban&page=1>
(retrieved 29 October 2020).

– *Het Nieuwe Instituut – Boerée, C.H.M.*
<https://zoeken.hetnieuweinstituut.nl/nl/archieven/scans/BOER/4/start/0/limit/25>
(retrieved 11 June 2018).

– *Het Nieuwe Instituut – Bond van Nederlandse Architecten*
<http://zoeken.hetnieuweinstituut.nl/nl/archieven/details/BNAR/keywords/>
(retrieved 29 December 2020).

– *Het Nieuwe Insituut – Bremer, G.C.*
<https://zoeken.hetnieuweinstituut.nl/nl/archieven/details/BREX/keywords/bremer> BREXpf1
(retrieved 27 September 2018).

– *Het Nieuwe Instituut – Bremer, G.C.,* BREXpf1
<https://zoeken.hetnieuweinstituut.nl/nl/archieven/details/BREX/keywords/bremer>
(retrieved 24 October 2018).

– *Het Nieuwe Instituut – Buijs, J.W.E.*
<https://zoeken.hetnieuweinstituut.nl/nl/personen/detail/712c3b41-f3fa-5374-a644-ce6e9ed17144>
(retrieved 6 March 2018).

– *Het Nieuwe Instituut – Collecting Otherwise*
< https://nieuweinstituut.nl/projects/collecting-otherwise/seenunseen>
(retrieved 2 May 2023).

– *Het Nieuwe Instituut – Kammer, H.* KAMM 110512230
<https://zoeken.hetnieuweinstituut.nl/nl/archieven/details/KAMM/keywords/kammer>
(retrieved 18 February 2020).

– *Het Nieuwe Instituut – Keegstra, J.F.*
<http://zoeken.hetnieuweinstituut.nl/nl/personen/detail/3d6fa8d8-00e6-57e0-8754-97cb71c01d21>
(retrieved 13 January 2021).

– *Het Nieuwe Instituut – Keegstra, J.F., publicaties*
<https://zoeken.hetnieuweinstituut.nl/nl/publicaties/?q=pot-keegstra>
(retrieved 12 March 2020).

– *Het Nieuwe Instituut – Kok, A.A. en Kok, Y.*
<https://zoeken.hetnieuweinstituut.nl/nl/archieven/details/KOKA/keywords/a.a.+kok>
(retrieved 9 november 2020).

– *Het Nieuwe Instituut – Nicolaï-Chaillet, C.*
<https://zoeken.hetnieuweinstituut.nl/nl/personen/detail/a59c720e-7193-55f0-a5e0-c46e1026fd2c>
(retrieved 10 July 2019).

– *Het Nieuwe Instituut – de 8 en Opbouw*
<https://zoeken.hetnieuweinstituut.nl/nl/archieven/details/ACOP/keywords/8+en+opbouw>
(retrieved 9 June 2020).

– *Het Nieuwe Instituut – Pot J.W.H.C. en Pot-Keegstra, J.F.*
<https://zoeken.hetnieuweinstituut.nl/nl/archieven/details/POTK/keywords/pot-keegstra>
(retrieved 21 July 2020).

– *Het Nieuwe Instituut – Rood, A.H. van*
<https://zoeken.hetnieuweinstituut.nl/nl/personen/detail/20602a4a-f398-5273-a2d6-65721d06ea90>
(retrieved 28 May 2020).

– *Het Nieuwe Instituut – Staal-Kropholler, M.*
<https://zoeken.hetnieuweinstituut.nl/nl/personen/detail/?q=m.%20staal-kropholler&page=1>
(retrieved 26 April 2021).

– *Het Nieuwe Instituut – Stadsplan Arnhem*
<https://zoeken.hetnieuweinstituut.nl/nl/projecten/detail/?q=bureau%20stadsplan%20arnhem&page=2>
(retrieved 11 June 2020).

– *Het Nieuwe Instituut – Tijen, W. van*
<https://zoeken.hetnieuweinstituut.nl/nl/archieven/details/TIJX/keywords/w.+van+tijen>
(retrieved 9 June 2020).

– *Huygens Instituut voor Nederlandse Geschiedenis – Koninklijke Nederlandse Akademie van Wetenschappen – Boeree, Theodoor Alexander*
<http://resources.huygens.knaw.nl/bwn1880-2000/lemmata/bwn3/boeree>
(retrieved 25 April 2018).

– *Huygens Instituut voor Nederlandse Geschiedenis – Koninklijke Nederlandse Akademie van Wetenschappen – Kropholler, Margaret*
<http://resources.huygens.knaw.nl/vrouwenlexicon/lemmata/data/Kropholler>
(retrieved 26 April 2021).

K

– *Kenniscentrum voor de Nederlandse Architecten Praktijk*
<https://www.architectenwerk.nl/architectenpraktijk02/Architectentitel#:~:text=De%20op%201%20October%201988,tuin%2D%20en%20landschapsarchitect%20en%20interieurarchitect>
(retrieved 10 May 2021).

– *Koninklijke Bibliotheek – Bijzondere vrouwen, bijzondere boeken*
<https://www.kb.nl/nieuws/2019/bijzondere-vrouwen-bijzondere-boeken>
(retrieved 1 February 2021).

– *Koninklijke Bibliotheek – Wereldoorlog 1 – Vrouwen aan het werk*
<https://www.kb.nl/themas/geschiedenis-en-cultuur/nederland-tijdens-de-eerste-wereldoorlog/wo-i-vrouwen-aan-het-werk>
(retrieved 1 March 2018).

– *Koninklijke Maatschappij tot Bevordering der Bouwkunst Bond van Nederlandse Architecten BNA*
<http://bna.instantmagazine.com/online-publicaties/175-jaar-bna#!/in-7-tijdvakken>
(retrieved 29 December 2020).

– *Krantenviewer Noord-Hollands Archief*
<https://nha.courant.nu/issue/JJVH/1935-01-01/edition/null/page/11?query=>
(retrieved 3 December 2018).

– *Kunstbus*
<http://www.kunstbus.nl/design/koen+limperg.html>
(retrieved 1 augustus 2018).

– *Kunsthal Rotterdam*
<https://www.kunsthal.nl/nl/plan-je-bezoek/tentoonstellingen/hereweare/>
(retrieved 27 April 2023).

L

– *Louis Kalff Instituut*
<https://www.louiskalffinstituut.nl/nl/louis-kalff/>
(retrieved 11 February 2021).

M

– *Musée d'Orsay*
<https://www.musee-orsay.fr/en/collections/women-art-and-power.html?cHash=1030a57d48>
(retrieved 2 February 2021).

N

– *Nationaal Archief, Archief Defensie/Dienst Gebouwen, Werken en Terreinen*
<http://www.gahetna.nl/collectie/archief/ead/index/eadid/2.13.96/anchor/descgrp-context-bioghist/open/c01%3A3.#c01:4.>
(retrieved 6 augustus 2018).

– *National Gallery*
<https://www.nationalgallery.org.uk/exhibitions/artemisia>
(retrieved 2 February 2021).

– *Nederland's Patriciaat*
<https://www.marres.nl/afb/Vollgraff_NP_36_1950.pdf>
(retrieved 30 March 2021).

– *De Nederlandse mijnstreek in het heden*
<https://www.demijnen.nl/actueel/artikel/hopel-een-mijnwerkerskolonie >
(retrieved 23 September 2019).

– *Nederlandse VrouwenRaad*
<http://www.nederlandsevrouwenraad.nl/html/index.php?paginalD=2224>
(retrieved 5 January 2021).

– *Noord-Hollandsarchief*
<https://noord-hollandsarchief.nl/bronnen/archieven/?mivast=236&mizig=210&miadt=236&miaet=1&micode=1314&minr=1024352&miview=inv2&milang=nl>
(retrieved 29 October 2020).

O

– *Overheid* a
<https://repository.overheid.nl/frbr/sgd/19601961/0000263683/1/pdf/SGD_19601961_0001912.pdf>
(retrieved 17 March 2020).

– *Overheid* b.
<https://repository.overheid.nl/frbr/sgd/19601961/0000262738/1/pdf/SGD_19601961_0001075.pdf>
(retrieved 17 March 2020).

P

– *Parlement – Ada Kuiper-Struyk*
<https://www.parlement.com/id/vg09ll2kc8zs/a_ada_kuiper_struyk>
(retrieved 15 February 2020).

– *Paul Mellon Centre*
<https://www.paul-mellon-centre.ac.uk/whats-on/aa-xx>
(retrieved 2 February 2021).

R

– *Reliwiki*
<https://reliwiki.nl/index.php/Hoogeveen,_Middenweg_14_-_Goede_Herderkerk>
(retrieved 4 November 2020).

– *Rijckheyt Centrum voor regionale geschiedenis*
<https://www.rijckheyt.nl/cultureel-erfgoed/boosten-alphons-architect>
(retrieved 26 June 2019).

– *Rijksmonumentenregister – 513736*
<https://monumentenregister.cultureelerfgoed.nl/monumenten/513736 >
(retrieved 26 June 2019).

– *Rijksmonumentenregister – 513743*
<https://monumentenregister.cultureelerfgoed.nl/monumenten/513743>
(retrieved 26 June 2019).

– *Rijksmonumentenregister – 513744*
<https://monumentenregister.cultureelerfgoed.nl/monumenten/513744>
(retrieved 26 June 2019).

– *Rijksmonumentenregister – 525416*
<https://monumentenregister.cultureelerfgoed.nl/monumenten/525416>
(retrieved 25 november 2019).

– *Rijksmonumentenregister – 528815*
<https://monumentenregister.cultureelerfgoed.nl/monumenten/528815>
(retrieved 25 November 2019).

– *Rijksmuseum*
<https://www.rijksmuseum.nl/nl/onderzoek/ons-onderzoek/overkoepelend/vrouwen>
(retrieved 27 April 2023).

– *Rijksmuseum Twenthe* a
<https://collectie.rijksmuseumtwenthe.nl/themas/detail/73a0dbb0-af73-4539-8e25-3a894d4f0d3e>
(retrieved 27 April 2023).

– *Rijksmuseum Twenthe* b
<https://www.rijksmuseumtwenthe.nl/content/3287/nl/nu-te-zien-sofonisba-anguissola>
(retrieved 27 April 2023).

– *Rijwielindustrie*
<http://www.rijwiel.net/vouwfietsen_n.htm>
(retrieved 9 November 2020).

– *RKD*
<https://rkd.nl/nl/over-het-rkd/actueel/nieuws/1099-vrouwen-in-de-nederlandse-kunstwereld-1780-1980>
(retrieved 27 April 2023).

S

– *See All This*
<https://seeallthis.com/post-magazine/no-10-zomer-2018/>
(retrieved 2 February 2021).

– *Staat in Groningen. Architectuur in stad – De Faun*
<http://www.staatingroningen.nl/116/de-faun>
(retrieved 26 September 2019).

– *Staat in Groningen. Architectuur in stad – Ter Schouw-Van Sanen-Stichting*
<http://www.staatingroningen.nl/1552/ter-schouw-van-sanenstichting>
(retrieved 23 September 2019).

– *Stedenbouw*
<https://www.stedenbouw.nl/artikel/arnhem-gelderse-rooslaan/>
(retrieved 11 June 2020).

– *Stichting "Eygelshoven door de eeuwen heen"*
<https://stichting-eygelshovendoordeeeuwenheen.nl/de-stichting/monumenten/het-oude-kerkje/>
(retrieved 19 September 2019).

– *Stylos*
<https://www.stylos.nl/nl/vereniging/geschiedenis>
(retrieved 28 February 2018).

U

– *Universiteit Utrecht*
<https://www.uu.nl/organisatie/alumni/anna-maria-van-schurman>
(retrieved 1 February 2021).

– *Het Utrechts Archief – Personen*
<https://www.archieven.nl/nl/zoeken?mivast=0&mizig=100&miadt=39&milang=nl&mizk_alle=barbera%20johanna%20wolffensperger&miview=tbl>
(retrieved 3 December 2018).

V

– *VACpunt Wonen*
<https://www.vacpuntwonen.nl/over-ons.html>
(retrieved 4 July 2019).

– *Vereniging Oud Oegstgeest, Voorstel tot aanwijzing van waardevolle gebouwen c.a.*, Oegstgeest 1987
<https://historischeverenigingoegstgeest.nl/1987/03/01/paarse-nota/>
(retrieved 6 April 2023).

– *Vereniging van vrouwen met hogere opleiding*
<https://www.vvao.nl/>
(retrieved 5 January 2021).

W

– *Wageningen University en Research Centrum (Wageningen UR)*
<http://www.wageningenur.nl/nl/Over-Wageningen-UR/Historie-van-Wageningen-UR.htm>
(retrieved 19 May 2016).

– *Wageningen University & Research – E. Blok, Jongere Tuinkunst 1900–1940*
<https://edepot.wur.nl/119354>
(retrieved 15 May 2021).

– *Wederopbouw Amsterdam*
<https://020apps.nl/kaart/wederopbouw/Haringvlietstraat/12-14>
(retrieved 27 July 2020).

– *Wikidata*
<https://es.wikipedia.org/wiki/Wikiproyecto:Mujeres/Art%C3%ADculos_faltantes/Editoras>
(retrieved 9 November 2020).

– Wikipedia – Aletta Jacobs
<https://nl.wikipedia.org/wiki/Aletta_Jacobs>
(retrieved 1 February 2021).

– *Wikipedia – Urbain Cassan*
<https://fr.wikipedia.org/wiki/Urbain_Cassan>
(retrieved 19 December 2019).

– *Wikipedia – Louis Plousey*
<https://fr.wikipedia.org/wiki/Louis_Plousey>
(retrieved 19 December 2019).

– *Wikipedia – Nieuw Amsterdam*
<https://nl.wikipedia.org/wiki/Kunstenaars_die_bijdroegen_aan_de_inrichting_van_de_Nieuw_Amsterdam>
(retrieved 9 June 2020).

Index

Illustrations

1 Introduction

1 Telegram offering congratulations from 'Grootje and Aunt Juul' to Wil Jansen, 17 December 1931, the date of her graduation. Source: archive owned by H.Th.F. Jansen.

2 The rise of women in furniture design, interior design and garden architecture

1 Interior (ca. 1939) based on design by Jo van Regteren Altena. Photo: *Binnenhuis en buitenwereld* 21 (1939) Nr. 2 (February), 13.

2 Design (1938) by Ida Falkenberg-Liefrinck of a sitting room / bedroom for a working woman, as published in *de 8 en Opbouw*. Source: *de 8 en Opbouw* 9 (1938) Nr. 3 (12 February), 26.

3 Teacher at the Huis te Lande Horticultural School for Girls in Rijswijk, 1930. Photo: City Archive of Delft, Image and Sound collection.

4 Pupils from the Huis te Lande Horticultural School for Girls in Rijswijk, 1928. Photo: Photo: City Archive of Delft, Image and Sound collection.

3 The pioneering women architects

1 a Drawing was considered of the utmost importance. J. Kret, *Grafostatica no. 3*, Delft 1928. Source: Het Nieuwe Instituut, Rotterdam.

1 b J. Kret, *Maassluis Waterboard Headquarters*, surveyed with fellow student Wil Jansen, second academic year at Delft, 1925–1926. Source: KAMM archive, Het Nieuwe Instituut, Rotterdam.

2 a W.C.M. Jansen, model of a design for a museum, undated. Photo: archive owned by H.Th.F. Jansen.

2 b W.C.M. Jansen, model of a design for a town hall, undated. Photo: archive owned by H.Th.F. Jansen.

3 a 'Girls in drafting studio', Oude Delft department of architecture, 1909. Photo: M.A. van Damme-van Weele and J.H.M. Ressing-Wolfert, *Vrouwen in techniek. 90 Jaar Delftse Vrouwelijke Ingenieurs*, Delft 1995, 32.

3 b Student of architecture, Delft, year and name unknown. Photo: F.L. Kristinsson-Reitsema (ed.), *Delfts Studenten Corps, 1904–1994. Ter gelegenheid van het 90-jarig jubileum van de Delftsche Vrouwelijke Studenten Vereniging*, s.l. undated. [1994], 2.

4 For the final examination, students had to design small public buildings. C.H.M. Boerée, *Hotel Café Restaurant*, elevation and floor plan, Delft 1924. Source: Het Nieuwe Instituut, Rotterdam.

5 Design for a public building, graduation project by J. Kret, *Bank building*, Delft 1930–1931. Source: Het Nieuwe Instituut, Rotterdam.

6 Roster for utility building exam, 1931. Photo: author. Source: archive owned by H.Th.F. Jansen.

7 a Title page of the programme by the architecture department for an excursion to France, 1929. Photo: author. Source: archive owned by H.Th.F. Jansen.

7 b Programme component, with notes by Wil Jansen. Photo: author. Source: archive owned by H.Th.F. Jansen.

7 c An excursion to Middelburg, 1927. Photo: KAMM archive, Het Nieuwe Instituut, Rotterdam.

8 Jan Kret, third from right in front, with four fellow women students in the fifth class of the Higher Civic School (HBS), 1923. Photo: Het Nieuwe Instituut, Rotterdam.

9 Drawing studio, first academic year at Delft, 1915–1916. Photo: Delft City Archives.

10 Front cover of list of members of the Delftsche Vrouwelijke Studenten Vereeniging, 1919. Source: *Almanak der D.V.S.V. 1919*, Delft 1918, 77.

11 a Beb Zeeman as president of the board of the Delftsche Vrouwelijke Studenten Vereeniging, 1917–1918. Photo: *Almanak der D.V.S.V. 1919*, Delft 1918, 25.

11 b Ko Mulder (centre) and Paula Rooseboom (second from left) as chair and first secretary of the board of the Delftsche Vrouwelijke Studenten Vereeniging, 1924–1925. Photo: *Almanak der D.V.S.V. 1926*, Delft 1925, 40.

11 c Wil van den Broek d'Obrenan (far right) as board member of the Delftsche Vrouwelijke Studenten Vereeniging, 1925–1926. Photo: *Almanak der D.V.S.V. 1927*, Delft 1926, 20.

11 d Chairwoman Toki Koeleman (centre) and Greet van der Poest Clement (left) on the board of the Delftsche Vrouwelijke Studenten Vereeniging, 1936–1937. Photo: Kristinsson-Reitsema undated. [1994], 62.

11 e To Strumphler (left) as board member of the Delftsche Vrouwelijke Studenten Vereeniging, 1934–1935. Photo: Kristinsson-Reitsema undated. [1994], 57.

12 Koos Keegstra as the first women to receive her diploma for Secondary and Higher Architecture Training (VHBO) in 1936. Source: Het Nieuwe Instituut, Rotterdam.

13 Koos Keegstra during her graduation assignment, *Residence for an Art Collector*, Amsterdam 1935. Photo: D. Wendt, *Academy of Architecture Amsterdam 1908–2008*, Rotterdam 2008, 85.

4 The professional practice of the first women architects in the Netherlands

1 Pot-Keegstra on a building site, undated. Photo: Het Nieuwe Instituut, Rotterdam.

2 Ko Mulder at the drawing board, undated. Photo: E. van Kessel and F. Palstra, *Ir Jakoba Mulder (1900–1988) urban designer and landscape architect*, Amsterdam 1994, 4.

3 Pot-Keegstra at work, undated. Photo: Het Nieuwe Instituut, Rotterdam.

4 Wil Jansen did not reveal she was a woman in a competition organized by the Architectura et Amicitia society, 1932. Tube containing competition material. Photo: author. Source: Schiedam Municipal Archives.

5 Grada Wolffensperger, the first women architectural engineer in the Netherlands

1 Shortly after successfully completing her final examination on 2 July 1915, Grada Wolffensperger made this drawing of a bell tower in Edam. Source: Noord-Hollands Archive, Haarlem, Provinciale Atlas collection.

2 L1917 membership list of the Delftsche Vrouwelijke Studenten Vereeniging, of which Grada Wolffensperger was a member throughout her time as a student. Source: *Almanak der D.V.S.V. 1917*, Delft 1916, 127.

3 After graduating in 1917, Grada Wolffensperger had her portrait taken by Henri Berssenbrugge. Photo: *De Kroniek, geïllustreerd maandblad voor Nederland en België* 4 (1918) Nr. 3 (March), 68.

4 The graduate Grada Wolffensperger in her living room in 1917, photographed for *De Vrouw en haar Huis*. Photo: *De vrouw en haar huis* 12 (1917) Nr. 5 (September), 1.

5 Grada's remuneration as deputy architect for Public Works was fully in line with salaries for civil servants. Source: Noord-Hollands Archive, Haarlem.

6 Grada's colleagues in permanent employment at the Public Works department in 1921. Source: *Adresboek van Haarlem*, Haarlem 1921, 11.
7 Grada Wolffensperger as the only woman among her colleagues at the Public Works department in Haarlem, 1921. Photo: Noord-Hollands Archive, Haarlem, Kennemerland collection.
8 The 'Dice' at the Grote Houtbrug bridge, 1909. Photo: Noord-Hollands Archive, Haarlem, Kennemerland collection.
9 The Stedelijk Gymnasium school on Prinsenhof for which Jan Buijs designed a new wing. Photo: Noord-Hollands Archive, Haarlem, Kennemerland collection.
10 Register of all Dutch Architects etc. 1934, which lists Grada Wolffensperger. Source: J. Diecke, *Register of all Dutch Architects, State & Municipal Architects, Directors of Municipal Works, Directors of Inspectorates of Housing and Building Control Department, all Architectural Engineers, the Construction Engineers or Carpenters in small towns, who sometimes act as Architects, the Board Members of the State & Provincial Water Management Departments, of the leading Firms in Reinforced Concrete, etc., all with many notes, as well as the Professors and Teachers in Technical Education, together with the Interior Architects and many Hydraulic Engineers*, The Hague 1934, unpaginated.

6 Riné Boerée, concrete specialist with the Army Corps of Engineers (Genie)

1 Henri Rijnier Boerée. Photo: Source: KB|National Library NL21E, H.P. van den Aardweg (ed.), *Persoonlijkheden in het Koninkrijk der Nederlanden in woord en beeld: Nederlanders en hun werk*, Amsterdam 1938, 174.
2 Riné Boerée in her final year of study, 1928. Photo: National Archives, The Hague.
3 C.H.M. Boerée, entrance, 1921. Source: archive owned by Ms J.C. Boerée.
4 C.H.M. Boerée, ornament, 1921. Source: Het Nieuwe Instituut, Rotterdam.
5 'RB', *Drommedaris gateway in Enkhuizen*, undated. Source: archive owned by Ms J.C. Boerée.
6 'RB', *Bell tower in Edam*, undated. Source: archive owned by Ms J.C. Boerée.
7 Unsigned, *St. Mary's Church Choir* (location not legible), undated. Source: archive owned by Ms J.C. Boerée.
8 Professor J.A.G. van der Steur as Rector Magnficus of the Technical College Delft, 1922. Photo: *Delftsche Studentenalmanak 1922*, Delft 1921, 10.
9 C.H.M. Boerée, *Detail of sliding window*, 1918. Source: Het Nieuwe Instituut, Rotterdam.
10 C.H.M. Boerée, *Interior door exterior door*, 1919. Source: Het Nieuwe Instituut, Rotterdam.
11 C.H.M. Boerée, *Seaside villa*, facade and floor plan, 1923–1924. Source: archive owned by Ms J.C. Boerée.
12 C.H.M. Boerée, *Seaside villa*, longitudinal and cross-section, 1923–1924. Source: archive owned by Ms J.C. Boerée.
13 C.H.M. Boerée, *Courthouse*, front and rear facades, undated. Source: Het Nieuwe Instituut, Rotterdam.
14 C.H.M. Boerée, *Courthouse*, cross-section and longitudinal section, undated. Source: Het Nieuwe Instituut, Rotterdam.
15 Riné Boerée (extreme left), second secretary of the board of the Delftsche Vrouwelijke Studenten Vereeniging, 1918–1919. Photo: *Almanak der D.V.S.V. 1920*, Delft undated. [1919], 18.
16 Unsigned, *Fort Prins Frederik*, Ooltgensplaat, floor plan, undated. Source: Het Nieuwe Instituut, Rotterdam.
17 Fort Prins Frederik, Ooltgensplaat, 1920–1930. Source: Netherlands Institute for Military History, The Hague.
18 C.H.M. Boerée, *Facade detail of Maarssen petrol station*, 1929. Source: Het Nieuwe Instituut, Rotterdam.
19 The Bammens complex in Maarssen, 1952. Photo: Koninklijke Bammens bv, Maarssen.
20 The Nirwana block of flats on Benoordenhoutseweg in The Hague, 1952. Photo: Department of City Development, collection of The Hague Municipal Archives.
21 The diploma for the course in Concrete Control, 1933. Source: Het Nieuwe Instituut, Rotterdam.
22 *Design for the construction of barracks for the army equestrian unit in The Hague*, or the design scheme for the Alexander barracks and the Frederik barracks, 1933. Source: Netherlands Institute for Military History, The Hague.
23 The Van Alkemade complex under construction, 1938. Photo: Netherlands Institute for Military History, The Hague.
24 Boerée, *The construction of barracks for the army equestrian unit in The Hague, building D1*, specification drawing, 1936. Source: The Hague Municipal Archive.
25 Riné Boerée (left of centre with hat) and her colleagues at the Army Corps of Engineers (Dienst der Genie), ca. 1936. Photo: Delft City Archives.
26 Concrete tension table, undated. Source: Het Nieuwe Instituut, Rotterdam.
27 *Graph for columns with eccentric loads*, undated. Source: Het Nieuwe Instituut, Rotterdam.
28 Reinforced concrete shelter according to the Wernink system. Source: website *Erfgoed Leiden en Omstreken* <https://www.erfgoedleiden.nl/collecties/beeldmateriaal>.
29 C.H.M. Boerée, *Strength calculation for Pentad hangar*, Deelen airport, 1946–1947. Source: Het Nieuwe Instituut, Rotterdam.

7 Wil Jansen, an enterprising women architect from Schiedam

1 Portrait of the Jansen family, ca. 1919. Wil attended a Higher Civic School (HBS) at the time. Photo: archive owned by H.Th.F. Jansen.
2 Wil Jansen with her father Herman in 1924, the year she began her studies. Photo: archive owned by H.Th.F. Jansen.
3 Wil Jansen (centre) as president of the Delftsche Vrouwelijke Studenten Vereeniging, 1927–1928. Photo: *Almanak der D.V.S.V. 1929*, Delft 1928, 20.
4 a W.C.M. Jansen, Student competition design of a residence for architects, 1932. Source: KB|National Library T232, *Bouwkundig Weekblad Architectura* 53 (1932) 23 (4 June), 198.
4 b Sketch of the facade composition of the architect's residence by Wil Jansen, unsigned and undated [1932]. Source: Schiedam Municipal Archives.
5 The early cardboard packaging factory on Oranjestraat, 1965. Photo: Cultural Heritage Agency of the Netherlands, Amersfoort.
6 Unsigned design by Wil Jansen, *Alternative plan for new Oranjebrug*, 1936. Source: Schiedam Municipal Archives.
7 Wil Jansen removed the stepped facades of the cardboard packaging factory on Noordvestsingel in 1951. Source: website *MijnAdres.org – Bouwdossiers online*.

8 a-d Possibly the first (undated and unsigned) designs by Wil Jansen for the new cardboard packaging factory of her brother Tup. Source: Schiedam Municipal Archives.
9 The factory and office complex of the Jansen family as surveyed by Wil Jansen, undated. Source: Schiedam Municipal Archives.
10 Unsigned design (1968) by Wil Jansen to extend the Valdelis perfume factory of her brother Guust. Source: Schiedam Municipal Archives.
11 a-c Wil Jansen designed interiors for off-licences owned by the Jansen family. Source: Schiedam Municipal Archives.
12 W.C.M. Jansen, interior design for the 'Pluk den dag' community centre, 1958. Source: Schiedam Municipal Archives.
13 The RVS block of flats in Rotterdam designed by Wil Jansen, circa 1958. Photo: Ary Groeneveld collection, Rotterdam City Archive.
14 The Bergpolderflat residential building in Rotterdam designed by Willem van Tijen, 1935. Photo: Rotterdam City Archive.
15 a-b W.C.M. Jansen, specification drawings (1956) for the bungalow in Meerssen, intended for her sister Ida and brother-in-law Edixhoven. Source: Meerssen Municipal Archives.
16 a-b W.C.M. Jansen, cupboard designs for living room and kitchen walls, 1956. Source: Schiedam Municipal Archives.
17 The design by Jansen, Wil of the living room with, next to the fireplace, three windows offering views of the undulating landscape, undated. Source: Schiedam Municipal Archives.
18 a-c Bungalow in Meerssen, 2019. Photos: author.
19 Design by Wil Jansen for the site layout of the Julia Mine in Eygelshoven, 1937. Source: Schiedam Municipal Archives.
20 Unsigned design by Wil Jansen for twelve drive-in dwellings with gardens in Heerlen, 1938. Source: Schiedam Municipal Archives.
21 Design by Wil Jansen of a pulpit for the John the Baptist Church in Eygelshoven, 1936. Source: Schiedam Municipal Archives.
22 Design by Wil Jansen of a kneeling chair. Source: Schiedam Municipal Archives.
23 Design of a new facade for the Van 't Hoff en Jongepier office supply factory in Schiedam, 1954. Source: Schiedam Municipal Archives.

8 Architect couples

1 Jan Kammer-Kret later became an advisor to her husband Harry. Photo: private archive of K.J. van Manen-Kammer.
2 The design for a village church with the motto 'Rest', with which Kammer-Kret won second prize, as published in the *Bouwkundig Weekblad Architectura*. Source: KB| National Library T232, *Bouwkundig Weekblad Architectura* 55 (1934) Nr. 13 (31 March), 121.
3 a Holiday home in Oostvoorne (1934), designed by Kammer-Kret. Source: KB| National Library T11574, *Het Landhuis* 30 (1935) Nr. 19 (9 October), 649, 660-661.
3 b The sober and modern interior of the holiday home. Photo: Het Nieuwe Instituut, Rotterdam.
4 a *Perspective*, undated design for a Montessori kindergarten (1936) in Schiebroek by husband-and-wife Kammer-Kret. Source: Het Nieuwe Instituut, Rotterdam.
4 b The school entrance. Source: Het Nieuwe Instituut, Rotterdam.
5 Front cover of *de 8 en Opbouw* with the Montessori kindergarten by husband-and-wife Kammer-Kret and the open-air school by Van Tijen. Source: *de 8 en Opbouw* 7 (1936) Nr. 6 (21 March).
6 a The glass wall of the south-east facade, circa 1936. Photo: J. Kamman, Het Nieuwe Instituut, Rotterdam.
6 b A music room was added to the school building 25 years after completion. Photo: Het Nieuwe Instituut, Rotterdam.
7 The luxury cabin (1937) designed by husband-and-wife Kammer-Kret on the *Nieuw Amsterdam* passenger liner. Source: *de 8 en Opbouw* 11 (1940) Nr. 13/14 (28 June), 132-133. Photos: J. Kamman, Het Nieuwe Instituut, Rotterdam
8 The private residence annex architecture office (1960) by husband-and-wife Kammer-Kret, Zuidbroekse Opweg 16, Berkenwoude, photo circa 1970. Photo: Het Nieuwe Instituut, Rotterdam.
9 Working drawing of private residence annex architecture office by husband-and-wife Kammer-Kret, 1960. Source: Midden-Holland Regional Archive.
10 The private residence annex architecture office (1954) by husband-and-wife Lammers-Koeleman, Monnikensteeg 20, Arnhem. Source: *Bouw* 10 (1955) Nr. 33, 677.
11 a The private residence annex architecture office (left part of the building) designed by husband-and-wife Pot-Keegstra, Haringvlietstraat 14, Amsterdam, 1955. Photo: Amsterdam City Archives.
11 b-c Living room and staircase by husband-and-wife Pot-Keegstra. Photos: Pot-Keegstra, Het Nieuwe Instituut, Rotterdam.
12 a-b The Bergerhof (1941–1942) by husband-and-wife Pot-Keegstra. Source: Het Nieuwe Instituut, Rotterdam.
13 Staff dwellings (1949) in Nijverdal, designed by Lammers-Koeleman. Source: KB| National Library 1374B15, J.H. van den Broek, G. Friedhoff and Vereniging van Delftse Ingenieurs, *Nederlandse architectuur. Uitgevoerde werken van bouwkundige ingenieurs*, Amsterdam 1956, 193.
14 Duplex dwellings (1948–1949) in De Steeg, designed by Lammers-Koeleman. Source: KB| National Library 1374B15, J.H. van den Broek, G. Friedhoff and Vereniging van Delftse Ingenieurs, *Nederlandse architectuur. Uitgevoerde werken van bouwkundige ingenieurs*, Amsterdam 1956, 194.
15 The post-war reconstruction plan for Arnhem-South. Source: *Bouwkundig Weekblad* 69 (1951) Nrs. 17-18 (1 May), 176.
16 a The Oranjehof (1941–1942) by husband-and-wife Pot-Keegstra, with the rear facade to Kostverlorenvaart, Amsterdam, 1953. Photo: Amsterdam City Archives.
16 b Interior of a dwelling in the Oranjehof, 1956. Photo: Pot-Keegstra, Amsterdam City Archives.
17 a Pot-Keegstra (in fur coat) in attendance as the first pile is driven into the ground for the retirement home on Cornelis Outshoornstraat, Amsterdam, 1966. Photo: Amsterdam City Archives.
17 b Geuzenveld, with centre left the retirement home designed by husband-and-wife Pot-Keegstra, Amsterdam 1975. Photo: Amsterdam City Archives.
18 a-b Exterior and hall with staircase of the Hoge Es Protestant Christian Retirement Home (1961–1963) on Bonteweg in Nijverdal, designed by Lammers-Koeleman. Source: *Bouwkundig Weekblad* 83 (1965) Nr. 20, 372-374.
19 a-b Coca-Cola bottling plant (1949) designed by Van Rood-van Rijswijk on Van Deventerstraat in Schiedam, 1957. Photo: Schiedam Municipal Archives Photo Collection.

20 Gasselte Transformer Station designed by Van Rood, 1935. Photo: KB| National Library 1374B15, J.H. van den Broek, G. Friedhoff and Vereniging van Delftse Ingenieurs, *Nederlandse architectuur. Uitgevoerde werken van bouwkundige ingenieurs*, Amsterdam 1956, 254.

21 Extension to Central Laboratory (1951–1952) Hoogovens, IJmuiden, designed by Van Rood-van Rijswijk. Photo: KB| National Library 1374B15, J.H. van den Broek, G. Friedhoff and Vereniging van Delftse Ingenieurs, *Nederlandse architectuur. Uitgevoerde werken van bouwkundige ingenieurs*, Amsterdam 1956, 255.

22 Model of the Bijlmerbajes prison. Photo: Het Nieuwe Instituut, Rotterdam.

23 The Bijlmerbajes prison by husband-and-wife Pot-Keegstra under construction, H.J.E. Wenckebachweg 48, Amsterdam, ca. 1976. Photo: ANEFO, Amsterdam City Archives.

24 A pavilion at the Bijlmerbajes prison with activity supervisor, 2000. Photo: M. Alberts, Amsterdam City Archives.

25 The walls were faced in materials that were warm to the touch, such as wood. Photo: Het Nieuwe Instituut, Rotterdam.

9 The 21 women architects

1 Lotte Beese, during her studies at the Bauhaus, Dessau, circa 1929. In the background Hartmut Schulze. Photo: Bauhaus-Archiv Berlin.

2 Riné Boerée, a year before her graduation, 1928. Photo: National Archives, The Hague.

3 Wil van den Broek d'Obrenan, 1928. Photo: National Archives, The Hague.

4 Joop Ferguson, circa 1925. Photo: Ferguson family collection.

5 Regrettably there is no known portrait of Ina Groenevelt.

6 Dé Heyting (centre), with hammer as chair of the board of the Delftsche Vrouwelijke Studenten Vereeniging, 1920–1921. Photo: *Almanak der D.V.S.V. 1922*, Delft 1921, 20.

7 Wil Jansen, 1927. Photo: archive owned by H.Th.F. Jansen.

8 Koos Keegstra, undated. Photo: Het Nieuwe Instituut, Rotterdam.

9 Co van der Kloet on the day of her wedding together with husband Pieter Stempels, 1 December 1926. Photo: Dordrecht Regional Archive, H.G. Beerman collection.

10 Toki Koeleman, ca. 1935. Photo: F.L. Kristinsson-Reitsema (ed.), *Delfts Studenten Corps, 1904–1994. Ter gelegenheid van het 90-jarig jubileum van de Delftsche Vrouwelijke Studenten Vereniging*, s.l. undated. [1994], 59.

11 Jan Kret, 1928. Photo: National Archives, The Hague.

12 Ko Mulder, undated. Photo: E. van Kessel and F. Palstra, *Jakoba Mulder (1900–1988) urban designer and landscape architect*, Amsterdam 1994, 4.

13 Greet van der Poest Clement, at the start of her studies at the Technische Hoogeschool in Delft, 1932. Photo: National Archives, The Hague.

14 Loes Pomes, 1928. Photo: National Archives, The Hague.

15 Jeanne van Rijswijk, 1928. Photo: National Archives, The Hague.

16 Paula Rooseboom, 1928. Photo: National Archives, The Hague.

17 Marie Snethlage, 1929. Photo: National Archives, The Hague.

18 To Strumphler, 1931. Photo: National Archives, The Hague.

19 Ada Struyck, 1928. Photo: National Archives, The Hague.

20 Grada Wolffensperger, after her graduation, 1918. Photo: *De Kroniek, geïllustreerd maandblad voor Nederland en België* 4 (1918) Nr. 3 (March), 68.

21 Beb Zeeman, during her tenure as chairwoman of the board of the Delft Female Student Society (DVSV), 1916–1917. Photo: F.L. Kristinsson-Reitsema (ed.), *Delfts Studenten Corps, 1904–1994. Ter gelegenheid van het 90-jarig jubileum van de Delftsche Vrouwelijke Studenten Vereniging*, s.l. undated. [1994], 32.

A word about the 21 portraits

When compiling the 21 photographic portraits of the women architects documented in this book, it was decided to colourize the original black-and-white photos. This process enables us to give the women in these pictures a palpable presence. We get a better idea of how they looked in reality, bringing them to life and forging a deeper bond with history. To respect that history, we have reproduced the original photographs here. Despite all our efforts, we have been unable to find a portrait of Ina Groenevelt. Indeed, tracking down the portraits presented a challenge in itself, since at that time women were often not documented, let alone photographed. Although the quality of the images varies, they are more about giving their subjects an identity than about achieving maximum sharpness of focus. Their presentation here is a means of acknowledging and celebrating the life and work of these women architects as well as building a bridge between present and past.

Lotte Beese

Riné Boerée

Wil van den Broek d'Obrenan

Joop Ferguson

Ina Groenevelt

Sophie (Dé) Heyting

Wil Jansen

Koos Keegstra

Co van der Kloet

Toki Koeleman

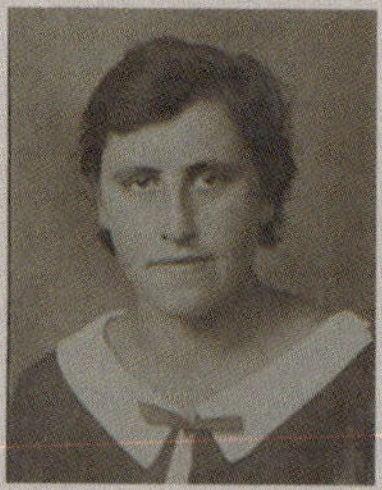
Jan Kret

Ko Mulder

Greet van der Poest Clement

Loes Pomes

Jeanne van Rijswijk

Paula Rooseboom

Marie Snethlage

To (Toot) Strumphler

Ada Struyk

Grada Wolffensperger

Beb (Bep) Zeeman

Credits

Author Erica Smeets-Klokgieters
Translation Billy Nolan and Joy Phillips
Copy editing Els Brinkman
Photo editing Erica Smeets-Klokgieters
Photo Erica Smeets-Klokgieters
© Brancheverening Nederlandse Architectenbureaus
Design Beukers Scholma
Printing and lithography NPN Printers Breda
Paper interior Edixion 80gr and Munken Print white 2.0 90gr, endpapers Sirio Color Pietra 140gr, cover Wibalin 500 White Satina
Production Laurence Ostyn, nai010 publishers
Publisher Laurence Ostyn, nai010 publishers

This publication was made possible by financial support from The Creative Industries Fund NL, Jaap Harten Fund, Van Eesteren-Fluck & Van Lohuizen Foundation

nai010 publishers is an internationally orientated publisher specialized in developing, producing and distributing books in the fields of architecture, urbanism, art and design. www.nai010.com

nai010 books are available internationally at selected bookstores and from the following distribution partners:

- North, Central and South America – Artbook | D.A.P., New York, USA, dap@dapinc.com
- Rest of the world – Idea Books, Amsterdam, the Netherlands, idea@ideabooks.nl

For general questions, please contact nai010 publishers directly at sales@nai010.com or visit our website www.nai010.com for further information.

Printed and bound in the Netherlands

ISBN 978 94 6208 815 3
NUR 648
BISAC ARC000000, ARC005000
THEMA AMX

Also available in Dutch:
Hulde aan onze kranige architecte! De opkomst van de eerste vrouwelijke architecten van Nederland
ISBN 978 94 6208 814 6